Lecture Notes in Computer Science 16841

The series Lecture Notes in Computer Science (LNCS), including its subseries Lecture Notes in Artificial Intelligence (LNAI) and Lecture Notes in Bioinformatics (LNBI), has established itself as a medium for the publication of new developments in computer science and information technology research, teaching, and education.

LNCS enjoys close cooperation with the computer science R & D community, the series counts many renowned academics among its volume editors and paper authors, and collaborates with prestigious societies. Its mission is to serve this international community by providing an invaluable service, mainly focused on the publication of conference and workshop proceedings and postproceedings. LNCS commenced publication in 1973.

Chia-Ju Lin · Andreja Istenic · Tien-Chi Huang · Yueh-Min Huang
Editors

Innovative Technologies and Learning

9th International Conference, ICITL 2026 Ljubljana, Slovenia, August 4–6, 2026 Proceedings, Part I

Springer

Editors
Chia-Ju Lin
National Chin-Yi University of Technology
Taichung, Taiwan

Tien-Chi Huang
National Taichung University of Science
and Technology
Taichung, Taiwan

Andreja Istenic
University of Ljubljana
Ljubljana, Slovenia

University of Primorska
Koper, Slovenia

Samarkand State University named after
Sharof Rashidov
Samarkand, Uzbekistan

Yueh-Min Huang
National Cheng-Kung University
Tainan, Taiwan

ISSN 0302-9743 ISSN 1611-3349 (electronic)
Lecture Notes in Computer Science
ISBN 978-3-032-32111-4 ISBN 978-3-032-32112-1 (eBook)
https://doi.org/10.1007/978-3-032-32112-1

This Springer imprint is published by the registered company Springer Nature Switzerland AG
The registered company address is: Gewerbestrasse 11, 6330 Cham, Switzerland

Preface

The *International Conference of Innovative Technologies and Learning* (ICITL) provides a platform for those in educational technology to exchange experiences. Benefiting from a wide range of emerging technologies, the e-learning environment has become increasingly diversified. These technologies have fueled the development of advanced learning environments through the adoption of appropriate pedagogies. Moreover, they not only facilitate learning but also help students achieve better learning outcomes. However, due to the rapid evolution of new technologies, how to integrate them with sound pedagogies to create adaptive and intelligent learning environments remains a challenge. Therefore, this conference aims to offer a forum for researchers in education, computer science, and educational technology to share their experiences in applying cutting-edge technologies to learning and to inspire new directions in the field. It is hoped that the work presented at the conference will inform researchers and practitioners seeking to build more effective learning environments. ICITL remains committed to sharing these efforts with the broader community.

This year's conference (ICITL 2026) was held at the University of Ljubljana in Ljubljana, Slovenia. We received 188 submissions from more than 30 countries worldwide, with each submission reviewed by at least three experts. Eighty-two papers from 27 countries were selected after a rigorous single-blind review process in which submissions received on average three reviews each. The acceptance rate was 44%. The accepted contributions represent the latest research across seven major areas: 1) Artificial Intelligence in Education; 2) Computational Thinking in Education; 3) Design and Framework of Learning Systems; 4) VR/AR/MR/XR in Education; 5) Pedagogies to Innovative Technologies and Learning; 6) STEM/STEAM Education; and 7) Application and Design of Generative Artificial Intelligence in Education. As educational technologies evolve, this year's conference highlighted the integration of generative AI, immersive technologies, and adaptive learning systems, reflecting increasing attention to innovation, pedagogical alignment, and personalized learning.

Moreover, ICITL 2026 featured two keynote presentations and one invited plenary presentation by renowned experts and scholars. Kinshuk and Frode Eika Sandnes provided insights into the future of technology-enhanced education with their keynote topics: "Emerging and disruptive technologies and the impact on the future of education" and "The Illusion of Inclusion: Can AI Fix the Broken Promise of Learner Participation in EdTech Research and Development?" The plenary topic, "Human-AI Collaboration in STEM Teaching and Assessment," was presented in detail by Kuen-Yi Lin. In addition, ICITL 2026 also featured a panel session titled "From AI Literacy to AI Competency: Preparing Learners for Human-AI Collaboration." This panel focused on how education can move beyond basic AI awareness toward developing learners' competencies for effective and responsible collaboration with generative AI. Discussions addressed how AI can support personalized learning, creativity, and knowledge construction, while also emphasizing critical thinking, academic integrity, and ethical AI use in future learning environments. The panel brought together Frode Eika Sandnes, David Jakobsen, Kinshuk, and Shu-Chen Cheng, who shared perspectives on AI-enhanced learning, educational innovation, and the evolving role of human-AI collaboration in education.

We would like to thank the Organizing Committee for their dedication and efforts in ensuring the success of the conference. We also express our sincere gratitude to the Program Committee members for their timely and constructive reviews. Last but not least, we thank all the authors for their contributions in maintaining the high academic quality of the conference. We look forward to your continued support in shaping the future of innovative technologies and learning.

August 2026

Yueh-Min Huang
Andreja Istenic
Tien-Chi Huang
Chia-Ju Lin

Organization

Honorary Chair

Yueh-Min Huang	National Cheng Kung University, Taiwan

Conference Co-chairs

Andreja Istenic	University of Ljubljana, Slovenia, University of Primorska, Slovenia, Samarkand State University named after Sharof Rashidov, Uzbekistan
Tien-Chi Huang	National Taichung University of Science and Technology, Taiwan

Technical Program Co-chair

Chia-Ju Lin	National Chin-Yi University of Technology, Taiwan

Program Committee

Celine Jost	Paris 8 University, France
Chantana Viriyavejakul	King Mongkut's Institute of Technology Ladkrabang, Thailand
Charuni Samat	Khon Kaen University, Thailand
Chi-Cheng Chang	National Taiwan Normal University, Taiwan
Chin Feng Lai	National Cheng Kung University, Taiwan
Claudia Motta	Federal University of Rio de Janeiro, Brazil
Davy Tsz Kit Ng	Education University of Hong Kong, China
Elmarie Kritzinger	University of South Africa, South Africa
Emanuele Bardone	University of Tartu, Estonia
Frode Eika Sandnes	Oslo Metropolitan University, Norway
George Ghinea	Brunel University of London, UK
Grace Qi	Massey University, New Zealand
Gwo-Dong Chen	National Central University, Taiwan

Hana Mohelska	University of Hradec Králové, Czech Republic
Hanlie Smuts	University of Pretoria, South Africa
Janne Väätäjä	University of Lapland, Finland
Jui-long Hung	Boise State University, USA
Jun-Ming Su	National University of Tainan, Taiwan
Kinshuk	University of North Texas, USA
Lisbet Ronningsbakk	UiT The Arctic University of Norway, Norway
Maiga Chang	Athabasca University, Canada
Margus Pedaste	University of Tartu, Estonia
Monika Frania	University of Silesia in Katowice, Poland
Mu-Yen Chen	National Cheng Kung University, Taiwan
Pao-Nan Chou	National Pingtung University of Science and Technology, Taiwan
Qing Tan	Athabasca University, Canada
Ru-Chu Shih	National Pingtung University of Science and Technology, Taiwan
Rustam Shadiev	Zhejiang University, China
Satu-Maarit Korte	University of Lapland, Finland
Shu-Chen Cheng	Southern Taiwan University of Science and Technology, Taiwan
Siri Sollied Madsen	UiT The Arctic University of Norway, Norway
Sumalee Chaijaroen	Khon Kaen University, Thailand
Synnøve Thomassen Andersen	UiT The Arctic University of Norway, Norway
Tacha Serif	Yeditepe University, Turkey
Tengel Aas Sandtrø	Oslo Metropolitan University, Norway
Ting-Sheng Weng	National Chiayi University, Taiwan
Ting-Ting Wu	National Yunlin University of Science and Technology, Taiwan
Tor-Morten Grønli	Kristiania University College, Norway
Wei-Sheng Wang	National Yunlin University of Science and Technology, Taiwan
Yu-Ju Lan	National Taiwan Normal University, Taiwan
Yu-Ping Cheng	National Chi Nan University, Taiwan
Yuping Wang	Griffith University, Australia

Organizers

Sponsored By

Contents

VR/AR/MR/XR in Education

Artificial Intelligence in Education

When AI Meets Autism: Integrating Large Language Models into Social Skills Training

Leon Yufeng Wu[1](✉), Yu-Hsuan Liao[1], Chia-Mao Peng[2], Wen-Lin Tsai[3], and Chang-Chih Pan[4]

[1] Graduate School of Education, Chung Yuan Christian University, Taoyuan City, Taiwan, ROC
leonwu@cycu.edu.tw

[2] Department of Business Administration, Chung Yuan Christian University, Taoyuan City, Taiwan, ROC

[3] Department of Mechanical Engineering, Chung Yuan Christian University, Taoyuan City, Taiwan, ROC

[4] Department of Earth Sciences, National Taiwan Normal University, Taoyuan City, Taiwan, ROC

Abstract. This study investigates the integration of AI Solly -a social skills conversational tool driven by large language models (LLMs) -into the social skills curriculum of an elementary school resource classroom. Using an action research design, the study examines how LLM-based interaction affects the learning motivation and social skill development of students with mild autism spectrum disorder (ASD). Three instructional cycles comprising twelve lessons were conducted with two Grade 2 students diagnosed with ASD. Data were collected through student feedback forms, classroom video recordings, AI Solly backend dialogue logs, instructional reflective journals, and post-lesson interviews. Results indicate that: (1) AI-assisted tools significantly enhanced students' participation motivation; (2) LLM-mediated dialogue supported improvements in verbal expression and social communication; and (3) teacher facilitation remained essential for ensuring response quality and strategy internalisation. The study offers evidence-based insights for educators designing AI-integrated social skills programmes in special education settings.

Keywords: Large Language Models · Autism Spectrum Disorder · Social Skills Training · AI-Assisted Learning · Action Research

1 Introduction

Students with autism spectrum disorder (ASD) face persistent challenges in social communication and peer interaction. According to DSM-5-TR, ASD is characterized by deficits in social communication across multiple contexts and by restricted and repetitive patterns of behavior [1]. These difficulties are particularly pronounced in school settings, where students must navigate complex social rules, regulate their emotions, and engage in reciprocal conversation [2]. In inclusive education environments, the

C.-J. Lin et al. (Eds.): ICITL 2026, LNCS 16841, pp. 3–10, 2027.
https://doi.org/10.1007/978-3-032-32112-1_1

gap between the communication style of ASD students and that of their neurotypical peers can lead to frequent conflicts, social rejection, and diminished learning quality, underscoring the importance of explicit, systematic social skills instruction.

Social skills training (SST) programmed - delivered through social stories, role-play, board games, and small-group instruction - have long constituted the primary intervention approach for ASD students. However, traditional methods struggle to provide the individualized, on-demand practice that many students with ASD require, particularly in resource-constrained classrooms where a single teacher may simultaneously support students with widely varying social skill profiles [3]. One student may struggle with initiating interaction, another with managing rejection, and a third with controlling impulsive physical contact - making uniform instruction inherently limited.

Advances in large language models (LLMs) present a promising alternative: LLM-powered conversational agents can sustain extended, patient, and contextually responsive dialogue with learners, effectively simulating the kind of peer interaction that is difficult to replicate in resource-constrained classroom environments [4]. Unlike scripted chatbots, LLMs can generate nuanced, contextually appropriate responses, providing immediate corrective feedback and emotional cues that support social learning.

The present study reports an action research project in which AI Solly - an LLM-based social skills companion - was integrated into a twelve-lesson SST programmed for two Grade 2 students with mild ASD. Three research questions guide the study: (1) Does LLM integration enhance students' motivation to participate in SST lessons? (2) Does it improve their social skill performance? (3) What teaching adjustments and professional reflections emerged throughout the implementation process?

2 Related Work

2.1 Social Skills Training for Students with ASD

Effective SST for ASD students requires repeated, individualized practice across multiple contexts. Gresham (2006) classified social skills into interpersonal, peer-relational, self-management, academic, and communication sub-domains [5]. Group-based instruction has been shown to increase generalization by exposing learners to authentic peer interactions [6]. Taiwan's 12-Year Curriculum Framework for Special Needs (2019) specifies learning outcomes across three domains - self-management, interpersonal interaction, and community participation - providing a competency-based structure for SST curriculum design. Despite these advances, traditional methods seldom allow students to practice at the pace and individualized level that ASD learners require.

2.2 LLMs in Special Education

A growing body of research has explored LLMs as interactive companions for students with ASD. Wang and Tang (2024) demonstrated that a personalized LLM-based chat companion improved communication skills and helped parents better understand their child's difficulties [7]. Zhu et al. (2024) developed an LLM-driven avatar system integrating discrete trial training (DTT), showing significant social skill gains and reduced therapist workload [8]. Lee et al. (2025) reported that Echo-Teddy, a low-cost LLM-powered social robot, increased student interaction and met educational safety standards [9]. Mishra et al. (2024) further demonstrated that human-mediated LLM robotic interventions improve personalized interaction without increasing student cognitive burden [13]. Collectively, these studies highlight LLMs' potential for scalable, individualized intervention while also emphasizing the continuing need for teacher oversight.

3 Methodology

3.1 Research Design

This study adopted an action research methodology, which enables practitioners to identify classroom problems and refine practice through iterative cycles of planning, acting, observing, and reflecting [10]. The study was conducted in the resource classroom of an elementary school in northern Taiwan, comprising three instructional cycles and twelve forty-minute lessons (two per week, approximately 2 months duration). Prior to the intervention, written informed consent was obtained from all participants and their legal guardians. Data analysis utilized thematic coding to extract recurring patterns from the collected data, and the findings were validated through data triangulation, converging evidence from Likert feedback forms, classroom video recordings, post-lesson interviews, and teacher reflective journals.

3.2 Participants

Two Grade 2 students with ASD served as the primary research participants. Student A (pseudonym: Xiao-Rui) presented with passive communication patterns, context-blind topic shifts, and difficulty reading social cues. Student B (pseudonym: Xiao-Yu) displayed ASD with ADHD comorbidity, impulsive verbal output, poor voice modulation, and conflict-prone peer interactions. Both students had been formally assessed and placed in the resource programmed by the district special education placement committee. A Grade 2 student with a learning disability was recruited as a peer partner in the third cycle to create more natural multi-participant interaction.

3.3 AI Solly: The LLM-Based Intervention Tool

AI Solly is a tablet-based social skills companion built on an LLM backend with a conversational interface featuring an animated character (Solly) capable of expressing four emotional states: happy, neutral, sad, and angry. Fifty-four scenario templates covering common school social situations were pre-configured in the system. Students typed or spoke responses within a selected scenario, and Solly reacted with contextually appropriate emotional feedback. Prompt cues (e.g., 'You could say it this way...') were embedded in the interface to scaffold student responses. Teachers monitored all dialogue logs through a backend dashboard and could flag system issues for the development team in real time.

3.4 Curriculum Design

Four thematic units were designed around social challenges identified through teacher observation and interviews with homeroom teachers and parents: (1) Joining a game or activity, (2) Stopping dangerous behavior, (3) Managing test anxiety, and (4) Responding to teasing or provocation. Each unit comprised three lessons aligned with indicators from Taiwan's Special Needs Curriculum Framework. Lessons followed a three-stage model: motivation (board games, videos, role-play, or timed worksheets to evoke the target emotion), strategy instruction and modelling, and AI-mediated practice. Students completed a five-point Likert feedback form at the end of each session. The 54 interactive AI scenario templates were rigorously developed and validated based on the core indicators of Taiwan's Special Needs Curriculum Framework. Furthermore, 'social skills improvement' was operationally defined through specific Task Checklists designed for each scenario. During the intervention, if the AI encountered logic loops or generated inappropriate responses, the teacher actively intervened using the system's prompt supports to guide the students to reorganize their conversational inputs, ensuring pedagogical safety.

3.5 Data Sources and Analysis

Qualitative data were collected from five sources: (1) student feedback forms, (2) classroom video recordings, (3) AI Solly backend dialogue logs, (4) teacher reflective journals, and (5) semi-structured post-intervention interviews with students, homeroom teachers, parents, and the peer partner. Data were coded thematically using a source–date convention (e.g., 「ref_01_1140301」 for the first reflective journal entry) and triangulated across sources to strengthen credibility.

4 Results and Discussion

4.1 Enhanced Participation Motivation Across Three Cycles

To substantiate the claims regarding student engagement, 5-point Likert scale feedback was collected after each session, which demonstrated a sustained high level of motivation (scoring consistently between 4 and 5) across the instructional cycles. Crucially, the iterative adjustments in this action research were directly driven by teacher reflective journals; for instance, reflections on student distraction in Cycle 1 prompted the immediate integration of Task Checklists in Cycle 2. Finally, post-intervention interviews with parents and homeroom teachers confirmed that the students' acquired social skills successfully transferred to real-world interactions outside the resource room (Fig. 1).

Both students consistently rated AI Solly-integrated lessons higher than non-AI sessions throughout the intervention. Post-intervention interviews confirmed that students valued Solly's encouraging language, emotional responsiveness, and gamified task structure. Xiao-Rui stated: '*It says supportive things. You talk back rudely and it still replies kindly.*' Xiao-Yu noted: '*I like setting my own scenario.*' These qualitative responses align with the findings of Kasneci et al. (2023) and Henriksen et al. (2025) that LLM systems enhance student engagement and willingness to interact [4, 11] (Fig. 2).

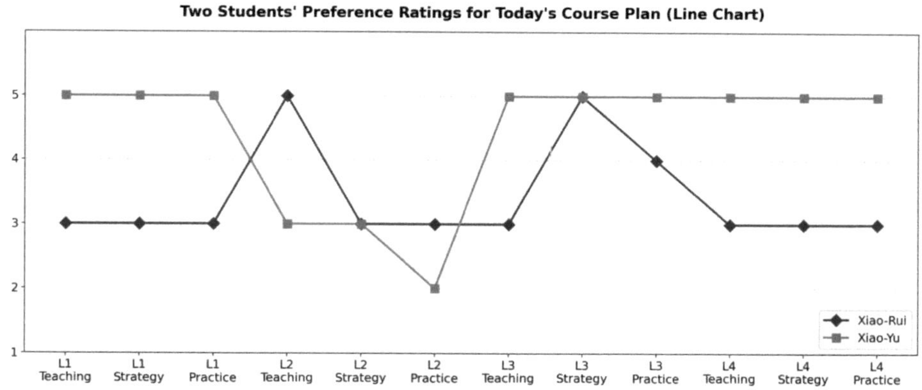

Fig. 1. Student Likert Feedback Trends Across Instructional Cycles.

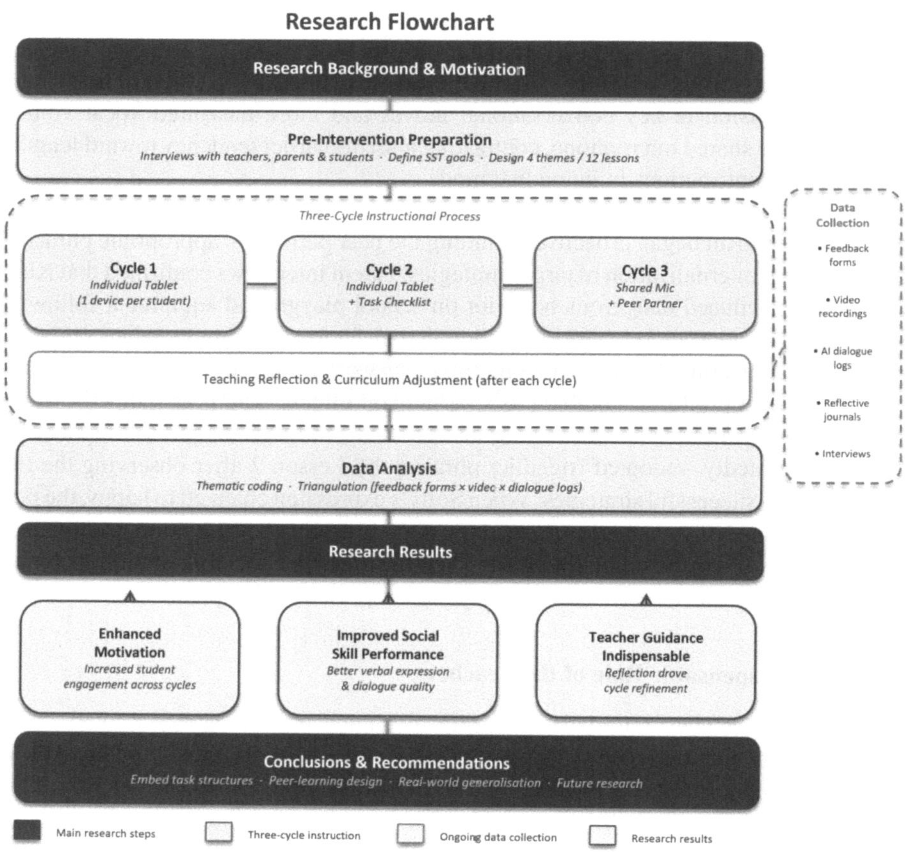

Fig. 2. The action research flowchart.

The three-cycle evolution of instructional modes illustrates how engagement can be progressively deepened. In Cycle 1 (individual tablet mode), novelty drove initial enthusiasm, but students quickly became confused about task goals and lost focus without clear structure. The teacher observed students saying '*I don't know what AI wants me to say*' and resorting to test inputs rather than practicing target language. In response, the addition of a task checklist in Cycle 2 provided goal clarity: Xiao-Rui reported *'the checklist helps me know what to do without asking the teacher*,' while Xiao-Yu's on-task time visibly increased. In Cycle 3, a shared microphone with turn-taking and a new peer partner produced the highest engagement ratings. Xiao-Rui - typically reticent - spontaneously explained the system to the new peer and adopted a peer-tutoring role, a behavior never observed in previous cycles.

4.2 Improvements in Social Skill Performance

Dialogue log analysis revealed measurable quality improvements across cycles for both students. For the 'joining a game' theme, Xiao-Rui progressed from context-blind utterances in Lesson 1 to appropriately framed requests by Lesson 3, producing language that consistently triggered Solly's positive emotional display. Xiao-Yu demonstrated improved precision in key conversational moves and more measured vocal volume when using the shared microphone, contrasting with his earlier tendency toward lengthy, disorganized contributions in individual mode.

Qualitative evidence further supported skill development. Teacher reflective journals noted that Xiao-Rui began proactively guiding the peer partner on appropriate phrasing, demonstrating internalization of target strategies. Parent interviews confirmed that Xiao-Yu displayed reduced dangerous behavior on school playground equipment following the '*stopping dangerous behavior*' unit, though transfer to off-campus settings remained incomplete, indicating the need for continued real-world practice [12].

Cycle 3 also produced notable cross-participant effects. The peer partner - whose blunt communication style ('None of your business') initially triggered Solly's angry response repeatedly - adopted friendlier phrasing by Lesson 2 after observing the two ASD students' successful strategies. When Solly's expression changed to happy, the peer partner exclaimed '*Teacher, look! It's happy now!*' - signaling both emotional attunement and awareness of conversational impact. This illustrates the social modelling potential of peer-inclusive LLM-based activities beyond the primary ASD population.

4.3 The Indispensable Role of the Teacher

Despite the tool's clear affordances, teacher mediation proved critical at every stage. When AI Solly entered repetitive-response loops, the teacher reframed the breakdown as a learning opportunity: 'Conversations don't always go as expected - *let's try a different way.*' This parallels Mishra et al.'s (2024) finding that human-mediated LLM interventions maintain student trust and learning stability [13]. Teachers also served as interpreters - helping students understand ambiguous AI responses - and as scaffolders, modelling target phrases before requiring independent production.

Critically, the teacher's reflective practice drove the cycle-to-cycle design adjustments that increased effectiveness. Comparing checklist completion rates, Likert scores, and dialogue transcripts after each lesson, the teacher identified that certain scenarios triggered disproportionate frustration (e.g., when the AI's emotional threshold was misaligned with students' language level) and requested backend calibration. This active troubleshooting role underscores that LLMs are pedagogical instruments requiring professional integration, not autonomous substitutes for teacher expertise.

5 Conclusion

This action research study demonstrates that LLM-powered conversational tools can meaningfully enrich social skills instruction for students with ASD by providing patient, individualized, and emotionally responsive practice partners. The progressive evolution of instructional design - from individual tablet use to peer-inclusive turn-taking - reveals how AI integration benefits from iterative, reflective refinement aligned with students' individual profiles.

Three practical recommendations emerge for educators: (1) embed explicit task structures such as checklists to reduce cognitive overload during LLM interaction; (2) incorporate peer-learning elements to maximize the social authenticity of AI practice; and (3) design explicit generalization activities that bridge AI-mediated practice and real-world application. However, it is important to acknowledge that the findings of this study are constrained by the very small sample size of only two participants. While this scale allowed for an in-depth, iterative exploration characteristic of action research, it inherently limits the generalizability of the results to the broader ASD population. Future research should extend these findings to larger and more diverse student populations, employ pre–post behavioral measures, and investigate long-term generalization effects beyond the instructional period. It would also be valuable to study how different disability profiles respond to LLM-based social skills tools, and to examine the professional development needs of teachers who implement AI-integrated special education programs.

References

1. American Psychiatric Association.: Diagnostic and statistical manual of mental disorders (5th ed., text rev.; DSM-5-TR). American Psychiatric Publishing (2022)
2. Gresham, F.M., Van, M.B., Cook, C.R.: Social skills training for teaching replacement behaviors: remediating acquisition deficits in at-risk students. Behav. Disord. **31**(4), 363–377 (2006)
3. Lin, C.Y.: Social skills training for adolescents with autism. Special Educ. Dev. J. **69**, 17–27 (2020)
4. Kasneci, E., et al.: ChatGPT for good? On opportunities and challenges of large language models for education. Learn. Individ. Differ. **103**, 102274 (2023)
5. Elliott, S.N., Gresham, F.M.: SSIS Classwide Intervention Program. Pearson Assessments (2007)
6. Hung, L.Y.: Social Skills Curriculum: Teaching Procedures and Examples. National Taiwan Normal University (2002)
7. Wang, Y., Tang, T. Y.: Position Paper: a personalized large language model (LLM)-based chat companion for autistic children early intervention. arXiv (2024)

8. Zhu, Y., et al.: Designing a LLM-driven avatar system to enhance social skills for autistic children in DTT learning. In: Companion of the 2024 on ACM International Joint Conference on Pervasive and Ubiquitous Computing (UbiComp 2024), pp. 697–700 (2024)
9. Lee, U., et al.: Echo-teddy: preliminary design and development of large language model-based social robot for autistic students. In: Generative Systems and Intelligent Tutoring Systems: 21st International Conference, ITS 2025, Proceedings, Part II, pp. 287–301. Springer (2025)
10. Niu, W.Y.: Action Research in Special Education: Practice and Methods. Psychological Publishing (2014)
11. Henriksen, D., Creely, E., Gruber, N., Leahy, S.: Social-emotional learning and generative AI: a critical literature review and framework for teacher education. J. Teach. Educ. **76**(3), 312–328 (2025)
12. Li, G., Zarei, M.A., Alibakhshi, G., Labbafi, A.: Teachers and educators' experiences and perceptions of artificial-powered interventions for autism groups. BMC Psychol. **12**, 199 (2024)
13. Mishra, R., Welch, K.C., Popa, D.O.: Human-mediated large language models for robotic intervention in children with autism spectrum disorders. arXiv (2024)

Can Artificial Intelligence Literature Review Tools Provide Reliable Overviews?

Besma Allagui(✉)

Rabdan Academy, Abu Dhabi, UAE
ballagui@ra.ac.ae

Abstract. Artificial Intelligence (AI) literature review tools like Elicit, consensus, and Scispace are gaining popularity among novice researchers, especially graduate and undergraduate students. Beyond retrieving a list of the most relevant research papers, these tools provide a synthesized overview of a research area. However, questions remain about the accuracy and reliability of AI-generated overviews. Therefore, this study compared the overviews produced by four user-friendly AI research assistants. I examined the citations used in the summaries based on three key criteria: (1) currency, (2) author expertise, and (3) diversity and bias. Additionally, I compared the content of the overviews based on their depth of analysis, supporting evidence, relevance, and language quality. Findings revealed several limitations in the effectiveness of AI research assistants for providing an overview of the research topic. The overviews were written based on the most recent publications (2009–2025). The AI research assistants often overlooked many seminal works in the field. Furthermore, the citations on the topic of teacher-written feedback were predominantly focused on university-based research and specific geographical regions. Most importantly, analysis demonstrated that AI-generated overviews lacked depth of analysis. Novice researchers wishing to use AI research assistants must be aware of the limitations of the AI-generated overviews.

Keywords: AI research assistant · General Overview · Reliability

1 Background

Writing a literature review can be time-consuming for novice researchers, especially graduate and undergraduate students [1]. To conduct a literature review, students should go through several steps, including searching for and selecting relevant articles, analyzing and synthesizing the information from the articles, and presenting it in the most organized and consistent way [2]. The emergence of innovative technologies, particularly AI-powered research assistants, has begun to transform the way students approach this process. At present, these tools can be categorized into two types: those that are citation-based literature mapping tools (Inciteful, Litmaps, Connected Papers and Research Rabbit) and those that are academic search engine-based tools (Consensus, Elicit, Luminar, Open scholar, Ask R Discovery, Evidence Hunt, etc..). Citation-based literature mapping tools use the traditional references between the papers to find out new papers; They can help students visualize the literature and understand how papers are related to

C.-J. Lin et al. (Eds.): ICITL 2026, LNCS 16841, pp. 11–18, 2027.
https://doi.org/10.1007/978-3-032-32112-1_2

each other's, but they do not analyze the content of papers. Academic search engines-based tools, however, use generative AI models to retrieve a list of relevant papers that are almost always real. This is because they use the Retrieval Augmented Generation (RAG) type systems ensures that the citations are actually found in the databases used [3]. In addition to generating a list of papers, many of these academic search engines-based tools can summarize abstracts, provide information about the papers such as limitations, methods, variables, and participants. These tools are also unique in providing researchers with a summary based on the most relevant citations to check if their questions have already been addressed.

Previous research assessing the effectiveness of AI tools in producing reliable sources has shown that some of these tools can identify relevant papers and generate summaries of topics [4–10]. For instance, [7] found that Scite.ai effectively retrieves relevant citations for specific research questions, such as the prevalence of diseases in particular populations [5]. claim that consensus enables researchers to compare and contrast views from multiple articles which is an important step in synthetizing the literature. A significant advantage of these tools is that they allow researchers to allocate more time to data analysis and results interpretation.

However, the use of AI literature search tools comes with several limitations. A significant challenge is that AI algorithms can be biased which leads to inaccurate conclusions [4, 6]. Additionally, concerns about the quality and accuracy of the content generated have been raised [3, 4]. For example, after a review of 21 apps for literature search according to 11 features, [3] found a considerable variation in the quality of the text generated by these tools, even when highly informative prompts were used. The authors suggested that these tools may be more useful for graduate students who are required to write shorter reviews rather than for researchers. While the effectiveness of AI tools in generating relevant sources has been extensively studied, there is limited research on the effectiveness of the AI-generated summaries as a starting point for gaining an overview of a topic. As AI research assistants become more widely adopted in educational settings, understanding their reliability and limitations is of critical importance for both educators and learners.

In this paper, I aim to contribute to the research on the effectiveness of AI literature searching tools. I illustrate whether AI-generated overviews can be used as a starting point for further review and analysis, when searching for evidence on the impact of teacher-written feedback on English as a Foreign Language (EFL) student writing. I propose some recommendations for guiding the use of AI literature searching tools for both students and novice researchers. In this study, a research overview is defined as a synthesized, field-level summary that identifies dominant themes, trends, gaps, and patterns across studies, rather than sequential summaries of individual papers.

2 Methodology

The objective of this paper was to evaluate AI-generated summaries to identify the benefits and challenges in using these summaries for obtaining an overview of the research topic. Given the large number of AI tools currently available, I have decided to focus on semantic-based tools that are user-friendly: Consensus, Elicit, SciSpace, and Ask R Discovery.

I used each tool to generate a summary based on the same prompt, "What evidence exists on the impact of teacher-written feedback on students' EFL writing performance EFL?" I selected a topic that is well-researched and debatable to minimize bias. I examined the summaries in terms of source currency (publication range), author expertise (journal quality, citation range), diversity (geographic distribution, type of study, and educational context). Data for each criterion were recorded into a spreadsheet for ease of analysis and clarity.

Content analysis was conducted to evaluate the relevance, depth of analysis, use of evidence, and language quality of the AI-generated overviews. The summaries were read closely to identify instances where the content oversimplified aspects of teacher feedback, omitted important complexities, or failed to acknowledge multiple perspectives. To evaluate evidence use, factual and interpretive claims in the summaries were cross-referenced with established literature and research on teacher feedback. In addition, the summaries were examined for overly assertive or excessively positive language, particularly statements that exaggerated the effectiveness or benefits of teacher-written feedback without sufficient evidentiary support. To enhance analytic reliability, a second researcher with expertise in applied linguistics independently coded the data using the same framework. Disagreements were resolved through discussion and iterative refinement of the codebook. Table 1 presents an example of a completed coding book.

Table 1. Example of a completed coding Framework

Dimension	Definition	Holistic Evaluation of the Overview
Relevance	The overview directly addresses the original question.	All examples and studies are directly connected to the topic.
Depth of Analysis	The overview provides multiple perspectives rather than superficial description.	The overview presents both positive and negative perspectives on teacher feedback. It discusses effectiveness conditions as well as limitations. Contextual differences such as age groups, subject areas, or digital versus in-person feedback are not discussed.
Evidence	Claims are supported with evidence, citations, or source attribution.	Six references are included. Claims are consistently linked to evidence.
Language	Language is appropriately cautious, hedged, and avoids overstatement.	Phrases such as "its impact depends critically," "positively affects," and "may limit broader learning benefits" are used consistently.

3 Results

The four tools enabled us to generate an overview of research relevant to the impact of teacher-written feedback on students' EFL writing performance EFL. Scispace and Consensus produced longer summaries based on 10 sources while Elicit provided a summary of 8 citations. Ask R discovery produced a summary based on 4 citations.

Critical Source Evaluation. Before analysing the content of the summaries, I first compared these sources in terms of currency, author expertise, and diversity or biases. It is important to note that all sources were not fake (Table 2).

Table 2. Comparison between the summaries in terms of currency, author expertise, and diversity.

Tool	Currency	Author expertise		Diversity		
		Journal Quality	Citation range	Geographic distribution	Type of study	Educational context
Consensus	2013–2025	Q1: 60% Unknown: 40%	36–01	Iran, China, Indonesia, Morocco	85.5% empirical	62% University context
Elicit	2011–2023	Q1: 10% Unknown: 90%	214–01	Predominantly Asian countries (Iran, China, Indonesia, Turkey)	85.5% empirical	87% University context
SciSpace	2021–2025	Q1:20% Unknown: 80%	4–01	Indonesia, Iran, Vietnam, Oman, Ecuador, Thailand, Saudi Arabia	100% empirical	66.6% University
Ask R discovery	2021–2023	Q1: 100%	180–11	China	60% empirical	80% University context

Currency. There is notable variation among the tools in the dates of publications retrieved. Consensus covered papers from 2013 to 2025. Elicit retrieved papers from 2009 to 2023, giving a wider timeline. SciSpace, on the other hand, retrieved only very recent publications, mostly from 2023 to 2025. Similarly, Ask R discovery provided sources from within the same range (2021–2023). Despite this variation, a substantial number of publications from the three tools are concentrated within the period from 2020 to 2025. While the focus on the latest research is essential for assessing the relevance of sources, it has overlooked key studies from earlier years that laid the groundwork on teacher written feedback.

Author Expertise. The evaluation of author expertise in the AI-generated sources reveals several key findings. In terms of publisher, the studies used in the Ask R discovery summary were all published in reputable journals, specifically those classified as Q1, such as Frontiers in Psychology and BMC Medical Education. Consensus retrieved many sources (60%) from reputable Q1 peer-reviewed journal articles that represent high quality research. However, both Elicit and SciSpace included a higher number of non-indexed sources from less well-known publishers. In terms of citations, Ask R discovery consistently included highly-cited papers. Elicit and consensus varied more in the number of citations. Elicit included sources with citation ranging from 0 to 36. Consensus retrieved some highly cited papers, including one with 214 citations. In contrast, Sicspace presented more sources with either zero citations or very few citations overall.

Diversity and Bias. I evaluated the differences between sources in terms of where the studies were conducted, the type of study and the educational context to examine bias in the search algorithms.

The geographical distribution reveals a strong focus on studies conducted in Asian countries across all three tools. Iran, China, and Indonesia appeared frequently in the results. Elicit returned studies conducted in China, Iran, Turkey, and Argentina. Consensus similarly identified studies conducted in Iran, China, Taiwan, Indonesia, and Morocco. Scispace provided studies conducted in Vietnam, Oman, Ecuador, Thailand, and Saudi Arabia. There is a notable underrepresentation of research from Western countries, African nations, and South American countries across all tools.

With regards to the type of study, it was found that empirical research constituted the majority of papers identified by all four tools, though both Elicit and Consensus also incorporated systematic reviews into their results. Furthermore, the educational context analysis demonstrated a consistent emphasis across all tools: the vast majority of studies were conducted in university settings.

Summary Content. I analysed the content of the summaries to see if the AI tool oversimplified a complex topic like teacher-written feedback, whether it included unproven claims, and whether it used overly positive and confident language.

Relevance. All the summaries provided by the different AI tools were highly relevant to the topic of teacher feedback in EFL writing. Summaries addressed various dimensions of teacher feedback, including its effectiveness and the factors that influence its impact, which are central to understanding how feedback shapes student outcomes.

Depth of Analysis. Elicit presented teacher feedback as having a straightforward "positive impact" without acknowledging the many mediating factors that influence feedback effectiveness (proficiency level, individual differences, task differences). Consensus presented a broader perspective on teacher feedback covering topics like self-regulated learning strategies, student engagement, long-term effects, peer feedback comparison, and anxiety and self-efficacy. However, it still lacked critical analysis of the topic. SciSpace identified different types of feedback (direct vs. indirect) and at the same time added nuance by mentioning individual differences. Ask R Discovery effectively synthesized key findings related to teacher-written feedback in EFL contexts and discussed two factors that influence its effectiveness. However, it lacked a comprehensive exploration of how specific types of feedback (e.g., written corrective feedback vs. peer feedback) affect different aspects of writing performance.

Evidence. The Elicit summary included more claims without evidence (has been shown to have a positive impact). The summary claims consensus where significant debate exists (linguistic and pedagogical consensus).

Scispace and Consensus summaries, by contrast relied on fewer unsupported or broad claims like "has a significant positive impact" and "teacher feedback generally leads to substantial improvements" as most sentences included numbered citations. The ask R Discovery summary made even fewer unsupported claims and offered more specific contextual details and research evidence.

Language. All four summaries exhibit a tendency toward overly positive language when discussing the impact of teacher-written feedback on EFL writing performance: positive impact," "effectively reduce," and "valuable tool". While such language highlights the benefits, it risks oversimplifying the nuanced realities of feedback implementation and its varying effectiveness across different contexts and student populations.

4 Discussion

The comparison of four AI-generated summaries on the impact of teacher-written feedback in EFL contexts revealed notable differences and similarities between the four tools. While most publications utilized in generating these summaries were recent, this focus on contemporary studies often came at the expense of ignoring seminal works that have laid the groundwork in the field. This oversight limited the overall understanding of the evolution of thought surrounding teacher feedback.

A significant limitation identified across the summaries is the absence of European and American contexts, with a predominant focus on studies from China and other Asian countries. This geographical bias restricts the generalizability of the conclusions drawn, as the dynamics of teacher feedback may vary significantly across different educational systems and cultures. Furthermore, the majority of studies included were empirical, with few conceptual papers or meta-analyses. This emphasis on empirical research, particularly in university settings, further narrows the applicability of findings to broader educational contexts, especially since very few studies were extracted from school settings.

Another finding of this comparison is the variation in the quality of the papers cited. Ask R Discovery emerged as the tool with the most highly cited and indexed sources, indicating a reliance on reputable research. In contrast, both SciSpace and Elicit included less reliable papers, which raises concerns about the validity of some claims made within their summaries.

Overall, these findings underscore the importance of prompt engineering; students should employ multiple prompts to enhance the quality and relevance of the summaries generated by these tools. Although prompt engineering may not mitigate the inherent bias in these tools, more nuanced prompts may help yield more diverse results.

In terms of content, while the summaries produced by SciSpace, Consensus, Elicit, and Ask R Discovery highlighted various aspects of teacher feedback—especially its positive effects on writing performance and self-efficacy—the depth and nuance of these discussions varied considerably. SciSpace, Consensus, and Ask R Discovery offered more comprehensive insights, while Elicit tended to simplify complex issues, presenting unproven claims without adequate evidence. In contrast, Ask R Discovery provided more contextual details, making it a more reliable resource.

Therefore, while AI-generated summaries can serve as a useful first step in exploring the impact of teacher-written feedback on EFL writing performance, students should avoid relying only on the output of a single tool. Each summary offers a different perspective, emphasizing the need for a critical approach to their content. Furthermore, students must recognize their limitations in depth of analysis and their use of overly positive language. Further exploration of original studies through manual Google search is essential for obtaining a more comprehensive understanding of the topic.

5 Implications

These findings carry important implications for educational practice. Instructors who incorporate AI research assistants into research projects should explicitly teach students to use them wisely and responsibly. First, it is important for students to report not only that they used an AI literature review tool but also which tool they used. This can foster transparency and epistemic accountability in the research process, helping students develop an awareness of how different tools retrieve, rank, and present information differently and why those differences matter for the quality and integrity of their literature review. Second, teachers may assign a reflection post-writing activity to help students think about how their decisions about the AI output influenced their literature review. This can enhance metacognitive awareness and self-regulated learning by prompting students to critically examine what they accepted, rejected, or modified from the AI-generated content and to articulate how those decisions shaped their final work. Such reflective practice aligns with the broader goals of academic writing and research development, encouraging students to position themselves as active, critical agents in the knowledge construction process rather than passive consumers of AI-generated output. Third, and most importantly, teachers should help students critically evaluate AI-generated overviews. The tendency of AI tools to employ overly positive language and provide biased content poses a particular risk for novice researchers and students, who may lack the disciplinary knowledge necessary to identify oversimplifications or biased output. This underscores the need for explicit instruction in source evaluation and critical reading as part of any course or program that incorporates AI research assistants. Without such guidance, students risk developing an uncritical dependence on AI-generated content that may undermine the development of essential research and synthesis skills.

6 Limitations and Conclusion

In this paper, I used a debatable topic to discuss the value of using AI-generated summaries as a starting point in research. This partially explains the bias in the AI generated summaries because the complexity inherent in controversial topics can lead the algorithms to favor certain perspectives or interpretations over others. Furthermore, this research relied on a single prompt to generate summaries from each tool which limited the range of responses generated by the AI tools. Thus, the results reflect tool behavior under one specific prompt condition and should not be read as a comprehensive assessment of each tool's full capabilities. Future research should systematically vary prompt types. During our study, I found that when I retyped the same prompt across different AI tools, the resulting summaries were similar, suggesting that these tools may produce repetitive outputs. This raises significant concerns about the potential for unintentional plagiarism if researchers or students were to copy and paste these summaries into their work without proper attribution. Future research should address the ethical implications of using AI-generated summaries.

Disclosure of Interests I declare no competing interests.

References

1. Chen, D.T.V., Wang, Y.M., Lee, W.C.: Challenges confronting beginning researchers in conducting literature reviews. Stud. Contin. Educ. **38**(1), 47–60 (2016)
2. Galvan, J.L., Galvan, M.C.: Writing Literature Reviews: a Guide for Students of the Social and Behavioral Sciences. Routledge (2017)
3. Bolaños, F., et al.: Artificial intelligence for literature reviews: opportunities and challenges. Artif. Intell. Rev. **57**, 259 (2024). https://doi.org/10.1007/s10462-024-10902-3
4. Fabiano, N., et al.: The effect of exercise on suicidal ideation and behaviors: a systematic review and meta-analysis of randomized controlled trials. J. Affect. Disord. **330**, 355–366 (2023). https://doi.org/10.1016/j.jad.2023.02.071
5. Farid, A., Van Welie, M., Olson, E., Nebeker, B., Salem, C. Consensus.app. [Computer software] (2022)
6. Jenko, N., Ariyaratne, S., Jeys, L., Evans, S., Iyengar, K.P., Botchu, R.: An evaluation of AI generated literature reviews in musculoskeletal radiology. Surgeon. (2024). https://doi.org/10.1016/j.surge.2023.12.005
7. Nicholson, J.M., et al.: Scite: a smart citation index that displays the context of citations and classifies their intent using deep learning. Quant. Sci. Stud. **2**(3), 882–898 (2021)
8. Ought.: Elicit. [Computer software] (2023)
9. Ge, L., et al.: Leveraging artificial intelligence to enhance systematic reviews in health research: advanced tools and challenges. Syst. Rev. **13**, 269 (2024). https://doi.org/10.1186/s13643-024-02682-2
10. Block, J., Kuckertz, A.: What is the future of human-generated systematic literature reviews in an age of artificial intelligence? Manag. Rev. Quart. **1** (2024). https://doi.org/10.1007/s11301-024-00471-8

A Systematic Review of Computer Vision-Based Approaches in Educational Contexts

Rustam Shadiev[1](✉), Meruert Aidaraly[2], Akerke Yermukhanbet[2], Zharkyn Naraly[2], Aigul Lukhmanova[2], Alima Abai[2], Gulnaz Salgarayeva[2], Altynshash Bekezhanova[2], and Serik Kenesbayev[2]

[1] Zhejiang University, No. 866, Yuhangtang Road, Hangzhou 310058, People's Republic of China
rustamsh@gmail.com
[2] Kazakh National Women's Teacher Training University, No. 114/8 Gogol Street, Almaty 050000, Republic of Kazakhstan

Abstract. Computer vision has emerged as an important artificial intelligence technology in educational research, enabling the automated analysis of visual learning data such as student behavior, movement, engagement, and interaction. Although an increasing number of empirical studies have explored its educational applications, existing research remains fragmented and insufficiently synthesized. To address this gap, this systematic review examines how computer vision technologies have been implemented across educational contexts. Guided by the PRISMA framework, empirical studies published between 2021 and 2025 were identified through searches of Scopus, Web of Science, and Google Scholar. Following a multi-stage screening and eligibility process, thirty studies were selected for in-depth analysis. The studies were coded according to technology type, educational domain, instructional tasks, learning outcomes, methodological design, advantages, and limitations. The findings show that deep learning-based computer vision models and pose estimation technologies are the most frequently used approaches, primarily supporting automated monitoring of student behavior and engagement, performance assessment, and classroom analytics. Applications were most common in higher education, STEM disciplines, physical education, and performance-based learning contexts. Learning outcomes predominantly focused on engagement, behavioral regulation, and motor skill development, while cognitive outcomes were reported less consistently. Despite clear advantages such as objective assessment, real-time feedback, and reduced teacher workload, challenges related to technical robustness, scalability, ethical concerns, and limited pedagogical integration were widely reported. The review highlights the need for theory-informed, pedagogy-driven, and ethically grounded research to advance the meaningful integration of computer vision in education.

Keywords: Computer vision · Artificial Intelligence in education · Systematic review

C.-J. Lin et al. (Eds.): ICITL 2026, LNCS 16841, pp. 19–28, 2027.
https://doi.org/10.1007/978-3-032-32112-1_3

1 Introduction

Computer vision (CV), a field of artificial intelligence that deals with deciphering information from visual input by machines, has rapidly expanded into educational research and practice [1]. Modern CV systems make use of methods such as deep learning, pose estimation, object detection, face and gaze tracking, and multimodal behavior recognition [2]. These technologies allow for the automated analysis of highly complex human activities, which currently include movement patterns, emotional expressions, attention, collaboration, motor coordination, and even subtle behavioral cues [3]. As CV becomes increasingly accessible its adoption within educational settings has markedly accelerated in recent years [4].

In contemporary educational contexts, CV has become an important tool for supporting teaching, assessment, classroom analytics, and personalized learning. CV-based systems can automatically assess the physical performance of students [1, 2], monitor engagement and attention [3–5], recognize emotions during instruction [6], detect cheating in online assessments [7], analyze artistic, linguistic, and musical practices [8], and support adaptive learning environments [9]. These applications position CV as one of the most promising technologies within emerging intelligent education systems [10].

Despite the growing number of studies, existing reviews of artificial intelligence in education rarely focus specifically on CV as a separable area of technology. Most reviews target broad AI categories, learning analytics, multimodal learning data, or XR-based environments without analyzing the distinct affordances and pedagogical implications associated with CV. At the same time, empirical studies using CV in schools and universities are rapidly expanding across varied domains such as physical education, STEM, language learning, art, special education, psychology, teacher education, and classroom effectiveness research. Yet, these studies have not been synthesized to reveal cross-cutting patterns in pedagogical applications, methodologies, technological approaches, and practical constraints.

A review of the existing body of research points to several critical gaps. First, although many studies demonstrate how CV can be technically implemented in educational settings to track motion accurately, recognize emotion, or identify objects, very few explicitly investigate how these technologies align with pedagogical approaches. Second, there is no comprehensive guideline that explains how teachers can meaningfully integrate CV technologies into instruction, assessment, and classroom management or how they might navigate concerns related to bias, privacy, and implementation constraints.

In view of these gaps, the present study provides a systematic review of the application of CV in education by synthesizing evidence from empirical studies. This review was guided by the following research questions: 1. What CV technologies and tools are used in educational research? 2. In which educational domains is CV applied, and for what purposes? 3. What pedagogical approaches underlie the use of CV in these studies? 4. What affordances, affective, cognitive, behavioral, or experiential, are associated with CV-based educational applications? 5. What learning outcomes or behavioral insights are reported? 6. What limitations, challenges, and ethical issues emerge in CV-based educational research? 7. What solutions or recommendations do researchers propose for improving the integration of CV into teaching and learning? 8. How can the synthesized findings inform a practical guide for teachers intending to implement CV technologies?

This systematic review therefore provides a comprehensive and timely analysis of the role of CV in education and outlines its potential, limitations, and implications for future pedagogical innovation.

2 Methodology

The Preferred Reporting Items for Systematic Reviews and Meta-Analyses (PRISMA) framework was used to ensure transparency and replicability throughout the review procedure [11–15]. Three academic databases, namely Scopus (n = 169), Web of Science (n = 20), and Google Scholar (n = 170), served as the primary sources for literature identification. Guided by previous review studies in artificial intelligence and educational technology, a set of search keywords was developed to locate research applying computer vision within learning environments. The search terms included "computer vision," "CV," "deep learning," "YOLO," "OpenCV," "MediaPipe," "pose estimation," "image recognition," "object detection," "OCR," "education," "learning," "teaching." These terms were entered across the selected databases using Boolean operators ("AND" and "OR") to retrieve peer-reviewed journal articles and conference publications relevant to the implementation of vision-based systems in educational settings.

Studies were included in the review based on the following several criteria: *1. Empirical studies.* Only empirical works employing a scientific research method and presenting original data on the use of CV in real educational contexts were selected. Theoretical discussions, conceptual frameworks, technical proposals without implementation, and opinion-based publications were excluded. *2. Studies involving CV in learning.* To be eligible, studies were required to explicitly implement CV technologies within teaching or learning environments. Relevance was determined according to whether the research examined educational outcomes supported by CV. *3. Academic rigor.* Selected articles were required to be published in peer-reviewed journals or reputable conference proceedings. Non-indexed sources, preprints without review, and workshop abstracts were excluded to ensure methodological reliability. *4. Scope.* The studies needed to provide sufficient detail regarding how CV technologies were applied, describe learner interaction with the system, and identify measurable outcomes or pedagogical implications. *5. Timeframe.* Only studies published between January 2021 and December 2025 were selected, ensuring the focus remained on contemporary developments in CV-enhanced education. *6. Language* - only studies published in English were included.

All selected studies underwent formal quality appraisal to ensure the credibility of their findings and the robustness of their evidentiary foundations.

The analytical framework developed for this review reflects the multi-stage selection process illustrated in the identification and screening diagram. A total of 359 records were initially retrieved from three major academic databases (Scopus, Google Scholar, Web of Science). After title- and abstract-level screening, 231 studies were excluded due to irrelevance, non-English publication, outdated timeline, or insufficient alignment with the research topic. The remaining 128 full-text articles were evaluated for methodological suitability, empirical rigor, and direct integration of CV in educational contexts. Following full eligibility assessment, 30 studies met all criteria and were coded in depth for final analysis.

The analytical framework developed for this review included four interconnected dimensions: *(1) technological approaches* - namely pose estimation, object detection, face and gaze recognition, multimodal learning analytics, neural rendering, and CV-based adaptive systems; *(2) pedagogical approaches* embedded within these tools, including project-based learning, inquiry-based learning, self-regulated learning, competency development, formative assessment, and personalized learning; *(3) educational domains*, such as STEM education, physical education, art and music education, language learning, teacher education, and classroom analytics; and *(4) outcomes and limitations* - including learning gains, behavioral insights, motivational effects, system accuracy, scalability concerns, occlusion issues, dataset limitations, and ethical considerations. So the review not only identifies how CV is currently being integrated into educational practice but also highlights emerging affordances that shape its pedagogical value: affective, cognitive, behavioral, experiential, and interactional. Furthermore, the synthesis reveals recurrent implementation challenges, including recognition errors, lighting sensitivity, privacy concerns, small datasets, difficulties in large classrooms, and limited generalizability. Unless these issues are adequately addressed, it will be difficult to design responsible, effective, and ethical learning environments.

Next, two researchers conducted a structured content analysis using an open-coding approach. They independently examined all selected studies, highlighted relevant fragments, and assigned initial codes aligned with the analytical framework developed for this review. The coded data were then compared, refined, and reorganized into thematic categories describing CV tools, application contexts, educational outcomes, and reported challenges. To ensure reliability and consistency, coding disagreements were discussed collaboratively until consensus was reached. In cases where disagreements or uncertainties persisted, an experienced professor in the field reviewed the coding decisions, provided expert judgment, and facilitated consensus. When necessary, the original articles were revisited and coding decisions were re-evaluated to maintain analytical rigor and accuracy.

3 Results

Type of Technology and Tools. The analysis indicates that CV technologies used in educational contexts can be categorized into several functional groups based on their technological characteristics and instructional purposes.

Deep learning–based CV models were the most frequently employed technologies, appearing in the majority of studies ($n = 21$). These included convolutional neural networks (CNNs), YOLO-based object detection models, recurrent neural networks (RNNs), GRU architectures, GANs, CRNNs, and hybrid deep learning frameworks. Such models were primarily used for behavior recognition, engagement detection, motion analysis, and automated assessment.

Pose estimation technologies constituted another prominent category ($n = 9$). Tools such as OpenPose, MediaPipe Pose, and skeleton-based representations were applied to track body posture, gestures, hand movements, and motor coordination in classroom, physical education, music, and sign language learning contexts.

Object detection and tracking methods, including YOLO, Viola-Jones, Haar cascade classifiers, and blob detection algorithms, were used in ten studies ($n = 10$).

These approaches enabled the recognition of learning-related objects, student–teacher interactions, gaze direction, cheating behavior, and classroom activities.

Facial expression and emotion recognition technologies were reported in eight studies (n = 8). These systems relied on facial landmarks, CNN-based emotion classifiers, and gaze tracking to analyze affective states, emotional engagement, and self-regulation in both face-to-face and online learning environments.

In addition, several studies implemented integrated or multimodal AI-CV systems (n = 11), combining CV with speech recognition, learning analytics, Bayesian knowledge tracing, or adaptive recommendation engines. A smaller number of studies incorporated augmented or mixed reality combined with CV (n = 4), as well as mobile or low-cost CV solutions suitable for real classroom deployment (n = 5).

Academic Levels and Participants. The reviewed studies were conducted across diverse educational levels. University and higher education contexts were the most frequently represented (n = 17), followed by secondary and high school settings (n = 7) and primary education (n = 4). In two studies, the academic level was mixed or not explicitly specified. Participant sample sizes varied substantially, ranging from small-scale pilot studies with fewer than ten participants to large classroom-based investigations involving more than 200 learners. While some studies did not report participant numbers in detail, most were conducted in authentic educational environments, reflecting real classroom, laboratory, or performance-based learning conditions.

Domain and Instructional Approach. CV technologies were applied across a wide range of educational domains. STEM education was the most frequently represented domain (n = 9), encompassing computer science, artificial intelligence education, science, engineering, and interdisciplinary STEM learning. Physical education constituted another major domain (n = 6), where CV was primarily used for movement analysis, fitness assessment, and motor skill evaluation. General education and classroom analytics studies accounted for seven investigations (n = 7), focusing on classroom behavior analysis, engagement monitoring, and instructional evaluation. Creative and arts-related domains, including music and art education, were represented in four studies (n = 4). Applied linguistics and language-related research appeared less frequently (n = 2), as did healthcare and psychology education (n = 2).

Skills and Learning Outcomes. Across the reviewed studies, CV technologies were predominantly used to support engagement-related and behavioral learning outcomes. Engagement-related skills, including attention, participation, motivation, and behavioral involvement, were the most frequently addressed outcomes (n = 18). Behavioral regulation and self-regulation skills, such as posture control, discipline, and learning behavior monitoring, were targeted in twelve studies (n = 12). Cognitive skills, including critical thinking, problem-solving, and conceptual understanding, were addressed in nine studies (n = 9). Motor and physical skills were emphasized in seven studies (n = 7), particularly in physical education, music performance, and gesture-based interaction contexts. Digital and computational skills, such as AI literacy, programming, and the use of CV tools, appeared in eight studies (n = 8). Emotional awareness and affective skills were examined in six studies (n = 6), while creative and expressive skills, including musical interpretation, sign language comprehension, and artistic expression, were reported in five studies (n = 5). Overall, the findings consistently indicated improvements in engagement, learning efficiency, assessment objectivity, and instructional effectiveness when CV technologies were integrated into educational practice.

Pedagogical Approaches. Although not all studies explicitly stated their pedagogical frameworks, several instructional approaches were identified. Data-driven and evidence-based teaching and evaluation approaches were the most frequently reported (n = 11), with CV systems supporting automated assessment, behavioral analytics, and instructional decision-making. Adaptive and personalized learning approaches appeared in seven studies (n = 7), where CV-based systems adjusted learning content, feedback, or task difficulty based on detected engagement or performance. Project-based and inquiry-based learning approaches were reported in six studies (n = 6), while practice-based or performance-oriented learning was identified in five studies (n = 5). Notably, a considerable number of studies did not clearly specify an underlying pedagogical approach (n = 9), highlighting a common gap between technological implementation and instructional design.

How CV Technologies Were Used. The reviewed studies demonstrated diverse applications of CV in education. Automated classroom monitoring and learning analytics were the most common uses (n = 14), enabling continuous observation of student behavior, attention, and interaction patterns. Engagement and attention detection systems were reported in thirteen studies (n = 13). CV technologies were also employed to support assessment and evaluation processes (n = 10), including performance scoring, behavior classification, and cheating detection. Performance and movement analysis applications appeared in eight studies (n = 8), particularly in physical education, music, and gesture-based learning. Real-time feedback systems were implemented in seven studies (n = 7), while adaptive recommendation and personalized learning systems were described in five studies (n = 5).

Reported Problems and Possible Solutions. Despite the reported benefits, several challenges were consistently identified. The most frequently reported problem was sensitivity to lighting conditions, occlusion, and camera placement (n = 17). Algorithmic limitations, including misclassification and reduced robustness in complex environments, were reported in thirteen studies (n = 13). Additional challenges included hardware and technical constraints (n = 9), limited generalizability across contexts (n = 8), and ethical or privacy concerns related to video recording and data collection (n = 4). Small sample sizes were also common (n = 14), limiting the generalizability of findings. To address these challenges, the reviewed studies proposed several solutions. The most common recommendations included the use of larger and more diverse datasets (n = 16), multi-camera setups and improved recording conditions (n = 12), algorithm optimization and hybrid modeling approaches (n = 11), and the integration of multimodal data sources such as audio or contextual information (n = 9). Teacher training and improved pedagogical integration of CV technologies were also emphasized (n = 7).

In summary, the results demonstrate that CV technologies play an increasingly significant role in educational research and practice. The reviewed studies highlight their effectiveness in enhancing engagement, supporting objective assessment, enabling adaptive learning, and improving instructional decision-making. At the same time, methodological, technical, and pedagogical challenges remain, underscoring the need for more robust study designs and closer integration between technology and educational theory.

4 Discussion

This systematic review examined how CV technologies are applied in educational contexts and identified clear patterns in technology selection, instructional use, and reported learning outcomes. Rather than demonstrating uniform adoption across pedagogical functions, the findings indicate that CV research is concentrated around monitoring, assessment, and performance analysis. This section interprets these patterns and explains why certain technologies and applications dominate current educational research.

Type of Technology and Tools. The predominance of deep learning-based CV models and pose estimation tools can be explained by their robustness and adaptability to real-world classroom environments. Deep learning approaches, particularly convolutional neural networks, are capable of handling variability in lighting, posture, and learner movement, which are common challenges in educational settings. As a result, these models are well suited for automated monitoring of student behavior and engagement. For instance, Kim et al. [3] demonstrated that CNN-based engagement detection systems could reliably identify on-task and off-task behavior in classroom videos, with outcomes closely aligning with teacher observations. Similarly, Vanneste et al. [4] employed gaze tracking and facial landmark detection to analyze student attention during instruction, showing that CV-based indicators can capture subtle engagement patterns that are difficult to observe manually. These examples help explain why behavioral monitoring is one of the most frequent applications of CV in education. Pose estimation technologies were especially prevalent in physical education and performance-based learning contexts. Liu and Lv [1] used pose estimation to evaluate exercise accuracy and provide real-time feedback, resulting in improved motor performance. The frequent use of pose estimation reflects the strong alignment between skeletal movement data and learning objectives in embodied learning domains, whereas more complex multimodal systems were less common due to higher implementation demands.

Educational Tasks and System Functions. The review shows that CV is most often applied to engagement detection, behavior analysis, and automated assessment. These tasks align closely with the core strength of CV: objective visual recognition. For example, Muratuly et al. [7] applied object detection and facial recognition techniques to identify suspicious behaviors during online examinations, illustrating how CV supports academic integrity monitoring. Likewise, Sulla-Torres et al. [2] used movement analysis to automate performance assessment in physical education, reducing subjectivity in evaluation. In contrast, relatively few studies integrated CV into adaptive or personalized instructional systems. This imbalance may be attributed to the difficulty of translating visual analytics into pedagogically meaningful real-time instructional decisions. Consequently, CV is more commonly positioned as a diagnostic and evaluative tool rather than as an adaptive teaching agent.

Skills and Learning Outcomes. The dominance of engagement-related and behavioral outcomes can be explained by the observable nature of visual data. CV is particularly effective at capturing attention, posture, gesture, and participation, which are directly visible learning behaviors. Studies such as Li et al. [5] reported increased participation and reduced off-task behavior when CV-based engagement monitoring was implemented. Similarly, Sulla-Torres et al. [2] found that visual feedback enhanced students' self-monitoring and motor skill accuracy. Cognitive outcomes, including conceptual understanding and problem-solving, were reported less frequently and often as indirect effects. When cognitive gains were observed, they were typically mediated by improved engagement or feedback rather than direct instructional input from CV systems. This suggests that CV primarily supports learning conditions rather than directly facilitating higher-order cognition.

Methodological Considerations. Methodological trends also help explain the observed outcome patterns. Many studies employed short-term or pilot designs focused on feasibility, accuracy, or usability rather than long-term learning impact. Small sample sizes and controlled environments were common, limiting the generalizability of findings. Although quantitative metrics were often complemented by qualitative data, the lack of longitudinal designs constrains conclusions about sustained learning effects.

Advantages and Constraints. Reported advantages, including objective assessment, real-time feedback, and reduced teacher workload, stem from the automation capabilities of CV. Classroom analytics studies (e.g., [9]) illustrate how automated observation supports instructional decision-making. However, technical constraints such as lighting sensitivity, occlusion, and camera placement remain significant barriers. Ethical concerns related to privacy and consent were addressed explicitly in only a small number of studies, further limiting large-scale classroom deployment.

Pedagogical Interpretation. A key limitation identified in this review is the weak articulation of pedagogical frameworks in many CV-based studies. While technological implementations were often sophisticated, their alignment with instructional theory was frequently implicit. Studies that explicitly connected CV tools to formative assessment or practice-based learning demonstrated clearer educational value, suggesting that pedagogy-driven design is essential for meaningful integration.

Overall, CV in education is currently used primarily for monitoring, assessment, and performance analysis due to its strong alignment with observable learning behaviors and technical feasibility. To advance the field, future research should prioritize theory-informed designs, longitudinal studies, and explicit ethical considerations to ensure that CV contributes meaningfully to teaching and learning.

5 Conclusion

This review examined the application of CV technologies in educational contexts by synthesizing empirical evidence. By analyzing studies that implemented vision-based systems in authentic learning environments, the review provides a focused and up-to-date overview of the technological approaches, educational domains, pedagogical practices, learning outcomes, and implementation challenges associated with CV-enhanced education. Unlike prior reviews that addressed artificial intelligence in education broadly, this study offers a targeted analysis of CV as a distinct and rapidly developing technological domain with unique pedagogical affordances.

The findings highlight the considerable potential of CV technologies to enhance educational practice through automated observation, objective assessment, real-time feedback, and data-driven instructional support. Across the reviewed studies, CV systems were most frequently applied to monitor student engagement, analyze behavior, assess performance, and support embodied and practice-based learning. Technologies such as deep learning-based vision models, pose estimation, object detection, and facial or gaze recognition were shown to improve learning efficiency, assessment accuracy, and instructional decision-making, particularly in domains where observable behaviors and physical actions are central to learning processes.

Beyond immediate performance and monitoring benefits, CV also demonstrated value in supporting affective, behavioral, and experiential dimensions of learning. Several studies reported improvements in student engagement, self-regulation, motivation, and awareness of learning behaviors when CV-based feedback or analytics were integrated into instruction. These findings suggest that CV primarily contributes to learning by shaping learning conditions, through enhanced feedback, visibility, and reflection, rather than directly delivering instructional content.

The review reveals important limitations that constrain the widespread adoption of CV in education. Methodological challenges such as small sample sizes, short study durations, and limited longitudinal evidence restrict the generalizability of reported outcomes. Technical constraints, including sensitivity to lighting conditions, occlusion, camera placement, and algorithmic misclassification, remain persistent barriers in real classroom settings. Furthermore, ethical concerns related to privacy, consent, data security, and potential bias were addressed explicitly in only a minority of studies, indicating the need for stronger ethical frameworks and institutional guidelines.

A notable gap identified is the limited articulation of pedagogical frameworks underlying CV-based educational interventions. While many studies demonstrated technically sophisticated implementations, their alignment with established instructional theories was often implicit or underdeveloped. This disconnect underscores the importance of pedagogy-driven design, where CV technologies are intentionally integrated to support clearly defined educational goals rather than functioning solely as monitoring or analytic tools.

CV represents a powerful and emerging component of intelligent educational systems, offering new possibilities for understanding, assessing, and supporting learning through visual data. However, its effective and responsible integration requires a careful balance between technological innovation and pedagogical intent. Future research should prioritize theory-informed designs, larger and more diverse samples, longitudinal evaluations, and explicit ethical considerations. By addressing these challenges, CV technologies can move beyond experimental applications and become sustainable, meaningful tools that enrich teaching and learning across diverse educational contexts. For future reviews, it is suggested to extend the time span of the literature coverage. Doing so would allow for a more comprehensive discussion of the developmental trajectory, research evolution, and changing trends of computer vision in education.

References

1. Liu, F., Lv, J.: Multidimensional analysis of physical education teaching based on big data action scenarios. J Sens. **2022**, 8123456 (2022)
2. Sulla-Torres, J., Martínez, A., López, R., García, P.: Multiplatform computer vision system to support physical fitness assessments in schoolchildren. Appl. Sci. **14**(16), 7140 (2024)
3. Kim, H., Park, J., Lee, S., Choi, Y., Kwon, D.: Evaluation of a computer vision-based system to analyse behavioral changes in high school classrooms. Int. J. Inf. Commun. Technol. Educ. **17**(4), 1–16 (2021)

4. Vanneste, P., Oramas, J., Tuytelaars, T.: Computer vision and human behaviour, emotion and cognition detection: a use case on student engagement. Sensors. **21**(9), 3128 (2021)
5. Li, C., Wang, L., Li, Q., Wang, D.: Intelligent analysis system for teaching and learning cognitive engagement based on computer vision in an immersive virtual reality environment. Appl. Sci. **14**(8), 3149 (2024)
6. El Bahri, N., Bensaid, A., Khaldi, M.: Emotion-aware education through affective computing and learning analytics: insights from a Moroccan university case study. Digital. **5**(3), 45 (2025)
7. Muratuly, D., Denissova, N., Krak, I.: Subject behavior detection and analysis based on computer vision technology. Sci. J. Astana IT University. **11**, 36–47 (2022)
8. Jia, H.: Design and implementation of personalized teaching system for ethnic vocal music learning resources based on computer vision. Int. J. Educ. Innov. Sci. **4**(1), 82–98 (2023)
9. Wu, T.-T., Lee, H.-Y., Chen, Y.-M.: Leveraging computer vision for adaptive learning in STEM education: effect of engagement and self-efficacy. Int. J. Educ. Technol. High. Educ. **20**(53), 1–26 (2023)
10. Shadiev, R., Wu, T.T., Huang, Y.M.: Using image-to-text recognition technology to facilitate vocabulary acquisition in authentic contexts. ReCALL. **32**(2), 195–212 (2020)
11. Zhang, L., Deng, X., Shadiev, R.: A meta-review of generative AI in education: synthesizing findings from systematic reviews. J. Educ. Comput. Res. **07356331261419689** (2026)
12. Shi, G., Li, Y., Shadiev, R.: A systematic review of online persistent learning: methodologies, findings and issues. Br. J. Educ. Technol. **57**(2), 395–422 (2026)
13. Liu, J.W., Shadiev, R.: A review of empirical research on game-based digital citizenship education. Educ. Inf. Technol. **30**, 19365–19417 (2025)
14. Lin, L., Shen, S.S., Shadiev, R., Yu, M.: Review of research on design thinking in K-12 education. Educ. Res. Rev. **47**, 100682 (2025)
15. Shadiev, R., Chen, X., Altinay, F.: A review of research on computer-aided translation technologies and their applications to assist learning and instruction. J. Comput. Assist. Learn. **40**(6), 3290–3323 (2024)

Dark Side of AI in Higher Education – A Scoping Review

Nkosikhona Theoren Msweli(✉) and Emmanuel Samuel Mtsweni

University of South Africa, Roodepoort, Johannesburg 1709, South Africa
mswelnt@unisa.ac.za

Abstract. Artificial intelligence (AI) is progressively transforming teaching and learning experiences in higher education. Some of the advances include simplified practices and smart processes, such as interactive learning content and grading assessments. Students are receiving instant support for complex problems and simplified approaches towards completing assignments or projects. However, there is a "dark side" that comes with the integration of AI, such as compromised academic integrity, among others. This study adopts a scoping review approach to examine the negative impact and challenges associated with the adoption of AI in higher education. Applying inclusion and exclusion criteria, 43 peer-reviewed articles from various databases were reviewed. Literature results demonstrate a rapid increase in studies focusing on AI, with academic integrity and ethical concerns emerging as the most frequently addressed topics. Key findings suggest many students use AI tools for academic work, specifically for assignments and exam questions. The review identifies critical gaps in institutional governance, policy frameworks, and the need for comprehensive AI literacy programs. The results also reveal concerns across four primary domains: ethical issues, algorithmic and implementation biases, negative impacts on student learning, and threats to academic integrity. The study provides recommendations on how the negative impact of AI can be addressed or minimized in education.

Keywords: Artificial Intelligence (AI) · Dark Side · Negative Impact · Higher Education · Ethics

1 Introduction

The integration of artificial intelligence (AI) in higher education is reshaping learning experiences and pedagogical practices. It has accelerated even more dramatically, following the release of advanced generative AI tools in late 2022. Generative AI (GAI) tools like ChatGPT and Bing Chat in higher education institutions (HEIs) are increasingly transforming the sector, benefiting both academics and students [1]. Especially for students, they are provided with individualized support and can get solutions to complex problems instantly. While AI has the potential to transform HEIs, the negative impact that comes with implementation is too much to ignore. The dark side of AI often refers to risks, and challenges associated with its integration in systems [2]. Some concerns

C.-J. Lin et al. (Eds.): ICITL 2026, LNCS 16841, pp. 29–38, 2027.
https://doi.org/10.1007/978-3-032-32112-1_4

arise from the integration of AI tools, often because there are no clear guidelines for learning institutions and students to follow when utilizing these tools [3]. There are also limitations in disclaimers that come with these tools, particularly when it comes to data sources and level of accuracy in data provided. Noting that data plays a critical role in AI solutions, it is of the utmost importance that the data used is of a good quality standard. Ivanov [4] admits that AI is imperfect and associated with numerous ethical and privacy concerns, including the potential for behavioral manipulation. Moreover, Aljuaid [5] questioned its ethical use, particularly paraphrasing versus plagiarism. As higher education continues to debate the integration of AI in teaching and learning practices, significant concerns arise regarding ethics, data privacy, and widening digital divide among students. While AI has numerous benefits, such as automating administrative tasks, its dark side includes critical risks, such as algorithmic bias, lack of transparency in decision-making, and the potential for surveillance [4].

Despite a growing interest among HEIs, especially students, the integration of AI presents substantial challenges, particularly given the lack of guidelines to inform responsible adoption and use [6]. This study acknowledges prior review studies that have investigated this area. For instance, Júnior et al. [7] and Moya et al. [8] investigates the ethical integration and academic integrity of AI in higher education, and recommends that learning institutions adopt a multi-stakeholder institutional framework to manage integration and to ensure transparency. Aljuaid [5] argued, while AI assists with improving grammar and style of writing for both students and academics, there are many concerns around creativity and critical thinking. The scholar suggests a balanced approach be adopted in integrating AI while preserving critical elements of academic writing. Chanpradit [9] also looked at AI in academic writing, focusing mainly on GenAI. The findings of this study are aligned with those of other scholars, identifying improved fluency and proficiency in academic writing. However, academic integrity, over-reliance on AI tools, and impact on creativity were identified as challenges.

The challenges identified are intensified by varying levels of AI literacy and access to technology among students, consequently increasing the educational gap. Therefore, it is imperative to investigate the negative impacts of AI in higher education to develop strategies that ensure equitable access, uphold ethical standards, and foster an inclusive learning environment. Existing research predominantly foregrounds ethical concerns, especially those related to academic integrity. This gap highlights the need for a more holistic understanding of the multifaceted challenges associated with AI deployment in higher education. Therefore, this study aims to identify the risks associated with the adoption of AI in higher education, moving beyond AI detection-centric approaches by exploring responsible mitigation strategies, recognizing the technical limitations of detection tools, and foregrounding data justice principles.

2 Methodology

This study adopts a scoping review approach and follows Preferred Reporting Items for Systematic reviews Meta-Analysis (PRISMA) reporting standards [10]. This review investigates the "dark side" of GAI in higher education, focusing on negative implications, challenges, and threats. The focus is on studies published between 2020 and

2025, as it aligns with the period when many learning institutions adopted educational technologies and the use of AI by stakeholders grew rapidly. Literature search was conducted from November to December 2025 using the following databases: IEEE Xplore Digital Library, Scopus, Science Direct, and ACM Digital Library. The search was restricted to peer-reviewed and English-language journal articles and conference papers. The following search string was used to identify metadata:

TITLE-ABS-KEY ((“generative artificial intelligence” OR “generative AI” OR “GAI” OR “genAI”) AND (“higher education” OR “tertiary education”) AND (“dark side” OR “drawback” OR “risk” OR “challenge” OR “threat” OR “negative impact”)) AND PUBYEAR > 2020 AND PUBYEAR < 2025 AND (LIMIT-TO (DOCTYPE, “ar”) OR LIMIT-TO (DOCTYPE, “cp”)) AND (LIMIT-TO (LANGUAGE, “English”))

Data Analysis: This review employed a rapid scoping methodology appropriate for emerging topics with rapidly expanding literature. Papers were analyzed using AI-assisted content extraction to identify themes, findings, and recommendations across.

Quality Assessment: Given the scoping nature and time constraints, formal quality assessment was not conducted. Papers were included based on relevance rather than methodological rigor, which is noted as a study limitation.

Synthesis Method: Thematic synthesis was used to identify recurring concerns, mechanisms, and recommendations across papers. Frequency estimates (e.g., “85% of studies”) represent approximate prevalence within the analyzed studies rather than precise meta-analytic calculations.

3 Results and Discussion

This section presents the results after the review process and data extraction. After reviewing 43 studies, the results reveal that their primary focus includes: 1. Academic integrity challenges 2. Fairness and bias concerns 3. Privacy and data protection 4. Institutional governance gaps. These results highlight broad consensus among researchers about the most pressing risks requiring attention from HEIs. The study analysis further shows clear temporal patterns in research focus as illustrated in Fig. 1.

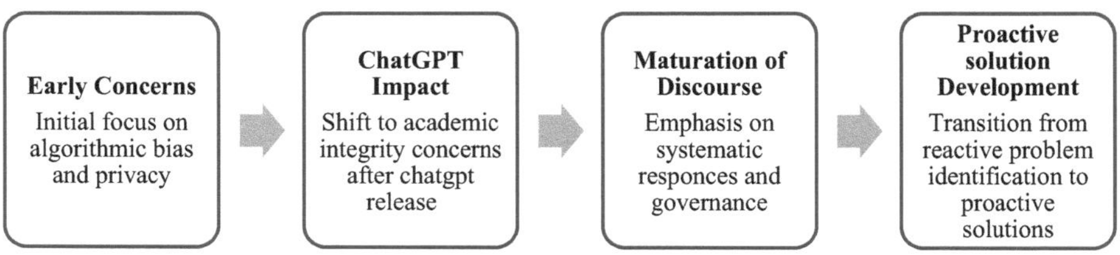

Fig. 1. Temporal evolution (2020–2025)

Between 2020 and 2021, the concerns that emerged were on algorithmic bias and privacy in learning systems. Some of the publications in this period called for early awareness and understanding of AI bias [11]. Then there was a period between 2022 and 2023 after the release of ChatGPT, where academic integrity became a dominant concern. Many publications documented the benefits of ChatGPT and the challenges it poses to academic integrity [12–14]. Williams [15] noted the rising concerns about plagiarism resulting from the AI-generated content. These developments probe for some level of AI literacy among the users and guidelines to ensure that assessment practices remain fair and transparent. The period (2024–2025) suggests the maturation of discourse, with emphasis on proactive responses, such as institutional governance frameworks and pedagogical adaptation, rather than technological solutions. Rather than focusing on AI disruptions, future research needs to focus on building sustainable mechanisms that support the responsible use of AI.

3.1 Negative Impact on the Use of AI in Higher Education

This review identified seven issues that recur across articles. These issues represent fundamental challenges that HEIs must address to ensure ethical integration of AI.

Privacy and data security are among the issues mentioned by the reviewed articles. Studies report issues relating to student data, behavioral data, and learning analytics collected by adaptive AI systems without any permission or informed consent. In many cases, institutional deployments lack data protection frameworks, creating vulnerabilities in how student data is collected, stored, and utilized [3, 16]. While the information may be used for teaching and learning purposes, access to sensitive data by third-party vendors interferes with privacy and confidentiality laws.

With regards to *fairness and bias* appear as a mostly cited concern. AI-driven decision-making systems can reproduce current social inequalities when models and datasets are not designed with justice-aware principles. The following patterns appeared in reviewed studies: unfair outcomes in admissions and grading [8], underrepresentation of marginalized groups in training data, and perpetuation of historical educational inequities [2, 17], unequal access to AI-supported learning resources [5]. Institutions may use AI systems to automate some of the processes, but there is a need to scrutinize the level of transparency and explainability in AI decisions.

Another growing concern is *academic integrity and the issue of authorship (including ghostwriting).* The traditional concept of creative writing has been overshadowed by new forms of automated cheating enabled by GenAI, which is the most debated concern in higher education [7, 8]. The key challenge is the difficulty in distinguishing AI-generated content or AI-paraphrased from student original work. This challenge destabilizes current academic integrity frameworks that have been put in place by institutions.

Transparency and explainability are other issues facing many learning institutions. Many educational institutions deploy AI systems with limited explainability, which undermines accountability on critical decisions such as student admissions, assessment grading, and student support interventions [3]. The major concerns include the reliance on black-box algorithms to make important decisions. Consequently, it becomes difficult to explain, contest or challenge AI-generated outcomes, as there is no algorithmic transparency for users [18]. Lack of transparency, coupled with insufficient documentation of system capabilities and limitations, further exacerbates these issues.

Pedagogical impact and overreliance were also mentioned by the reviewed articles. The increased dependence on AI tools can reduce opportunities for skills and knowledge development, potentially producing weaker learning outcomes [8]. This could result in the underdevelopment of fundamental academic skills or reduced engagement with challenging learning tasks. Over-reliance on AI poses a risk to students accepting AI solutions without any understanding, reducing opportunities for student-lecture engagements and mentorship.

Surveillance issues. Learning institutions are working hard to maintain academic integrity by implementing monitoring systems. Comprehensive surveillance, or excessive use of automated systems (proctoring technologies) to monitor students, may raise ethical concerns [19].

Gaps in institutional readiness. Literature shows that governance structures (including policy and frameworks) and training programs lag significantly behind AI adoption rates, producing inconsistent protections and guidance across learning institutions [16]. In addition, there are limited ethical review processes for AI deployments and resources for responsible AI implementation.

3.2 Classification of Bias in Educational AI Systems

AI systems in higher education show multiple, distinct forms of bias that operate at different stages of development and deployment. Understanding the types of biases that exist is important to come up with mitigation strategies. Literature shows that these biases do not operate in isolation. These types of biases often compound, multiplying the negative effects for already marginalized groups. Therefore, mitigation strategies need to address all three dimensions simultaneously [16] (Table 1).

Evidence in the literature shows that these biases do not operate in isolation. These types of biases often compound, multiplying the negative effects for already marginalized groups. Therefore, mitigation strategies require addressing all three dimensions simultaneously [2, 8, 22].

3.3 Risk of AI on Student Learning

Literature documents several negative outcomes for student learning associated with AI use in higher education. These impacts are often mediated by implementation choices and student beliefs about appropriate AI use. Figure 2 summarises risks to student learning:

Reduced critical thinking can be assumed as a high-severity risk, with multiple scholars warning that it may affect students' independence over time. This concern stems from a lack of AI literacy, and engaging less with tasks that require problem-solving skills, and bypassing the cognitive struggle required for deeper learning [23]. Students need guidance on how AI can be used to complement their skills and augment their intelligence in solving complex and analytical problems. This will also address issues of *AI de-skilling and competency erosion* as students overuse AI tools. Scholars have documented concerns, including declining information literacy, new knowledge generation, creative writing, and weakened domain-specific knowledge acquisition [4, 7]. These challenges may ultimately undermine the credibility of qualifications obtained by students due to incompetence and inadequate knowledge acquisition. *Poor quality or incorrect/misleading feedback* is another growing concern in teaching and learning environment. Common issues include AI "hallucinations," contextually inappropriate answers, feedback lacking pedagogical depth, and reinforcement of misconceptions [9, 24]. Students lacking AI

Table 1. Types of AI Biases in Education

Type of Bias and explanation	Mechanisms	User cases
Algorithmic Bias – embedded in mathematical models, algorithms, or optimization objectives that drive AI system outputs.	Model architecture that amplifies disparities in predictions. Objective functions that prioritize efficiency over equity Feature selection that encodes discriminatory patterns.	Unfair predictions in admissions systems [2, 3]. Biased automated grading that disadvantages certain writing styles.
Data Bias – arise from training or operational datasets that underrepresent groups, encode historical harms, or reflect existing inequalities.	Historical data reflecting past discriminatory practices. Underrepresentation of minority groups in training datasets. Sampling bias in data collection processes. Labeling bias in annotated datasets.	Training datasets omitting or misrepresenting minority students [16, 20]. Language models are trained predominantly on Western, English-language content. Historical grade data reflecting biased human evaluation.
Implementation bias is introduced through deployment choices, institutional practices, and contextual factors during AI system implementation	Inappropriate use cases for AI tools. Poor human oversight and intervention protocols, Inadequate training for system users. Policy gaps allow misuse.	Using general-purpose language models for high-stakes grading [7, 21]. Deploying AI systems without cultural adaptation. Insufficient human review of AI-generated decisions. Unequal access to AI tools across student populations.

Fig. 2. Negative impact on student learning

literacy while using AI for guidance may fail to recognize gaps in their own knowledge. This also has a negative impact on *assessment validity.* This emerges as a significant risk, particularly where students use AI detection-avoidance and paraphrasing tools to disguise AI-generated content, thereby compromising the authenticity, originality, and reliability of student assessments. Assessments should be structured in a manner that incorporates critical thinking, practical application, and authentic learning activities that are difficult to replicate using AI tools alone. *Reduced practice opportunities* arise when students are less inclined to attempt assignments, relying instead on available tools to complete tasks on their behalf. This limits the essential repetition required for skill and technique mastery, reduces opportunities to learn from errors, and ultimately leads to lower engagement with course materials [2, 23]. Such risks undermine the core purpose of teaching and learning, as intended learning outcomes may not be fully achieved.

3.4 Strengths and Limitations in Current Frameworks

Literature has highlighted the importance of having risk frameworks when implementing AI in educational settings. Various frameworks have been proposed, and Fig. 3 highlights their strengths.

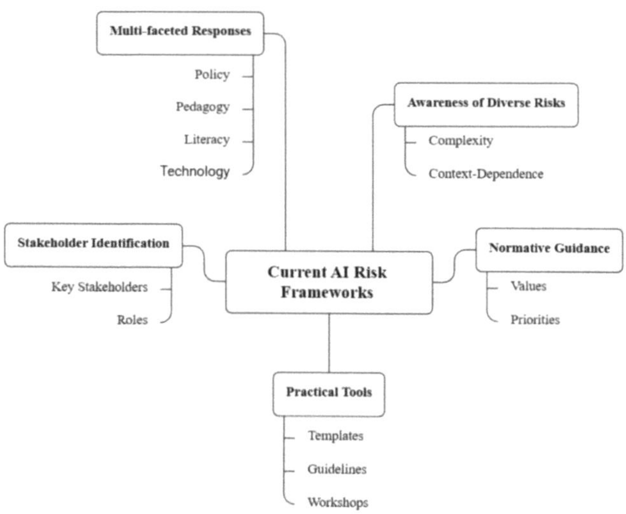

Fig. 3. Strengths in current AI risk frameworks

While these strengths address important elements of implementing AI in higher education, there are also limitations identified within these frameworks. Firstly, the current frameworks lack concrete enforcement mechanisms, leaving policies aspirational without any accountability [8]. Second, they fail to address resource equity, potentially widening inequality between well-resourced and under-resourced institutions [19]. Third, they lack cross-institutional coordination, producing inconsistent standards across institutions and their faculties [8, 25]. Fourth, they lack long-term sustainability mechanisms, focusing on immediate response rather than ongoing evolution [4, 25, 26]. Fifth, they lack rigorous evidence of effectiveness, making it unclear whether they actually work [8, 23]. Sixth, they marginalize student voice, developing policies without meaningful student participation [22]. Seventh, they lack disciplinary specificity, applying one-size-fits-all approaches despite legitimate variation [25]. Eighth, they lack integration across domains, creating fragmented responses [7, 25]. Ninth, they fail to govern vendors and technology, ignoring external actors who shape AI systems [7, 22]. Tenth, they lack measurement and evaluation mechanisms, preventing continuous improvement [8, 26]. These limitations are not minor oversights but fundamental challenges that the field has not yet solved. Addressing them requires not incremental improvements to existing frameworks but a fundamental reconceptualization of AI governance in higher education.

3.4.1 Recommendations

AI will be part of education and many other sectors for a long time. Strategies need to be in place to minimize the identified risk, particularly in educational settings. Some recommendations have been proposed before, but they concentrate more on educational and institutional responses rather than technical fixes [4, 8, 19, 24]. With that being said, this study makes the following recommendations to minimize the negative impact of AI:

1. **Pedagogical alignment and Assessment Redesign.** AI should be integrated as a learning aid rather than a surveillance tool. This includes creating AI-resistant evaluation methods and also assessments that feature AI without compromising the learning outcomes.
2. **AI Literacy Programs.** The programs should be designed for all relevant stakeholders (including students, administrators, and faculty members) on how to use AI ethically, responsibly, and appropriately. AI policy is not sufficient without awareness.
3. **Governance Frameworks.** Effective governance ensures that clear and transparent policies, procedures, and accountability mechanisms are in place to guide the responsible development, deployment, and use of AI systems. Governance should also support risk management, and this can be achieved by having a risk strategy for AI integration in education.
4. **Detection Limitation Recognition.** Acknowledging the technical limitations of AI detection tools is critical, as such systems are often prone to false positives, false negatives, and contextual inaccuracies. Institutions need to acknowledge that over-reliance on AI detection systems may lead to unfair academic judgments, erosion of trust, and inconsistent enforcement of academic integrity policies.
5. **Data Justice Focus.** Targeting equity in AI deployment decisions needs to be prioritised to prevent the reproduction or amplification of existing social, cultural, and educational inequalities. The approaches adopted should consider how data are collected, represented, relevant, and used, ensuring that AI systems do not disadvantage any student cohorts. Embedding data justice principles within AI governance and pedagogical practices may support inclusive, fair, and socially responsible educational outcomes.

Acknowledgments. None.

Disclosure of Interests Authors have no competing interests to declare.

References

1. Shanto, S., Ahmed, Z., Jony, A.: PAIGE: a generative AI-based framework for promoting assignment integrity in higher education. STEM Educ. **3**(4), 288–305 (2023). https://doi.org/10.3934/steme.2023018
2. Wach, K., et al.: The dark side of generative artificial intelligence: a critical analysis of controversies and risks of ChatGPT. Entrep. Bus. Econ. Rev. **11**(2) (2023). https://doi.org/10.15678/EBER.2023.110201
3. Shamsi, S.A., Hamami, R.A., Ali, S., Elsayary, A.: Impacts of AI usage ethically on students. J. Syst. Cyber. Inf. **23**(2), 7–14 (2025). https://doi.org/10.54808/JSCI.23.02.7
4. Ivanov, S.: The dark side of artificial intelligence in higher education. Total Qual. Manag. Bus. Excell. **34**(15–16), 1055–1082 (2023). https://doi.org/10.1080/02642069.2023.2258799
5. Aljuaid, H.: The impact of artificial intelligence tools on academic writing instruction in higher education: a systematic review. Arab World English J., 26–55 (2024). https://doi.org/10.24093/awej/ChatGPT.2
6. Yusuf, F.A.: Trends, opportunities, and challenges of artificial intelligence in elementary education: a systematic literature review. J. Integr. Elementary Educ. **5**(1), 109–127 (2025). https://doi.org/10.21580/JIEED.V5I1.25594
7. Cruvinel Júnior, L., Ascama, O.H., Marques da Silva, M.: AI ethics in higher education: a review of ethical challenges. In: International Conference on the Ethical and Social Impacts of ICT, pp. 192–203. Springer, Cham (2026). https://doi.org/10.1007/978-3-032-01429-0_17
8. Moya, B., et al.: Academic integrity and artificial intelligence in higher education contexts: a rapid scoping review. Canadian Perspect. Acad. Integr. **7**(3) (2024). https://doi.org/10.55016/ojs/cpai.v7i3.78123
9. Chanpradit, T.: Generative artificial intelligence in academic writing in higher education: a systematic review. Edelweiss Appl. Sci. Technol. **9**(4), 889–906 (2025). https://doi.org/10.55214/25768484.v9i4.6128
10. Siddaway, A.P., Wood, A.M., Hedges, L.V.: How to do a systematic review: a best practice guide for conducting and reporting narrative reviews, meta-analyses, and meta-syntheses. Annu. Rev. Psychol. **70**, 747–770 (2019). https://doi.org/10.1146/annurev-psych-010418-102803
11. Ramachandran, S., Cutchin, S.M., Fu, S.: Raising algorithm bias awareness among computer science students through library and computer science instruction. In: ASEE Annual Conference and Exposition Proceedings. ASEE (2021). https://doi.org/10.18260/1-2-37634
12. Gallent-Torres, C., Zapata-González, A., Ortego-Hernando, J.L.: The impact of generative artificial intelligence in higher education: a focus on ethics and academic integrity. RELIEVE – Revista Electrónica de Investigación y Evaluación Educativa. **29**(2) (2023). https://doi.org/10.30827/relieve.v29i2.29134
13. Baidoo-Anu, D., Owusu Ansah, L.: Education in the era of generative artificial intelligence: understanding the potential benefits of ChatGPT in promoting teaching and learning. J. Artif. Intell. **52**(7), 52–62 (2023)
14. Mironova, J., Djakona, V., Riashchenko, V., Dimitrova, S.I., Kinderis, R.: Ethical concerns in using generative tools in higher education: a cross-country study. In: ETR 2024 Proceedings, vol. II, pp. 444–447 (2024). https://doi.org/10.17770/etr2024vol2.8097
15. Williams, R.T.: The ethical implications of using generative chatbots in higher education. Front. Educ. **8**, 1331607 (2024). https://doi.org/10.3389/feduc.2023.1331607

16. Francis, N.J., Jones, S., Smith, D.P.: Generative AI in higher education: balancing innovation and integrity. Br. J. Biomed. Sci. **81**, 14048 (2025). https://doi.org/10.3389/bjbs.2024.14048
17. Ogalo, E.O., Mtenzi, F.: Leveraging artificial intelligence tools for learning: academic integrity and ethics in higher education in Kenya. In: Artificial Intelligence, Digital Learning, and Leadership: Redefining Higher Education, pp. 1–36. IGI Global (2024). https://doi.org/10.4018/979-8-3373-0025-2.ch001
18. Elliott, K., et al.: Towards an equitable digital society: artificial intelligence and corporate digital responsibility. Society. **58**, 179–188 (2021). https://doi.org/10.1007/s12115-021-00594-8
19. Sharma, D.: Balancing innovation and integrity in the Pacific: exploring the dual impact of AI on tertiary education in Fiji. Int. J. Soc. Sci. Lang. Linguist. **5**(9), 14–21 (2024)
20. Ardito, C.G.: Generative AI detection in higher education assessments. New Dir. Teach. Learn. **2025**(182), 11–28 (2025). https://doi.org/10.1002/tl.20624
21. Slimi, Z., Carballido, B.V.: Navigating the ethical challenges of artificial intelligence in higher education: an analysis of seven global AI ethics policies. TEM J. **12**(2), 590–602 (2023). https://doi.org/10.18421/TEM122-02
22. Pechenkina, E.: Artificial intelligence for good? Challenges and possibilities of AI in higher education from a data justice perspective. In: Higher Education for Good: Teaching and Learning Futures, pp. 239–266. Open Book Publishers (2023). https://doi.org/10.11647/OBP.0363.09
23. Mannuru, N.R., et al.: Artificial intelligence in developing countries: the impact of generative artificial intelligence technologies for development. Inf. Dev. **41**(3), 1036–1054 (2025). https://doi.org/10.1177/02666669231200628
24. Gruenhagen, J.H., Sinclair, P.M., Carroll, J.A., Baker, P.R.A., Wilson, A., Demant, D.: The rapid rise of generative AI and its implications for academic integrity: students' perceptions and use of chatbots for assistance with assessments. Comput. Educ. Artif. Intell. **7**, 100273 (2024). https://doi.org/10.1016/j.caeai.2024.100273
25. Wang, H., Dang, A., Wu, Z., Mac, S.: Generative artificial intelligence in higher education: viewing ChatGPT through universities' policies, resources, and guidelines. Comput. Educ. Artif. Intell. **7**, 100326 (2024). https://doi.org/10.1016/j.caeai.2024.100326
26. Wohn, D.Y., Carroll, J.M.: Generative AI in virtual reality communities: a preliminary analysis of the VRChat discord community. In: Extended Abstracts of the CHI Conference on Human Factors in Computing Systems, pp. 1–11. ACM (2025). https://doi.org/10.1145/3706599.3720120

AI-Assisted Speech-Based Corrective Feedback System and Its Application to Facilitate Intercultural Competence Development

Asror Muhamedov[1], Rustam Shadiev[2](✉), Bayarmaa Dashnyam[3], Narzikul Shadiev[4], Mirzaali Fayziev[4], Fahriye Altınay[5], Nurassyl Kerimbayev[6], Laura Smagulova[7], and Elena Gaevskaia[8]

[1] Vatan University, Tashkent 100100, Republic of Uzbekistan
[2] Zhejiang University, Hangzhou 310058, People's Republic of China
rustamsh@gmail.com
[3] National University of Mongolia, Ulaanbaatar 210648, Mongolia
[4] Samarkand State Pedagogical Institute, Samarkand 140100, Republic of Uzbekistan
[5] Near East University, Nicosia 99138, Cyprus
[6] Al-Farabi Kazakh National University, Almaty 050040, Republic of Kazakhstan
[7] Zhetysu University, Taldykorgan 040000, Republic of Kazakhstan
[8] Saint Petersburg State University, Saint Petersburg 199034, Russian Federation

Abstract. This study addressed linguistic challenges that frequently arise in intercultural spoken communication, particularly when interlocutors rely on a shared lingua franca such as English. In intercultural exchanges where participants possess differing levels of language proficiency, inaccuracies in pronunciation, grammar, and lexical choice may disrupt mutual understanding, constrain meaningful interaction, and ultimately limit the development of intercultural competence. To mitigate such challenges, we integrated an AI-Assisted Speech-Based Corrective Feedback System (AISCF) designed to provide automated, real-time feedback on spoken language performance. The system transcribed participants' speech and delivered corrective guidance to enhance linguistic accuracy prior to and during intercultural exchanges. The study involved university students from China and Kazakhstan who engaged in online spoken communication and cultural information sharing in English. Given that English was not the first language of the participants, AISCF support was incorporated to facilitate clearer expression and more effective interaction. The primary objective was to examine the extent to which integrating AISCF technology into cultural exchanges could support the development of intercultural competence. In addition, the study explored participants' perceptions of the technological support provided. Findings indicated significant gains in participants' intercultural competence following the intervention. Moreover, students reported favorable attitudes toward the AISCF system, emphasizing its usefulness in enhancing spoken clarity and confidence during intercultural communication. Based on these results, the study offers theoretical and pedagogical implications for the integration of AI-supported corrective feedback technologies in online intercultural learning environments.

Keywords: AI-Assisted Speech-Based Corrective Feedback System · Intercultural Competence · Perception

C.-J. Lin et al. (Eds.): ICITL 2026, LNCS 16841, pp. 39–45, 2027.
https://doi.org/10.1007/978-3-032-32112-1_5

1 Introduction

In an era characterized by rapid globalization and digital connectivity, communication across cultural boundaries has become both commonplace and essential [1]. Individuals from diverse linguistic and cultural backgrounds increasingly interact for academic, professional, and social purposes [2]. While such interaction creates valuable opportunities for mutual understanding and collaboration, it also presents challenges [3, 4]. Differences in cultural norms, values, and communicative styles may lead to misunderstanding or conflict if not navigated appropriately [5]. Developing intercultural competence, encompassing cultural knowledge, awareness, sensitivity, and the ability to act effectively across cultural contexts, has therefore become a central objective of contemporary education [6, 7].

Intercultural learning is widely understood as a dynamic process that unfolds through communication and the exchange of culture-related information [8]. When learners from different cultural backgrounds engage in meaningful dialogue, they gradually expand their understanding of one another's perspectives and social realities [9]. Through such interaction, they develop knowledge of cultural practices, awareness of similarities and differences, sensitivity to contextual nuances, and the competence required to collaborate across cultural boundaries [3, 4, 6, 7]. Online intercultural learning environments, in particular, offer structured yet authentic spaces in which learners can communicate with real partners beyond their immediate context [8, 9]. These environments combine guidance from instructors with genuine intercultural interaction, thereby supporting both safety and authenticity [10].

However, language remains a critical factor influencing the quality and effectiveness of intercultural exchanges [2, 10]. In many intercultural learning activities, English functions as a lingua franca among participants who do not share a common first language [10]. Differences in pronunciation, grammatical accuracy, and lexical choice may impede comprehension, reduce confidence, and constrain the depth of cultural discussion. When communication breakdowns occur, opportunities for meaningful intercultural learning may be diminished. Moreover, in traditional instructional settings, providing individualized corrective feedback on spoken language can be time-consuming and difficult to sustain, particularly in large-scale or online exchanges [10].

Recent advances in artificial intelligence and machine learning have introduced new possibilities for addressing such challenges [11]. Speech-to-text recognition technologies can transcribe spoken input into written text with high levels of accuracy, enabling learners to visualize their oral production [12]. Automated corrective feedback systems can then identify linguistic errors and provide immediate explanations and suggestions for improvement [13, 14]. While these technologies have been widely explored independently in language learning contexts, their integrated application to support spoken intercultural communication remains underexplored.

To address this gap, the present study implemented an AI-Assisted Speech-Based Corrective Feedback System (AISCF), which combines speech-to-text recognition with automated corrective feedback to enhance the clarity and accuracy of spoken English during intercultural exchanges. University students from China and Kazakhstan participated in online intercultural learning activities in which they exchanged culture-related information through verbal communication. By using AISCF technology, participants received real-time feedback on pronunciation, grammar, and word choice, enabling them to refine their spoken content and engage more confidently in dialogue.

This study aimed to investigate whether integrating AISCF technology into online intercultural learning activities could facilitate the development of participants' intercultural competence. Additionally, it sought to explore learners' perceptions of AISCF support and its role in shaping their communication experience. By examining the pedagogical potential of speech-enabled corrective feedback in intercultural learning activities, this research contributes practical and theoretical insights into the integration of AI technologies for enhancing intercultural learning in digitally mediated environments.

2 Method

A total of 28 university students participated in the study, including 14 students from China and 14 from Kazakhstan. The majority were first-year students majoring in social sciences. Participants were recruited through official university social media groups, which facilitated voluntary participation and ensured a diverse representation within the sample.

Participants engaged in a structured online intercultural learning project centered on the exchange of culture-related knowledge through spoken communication. Each student selected a cultural topic of personal interest (e.g., historical figures, traditions, or cultural landmarks) and conducted independent research to gather relevant information, images, and contextual details. To support preparation, researchers provided sample manuscripts and example videos that guided participants in effectively introducing their own cultures. In some cases, participants also explored relevant cultural sites or resources firsthand to deepen their understanding. Based on this preparation, participants organized their findings into scripts and used the technology to practice, refine, and improve their pronunciation, grammar, and word choice before recording video presentations. These videos introduced cultural artifacts, traditions, and culturally significant topics to foreign peers while also including questions designed to encourage intercultural dialogue. All video content was reviewed by researchers before submission to ensure quality and accuracy. Chinese and Kazakh students who selected similar topics were paired and exchanged their recorded videos asynchronously. After viewing their partners' presentations, they responded to questions and comments, participated in follow-up exchanges, and completed reflective tasks comparing cultural similarities and differences. Because the feedback was private and used only during preparation, it enhanced speaking quality without interrupting the natural flow of authentic intercultural communication.

To facilitate the exchange of videos and related materials, participants used WeTransfer, an online file-sharing platform that enabled efficient transfer of large files. After sharing and receiving their partners' videos, participants engaged in asynchronous question-and-answer (Q&A) interactions, asking about cultural content, clarifying details, and responding to comments. This process promoted active engagement, deeper exploration of presented cultural topics, and more meaningful intercultural dialogue. Following these exchanges, participants completed reflective activities in which they evaluated what they had learned, considered their intercultural experiences, and compared similarities and differences between their own cultural presentations and those of their partners. They also provided reflections on their use of the technology, offering insights into its effectiveness in supporting spoken communication, language improvement, and cross-cultural learning.

To support the quality of spoken communication, the project integrated the AISCF tool, which combines speech-to-text recognition with automated corrective feedback. When students practiced their scripts orally, the system first transcribed their speech into text in real time using AI-based speech recognition, and then analyzed the transcribed content for pronunciation, grammar, and word choice issues through an automated feedback mechanism. Detected errors were highlighted with explanations and suggested revisions, enabling learners to clearly understand the nature of their mistakes and refine their spoken content before recording their final videos. For example, if a learner mispronounced a word or used an inappropriate grammatical structure, the system could identify the issue, explain why it was problematic, and recommend a more accurate alternative. This process allowed students to repeatedly practice, review, and selectively accept or ignore feedback based on their own judgment, thereby strengthening learner autonomy while improving communication quality. Importantly, corrective feedback remained private and was not visible to communication partners, ensuring that interaction flowed naturally without interrupting authentic cross-cultural exchange.

By allowing participants to rehearse, self-correct, and improve linguistic accuracy prior to intercultural exchange, AISCF functioned as a scaffold for clearer expression and greater confidence. The integration of this system supported meaningful communication while minimizing language-related misunderstandings.

At the beginning of the study, participants completed a background questionnaire and a pre-test measuring their initial level of intercultural competence (IC). During the preparatory phase, researchers introduced the AISCF technology, provided detailed instructions, and conducted training sessions to ensure that participants could use the system effectively in their language learning activities. The procedures and expectations of the intercultural learning project were also clearly explained.

Participants then carried out the culture-learning tasks, engaging in online intercultural communication while using AISCF to improve pronunciation, grammar, and word choice. After completing the activities, they took a post-test to assess changes in their intercultural competence. Finally, selected participants took part in interviews to share their reflections and provide qualitative feedback on their learning experience and the usefulness of the AISCF technology.

Data were collected using three instruments. (1) Intercultural Competence Questionnaire: Intercultural competence was measured using an instrument adapted from Fantini (2009). The questionnaire included 39 items covering four dimensions: knowledge (10 items), attitude (11 items), skills (8 items), and awareness (10 items). Responses were recorded on a five-point Likert scale ranging from 0 ("incompetent") to 5 ("highly competent"). (2) Perceptions of AISCF Technology Questionnaire. Participants' perceptions of the AISCF system were assessed using a questionnaire adapted from Davis (1989). This instrument consisted of 19 items examining perceived usefulness (6 items), perceived ease of use (6 items), and intention to continue using the technology (7 items). All items were rated on a seven-point Likert scale ranging from 0 ("strongly disagree") to 7 ("strongly agree"). (3) One-on-One Structured Interviews. Upon completion of the learning activities, individual structured interviews were conducted with each participant. The interviews included open-ended questions designed to explore participants' experiences of intercultural competence development and their views on the effectiveness and practicality of the AISCF technology.

3 Results and Discussion

The results of the paired-samples t-tests indicated statistically significant differences between pre-test and post-test scores across all four dimensions of intercultural competence: knowledge ($t = 7.199$, $p < .001$), attitude ($t = 5.435$, $p < .001$), skills ($t = 5.425$, $p < .001$), and awareness ($t = 5.381$, $p < .001$). In each case, post-test scores were significantly higher than pre-test scores.

These findings provide strong evidence that the online intercultural learning activities supported by AISCF technology positively contributed to participants' intercultural competence development. Following the intervention, students demonstrated enhanced cultural knowledge and a greater capacity to identify and compare similarities and differences between their own culture and that of their partners. They also exhibited more favorable attitudes and increased curiosity toward the target culture. Improvements in intercultural skills and awareness further suggest that participants became more capable of engaging thoughtfully and effectively in cross-cultural interactions.

Generally, the results underscore the effectiveness of integrating AISCF technology into online intercultural learning environments, particularly in strengthening learners' cultural knowledge, attitudes, skills, and awareness.

Results from the perceptions questionnaire showed that participants held generally positive views of the AISCF technology, with mean scores exceeding 5.38 across all measured dimensions. Participants perceived the system as useful for supporting their intercultural learning, easy to operate, and expressed a clear intention to continue using it in the future. These quantitative findings were consistent with insights obtained from interviews.

In interviews, the participants reported that AISCF facilitated their speaking practice by converting spoken input into text and providing immediate feedback on pronunciation, grammar, and word choice. This process enabled them to identify errors, review explanations, and apply suggested corrections before engaging with their partners. As a result, they felt more confident and better prepared for intercultural communication. Many participants emphasized that the system helped them produce clearer and more accurate spoken content, thereby enhancing the effectiveness of their exchanges.

The technology was also regarded as user-friendly. After receiving training and instructions, most participants quickly understood how to integrate AISCF into their preparation process. Its perceived usefulness and accessibility motivated most of the participants to adopt it in future learning activities.

Nevertheless, several limitations were noted. A few participants reported occasional inaccuracies in speech recognition, which sometimes led to irrelevant feedback. These issues were primarily associated with mispronunciation; once pronunciation improved, recognition accuracy also increased and such inaccuracies largely disappeared. Some participants also mentioned technical constraints related to device performance and internet connectivity, which occasionally caused delays in feedback generation. In most cases, these delays were linked to unstable connections or the limited processing capacity of older devices and tools with lower memory. When participants used more stable internet access and newer tools or devices, these problems were substantially reduced or eliminated. Despite these concerns, the overall evaluation remained positive, highlighting AISCF's practical value in supporting intercultural spoken communication.

4 Conclusion

This study examined the integration of the AISCF technology into online intercultural learning activities between Chinese and Kazakh students. Intercultural communication offers meaningful opportunities for competence development; however, linguistic limitations often constrain the quality of such exchanges. By incorporating AISCF to support pronunciation, grammar, and word choice during spoken preparation, the project sought to reduce language-related barriers and enhance communication clarity.

The findings indicated significant improvements across all dimensions of intercultural competence (i.e. knowledge, skills, attitudes, and awareness) following participation in the AISCF-supported activities. Participants also reported positive perceptions of the technology, emphasizing its usefulness, ease of use, and value in improving spoken accuracy. Many expressed willingness to continue using the system in future learning contexts. These results suggest that AISCF can serve as an effective scaffold for intercultural spoken communication in online intercultural learning settings.

From a pedagogical perspective, educators may consider integrating AISCF or similar AI-supported feedback tools into intercultural communication tasks, particularly for speaking practice. Providing high-accuracy systems with localized language interfaces may further enhance learner engagement and acceptance. Future research could explore the impact of AISCF on learner engagement, emotional experience, and long-term development, as well as its applicability in other content areas delivered through a foreign language.

Nevertheless, certain limitations should be acknowledged. The sample size was relatively small, the project duration was limited, and participants were recruited through convenience sampling without a control group. Future studies should employ larger and more diverse samples, include comparison groups, conduct power analyses, and examine learners' behavioral interaction data with AISCF to provide a more comprehensive evaluation of its effectiveness. It is also recommended that future studies incorporate qualitative interviews to gain in-depth insights into users' specific perceptions.

Acknowledgments. N/A

Disclosure of Interests The authors have no competing interests to declare that are relevant to the content of this article.

References

1. Enny, F.S., Mannan, M., Maruf, T.I.: The impact of globalization on intercultural communication and education: a qualitative study. ABC J. Adv. Res. **14**(1), 1–14 (2025)
2. Shadiev, R., Feng, Y., Zhussupova, R., Altinay, F.: Effects of speech-enabled corrective feedback technology on EFL speaking skills, anxiety and confidence. Comput. Assist. Lang. Learn. **1-37** (2024)
3. Shadiev, R., Hwang, W.Y., Nguyen, R.G.: AI-enhanced cross-cultural learning with contextualization, personalization, and socialization in authentic contexts. Interact. Learn. Environ. **1-29** (2026)
4. Shadiev, R., et al.: Enhancing global artificial intelligence literacy, innovation and entrepreneurship through an exploratory cross-cultural study: interactions with pedagogical agents in immersive virtual reality environments. J. Educ. Comput. Res., 1–37 (2026)
5. Guo, W.: Conflict resolution in intercultural communication: strategies for managing cultural conflicts. Humanit. Soc. Sci. Commun. **12**(1), 1–10 (2025)
6. Shadiev, R., et al.: Facilitating cross-cultural competence of students in an interactive VR learning environment. Educ. Technol. Soc. **28**(1), 78–108 (2025)
7. Shadiev, R., Wang, X., Shen, S.: Effects of immersion and interactive strategies on students' intercultural competence in virtual learning environments. Educ. Inf. Technol. **30**(5), 5883–5919 (2025)
8. Çiftçi, E.Y., Savaş, P.: The role of telecollaboration in language and intercultural learning: a synthesis of studies published between 2010 and 2015. ReCALL. **30**(3), 278–298 (2018)
9. Cai, L., Yun, H.: The cultivation of intercultural communicative competence in senior high school English teaching-based on China's standards of English ability. J. Lang. Teach. Res. **11**(4), 616–622 (2020)
10. Shadiev, R., Yu, J.T.: Review of research on computer-assisted language learning with a focus on intercultural education. Comput. Assist. Lang. Learn. **37**(4), 841–871 (2024)
11. Zhang, L., Deng, X., Shadiev, R.: A meta-review of generative AI in education: synthesizing findings from systematic reviews. J. Educ. Comput. Res., 1–25 (2026)
12. Ryba, K., McIvor, T., Shakir, M., Paez, D.: Liberated learning: analysis of university students' perceptions and experiences with continuous automated speech recognition. J. Instr. Sci. Technol. **9**(1), 1–19 (2006)
13. Shang, H.: Exploring online peer feedback and automated CF on EFL writing performance. Interact. Learn. Environ. **30**(1), 4–16 (2022)
14. Shadiev, R., Feng, Y.: Using automated corrective feedback tools in language learning: a review study. Interact. Learn. Environ. **32**(6), 2538–2566 (2024)

Systematic Review and Meta-Analysis of the Effects of High-Fidelity Simulation-Based Education on Learning Outcomes in Undergraduate Nursing Education

I-Fan Liu(✉)

Department of Allied Health Education and Digital Learning, National Taipei University of Nursing and Health Sciences, No. 365, Ming-te Rd, Taipei City, Taiwan
ifliuG@gmail.com

Abstract. As healthcare environments become increasingly complex and clinical placement opportunities become more limited, high-fidelity simulation (HFS) has emerged as an important instructional strategy in nursing education. This study aimed to systematically evaluate the effects of HFS interventions on learning outcomes among undergraduate nursing students. Following the PRISMA guidelines, randomized controlled trials (RCTs) published up to February 2026 were included and synthesized through meta-analysis. A total of nine RCTs involving 691 nursing students were analyzed. The results demonstrated that HFS had a statistically significant moderate effect on improving critical thinking, with moderate heterogeneity. However, although positive trends were observed for knowledge, clinical skills, satisfaction, and self-confidence, these effects did not reach statistical significance and were associated with high heterogeneity. The findings indicate that HFS has a stable and significant effect on enhancing critical thinking among nursing students. These results provide evidence to inform future curriculum planning and instructional decision-making in nursing education.

Keywords: High-fidelity simulation · Nursing education · Critical thinking · Meta-analysis

1 Introduction

As healthcare systems become increasingly complex, high-risk medical interventions continue to rise, and patient safety awareness intensifies, traditional lecture-based instruction and opportunistic clinical learning are no longer sufficient to ensure that undergraduate nursing students acquire the competencies required for contemporary clinical practice. Nursing education is therefore confronted with the dual challenges of restricted clinical placement opportunities and increasing pressure to maintain teaching quality [1]. In recent years, clinical training opportunities have been further limited due to excessive workloads in healthcare institutions, COVID-19 infection control policies, and growing awareness of patients' rights, resulting in fewer hands-on practice opportunities for nursing students in real clinical settings [2]. Consequently, how to provide

C.-J. Lin et al. (Eds.): ICITL 2026, LNCS 16841, pp. 46–57, 2027.
https://doi.org/10.1007/978-3-032-32112-1_6

systematic, repeatable, and standardized clinical learning experiences while ensuring patient safety has become a critical issue in modern nursing education.

Against this background, simulation-based teaching has gradually become one of the core strategies in nursing education. It refers to the recreation of realistic clinical scenarios within a safe and controlled environment, enabling nursing students to learn without threat or harm. Importantly, simulation does not pose direct risks to patients and allows students to accumulate experience through experiential learning [3, 4]. However, in increasingly complex healthcare environments, simulation approaches must vary in levels of fidelity to meet evolving clinical training needs. According to Kolb's (1984) Experiential Learning Theory, learning occurs through a cyclical process involving four stages: concrete experience, reflective observation, abstract conceptualization, and active experimentation [5]. Simulation teaching with varying levels of fidelity aligns closely with this framework, as realistic clinical scenarios and computerized full-body patient simulators provide students with concrete experiences that facilitate reflection, conceptual understanding, and behavioral adjustment during practice.

Simulation fidelity is generally categorized into three levels: low, medium, and high fidelity. To address the challenges associated with limited clinical placements, high-fidelity simulation (HFS) has become an increasingly prevalent and central instructional strategy in contemporary nursing education [1]. In HFS-based courses, full-body computerized patient simulators are used to replicate realistic clinical conditions and patient responses, aiming to closely mirror authentic clinical scenarios. This highly immersive approach has gained widespread adoption in nursing education [1, 6, 7]. Through repeated practice within simulated scenarios, students are able to identify and correct errors in a safe learning environment. Consequently, HFS not only provides learning experiences that closely approximate real clinical settings but has also been reported to substitute for up to half of traditional clinical training time, contributing to its growing popularity in nursing education [8].

Regarding learning outcomes, the literature indicates that high-fidelity simulation (HFS) can significantly enhance multiple competencies. First, in terms of critical thinking, simulated scenarios provide students with both active and passive learning opportunities. Through group discussions, interactive exercises, and structured feedback, learners are encouraged to engage in reflective analysis and clinical reasoning, thereby fostering critical thinking [9]. Second, HFS offers a contextualized learning environment that helps bridge gaps in students' theoretical knowledge and limited clinical experience, leading to improvements in clinical knowledge performance [10]. Third, by replicating realistic clinical situations, HFS enables students to learn from mistakes in a safe environment. Error analysis and instructor-guided debriefing further strengthen clinical skill performance [11]. Additionally, HFS training has been shown to enhance clinical reasoning ability and self-confidence among nursing students, empowering them to provide patient care with greater assurance and increasing their learning satisfaction [12]. Therefore, beyond building a solid theoretical foundation, nursing students aspire to master essential clinical care skills during their academic training, which not only enhances professional confidence but also effectively stimulates learning interest and intrinsic motivation [8].

In summary, although [7, 11] have conducted systematic reviews and meta-analyses on the effects of high-fidelity simulation (HFS) in nursing education, limitations remain in the existing body of evidence. Therefore, the present study aims to examine the effectiveness and implementation characteristics of HFS interventions in enhancing undergraduate nursing students' critical thinking, knowledge, clinical skills, satisfaction, and self-confidence. By providing a comprehensive and systematic synthesis of current evidence, this study seeks to offer a more robust empirical foundation and practical recommendations for future nursing practice education and curriculum development.

2 Methods

The included studies were required to meet the following criteria: (1) randomized controlled trial (RCT) design; (2) participants were undergraduate nursing students; (3) the intervention in the experimental group was high-fidelity simulation (HFS); and (4) the full text was published in English. Studies were excluded if: (1) the participants were not enrolled in a nursing degree program or were taking courses unrelated to nursing; or (2) the data were incomplete or insufficient for analysis.

Based on the predefined inclusion and exclusion criteria, a systematic search was conducted in PubMed, Embase, Cochrane Library, and CINAHL. The search covered all relevant English-language studies published from database inception through February 28, 2026, without restrictions on country of origin or year of publication. All studies that appeared to meet the inclusion criteria after initial screening were subjected to full-text review. In addition, manual searches were performed to ensure that no potentially eligible studies were overlooked. The search terms encompassed all subject terms and free terms "High-fidelity simulation", "Nursing students", and "Nursing education".

All relevant studies were independently screened and assessed by two reviewers. In cases of disagreement that could not be resolved through discussion, a third reviewer was consulted to reach a final decision. Only randomized controlled trials (RCTs) were included. In the selected RCTs, the experimental group received high-fidelity simulation (HFS) as the primary intervention, while the control group received traditional education. The outcome measures included critical thinking, knowledge, clinical skills, satisfaction, and self-confidence.

Data extraction was independently conducted by two reviewers using a predefined data extraction form. The extracted information included the author(s), country of origin, year of publication, intervention details for each group, sample size, measurement instruments, and outcome indicators. Only outcome measures reported in at least two studies were included in the meta-analysis. The methodological quality of the included studies was assessed using the Cochrane Collaboration's Risk of Bias tool (RoB 2.0). This tool evaluates potential bias across five domains: the randomization process, deviations from intended interventions, missing outcome data, measurement of the outcome, and selection of the reported result.

Statistical analyses were performed using Cochrane Review Manager software (RevMan version 5.4). Because the included studies employed different measurement scales, a random-effects model was applied. For continuous outcomes, effect sizes were calculated using standardized mean differences (SMDs). Heterogeneity was assessed using the I^2 statistic. I^2 values of 25%, 50%, and 75% were interpreted as indicating low, moderate, and high heterogeneity, respectively [13].

3 Results

3.1 Studies Selection

A total of 1,625 English-language articles were initially identified. After removing 972 duplicates using EndNote X9 and an additional 166 duplicates through manual screening, 1,138 duplicate records were excluded. Following title and abstract screening, 52 potentially relevant studies were identified for further assessment. After full-text review, 43 studies were excluded, and nine randomized controlled trials (RCTs) were ultimately included in the final analysis. The study selection process is illustrated in Fig. 1.

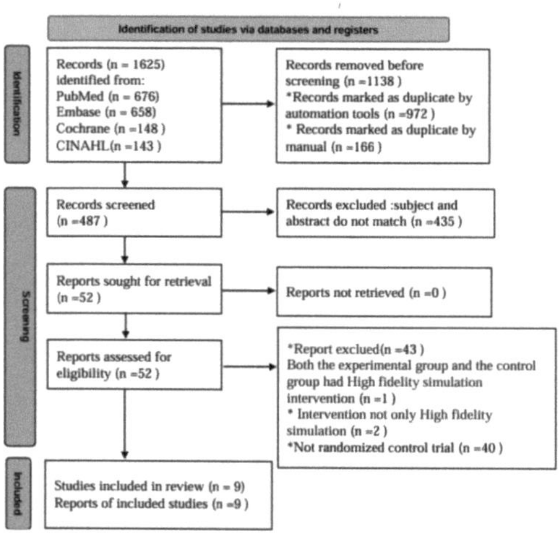

Fig. 1. Flow diagram of literature search and study selection

3.2 Studies Characteristics

A total of nine studies published up to 2026 were included in the analysis. Of these, one study was conducted in Norway, one in Portugal, one in Jordan, one in Spain, one in Taiwan, and four in Turkey. Sample sizes ranged from 17 to 53 participants. In total, 691 undergraduate nursing students were recruited across all included studies, with 353 assigned to the experimental groups and 338 to the control groups. All participants were undergraduate nursing students from different academic years, and all interventions in the experimental groups involved high-fidelity simulation (HFS). The outcome measures assessed included knowledge, clinical skills, critical thinking, satisfaction, and self-confidence. The characteristics of the included studies are presented in Table 1.

Table 1. The characteristics of the included randomized controlled trials (RCT)

Author/year	Country	Academic year	Average age	Simulation	E.G.	C.G.	Study design	Sample size (E.G. /C.G.)	Outcome
Tosterud et al., 2013	Norway	y1, y2, y3	NA	Respiratory system	HFS	Traditional teaching	RCT	30/28	Satisfaction, Self-confidence
Baptista et al., 2016	Portugal	y1, y2, y3, y4	NA	Respiratory system, Circulatory system, Nervous system	HFS	Traditional teaching	RCT	49/36	Technical/practical
Mert Karadas & Terzioglu, 2019	Turkey	y3	NA	Preeclampsia	HFS	Traditional teaching	RCT	53/54	Clinical skills, Self-confidence
Tawalbeh, 2020	Jordanian	Undergraduate students	20	Cardiovascular system, Respiratory system, Nervous system	HFS	PPT + Traditional teaching	RCT	38/38	Knowledge, Self-confidence
Ozdemir & Kaya, 2023	Turkey	y1	19	Urinary catheterization	HFS	Traditional teaching	RCT	40/40	Knowledge, Satisfaction, Self-confidence
Peng & Wu, 2024	Taiwan	y3	21	Endotracheal intubation, 12-lead electrocardiogram (ECG), Personal protective equipment (PPE) for droplet precautions	HFS	Traditional teaching	RCT	41/43	Clinical skills, Critical thinking, Self-confidence

(continued)

Table 1. *(continued)*

Author/year	Country	Academic year	Average age	Simulation	E.G.	C.G.	Study design	Sample size (E.G. /C.G.)	Outcome
Chabrera et al., 2025	Spain	y2	NA	Droplet isolation, Peripheral intravenous (IV) catheter insertion, Urinary catheterization, Nasogastric tube insertion, Respiratory pattern assessment	HFS	Traditional teaching	RCT	34/33	Knowledge, Clinical skills, Critical thinking
Eyüboğlu et al., 2025	Turkey	y2	20	Cardiac auscultation	HFS	Traditional teaching	RCT	17/17	Satisfaction
Ceylan et al., 2025	Turkey	undergraduate students	20	Breast feeding	HFS	Traditional teaching	RCT	51/49	Knowledge, Self-Efficacy Scale, Breastfeeding Counseling Skills

E.G. = Experimental group; **C.G.** = Control group

3.3 Studies Quality Appraisal

Using the RoB 2.0 tool, the risk of bias in the included studies was categorized into three levels: low risk, some concerns, and high risk. Overall, the majority of the included studies demonstrated acceptable methodological quality with a generally low risk of bias. The detailed risk of bias assessment is presented in Fig. 2.

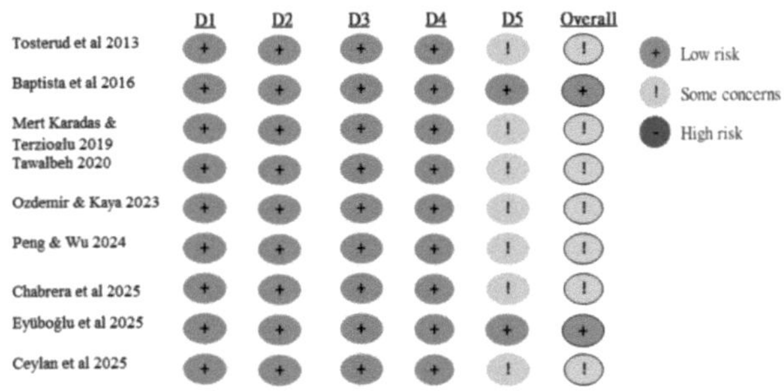

Fig. 2. Risk of bias summary

3.4 Effects on Learning Outcomes

3.4.1 Effects on Critical Thinking

Three studies [9, 14, 15] reported that high-fidelity simulation (HFS) significantly improved critical thinking among undergraduate nursing students. Using a random-effects model for pooled analysis, the results demonstrated a statistically significant positive effect of HFS on critical thinking (SMD = 0.54, 95% CI [0.21, 0.87], p = 0.001), with moderate heterogeneity ($I^2 = 43\%$) (Fig. 3).

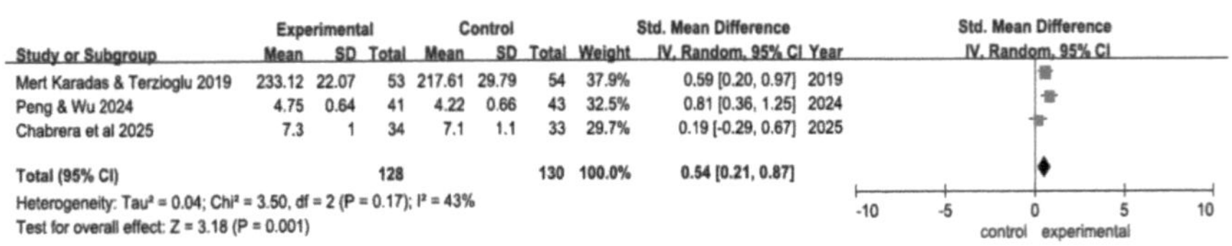

Fig. 3. Effect of high-fidelity simulation on nursing students' critical thinking

3.4.2 Effects on Knowledge

Four studies [15–18] examined the effects of high-fidelity simulation (HFS) on knowledge outcomes among undergraduate nursing students. The pooled analysis indicated that HFS did not produce a statistically significant improvement in knowledge (SMD = 0.45, 95% CI [−0.31, 1.20], $p = 0.25$), with substantial heterogeneity observed across studies ($I^2 = 91\%$) (Fig. 4).

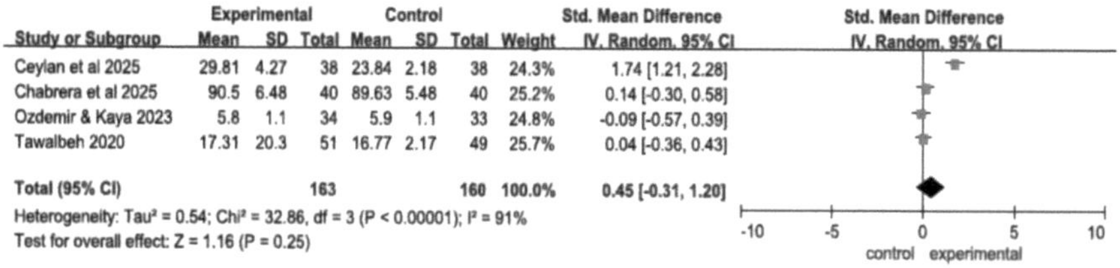

Fig. 4. Effect of high-fidelity simulation on nursing students' knowledge

3.4.3 Effects on Clinical Skills

Four studies [9, 15, 18, 19] investigated the effects of high-fidelity simulation (HFS) on clinical skills among undergraduate nursing students. The pooled analysis showed that HFS did not result in a statistically significant improvement in clinical skills (SMD = 0.36, 95% CI [−0.17, 0.89], $p = 0.18$), with substantial heterogeneity observed across studies ($I^2 = 78\%$) (Fig. 5).

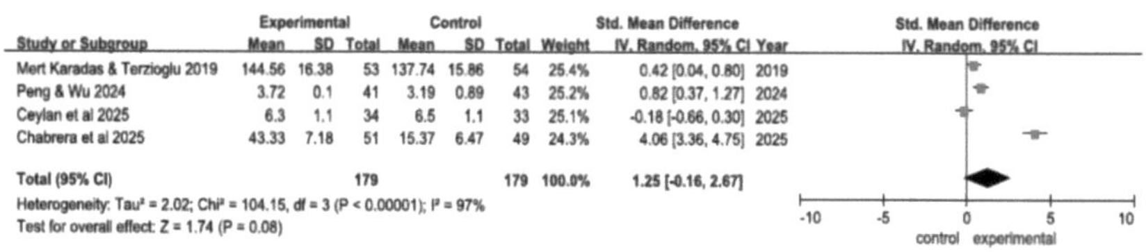

Fig. 5. Effect of high-fidelity simulation on nursing students' clinical skills

3.4.4 Effects on Satisfaction

Three studies [17, 20, 21] examined the effects of high-fidelity simulation (HFS) on satisfaction among undergraduate nursing students. The pooled results indicated that HFS did not produce a statistically significant improvement in satisfaction (SMD = 0.86, 95% CI [−1.16, 2.88], $p = 0.40$), with considerable heterogeneity observed ($I^2 = 97\%$) (Fig. 6).

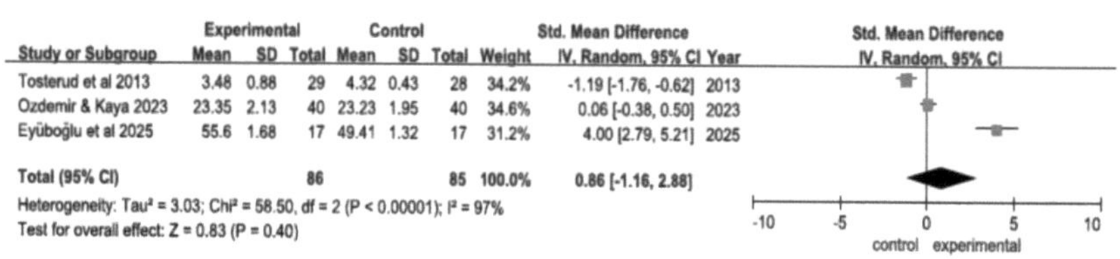

Fig. 6. Effect of high-fidelity simulation on nursing students' satisfaction

3.4.5 Effects on Self-Confidence

Five studies [9, 14, 16, 17, 19] examined the effects of high-fidelity simulation (HFS) on self-confidence among undergraduate nursing students. The pooled analysis indicated that HFS did not result in a statistically significant improvement in self-confidence (SMD

$= 0.65$, 95% CI $[-0.28, 1.57]$, $p = 0.17$), with substantial heterogeneity observed across studies ($I^2 = 95\%$) (Fig. 7).

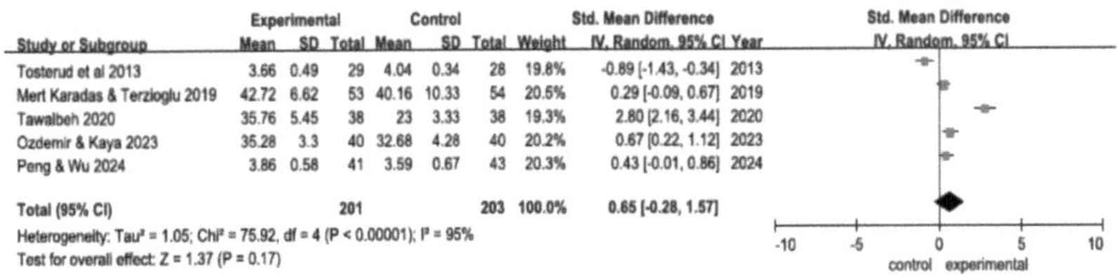

Fig. 7. Effect of high-fidelity simulation on nursing students' Self-confidence

4 Discussion

The present study demonstrated that HFS significantly enhances students' critical thinking ability, a finding consistent with the results reported by [7] ($p = 0.002$, $I^2 = 94\%$). Through scenario-based decision-making, real-time responses, and clinical reasoning processes, HFS encourages students to engage in problem analysis and prioritization within authentic experiential contexts. This finding can also be explained by Kolb's Experiential Learning Theory. Simulation scenarios provide concrete experiences, followed by reflective observation through structured debriefing, which facilitates abstract conceptualization and active experimentation, thereby completing the learning cycle [5]. Compared with traditional lecture-based teaching, HFS is more effective in creating high-pressure, dynamic environments that require immediate clinical decision-making, fostering the development of higher-order cognitive skills. Notably, even after restricting inclusion to RCTs only, the significant effect remained, suggesting that the finding is relatively robust and stable.

The findings of this study indicate that HFS interventions did not produce statistically significant improvements in knowledge (SMD $= 0.45$, $p = 0.25$, $I^2 = 91\%$) or clinical skills (SMD $= 0.36$, $p = 0.18$, $I^2 = 78\%$), and both outcomes demonstrated substantial heterogeneity. These results differ from the conclusions reported by [7, 11], who suggested that HFS significantly enhances knowledge and clinical skills. One possible explanation for this discrepancy may be the more stringent inclusion criteria applied in the present study. By excluding quasi-experimental designs and including only high-quality randomized controlled trials (RCTs), the pooled effect sizes were reduced, suggesting that previous estimates may have been inflated due to variations in study design and methodological rigor.

The substantial heterogeneity observed in this study may be attributed to several factors. First, variations in measurement instruments may have contributed to inconsistent findings, as different studies employed diverse tools to assess knowledge and clinical skills, lacking standardized evaluation criteria. Second, differences in students' academic levels may have influenced the intervention effects, as some studies included junior students with limited foundational knowledge, potentially affecting the impact of HFS. Third, variability in scenario design may have played a role, with some studies implementing only a single simulation session, thereby limiting opportunities for repeated practice. Moreover, knowledge acquisition can often be effectively achieved through traditional lecture-based instruction, which may dilute the observable differences between experimental and control groups. Regarding clinical skills, although HFS is theoretically expected to enhance skill proficiency [10], its advantages may not become immediately apparent in the short term without repeated practice sessions and structured debriefing to reinforce learning outcomes.

The present study found that neither satisfaction (SMD $= 0.86$, $p = 0.40$, $I^2 = 97\%$) nor self-confidence (SMD $= 0.65$, $p = 0.17$, $I^2 = 95\%$) reached statistical significance, and both outcomes exhibited extremely high heterogeneity. These findings are consistent with those reported by [7, 11]. Notably, although statistical significance was not achieved, the direction of the effect sizes for both satisfaction and self-confidence remained positive, suggesting that HFS may have a potential beneficial effect. However, the lack of statistical significance may be attributable to limited sample sizes and variations in study quality across the included trials.

The studies by [7, 11] included quasi-experimental designs and generally reported more pronounced effects. In contrast, by restricting inclusion to randomized controlled trials (RCTs), the present study yielded more conservative effect estimates, suggesting that previous findings may have overestimated the effectiveness of HFS. Nevertheless, this study updates the evidence base through 2026 and focuses exclusively on high-quality RCTs, thereby providing a more rigorous foundation for interpretation. The results indicate that critical thinking currently represents the most robust and stable outcome associated with HFS, whereas other learning outcomes require further confirmation through high-quality, large-scale research.

5 Conclusion and Limitations

This systematic review and meta-analysis demonstrate that high-fidelity simulation (HFS) has a significant positive effect on improving critical thinking among undergraduate nursing students, supporting its role as an effective instructional strategy for developing higher-order clinical reasoning skills. However, although positive trends were observed for knowledge, clinical skills, satisfaction, and self-confidence, these outcomes did not reach statistical significance and were associated with substantial heterogeneity. This study emphasizes that HFS should not be regarded as a comprehensive replacement for traditional teaching methods, but rather as a complementary and enhancement strategy, particularly suitable for educational objectives that require the development of clinical judgment and real-time decision-making abilities. Future nursing education should integrate theoretical coursework, clinical placements, and structured high-fidelity simulation, supported by standardized design and quality control measures to strengthen educational effectiveness and evidence quality. By providing updated and methodologically rigorous evidence, this study offers an empirical foundation for curriculum planning and instructional decision-making in nursing education, while also identifying directions for future research.

Regarding the limitations, only nine studies were included in this meta-analysis, which may have resulted in limited statistical power for certain outcomes. Additionally, the high heterogeneity observed across several results may have affected the stability and generalizability of the findings. Variations in simulation scenarios and intervention designs among the included studies also precluded the performance of subgroup analyses. Future research is recommended to conduct multicenter, large-scale randomized controlled trials (RCTs) and to standardize HFS design and evaluation instruments in order to reduce heterogeneity and strengthen the overall quality of evidence.

References

1. Alharbi, A., Nurfianti, A., Mullen, R.F., McClure, J.D., Miller, W.H.: The effectiveness of simulation-based learning (SBL) on students' knowledge and skills in nursing programs: a systematic review. BMC Med. Educ. **24**(1), 1099 (2024)
2. Ulenaers, D., Grosemans, J., Schrooten, W., Bergs, J.: Clinical placement experience of nursing students during the COVID-19 pandemic: a cross-sectional study. Nurse Educ. Today. **99**, 104746 (2021)
3. Akalin, A., Sahin, S.: The impact of high-fidelity simulation on knowledge, critical thinking, and clinical decision-making for the management of pre-eclampsia. Int. J. Gynecol. Obstet. **150**(3), 354–360 (2020)
4. Soghier, L.: Improving neonatal patient outcomes using simulation-based education. J. Pediatr. **266**, 113875 (2024)
5. Wijnen-Meijer, M., Brandhuber, T., Schneider, A., Berberat, P.O.: Implementing Kolb's experiential learning cycle by linking real experience, case-based discussion and simulation. J. Med. Educat. Curri. Develop. **9**, 23821205221091511 (2022)
6. Tong, L.K., Li, Y.Y., Au, M.L., Wang, S.C., Ng, W.I.: Prebriefing for high-fidelity simulation in nursing education: a meta-analysis. Nurse Educ. Today. **119**, 105609 (2022)
7. Tong, L.K., Li, Y.Y., Au, M.L., Wang, S.C., Ng, W.I.: High-fidelity simulation duration and learning outcomes among undergraduate nursing students: a systematic review and meta-analysis. Nurse Educ. Today. **116**, 105435 (2022)
8. Lei, Y.Y., Zhu, L., Sa, Y.T.R., Cui, X.S.: Effects of high-fidelity simulation teaching on nursing students' knowledge, professional skills and clinical ability: a meta-analysis and systematic review. Nurse Educ. Pract. **60**, 103306 (2022)
9. Peng, Y.C., Wu, H.S.: The efficacy of high-fidelity telesimulation in preparing nursing students for emergency and critical patient care: a prospective study. J. Nurs. Res. **32**(5), e348 (2024)
10. Cura, Ş.Ü., Kocatepe, V., Yıldırım, D., Küçükakgün, H., Atay, S., Ünver, V.: Examining knowledge, skill, stress, satisfaction, and self-confidence levels of nursing students in three different simulation modalities. Asian Nurs. Res. **14**(3), 158–164 (2020)
11. Li, Y.Y., Au, M.L., Tong, L.K., Ng, W.I., Wang, S.C.: High-fidelity simulation in undergraduate nursing education: a meta-analysis. Nurse Educ. Today. **111**, 105291 (2022)
12. Guerrero, J.G., Ali, S.A.A., Attallah, D.M.: The acquired critical thinking skills, satisfaction, and self confidence of nursing students and staff nurses through high-fidelity simulation experience. Clin. Simul. Nurs. **64**, 24–30 (2022)
13. Higgins, J.P., Thompson, S.G., Deeks, J.J., Altman, D.G.: Measuring inconsistency in meta-analyses. BMJ. **327**(7414), 557–560 (2003)
14. Mert Karadas, M., Terzioglu, F.: The impact of the using high-fidelity simulation and standardized patients to management of postpartum hemorrhage in undergraduate nursing students: a randomized controlled study in Turkey. Health Care Women Int. **40**(5), 597–612 (2019)
15. Chabrera, C., Curell, L., Rodríguez-Higueras, E.: Effectiveness of high versus mixed-level fidelity simulation on undergraduate nursing students: a randomised controlled trial. Nurse Educ. Pract. **82**, 104206 (2025)

16. Tawalbeh, L.I.: Effect of simulation modules on Jordanian nursing student knowledge and confidence in performing critical care skills: a randomized controlled trial. Int. J. Afr. Nurs. Sci. **13**, 100242 (2020)
17. Ozdemir, N.G., Kaya, H.: The effectiveness of high-fidelity simulation methods to gain Foley catheterization knowledge, skills, satisfaction and self-confidence among novice nursing students: a randomized controlled trial. Nurse Educ. Today. **130**, 105952 (2023)
18. Ceylan, S., Pardes, B.B., Erdoğan, E.N., Güvenç, G., Kök, G., Kurt, G.: The effect of different simulation approaches in breastfeeding education on nursing students' knowledge, skills, and clinical self-efficacy: a randomized controlled trial. Breastfeed. Med. **20**(12), 931–938 (2025)
19. Baptista, R.C., Paiva, L.A., Goncalves, R.F., Oliveira, L.M., Pereira, M.D.F.C., Martins, J.C.: Satisfaction and gains perceived by nursing students with medium and high-fidelity simulation: a randomized controlled trial. Nurse Educ. Today. **46**, 127–132 (2016)
20. Tosterud, R., Hedelin, B., Hall-Lord, M.L.: Nursing students' perceptions of high-and low-fidelity simulation used as learning methods. Nurse Educ. Pract. **13**(4), 262–270 (2013)
21. Eyüboğlu, G., Sarıtaş, E., Çalışkan, N., Baykara, Z.G.: The effect of psychoacoustic learning method and high-fidelity simulation on the cardiac auscultation competence of nursing students: a randomized controlled study. Nurse Educ. Pract., 104475 (2025)

Evaluating Students' AI Literacy and Reflective Capacity in an Entrepreneurship Course Using Professor E

Jac Ka Lok Leung[1(✉)], Joyce Ching Yan Wong[2], and Davy Tsz Kit Ng[3]

[1] Division of Integrative Systems and Design, The Hong Kong University of Science and Technology, Clear Water Bay, Kowloon, Hong Kong, China
egjac@ust.hk

[2] Department of Hospitality and Business Management, The Technological and Higher Education Institute of Hong Kong, 133 Shing Tai Road, Chai Wan, Hong Kong, China
joycewong@thei.edu.hk

[3] Department of Mathematics and Information Technology, The Education University of Hong Kong, 17 10 Lo Ping Road, Tai Po, New Territories, Hong Kong, China
davyngtk@eduhk.hk

Abstract. Generative artificial intelligence (GenAI) has the potential as a powerful tool to enhance and strengthen student learning experiences. Students depend on GenAI for immediate answer generating rather than cultivating genuine reflection. To fill this gap, the researchers created a retrieval-augmented generation (RAG)-enabled chatbot, Professor E, which assists students in reflection using Gibbs's reflective cycle. The researchers used an exploratory methodology to assess students' AI literacy, reflective capabilities, and their impressions of the system's educational design. This exploratory study examines students' AI literacy and reflective capacity, as well as their impressions of the system's educational design. The researchers gathered data through AI-student conversations to discern the principal themes arising from collaborations between students and AI in an entrepreneurship course in a Hong Kong business school. The focus group interview results highlighted students' concerns on technical, practical, critical, and ethical factors when utilising Professor E for reflective purposes. The implementation of protected systems, role-playing, and RAG creation helped students in articulating personal thoughts, fostering empathy, and obtaining relevant, customised guidance linked with their project endeavours. This work advances the field of AI-human collaboration by highlighting how pedagogically built GenAI systems can improve students' reflective thinking abilities.

Keywords: AI Literacy · Generative AI · Entrepreneurship · Gibbs' Reflective Cycle

1 Introduction

The metacognitive capacity of students to review previous learning and experiences, helping them to analyse and respond cautiously to new challenges, is sometimes referred to as reflective thinking [1, 2]. This process entails analysing material, establishing links

C.-J. Lin et al. (Eds.): ICITL 2026, LNCS 16841, pp. 58–67, 2027.
https://doi.org/10.1007/978-3-032-32112-1_7

between concepts, and identifying how to implement most effectively. It also includes the capacity to employ previous information and experience to make educated decisions. Research indicates that Students who participate in reflective writing improve abilities to critically evaluate their experiences, so fostering greater understanding, critical thinking, self-regulated learning, lifelong learning, and personal growth [3, 4]. Although introspective thinking and critical thinking are similar, they are differentiated by certain characteristics. Critical thinking is a methodical and intentional kind of judgement that encompasses interpretation, analysis, assessment, and inference, frequently directed at uncovering deficiencies in arguments. Cognitive abilities including reasoning, inference, correlation, and analysis are important for the learning procedure. Reflective thinking, in contrast, emphasises the analysis of students' previous experiences, knowledge, perceptions, reasoning, and understanding. Through this reflective approach, learners can discern facts, investigate potential solutions, and spot patterns, so enhancing their ability to tackle complicated issues and tasks more successfully [5]. In contrast, reflective thinking is an active process that involves examining the assumptions essential for the content or approach of problem-solving. The researchers defined four dimensions: knowledge and comprehension, application and utilisation, assessment and reasoning, and ethical considerations. These can be implemented to enhance AI literacy by transforming traditional AI literacy [6].

Reflections allow students to express their thoughts and experiences in a coherent and organised manner, thereby improving their learning outcomes and performance [7]. classified the identified competencies into four dimensions to assess students' literacy development: (1) affective learning (intrinsic motivation and self-efficacy/confidence), (2) behavioural learning (behavioural commitment and collaboration), (3) cognitive learning (knowledge and understanding; application, evaluation, and creation), and (4) ethical learning. Students possessing heightened reflective literacy can enhance their learning through experience and connect new knowledge to their prior learning. Reflective literacy combines the integration of classroom instruction with practical application, promotes self-awareness of actions, strengths, and shortcomings, and assists both students and educators in recognising learning requirements [8]. Reflective literate learners possess enhanced capabilities to handle uncertainty and difficult situations, enabling them to create personal solutions to address problems [3]. They can evaluate their learning processes and critically reflect on their performances. They can also acquire additional transferable abilities, including feedback, self-awareness, self-assessment, critical thinking, and problem-solving through the development of reflections [9]. Additionally, students can assume greater ownership and responsibility for their education and become self-directed lifelong learners.

1.1 AI Literacy and Reflective Thinking

A fundamental skill in interacting with AI is reflective thinking, especially when students depend excessively on AI without critically assessing their learning processes. Previous studies indicate that AI may result in cognitive offloading and diminished involvement in cognitively intensive activities [10]. Guided models are essential for influencing AI behaviour to enhance students' reflection and learning processes effectively, rather than permitting students to produce final outputs directly from AI. For instance, [11] discovered that GenAI offered feedback to 74 undergraduate students during essay writing to facilitate their reflections.

[10] discovered that GenAI assists students with notetaking, summarisation, and inquiry after giving automated writing criticism. GenAI transcends linguistic barriers and enhances students' English writing proficiency and drive for self-reflection [13]. Students can engage in metacognitive reflections to enhance their internal observation, awareness, monitoring, and manage their knowledge, experiences, and emotions [14]. Consequently, GenAI enhances students' reflective processes by providing customised feedback, clarifications, and recommendations relevant to their educational experiences [15, 16].

ChatGPT in particular can enhance reflective thinking and writing in various manners. Automated feedback can offer students prompt and individualised recommendations to improve their reflective writing [12, 17]. By means of fast engineering, GenAI can instruct learners to take notes, summarise essential points, and critically evaluate their assumptions after receiving their responses.

A GenAI-enabled chatbot can engage learners through reflective dialogue, prompting students to elaborate on their views, consider alternative perspectives, and deepen their reflections [18]. by GenAI can enhance reflective literacy by assisting students in organising their thoughts, emphasising key topics, and expressing their personal connections to the topic. This might be especially useful for studemts who are unfamiliar with introspection and require assistance in developing fundamental competencies. GenAI can enhance learners' English proficiency and elevate their reflective writing abilities, allowing them to express their ideas more efficiently, tackling the linguistic obstacles second language learners face [20]. Nonetheless, there is little research pertaining to the capacity of GenAI to enhance contemplation. Further investigation is required to comprehend the influence of AI-assisted reflective writing in terms of enhancing students' cognitive and metacognitive learning [21].

1.2 Research Gap

To bridge this research gap, the researchers investigated the potential of GenAI to cultivate students' reflective literacy. They created a retrieval-augmented generation (RAG) enhanced chatbot named Professor E, with 'E' symbolising openness to creativity. Professor E is meant to augment reflection among university students enrolled in an entrepreneurial course. The study concentrated on enabling students to adopt effective reflection tactics and examine the application of prompt engineering guidelines to enhance their reflection and social entrepreneurship. This study explores the primary themes of students' impressions of Professor E's implementation of reflections in Social Innovation Education (SIE) learning. The research topic is: What are students' perceptions of their reflective interactions with Professor E utilising Gibbs's reflective cycle?

2 Methods

2.1 Research Design

This research investigates the incorporation of a GenAI-enhanced educational platform in a Securities and Investment Environment course at a university in Hong Kong throughout the course of a semester. The researchers analysed experiences from two distinct classes. The study involved 50 third-year undergraduate classes. One class, supported by Professor E, comprised 50 students (28 males and 22 females). The alternative class, which used a traditional chatbot, included 37 students (18 males and 19 females). In both classes, students studied SIE-related topics such as entrepreneurial spirit and design thinking and worked collaboratively on a project to endorse products for their intended target demographics. Five entrepreneurs were asked to discuss their accomplishments, mistakes, and insights regarding social entrepreneurship. Following these sharing sessions, students were prompted to contemplate any insights that they could apply to their own learning. Students first gave informed consent and were subsequently told how to utilise Professor E and acquired pertinent AI literacy abilities for crafting reflections (e.g., prompt engineering, AI knowledge). Figure 1 depicts a methodology for enhancing reflection in social innovation education through the utilisation of AI. The study consists of two groups: an experimental group employing the Gibbs Reflective Cycle alongside topic knowledge, and a control group using solely subject knowledge. The instructor integrates these groups and directs the students, Professor E facilitates student engagement and reflection, and students motivate entrepreneurs. Professor E formulates ideas for enhancing reflections in social innovation education, which are critically reviewed in a cyclical process. These guidelines facilitate the refinement and development of final mobile applications. The applications augment reflective capacity, artificial intelligence literacy, and the likelihood of using AI for reflection.

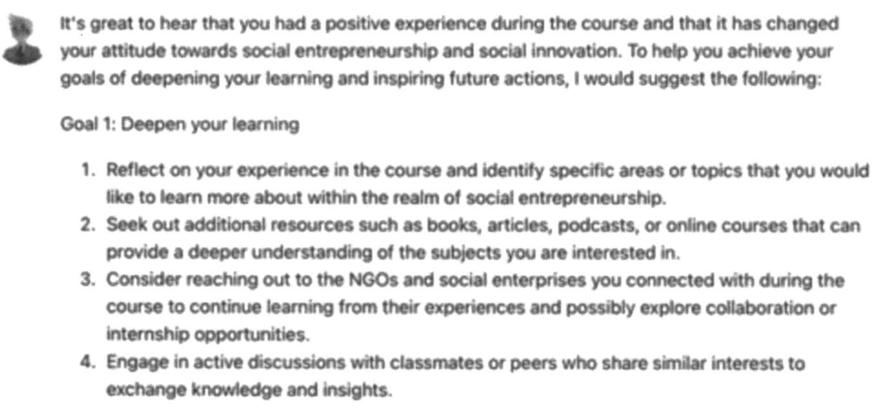

Fig. 1. An example of Professor E chatbot's response

The researchers used Gibbs's Reflective Cycle (GRC) to inform AI's responses in guiding students' reflective techniques regarding their learning experiences, encompassing six phases: (a) description of the learning experience, (b) feelings and thoughts about the experience (c) evaluation of the experience, (d) analysis to comprehend the learning, (e) conclusions about what was learned and potential alternative actions, and (f) action plans for addressing similar knowledge and challenges in the future, along with proposed changes and strategies. For instance, inquiries were posed in accordance with GRC (For example: What transpired during your learning? What emotions did you experience throughout the process? What aspects were positive and negative about the experience? What factors contributed to the success of your learning?). This strategy promotes active, reflexive, and experiential learning to enhance students' professional development as entrepreneurs. Students may face challenges with integrating new knowledge with previous experiences or difficulties applying learnt concepts For coursework and project creation, they may request assistance from Professor E for support and reflection.

2.2 Instruments, Instructional Design, and Data Analysis

The researchers utilised a qualitative design methodology to investigate student perceptions. Considerations of AI platform design. The instructional design framework consists of two essential components: (a) pedagogical and technological design, and (b) material related to learning about and utilising AI, including how students employ GenAI for reflections on domain-specific applications expertise and AI ethics, as well as learning outcomes, including AI literacy, intention to engage in reflection, and the quality of that reflection. GenAI facilitated text-based conversational exchanges to improve students' reflective writing. Students submitted dialogues with Professor E as part of their assignments at the end of the course. Figure 2 presents a summary of Professor E's approach to student reflective writing.

To enhance students' critical thinking in an entrepreneurial sense, they must engage in activities and thought processes to develop design thinking by asking, "How can we devise a solution for specific target audiences to effectively address a particular problem?" and "What insights have I gained from the entrepreneurs?" or "What elements contribute to their success?". The chatbot responses to these help students gain new perspectives on entrepreneurship. The researchers utilised the log files for additional analysis of student interactions with GenAI. To guarantee the dependability of qualitative outcomes, the researchers transcribed and categorised students' dialogues in accordance with GRC. They gathered data through multiple methods, including student interviews, which are corroborated through student-AI interactions. Education undergoes critical examination in a cyclical process. These guidelines facilitate the refinement and development of students' applications. Minor pictures depict an educator at a chalkboard, two students engaged in study, and an entrepreneur in celebration, visually connecting responsibilities within the process. Arrows denote the progression and connections among each phase illustration.

Professor E implemented GPT-4.1 as a RAG-enhanced reflective thinking tool, increasing students' ability to produce contextually relevant prose and engage in reflection. RAG is fundamental to the platform's architecture as it facilitates the model's retrieval and integration of pertinent educational resources that educators and learners submit. The tool's training data comprises a varied collection of students' reflective writings from previous lessons, guidelines for GRC, and additional materials that illustrate the linguistic patterns and cognitive frameworks related to reflective thinking. This

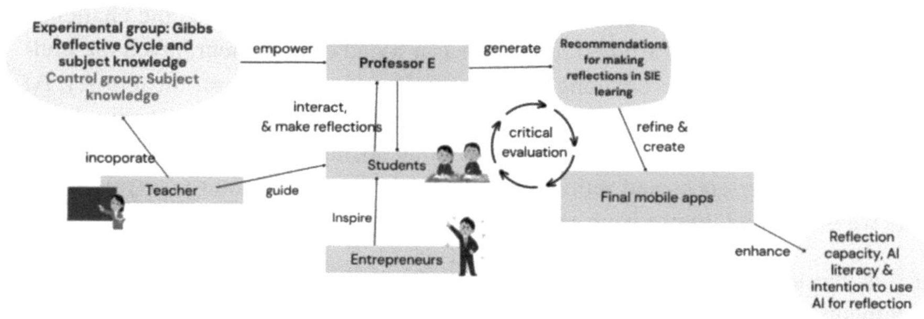

Fig. 2. Pedagogical design of learning intervention with Professor E

facilitates the model's acquisition of information through RAG, enabling it to respond according to Gibbs's reflective process. The AI tool features a collection of meticulously designed prompts that help students navigate the many levels of GRC. These prompts encompass self-assessment, the identification of learning objectives, the analysis of experiences, and the synthesis of insights. The prompts purposely align with the unique learning objectives and the AI literacy level of the intended student demographic.

3 Results

3.1 Perceptions of Professor E with Gibbs's Reflective Cycle

Professor E creates guided reflection templates and scaffolded prompts that incorporate structured Gibbs's Reflective Cycle into the chat flow, ensuring that each AI output is accompanied with prompts that enhance students' reflective abilities. Here are several benefits of integrating GRC into a GenAI system.

First, students discovered that Gibbs's stages (What? So what? Now what?) in the AI chat provided them with a systematic reflection framework and alleviated uncertainty when reflecting with AI. The GRC-enhanced chatbot facilitated their transition to interpretative and progress-oriented reflection. S03 stated, "Educators recommended employing the Gibbs model, which offered explicit guidelines integrated within the chat flow." The utility of AI output increased alongside prompts that required interpretation, critique, and planning. S07 remarked, "Initially, I lacked guidance for engaging in reflection with AI." AI offered specific Gibbs's guides integrated inside the chat flow. The utility of AI output increased when accompanied by leading questions that prompt me to understand, criticise, and strategise my learning."

Secondly, students believed that GenAI facilitates the initiation of reflection and the maintenance of this practice. They kept using the same reflective bot post-course completion, since the Gibbs-based prompts facilitated their continuous reflections. Records indicated that prolonged usage suggests effective adoption when the instrument facilitates a definitive approach. E01 expressed, "Following the lesson, I remain enthusiastic and keen to investigate the realm of entrepreneurship." and "AI offered me invaluable guidance to enhance my project." E06 described how AI-assisted prompts facilitated her connection of theory to practice and enabled her to devise specific subsequent actions following lessons:

> AI prompted me to consolidate knowledge, ponder, and recognise the challenge of defining a singular formula for success as a social entrepreneur, given the multitude of obstacles faced challenges and setbacks encountered over the journey. AI provided me with initial recommendations for launching a social enterprise. I will persist in conversing with founders of particular social enterprises to gain insights from their experiences and motives including the origins of their enterprises and the ways in which their vision sustains them.

Third, some students claimed that they used AI to expedite the completion of their assignments and embraced AI recommendations without critical evaluation. Students discovered that the GRC-enhanced chatbot prompted them to understand their learning processes rather than simply doing tasks, diminishing cognitive offloading. For instance, E02 described:

> AI requested that I recount the events that transpired in the lesson and the way we acquired knowledge. The ideation sessions with my colleagues were my preferred aspect. This was my initial encounter in which significant obstacles during discussions were consequential particularly for concepts that were merely preliminary and inadequately developed. It also instructed me on transitioning between interrogation and criticism as we honed our solutions and established our new social venture.

Students appreciated scaffolded prompts that necessitated evidence-based connections. For instance, "Which user quotations or theories substantiate this insight?" and critical follow-up enquiries such as, "If I were to repeat this process [e.g., project design], what alterations would I implement?" These categories of prompts transformed the utilisation of AI from the transition from task completion to metacognitive processing.

4 Other Perceptions of Professor E Usage

Students value technologies that offer digital advantages to their SIE education. S12 emphasised the practical utility of the RAG feature in Professor E, stating, "I find the RAG feature (the knowledge base function) to be beneficial." AI may provide unhelpful guidance in the absence of the syllabus, and it is necessary to configure its responses based on the knowledge base. This necessitates the adoption of RAG to link the model to specified resources (e.g., user interviews, online sources). Course resources ensure that AI responses are pertinent, evidence-based, and connected with instructional objectives. RAG improved evidence-based sense-making by integrating grounded data with local contextual resources, anchoring replies in students' own data via the knowledge base. Secondly, role-playing simulators featuring customisable personas allow students to practice stakeholder interviews, pitching, and negotiating using AI-generated personas. Role-play exposes students to varied views, facilitates practice and produces test cases and reflective debriefs. S11 proposed that AI can role-play, stating, "Professor E can acquire skills to enhance inventions alongside end-users, present and negotiate with AI-driven personas (e.g., elderly users in Cantonese, company founders, funders) to elicit reflections and emphasise pain points." Furthermore, data-to-insight visualisation and synthesis tools can autonomously extract summaries of reading materials and key themes from interview data, generating thematic or empathy maps that reduce cognitive load and facilitate students' reflections based on synthesised evidence.

The researchers recognized poor self-regulated learning (SRL) skills as an impediment to reflective involvement. Certain students emphasised task completion rather than planning, monitoring, and assessing their learning strategies; for instance, S12 stated, "I do not monitor my understanding or modify my strategies, I concentrate solely on task completion. While AI can alleviate cognitive burden to enhance understanding, students can perceive it as a mere external shortcut, resulting in cognitive offloading and superficial processing". S7 stated, "I merely utilise the AI to expedite task completion." However, others deemed this approach questionable. S10 contended, "We should not solely concentrate on merely fulfilling assignments. We must comprehend the AI feedback."

E03 expressed concerns over intellectual property theft "As an entrepreneur, I refrain from disclosing excessive information to AI."or apprehensions about the implications of plagiarism, while E04 sought assurances on privacy and permissible usage prior to participation. Furthermore, students want private concept spaces and customisable disclosure settings to manage what is stored, shared, or utilised for model training. The researchers handled dialogues over a private, local server to mitigate privacy issues. One student expressed, "I am apprehensive about being monitored and accused of plagiarism." Privacy and local data storage are essential."

5 Conclusions and Discussion

5.1 Implications for Educators

Educators believe that as a tool, GenAI's capabilities fulfil their expectations [22]. Technical obstacles, including unforeseen functionalities or insufficient explainability, can impede effective interactions. Consequently, AI has to demonstrate consistency and transparency in its actions, while features like RAG and an extensive dialogue history are crucial to enhance students' inclination to utilise AI for reflection. Instructional designers must enhance technical skills to cultivate trust and reduce conflict [23].

A statement like, "I utilise AI to expedite task completion," demands instructional design that actively fosters tasks that require higher-order (e.g., categorising interview data, modelling assumptions) and compels students to analyse and validate AI outputs (e.g., fact-checking, evidence-based justification). This technique guarantees that AI enhances analytical reasoning instead of obstructing it. Age-related inactivity is acknowledged as a constraint caused by over dependence on AI assistance.

E02 articulated ethical doubts and critical issues that directly influential figure, such as, "I am reluctant to share original concepts due to apprehensions over appropriation or plagiarism, while possessing considerable AI literacy." and "As an entrepreneur, I endeavour to limit the information I disclose to AI." These concerns correspond with previous studies demonstrating that transparency and the abuse of concepts are prominent challenges in talks around trustworthy AI [24]. Cultivating trust requires systems that are both dependable and comprehensible, indicating that future AI solutions must tackle the emotional dimensions of user experience to cultivate comfort and assurance [23].

5.2 Concluding Remarks

This study emphasises the pioneering potential of GenAI technologies through the deployment of Professor E chatbot, insofar as augmenting students' introspective abilities. By facilitating personalised prompts and guided reflections based on GRC, Professor E promotes enhanced progress-oriented reflection, introspection, and self-analysis among university students investigating SIE. The findings indicate that effective engagement with GenAI encourages students to cultivate both AI literacy and introspective abilities, enabling them to interact more profoundly with the technology and obtain personalised instruction. Furthermore, the involvement of educators is essential in establishing a collaborative AI-enhanced learning environment that facilitates this reflective process. As students engage in their educational journeys, GenAI enhances their cognitive abilities while fostering proficiency in AI literacy.

This research enhances the understanding of AI-human collaboration, highlighting GenAI's potential to promote significant educational outcomes and improve reflective behaviours in higher education. This research possesses several limitations. The results were affected by the distinct attributes of Professor E and the AI platform, potentially restricting generalisability to other systems with varying features and engagement methods. More stringent analytical methods, such as clustering and latent profile analysis, could yield profound insights on student interactions with AI tools. Longitudinal research may elucidate the evolution of learning experiences, emphasising the enduring effects of AI technologies. Integrating experimental and control groups with quantitative methodologies would also provide comparisons of student experiences prior to and following the implementation of GenAI.

References

1. Choy, S., Yim, J., Sedhu, D.: Pre-service teachers' reflection on reflective practices: a Malaysian perspective. Univ. J. Educ. Res. **7**(12A), 18–26 (2019). https://doi.org/10.13189/ujer.2019.071903
2. Sullivan, S., Gaydon, M., Panton, S., Nguyen, X., Richardson, J.: Perceptions of feedback: the use of self-reflection to improve student satisfaction. Assess. Eval. High. Educ. **51**(2), 301–314 (2026). https://doi.org/10.1080/02602938.2025.2572034
3. Chan, C., Lee, K.: Reflection literacy: a multilevel perspective on the challenges of using reflections in higher education through a comprehensive literature review. Educ. Res. Rev. **32**, 100376 (2021). https://doi.org/10.1016/j.edurev.2020.100376
4. Chan, C., Lee, K.: The balancing act between AI and authenticity in assessment: a case study of secondary school students' use of GenAI in reflective writing. Comput. Educ. **105399** (2025). https://doi.org/10.1016/j.compedu.2025.105399
5. Liao, H., Wang, H.: Storytelling in medical education: narrative medicine as a resource for interdisciplinary collaboration. Int. J. Environ. Res. Public Health. **17**(4), 1135 (2020)
6. Tsingos, C., Bosnic-Anticevich, S., Smith, L.: Learning styles and approaches: can reflective strategies encourage deep learning? Curr. Pharmacy Teach. Learn. **7**(4), 492–504 (2015)
7. Ng, D., Leung, J., Chu, S., Qiao, M.: Conceptualizing AI literacy: an exploratory review. Comput. Educ. Artif. Intell. **2**, 100041 (2021)
8. Ng, D., Wu, W., Leung, J., Chiu, T., Chu, S.: Design and validation of the AI literacy questionnaire: the affective, behavioural, cognitive and ethical approach. Br. J. Educ. Technol. **55**(3), 1082–1104 (2024)

9. Venter, J., Coetzee, S.A., Schmulian, A.: Exploring the use of artificial intelligence (AI) in the delivery of effective feedback. Assess. Eval. High. Educ. **50**(4), 516–536 (2025). https://doi.org/10.1080/02602938.2024.2415649
10. Klingbeil, A., Grützner, C., Schreck, P.: Trust and reliance on AI—an experimental study on the extent and costs of overreliance on AI. Comput. Hum. Behav. **160**, 108352 (2024). https://doi.org/10.1016/j.chb.2024.108352
11. Banihashem, S., Kerman, N., Noroozi, O., Moon, J., Drachsler, H.: Feedback sources in essay writing: peer-generated or AI-generated feedback? Int. J. Educ. Technol. High. Educ. **21**(1), 23 (2024). https://doi.org/10.1186/s41239-024-00455-4
12. Liu, C., Hou, J., Tu, Y.F., Wang, Y., Hwang, G.J.: Incorporating a reflective thinking promoting mechanism into artificial intelligence-supported English writing environments. Interact. Learn. Environ. **31**(9), 5614–5632 (2023)
13. Kasneci, E., et al.: ChatGPT for good? On opportunities and challenges of large language models for education. Learn. Individ. Differ. **103**, 102274 (2023). https://doi.org/10.1016/j.lindif.2023.102274
14. Ng, D., Cheung, K.: Interweaving generative AI technological and pedagogical design: enhancing students' motivation, intentions, and AI literacy for feedback seeking. Educ. Psychol. **46**(1), 1–22 (2026)
15. Merkebu, J., Veen, M., Hosseini, S., Varpio, L.: The case for metacognitive reflection: a theory integrative review with implications for medical education. Adv. Health Sci. Educ. **29**(4), 1481–1500 (2024). https://doi.org/10.1007/s10459-023-10310-2
16. Maier, U., Klotz, C.: Personalized feedback in digital learning environments: classification framework and literature review. Comput. Educ. Artif. Intell. **3**, 100080 (2022)
17. Chiu, T.: The impact of generative AI (GenAI) on practices, policies and research direction in education: a case of ChatGPT and Midjourney. Interact. Learn. Environ. **32**(10), 6187–6203 (2024). https://doi.org/10.1080/10494820.2023.2253861
18. Ng, D., Tan, C., Leung, J.: Empowering student self-regulated learning and science education through ChatGPT: a pioneering pilot study. Br. J. Educ. Technol. **55**(4), 1328–1353 (2024)
19. Šedlbauer, J., Činčera, J., Slavík, M., Hartlová, A.: Students' reflections on their experience with ChatGPT. J. Comput. Assist. Learn. **40**(4), 1526–1534 (2024). https://doi.org/10.1111/jcal.12967
20. Ramli, A., Rasul, M., Omar, M.: Issues and challenges in the implementation of professional development programs for design and technology teachers. Int. J. Learn. Teach. Educ. Res. **23**(7), 64–83 (2024)
21. Lo, A.: Students' self-regulatory processes in content and language integrated learning: a vignette-based microanalytic study. Int. J. Bilingual Educ. Biligualism. **28**(1), 19–35 (2025)
22. Ng, D., Chan, E., Lo, C.: Opportunities, challenges and school strategies for integrating generative AI in education. Comput. Educ. Artif. Intell. **8**, 100373 (2025)
23. Nazaretsky, T., Ariely, M., Cukurova, M., Alexandron, G.: Teachers' trust in AI-powered educational technology and a professional development program to improve it. Br. J. Educ. Technol. **53**(4), 914–931 (2022). https://doi.org/10.1111/bjet.13232
24. Li, H., Wang, Y., Luo, S., Huang, C.: The influence of GenAI on the effectiveness of argumentative writing in higher education: evidence from a quasi-experimental study in China. J. Asian Public Policy. **18**(2), 405–430 (2025)

Fostering "Smart People" for the Digital Metropolis: Pedagogical Models of AI-Enhanced Cultural Heritage Preservation at Saint Petersburg State University and Russian Museum

Elena Gaevskaya[1(✉)], Nikolay Borisov[1], and Rustam Shadiev[2]

[1] Saint Petersburg State University, 7/9 Universitetskaya nab, St. Petersburg 199034, Russia
{e.gaevskaya,n.borisov}@spbu.ru

[2] Zhejiang University, 866 Yuhangtang Road, Hangzhou 310058, China

Abstract. This paper explores the synergetic potential of university-museum collaborations within the framework of a Human-Centric Smart City. The research aims to transform traditional pedagogical approaches into a multimodal framework for actualizing cultural heritage through Artificial Intelligence (AI). Methodology (Research Design): the study implemented a structured six-stage workflow integrated into the University's LMS, focusing on the transition from passive archival study to the creation of high-fidelity multimedia prototypes. The design emphasizes technological transformation, competency growth, and institutional integration. Results: the implementation yielded the creation of a "Digital Twin of Cultural Memory" for the museum's media library, including AI-driven animated narratives and inclusive digital resources. Quantitative assessments confirmed that 92% of participants achieved advanced proficiency in Prompt Engineering and AI-content curation. Furthermore, the project evolved the partnership between Saint Petersburg State University and the "Virtual Russian Museum" into a continuous knowledge-sharing ecosystem, significantly enhancing the metropolis's digital resilience and global cultural competitiveness. Practical Implications: the findings demonstrate that micro-group collaboration and AI-enhanced toolsets not only foster professional socialization and soft skills but also position students as "Digital Heritage Architects" capable of solving complex urban and cultural challenges.

Keywords: Human-Centric Smart City · AI Pedagogy · Digital Humanities

1 Introduction

A modern Smart City transcends the conventional definition of a digital service hub designed for comfort and security. It has evolved into a sophisticated cyber-physical ecosystem that encompasses virtual repositories of library and museum collections, integrated educational portals, and social networks that form the bedrock of informal digital

C.-J. Lin et al. (Eds.): ICITL 2026, LNCS 16841, pp. 68–76, 2027.
https://doi.org/10.1007/978-3-032-32112-1_8

communities and open data repositories. The proliferation of these services enables citizens to seamlessly integrate their physical routines with life in virtual communities, a phenomenon that has catalyzed a surge in interdisciplinary research across the humanities and social sciences

Global precedents highlight the shift toward "human-centric" urbanism through the creation of Digital Twins of Cultural Memory. A prominent example is the development of the Xiongan New Area in China, where the "city of the future" is being built simultaneously in physical and digital dimensions. Within this framework, the "Digital Xiongan" project integrates massive cultural data and historical archives into the city's unified operating system, allowing residents to interact with heritage through augmented reality (AR) and ubiquitous digital interfaces [1]. Similarly, the Cleveland City History project in the USA exemplifies the democratization of historical preservation, leveraging personal digital devices to build a shared urban narrative. These initiatives mirror the large-scale "Smart Heritage" strategies where cultural memory is treated as a strategic urban asset [2].

In the Russian Federation, the "Virtual Russian Museum" [3] stands as a pioneering benchmark. Since 2003, it has evolved from a repository into a massive virtual community uniting over a hundred cities globally. The involvement of students from the "Applied Informatics in Arts and Humanities" program at Saint Petersburg State University (SPbU) in exploring these multimedia resources represents a critical intersection of Digital Humanities and urban development [4]. Since 2022, educational internships at the Russian Museum's Multimedia Center have enabled young scholars to not only reflect on Russia's cultural potential but also to develop high-level professional competencies [5].

The advancement of urban infrastructure is now inextricably linked to the integration of neural networks and Generative AI (GenAI). The application of artificial intelligence in higher education ensures the cultivation of "Smart People"—the intellectual capital essential for a resilient digital economy. Consequently, there is an urgent academic demand for robust methodologies that leverage AI-driven tools within university-museum partnerships to ensure that cultural heritage remains a vibrant, interactive component of the unified digital fabric of the city [6].

2 Literature Review

The development of global smart city models and the digitalization of cultural heritage represent one of the most rapidly evolving frontiers in interdisciplinary research. The conceptual framework was established through the seminal works of Giffinger et al. (2007), who proposed a multidimensional model consisting of six core axes: Smart Economy, Smart Mobility, Smart Environment, Smart People, Smart Living, and Smart Governance [7]. Building on these foundations, Townsend (2013) shifted the discourse toward the role of Big Data and civic engagement, arguing that true urban intelligence lies in empowering citizens through information—a perspective vital for analyzing decentralized models in the USA today [8].

Modern Chinese urbanism, exemplified by the Xiongan New Area, represents a high-tier state-led model. Recent studies by Li et al. (2024) analyze Xiongan as a paradigm shift toward "Digital Twin" urbanism, where virtual modeling precedes physical reality [1]. In the cultural sphere, China emphasizes Smart Heritage (e.g., the "Digital Library Cave" of Dunhuang), using AI for both visualization and automated scholarly deciphering of ancient artifacts, effectively integrating cultural code into the national IT infrastructure.

The "SENSEable City" concept pioneered by Carlo Ratti (2014) offers a theoretical basis for the sensor-rich, hyper-connected environments of the Middle East [9]. Ahmed (2025) discusses the emergence of networked architectures in the UAE, where AI and IoT optimize occupant experience [10]. Projects like Burj Azizi (Dubai) illustrate the "Vertical Smart City" model, integrating high-density architectural innovation with AI-driven building management systems (BMS), shifting the focus toward ultra-personalized "Smart Living."

The Russian experience showcases a transition toward "Smart City 3.0," characterized by high citizen engagement through centralized platforms. Cherepanov and Sokolov (2025) observe that Moscow leads in creating digital ecosystems where cultural projects are an integral part of the educational environment [11]. The Virtual Russian Museum directly aligns with Giffinger's "Smart People" dimension, acting as a tool for "Digital Enlightenment" and bridging the geographical divide between regions through cloud technologies [12].

A modern "Smart City" strategy is inconceivable without the proactive training of specialists in AI, data analytics, and cyber-physical systems. In the PRC, this is achieved through the establishment of university clusters within new urban areas; for instance, leading Beijing universities are opening branches in Xiongan to form the city's scientific core. The UAE focuses on international cooperation—the establishment of the Mohamed bin Zayed University of Artificial Intelligence (MBZUAI) in Abu Dhabi exemplifies the nation's ambition to become a global exporter of knowledge. In Russia, "Digital Departments" and university partnerships with IT giants play a pivotal role, allowing students to integrate into real-time urban data management. Consequently, higher education is transforming from a knowledge transmission system into a functional component of urban infrastructure [13].

In contrast to centralized models, the USA prioritizes municipal-level innovation and open data. Recent reports by Smart Cities Dive (2026) highlight leading hubs like Seattle and Austin, which utilize IoT networks for environmental resilience [14]. The cultural sphere is dominated by private initiatives and global platforms (Google Arts & Culture), striving to create "metaverses" where heritage is separated from the physical boundaries of the city.

The synthesis of classical theories and contemporary data (2022–2026) reveals that while technical tools (AI, VR, IoT) are increasingly uniform, strategic objectives diverge: from state-level planning (PRC) to social equity (Russia) or innovative commercial environments (UAE, USA).

3 Research Design and Problem Statement

To achieve the set goal and address the identified problems, the following objectives have been established:

Development and Testing of Technological Solutions (Smart Heritage): to transition from traditional archival studies to the multimodal actualization of resources. This involves creating a series of high-fidelity AI-driven prototypes (animated narratives, inclusive interfaces, and search optimization systems) that form a "Digital Twin of Cultural Memory" for the museum's media library.

Formation and Assessment of Digital Competencies (Smart People): to implement a structured six-stage workflow within the Learning Management System (LMS) to develop advanced skills in prompt engineering and AI-driven content curation. The objective is to ensure high levels of cognitive ergonomics while training students as "Digital Heritage Architects".

Integration into the Smart City Ecosystem: to develop a framework for university-museum collaboration as a vital node in a human-centric Smart City. This includes modernizing the "Virtual Russian Museum" resources to enhance the digital resilience and cultural competitiveness of the metropolis.

Transformation of Institutional Collaboration: to expand the modalities of cooperation between the university and the cultural institution, moving beyond standard internships toward a continuous knowledge-sharing ecosystem (through joint AI-project mentoring and the integration of practitioners into the curriculum).

Professional Socialization and Soft Skills Development: to create an environment for micro-group project activities that foster student integration into the professional expert community. This objective includes evaluating the effectiveness of team collaboration and identifying strategies to overcome time-management challenges.

4 Research Methodology and Conceptual Framework

The research methodology is centered on examining the long-term impact of university-museum collaboration on the development of the Smart City ecosystem. The current stage focuses on analyzing the pedagogical component, which serves as the foundation for an expanded research agenda in the field of Smart City integration.

To facilitate this study, the following instruments were developed: a comprehensive AI competency framework and a specialized course curriculum specifically adapted for sustainable inter-institutional cooperation. These tools were validated through expert consultations with Prof. N. Borisov (Educational Technology) and A. Nikonova (Head of the Department of Museum Studies and Heritage Protection). Following a preliminary trial with a group of 7 students, a pilot experiment is currently underway to further evaluate the toolkit's effectiveness within a live academic environment.

The study evaluates the growth of student competencies in leveraging Artificial Intelligence to analyze and actualize digital cultural heritage assets. This collaboration between Saint Petersburg State University (SPbU) and the State Russian Museum aligns directly with the Smart City concept, where culture and education become integral components of a metropolis's unified digital ecosystem.

The project integrates several key Smart City dimensions:

Smart Governance & Education: the partnership establishes a model for inter-institutional interaction where students do not merely undergo internships but actively create "digital capital," integrating the educational process into real urban infrastructure.

Smart Living (Digital Accessibility and Inclusivity): by developing virtual tours and mobile applications (e.g., the "Artifact Platform"), students implement the principle of a barrier-free environment, making cultural heritage accessible 24/7 regardless of physical location.

Smart Culture: the museum is transformed from a repository into an interactive space. Student developments in 3D modeling and Augmented Reality (AR) utilize visualization technologies that form the technological core of a Smart City.

Smart People (Human Capital): the project redefines students as actors (creators) of the urban environment rather than passive consumers, increasing technological literacy and citizen engagement in the development of St. Petersburg.

Creation of a "Permeable" Cultural Space: digital resources bridge the gap between the museum's physical objects and city-wide information flows. This creates a unified information fabric, integrating museum data into urban services and educational portals.

5 Smart Heritage: Pedagogical Strategies and Outcomes

The framework utilizes the "Media Library of the Russian Museum" (part of the "Virtual Branch" project) as an authentic resource. This collection of 400+ multimedia programs includes: Virtual Tours (Mikhailovsky Palace, Benois Wing, Marble/Stroganov Palaces, Mikhailovsky Castle); Digital Catalogues (annotated high-quality reproductions); Educational Content (expert lectures and art theory materials); and Edutainment (gamified tools for restoration and attribution).Technological Specifications: the open-source database supports High Resolution for detailed examination, Interactivity for comparative analysis, and Versatility for access via both local virtual branches and the online portal.

Student Tasks and Autonomy. The Russian Museum Media Library serves as a vital tool for the sociocultural actualization of heritage by integrating museum content into the modern educational environment and ensuring global access to masterpieces of Russian art. As a unique digital cultural heritage site, it requires both careful preservation and sustainable management. Within this framework, students were tasked with bridging the gap between historical preservation and modern technology through the following objectives: (1) Developing a conceptual framework for the sociocultural actualization of self-selected multimedia resources (focusing on assets created between 2000 and 2020);(2) Designing an AI-enhanced multimedia presentation aimed at increasing sociocultural engagement with the chosen digital artifacts; (3) Exploring digital cultural heritage by utilizing specialized resources curated by experts from the Russian Museum; (4) Engaging in collaborative microgroup activities, focusing on reflective problem-solving and critical analysis of emerging challenges.

To encourage creative agency, students were granted maximum independence in selecting their research topics, project themes, and work formats (individual or group). The project workflow was structured into six progressive stages:

Selection: identifying a specific digital resource for updating.

Format determination: deciding between a collaborative or individual approach.

Conceptualization: developing a formal concept for the resource's actualization.

Implementation: building a functional demo version based on the proposed concept.

Documentation: compiling a comprehensive internship report.

Table 1. Adherence to the "Introductory Internship" Work Schedule (n = 18)

	Stage	Activity	On time	Late	Not finished
1	Selection	Resource selection via technical criteria,	18		–
2	Format	Plan approval and group coordination	16	2	–
3	Concept	Tool selection and AI-prompt strategy	16	2	–
4	Implementation	Functional demo and error correction	10	8	
5	Documentation	Internship report compilation	8	10	
6	Examination	Final presentation to the committee	18	–	–

Examination: presenting the final results to the committee of the educational program (09.03.03).

Student Project Thematic Areas and Outcomes All participants integrated AI into their work across five key areas: Inclusion (accessibility for hearing-impaired); Museum Tribute (Kuindzhi/Hero-image projects); Tech Modernization (video scaling/subtitling for Shubin, Levitan, Vrubel); UX Enhancement ("Art Workshop" app); and AI-Driven Management (search engines and recommender systems). A notable project was an AI-based Telegram Bot for the Media Library. Tasks and assessment tools (Technical Assignments, reports) were co-developed with students and managed via the SPbU Blackboard portal.

6 Competency Framework for Student Engagement with Digital Cultural Heritage

The curriculum for the 'Introductory Internship' course is based on a set of developed professional competencies that comply with both Russian national requirements [15] and international standards [16]. Eighteen fourth-year undergraduate students from St. Petersburg University (SPbU) participated in an experiment to validate the developed competencies". Professional competencies included identifying the effectiveness of technological aspects of working with neural networks (Competency 1). The study also examined sociocultural issues arising when working with neural networks (Competency 2). The development of general cultural competencies included studying materials on artistic heritage displayed at the Russian Museum Competency 3).

AI Competency 1: Functional Updating and Authentic Reproduction of DCH. Statement: Ability to apply digital technologies and AI to preserve, restore, and promote heritage, ensuring inclusivity and digital sustainability. IDK-1 (Knowledge): Visualization and verification technologies; technical risks (attribution errors in AI); standards for digital sustainability. IDK-2 (Skills): Analyzing IT trends in museology. IDK-3 (Abilities): Systematic approach to formalizing solutions for DCH problems.

AI Competency 2: Sociocultural Actualization of Cultural Heritage. Statement: Capability to conduct humanitarian expertise, interpret cultural values, and design ethical representation formats. IDK-1 (Knowledge): Digital Humanities foundations; methods for interpreting cultural codes; ethical and legal frameworks for digital copies. IDK-2 (Skills): Socio-humanitarian assessment of VR/AR/AI projects; developing narratives for educational representation.IDK-3 (Abilities): Designing human-centered UX for archives; critical analysis and verification of digital interpretations.

Competency 3: General Cultural Competence (Russian Museum Collection). Statement: Ability to navigate cultural spaces and define identity using museum resources. IDK-1 (Knowledge): Artistic styles (Academicism to Avant-garde); distinction between digitized and "born-digital" resources. IDK-2 (Skills): Recognizing artistic styles; independent planning of exhibition routes via navigation tools. IDK-3 (Abilities): Intercultural communication in Multimedia Centers; proficiency in digital resources for art-related data processing.

7 Experimental Results and Discussion

The experiment involved18 fourth-year students, all of whom successfully defended their internship reports for the "Introductory Internship" course. The high quality of the developed subtitles, submitted reports, and final presentations indicates overall positive learning outcomes. Quantitative data regarding competency mastery are summarized in Tables 1 and 2. Additionally, qualitative insights are drawn from the report of student A.I. Latipov, excerpts of which are analyzed below.

Data indicate that most students achieved Advanced (B) or High (A) levels across all competencies. Key highlights:

AI Competency 1: 94% of students successfully integrated AI into DCH preservation; only one remained at the basic level.

Table 2. Student Competency Mastery (Applied Informatics Program, n = 18)

Competence	Key Focus / Statement Summary	A high	B adv	C basic
AI comp.1	Use of AI/IT for DCH preservation & restoration	8	9	1
AI comp. 2:	Humanitarian expertise & ethical heritage design	8	10	–
Cultural Comp.	Navigation of Russian Museum space & identity	12	6	–

AI Competency 2: 100% mastery of sociocultural and ethical heritage representation, confirming strong humanitarian expertise in digital environments.

General Cultural Competence: peak performance area with 66% at the "High" level, validating authentic museum collections as vital for professional identity and navigation.

8 Research Outcomes

The project validated the proposed framework through five vectors: (1) Smart Heritage: 9 prototypes (AI-narratives, inclusive tools, search models) created a "Digital Twin of Cultural Memory." (2) Smart People: 92% of students mastered Prompt Engineering, becoming "Digital Heritage Architects." (3) Urban Integration: the collaboration acts as a Smart City node, enhancing the metropolis's digital resilience. (4) Collaboration: potential was confirmed, though co-mentoring failed due to administrative barriers. (5) Soft Skills: despite 20% deadline slippage, micro-group work fostered professional socialization within the Multimedia Center.

9 Discussion

The project results confirm the validity of the proposed framework, yet several areas require critical reflection. While the "Digital Twin of Cultural Memory" was successfully prototyped, the limitations of the current study must be acknowledged.

First, the small sample size of participants restricts the broader generalization of the quantitative data. Second, the methodology relied heavily on descriptive analysis, which, while providing deep qualitative insights, lacks the rigor of large-scale statistical validation. Future iterations of the project should prioritize expanding the participant pool and integrating more robust quantitative metrics. Furthermore, the identified administrative barriers that prevented the full integration of museum specialists into the curriculum highlight the need for a more flexible institutional roadmap.

10 Conclusion

In conclusion, the experiment demonstrated that the synergy between a university and a museum acts as a powerful catalyst for the "Human-Centric Smart City". The project successfully transformed students into "Digital Heritage Architects", equipped with advanced AI competencies and a proactive approach to cultural preservation. While goals such as co-mentoring and full institutional practitioner integration were not entirely met at this stage, the identified growth points—scaling technological prototypes and optimizing AI-driven workflows—provide a clear trajectory for future development.

The proposed methodology establishes an innovative trajectory in interdisciplinary research, translating the theoretical concepts of the smart city into the practical plane of professional talent development. The scientific originality of this work lies in substantiating the synergy between the virtual environments of Saint Petersburg State University and the State Russian Museum as a critical factor in forming a "Digital Twin of Cultural Memory" for the metropolis.

In contrast to traditional approaches that limit the "Smart City" scope to logistics and utilities, this study demonstrates that the socio-cultural sphere and higher education form the bedrock of urban resilience. University portals and museum media libraries cease to be passive repositories, evolving into active nodes within the urban neural network. The integration of AI technologies into humanities education not only preserves historical identity but also generates high-tech intellectual capital. Ultimately, this approach ensures the sustainable development and global competitiveness of the metropolis amidst the transition to a new technological paradigm.

References

1. Li, Y., et al.: Spatiotemporal differentiation and evolution pattern of digital twin cities: the case of Xiongan. Cities J. (2024)
2. Clevelend History Centre. https://www.wrhs.org/plan-visit/places-to-visit/cleveland-history-center
3. Virtual Russian Museum, https://rusmuseumvrm.ru/
4. Gaevskaya, E.: Nikolay Borisov Digital Cultural Heritage. Textbook for University, p. 183. Saint Petersburg State University, Saint-Petersburg (2025)
5. Gaevskaya, E.G., Prokudin, D.E., Kononova, O.V.: Development of methods for studying the image of culture in the digital era. Vestnik Sankt-Peterburgskogo Universiteta, Filosofia I Konfliktologia. **40**(1), 134–144 (2024)
6. Duggan, S.: AI in education: change at the speed of learning. In: Knyazeva, S. (ed.) The Policy Brief of UNESCO IITE. UNESCO IITE, Moscow (2020)
7. Giffinger, R., et al.: Smart Cities: Ranking of European Medium-Sized Cities. Vienna University of Technology (2007)
8. Townsend, A.M.: Smart Cities: Big Data, Civic Hackers, and the Quest for a New Utopia. W. W. Norton & Company (2013)
9. Ratti, C., Claudel, M.: The City of Tomorrow: Sensors, Networks, Hackers, and the Future of Urban Life. Yale University Press (2014)
10. Ahmed, O.G.: Smart building systems: a confluence of architecture and technology. J. Adv. Urbanism. (2025)
11. Cherepanov, V., Sokolov, A.: Smart cities in Russia: current situation and insights for future development. Urban Anal. Rev. (2025)
12. Shadiev, R., Wang, X., Chen, X., Gayevskaya, E., Borisov, N.: Research on the impact of the learning activity supported by 360-degree video and translation technologies on cross-cultural knowledge and attitudes development. Educ. Inf. Technol. **29**(7), 7759–7791 (2024)
13. Yigitcanlar, T.: Smart City Schools and Universities: the Role of Education in Urban Intelligence. Educational Technology & Society (2024)
14. Smart Cities Dive 8 Trends that will Shape Cities in 2026. Industry Report (2026).
15. Federal State Educational Standard (3++) for Bachelor's Degree Programs. https://fgosvo.ru/fgosvo/index/24 (2026)
16. AI Competency Framework UNESCO 2024

AI Avatars in University Education: Literature Review

Radim Dolak(✉), Petr Suchanek, and Josef Botlik

School of Business Administration in Karvina, Silesian University in Opava, 733 40, Karvina, Opava, Czechia
{dolak,suchanek,botlik}@opf.slu.cz

Abstract. The role of AI avatars in university education is emerging as a transformative component within the academic ecosystem, driven by their potential to enhance personalized learning, improve engagement, and streamline educational processes. The integration of AI avatars is recognized for their multifaceted benefits, which are evident through various case studies and research findings. This paper discusses the possibility of use of AI avatars in university teaching. The main aim is to highlight the potential to enhance students' understanding and also to identify limits and potential problems. There will be mentioned role of AI avatars aspects in university education, role of AI avatars in personalized learning, ethical considerations, realism and authenticity of AI avatars and finally possible integration of AI avatars into university education framework.

Keywords: AI avatars · university education · teaching

1 Introduction

The implementation of Artificial Intelligence (AI) avatars, particularly in the form of chatbots and virtual tutors, has gained momentum in educational settings, largely driven by their potential to enhance student engagement. Research indicates a multifaceted impact of these technologies, primarily by providing personalized learning experiences, fostering interactive learning environments, and addressing individual student needs efficiently.

The integration of AI avatars into university education presents transformative opportunities to enrich the learning experience by personalizing instructional delivery, enhancing engagement, and providing real-time feedback. These avatars serve not only as teaching aids but also as proactive educational partners that facilitate a deeper connection with course material and foster student autonomy.

2 AI Avatars

The integration of AI-generated avatars in university education courses is becoming increasingly important in enhancing learner engagement and optimizing the educational experience. These virtual entities, when used appropriately, can foster a more interactive and personalized learning environment. Several studies elucidate the impact of AI avatars on educational outcomes and user experience.

C.-J. Lin et al. (Eds.): ICITL 2026, LNCS 16841, pp. 77–84, 2027.
https://doi.org/10.1007/978-3-032-32112-1_9

AI avatars facilitate personalized learning experiences by adapting to individual students' needs and learning preferences. By leveraging machine learning and data analytics, these avatars can tailor feedback and resources, creating a more engaging educational environment. Avatars utilize algorithms that analyse student performance and learning patterns, enabling them to adjust instructional materials in real time to ensure that content resonates with the learner's pace and style [25, 36]. This personalization is crucial as students often exhibit diverse learning pathways, particularly in university education settings where demographics vary significantly, such as with adult learners balancing education and life commitments [19, 23].

2.1 AI Avatars Aspects in University Education

One significant aspect is the user experience associated with AI-generated avatars in educational videos. Research indicates that the appearance, behaviour, and emotional expressiveness of these avatars play a critical role in engaging students. For instance, Zhang and Wu demonstrated that visually appealing avatars can significantly increase average viewing times and interaction rates, suggesting that well-designed avatars help maintain learner interest during educational content delivery [38]. Vallis et al. [35] also noted that qualitative experiences of students using AI avatars revealed mixed feelings towards their effectiveness in conveying complex ethical business concepts, underscoring that while avatars can engage, their ability to resonate ethically remains a challenge.

Engagement is another critical factor where AI avatars show promise. Students have expressed positive perceptions regarding the use of AI-generated avatars as educational presenters. A study examining student responses to an avatar employed in business ethics courses found that participants noted these avatars were often preferred for conveying lecture material, thus validating the effectiveness of synthetic media [35]. Moreover, Vallis [33] documents the use of avatars in facilitating critical discussions among students, reflecting their growing role in enhancing interactive learning experiences.

Furthermore, the development of distinct personality traits in avatars significantly influences educational outcomes and student engagement. Research suggests that avatars imbued with positive personality traits, such as approachability and creativity, can enhance the learning experience by fostering a more relatable interaction [22]. This aligns with findings from various studies indicating the importance of emotional and psychological elements in learning environments that utilize AI avatars [4].

While AI avatars offer advantages in educational settings, their implementation also raises ethical considerations and challenges. Institutions must navigate the complexities of ethical implications and pedagogical principles when integrating AI technologies. Literature indicates that guidelines for responsible AI use are essential to ensure fairness and transparency within educational applications. Experiences from various universities, including innovative approaches discussed by Britton and Vallis [5], highlight the need for strategic frameworks that effectively balance technological advancement with ethical responsibility.

2.2 AI Avatars and Personalized Learning

AI avatars can tailor educational resources to fit individual learning styles, thereby increasing engagement and motivation among students. One of the significant aspects of AI avatars in university education is their ability to provide personalized educational experiences. Research indicates that digital avatars can be employed to adapt learning content to students' needs and preferences, fostering an environment where students receive tailored guidance and support [3]. Additionally, personalized learning is enhanced through intelligent tutoring systems that leverage AI-driven avatars, creating immersive educational environments, as highlighted by Khalil and Thakur [16].

Furthermore, the personalized learning opportunities afforded by AI avatars are of paramount importance. As discussed by Fink et al. [11], these avatars can provide individualized and contextualized instruction, adapting to learners' needs and preferences, which can facilitate deeper understanding and retention of material. The need for ethical and pedagogical guidelines surrounding the use of these avatars has also been emphasized by Britton and Vallis [5], as educational institutions strive to navigate the potential challenges alongside the advantages.

In addition to personalized support, AI avatars encourage collaboration and communication among students and instructors. By creating a more socially connected learning environment, avatars can mitigate feelings of detachment often associated with online learning [8, 29]. They serve as facilitators of group discussions and collaborative projects, boosting peer interaction and ensuring that all voices are heard. This aligns with the principles of inclusive education, where diverse perspectives contribute to a richer learning experience [14, 30].

2.3 Ethical Considerations, Realism and Authenticity

Ethics and accountability also play a pivotal role in the deployment of AI avatars in university education. Institutions must ensure that the technology is implemented responsibly, balancing the benefits of AI with considerations around data privacy, algorithmic bias, and equitable access [10, 26]. Training for educators on the effective use of AI tools is essential to harness the full potential of technology while maintaining an ethical framework [1, 2]. Furthermore, as AI avatars become integral to the learning landscape, ongoing research and feedback from users—both students and educators—are imperative to refine AI applications and address any emerging challenges [15, 20].

Despite their potential, the use of AI avatars raises ethical considerations and questions about representation and authenticity. Vallis [33] emphasized the importance of ethical frameworks when integrating AI technologies in education, advocating for careful consideration of the implications these avatars have on both teaching and learning processes. Moon's research [24] indicated a mixed reception among students, who often felt that interactions with AI avatars lacked the emotional connection found in human instructors, underscoring the necessity for nuanced integration of technology in pedagogy.

Challenges persist in the implementation of avatars in educational settings, particularly regarding their fidelity and realism. High-fidelity avatars, which closely resemble human figures, have been shown to enhance user engagement by conveying professionalism and credibility. Chae et al. [13] highlighted that human-like avatars seem to elicit a greater sense of psychological closeness, which is beneficial in educational contexts. However, Cao et al. [6] posed critical questions regarding whether high-fidelity avatars are necessary for effective interactions, suggesting that simpler avatars might still achieve desired engagement levels under certain conditions.

Moreover, the implementation of AI avatars can significantly address the challenges of student engagement and retention. The interactive nature of these avatars encourages students to participate actively in their learning processes, fostering not only content mastery but also critical thinking skills [21, 27]. The ability of AI avatars to simulate conversation and provide immediate responses can replicate the effect of traditional tutoring while making learning accessible at any time [12]. This capability becomes particularly beneficial in hybrid or remote learning environments, where students may feel isolated from their instructors and peers [30].

2.4 The Integration of AI Avatars into University Education

The integration of AI avatars into university education has emerged as a transformative trend, particularly with the rise of platforms for creating engaging video content tailored for educational purposes. This synthesis highlights the capabilities, challenges, and implications of employing AI avatars in instructional design.

AI-generated avatars are increasingly recognized for their capacity to enhance student engagement and communication clarity in educational videos. In the context of Massive Open Online Courses (MOOCs), Conto et al. [7] analysed the integration of AI-generated avatars as communication tools in educational videos and found that students exhibited increased acceptance and perceived empathy from avatars, which played a crucial role in maintaining attention and facilitating knowledge retention during video lectures. Similarly, Vallis and Britton [34] reported on the efficacy of AI avatars in promoting critical discussions among students, particularly regarding ethical decision-making, and noted the positive impact avatars had on engaging students in complex topics such as business ethics.

Platforms such as D-ID Studio leverage advancements in AI to create lifelike avatars that enhance language learning experiences. Wang and Zou [37] highlighted how such technology allows for improved language instruction through contextually relevant speaking practice, thereby facilitating second language acquisition. Furthermore, the personalization of learning experiences through AI avatars has been linked to enhanced motivation and engagement in students, as detailed in studies examining their application across diverse educational settings [22, 28]. This personalization often correlates with improved learning outcomes and student satisfaction.

2.5 AI Avatars and Its Future in University Education

The ongoing evolution of AI technologies, particularly in natural language processing and machine learning, continues to reshape university education. Tools like intelligent tutoring systems and AI avatars not only facilitate learning but also administrative efficiency, demonstrating the broad applicability of AI in educational contexts [17, 31]. As higher education institutions explore AI's transformative potential, case studies emphasize the necessity of adapting curricula to incorporate these innovative tools effectively [18, 32].

The challenges of AI avatars also extend to practical implementation aspects. Drobnjak and Botički [9] examined the technological considerations necessary for developing virtual educational avatars. They stressed the importance of aligning technological capabilities with educational pedagogies to ensure effective utilization in learning environments. Moreover, realism in avatars—specifically how closely they mimic human characteristics—remains a focal point in ongoing research, as noted by Fink et al. [11]. Their findings suggested that while avatars can significantly enhance personalized learning, improvements in the realism of their presentations are required for maximizing effectiveness

3 Conclusion

The evolution of AI avatars in higher education presents both promising opportunities and considerable challenges. While the benefits of increased engagement, personalized learning experiences, and potential ethical guidelines are well-documented, ongoing research is critical to optimize their effectiveness and mitigate issues of user perception and representation. As educational environments continue to evolve, the effective integration of these avatars will likely depend on a blend of technological advancement, pedagogical strategies, and ethical considerations.

In summary, AI avatars are transforming how instructional content is delivered in university education. They offer enhanced engagement and personalized learning pathways but also necessitate a careful and ethical approach to their design and implementation. As educational institutions increasingly adopt these technologies, ongoing assessments of their impact on learning outcomes and student perceptions will be essential to optimize their use in academic settings.

AI avatars can create an enriched educational experience that prepares students for the complexities of modern professions. This transformation demands continuous research and adaptation, ensuring that educational technology serves as a powerful tool for inclusive and effective learning.

Acknowledgments. This paper was supported by the Ministry of Education, Youth and Sports within the Institutional Support for long-term Development of a Research Organization Silesian University in Opava in 2026.

Disclosure of Interests The author has no competing interests to declare that are relevant to the content of this article.

References

1. Adigun, O.T., Haihambo, C.K., Veii, K.K., Hengari, J.K., Simasiku, E.L.: A perspective of requirements for trainers in the application of artificial intelligence in inclusive education. In: Du, S., Sanmugam, M., Mohd Barkhaya, N., Chen, C., Wang, J. (eds.) Assessing Educational Digital Transformation in the AI Era, pp. 1–24. IGI Global Scientific Publishing, Hershey (2026). https://doi.org/10.4018/979-8-3373-7508-3.ch001
2. Asrifan, A., Sudirman, R., Rosmayanti, V., Sulolipu, A.A.: Navigating ethical AI: ensuring fairness in educational technologies. In: Wang, V. (ed.) Foundations and Frameworks for AI in Education, pp. 27–52. IGI Global Scientific Publishing, Hershey (2026). https://doi.org/10.4018/979-8-3373-2397-8.ch002
3. Bobro, N.: Economic feasibility of implementing teachers' digital avatars in the higher education system. Econ. Synergy. **3**, 8–23 (2025). https://doi.org/10.53920/es-2025-3-1
4. Bozkurt, A., Karadeniz, A., Bañeres-Besora, D., Guerrero-Roldán, A., Rodríguez, M.: Artificial intelligence and reflections from educational landscape: a review of AI studies in half a century. Sustainability. **13**(2), 800 (2021). https://doi.org/10.3390/su13020800
5. Britton, B., Vallis, C.: Digital facelift. Ascilite Publications (2023). https://doi.org/10.14742/apubs.2023.552
6. Cao, Q., Yu, H., Charisse, P., Qiao, S., Stevens, B.: Is high-fidelity important for human-like virtual avatars in human computer interactions? Int. J. Network Dyn. Intell., 15–23 (2023). https://doi.org/10.53941/ijndi0201008
7. Conto, J., Soto, G., Valarezo-Álvarez, G., Arévalo, F., Valdiviezo-Ortiz, J.: Construcción de MOOC con avatares generados mediante ia: Estudio de caso aplicado y evaluación de percepciones. Revista Tecnológica. **36**(E1), 215–233 (2024). https://doi.org/10.37815/rte.v36ne1.1210
8. Cusnir, C., Surugiu, R.: It's a social practice, and schools cannot ignore it: exploring the usage of GenAI in media and communication higher education. In: Duarte, A., Andrade, J., Dias, P. (eds.) AI as Help and Hindrance in Education, pp. 361–382. IGI Global Scientific Publishing, Hershey (2026). https://doi.org/10.4018/979-8-3373-6018-8.ch014
9. Drobnjak, A., Botički, I.: Technology considerations in building virtual educational avatars. Int. Conf. Comput. Educ. (2024). https://doi.org/10.58459/icce.2024.4887
10. Eunkyung, H. AI-based Edutech for adaptive teaching and learning. In Artificial Intelligence. IntechOpen, London (2024). doi: https://doi.org/10.5772/intechopen.1004952
11. Fink, M., Robinson, S., Ertl, B.: AI-based avatars are changing the way we learn and teach: benefits and challenges. Front. Educ. (2024). https://doi.org/10.3389/feduc.2024.1416307
12. Goenka, N., Patnaik, D., Pradhan, B.B.: Impact of artificial intelligence on virtual teacher learner engagement: redefining educational dynamics. In: Bansal, R., Chakir, A., Hafaz Ngah, A., Rabby, F., Jain, A. (eds.) AI Algorithms and ChatGPT for Student Engagement in Online Learning, pp. 192–207. IGI Global Scientific Publishing, Hershey (2024). https://doi.org/10.4018/979-8-3693-4268-8.ch013
13. Chae, R., Lee, H., Kim, E.: The effects of avatar human-likeness on psychological closeness in virtual-reality. Psychol. Mark. **42**(4), 1132–1145 (2024). https://doi.org/10.1002/mar.22168
14. Jafary, M., Kotamjani, S.S.: The role of artificial intelligence in supporting Canadian Plurilingual graduate students: opportunities, challenges, and implications for inclusive education. In: Sorayyaei Azar, A., Shakib Kotamjani, S., Milad, M., Sharatol Ahmad Shah, S. (eds.) AI-Powered Solutions for Bilingual Proficiency and Communication, pp. 279–310. IGI Global Scientific Publishing, Hershey (2026). https://doi.org/10.4018/979-8-3373-0275-1.ch009
15. Jaya, K., Raghuvaran, A.P., Natarajan, S.: Mind the gap: examining the disadvantages of AI writing tools in education, focusing on originality. In: Pandey, J. (ed.) Developing AI Literacy in Students, pp. 181–202. IGI Global Scientific Publishing, Hershey (2026). https://doi.org/10.4018/979-8-3373-2297-1.ch006

16. Khalil, A., Thakur, I.: Beyond reality: leveraging AI and educational metaverse for immersive learning experiences in education. In: Demircioğlu, A. (ed.) AI Use in Social Sciences, pp. 429–456. IGI Global Scientific Publishing, Hershey (2025). https://doi.org/10.4018/979-8-3373-2612-2.ch016
17. Kiran, A.K.: Applications and Impacts of AI Tools in Education, vol. I, 1st edn. Magestic Technology Solutions (P) Ltd. (2025). https://doi.org/10.47716/978-93-92090-38-7
18. Kotsis, K.: Integrating artificial intelligence into higher education curricula: challenges and opportunities for science-based programs. IJAIET. **6**(1), 4–12 (2025). https://doi.org/10.54660/ijaiet.2025.6.1.04-12
19. Love, A.S., Labay-Marquez, J., Valadez, R.: Understanding adult learners' needs and integrating technology for effective online education: adult-centered approaches for teaching and learning. In: Keengwe, J. (ed.) Handbook of Research on Innovative Frameworks and Inclusive Models for Online Learning, pp. 172–193. IGI Global Scientific Publishing, Hershey (2023). https://doi.org/10.4018/978-1-6684-9072-3.ch009
20. Machicao, J.C.: Artificial intelligence as a general resource for all professions: towards a higher education pedagogy framework. In: Almaraz-Menéndez, F., Maz-Machado, A., López-Esteban, C., Almaraz-López, C. (eds.) Strategy, Policy, Practice, and Governance for AI in Higher Education Institutions, pp. 156–180. IGI Global Scientific Publishing, Hershey (2022). https://doi.org/10.4018/978-1-7998-9247-2.ch007
21. Mafarja, N., Zulnaidi, H., Mohamad, M.M.: Developing critical thinking skills through AI-enhanced science education for sustainability. In: Chinedu, C., Mafarja, N., Hussein, M., Saleem, A. (eds.) Rethinking the Pedagogy of Sustainable Development in the AI Era, pp. 173–196. IGI Global Scientific Publishing, Hershey (2025). https://doi.org/10.4018/979-8-3693-9062-7.ch009
22. Majgaard, G., Andersen, M.: From code to character: investigating personality in generative AI-driven educational avatars. Eur. Conf. Games Based Learn. **19**(2), 543–551 (2025). https://doi.org/10.34190/ecgbl.19.2.4002
23. Maharjan, S., Espinoza, M., Robles, T., Strayer, L.P.: Revolutionizing CTE: AI-driven Andragogical practices for social justice in urban education. In: Wang, V. (ed.) AI Integration into Andragogical Education, pp. 255–282. IGI Global Scientific Publishing, Hershey (2025). https://doi.org/10.4018/979-8-3373-0502-8.ch011
24. Moon, H.: Exploring the acceptance of AI video technology in distance learning environments. J. Appl. Instruct. Design. **14**(2) (2025). https://doi.org/10.59668/2222.20828
25. Rao, M.N., Al-Obaidi, J.A.: Embracing how AI responsibly empowers students and faculty in higher education: theoretical perspectives. In: Boivin, J., Al-Obaidi, J., Rao, M. (eds.) Emerging Technologies Transforming Higher Education: Instructional Design and Student Success, pp. 1–32. IGI Global Scientific Publishing, Hershey (2025). https://doi.org/10.4018/979-8-3693-3904-6.ch001
26. Salendab, F.A., Cogo, D.A., Catipay, A.Z., Millendez, G.J.: The role of artificial intelligence (AI) in personalized learning and adaptive assessments. In: Moore, J., Gupta, S., Sharma, M., Garg, A., Josephine, V.L. (eds.) Transforming Education with Data Science in the AI Era, pp. 93–122. IGI Global Scientific Publishing, Hershey (2026). https://doi.org/10.4018/979-8-3373-2185-1.ch004
27. Samaty, M.: Beyond AI-enabled classrooms: fostering critical thinking in the age of generative artificial intelligence. In: ElSayary, A. (ed.) Prompt Engineering and Generative AI Applications for Teaching and Learning, pp. 527–546. IGI Global Scientific Publishing, Hershey (2025). https://doi.org/10.4018/979-8-3693-7332-3.ch030
28. Sanders, E., Llantuy, N., Li, J.: AI avatars in hospitality employee training: transforming learning through innovation. ICHRIE Research Reports. **10**(4) (2025). https://doi.org/10.61701/736487.462

29. Sotiriou, S., Bogner, F.: Discovery space: a technology-enhanced classroom for deeper learning in STEM. In: Reimagining Education - the Role of E-Learning, Creativity, and Technology in the Post-Pandemic era. IntechOpen, London (2023). https://doi.org/10.5772/intechopen.1002649
30. Tahura, S., Kalaiyarasan, G., Sarkar, S.R.: From exclusion to inclusion AI as a catalyst for equal access to education. In: Awashreh, R. (ed.) Democratizing Education with AI and the Future of Personalized Learning, pp. 29–66. IGI Global Scientific Publishing, Hershey (2026). https://doi.org/10.4018/979-8-3373-2302-2.ch002
31. Thuy, P.: Empowering student research with artificial intelligence: transforming education through AI applications. J. Inf. Syst. Eng. Manag. **10**(15), 734–741 (2025). https://doi.org/10.52783/jisem.v10i15s.2514
32. Toktarova, V., Rebko, O.: Educational audio and video content in the practice of university lecturers: intelligent tools and approaches to development and implementation. Inf. Educ. **40**(2), 5–15 (2025). https://doi.org/10.32517/0234-0453-2025-40-2-5-15
33. Vallis, C.: It's not just about text: AI-generated video in education. Pacific J. Technol. Enhanced Learn. **7**(2) (2025). https://doi.org/10.24135/pjtel.v7i2.211
34. Vallis, C., Britton, B.: From script to screen: an emergent view of AI-generated avatars. Proc. Int. Conf. Network. Learn. **14**(1) (2024). https://doi.org/10.54337/nlc.v14i1.8055
35. Vallis, C., Wilson, S., Gozman, D., Buchanan, J.: Student perceptions of AI-generated avatars in teaching business ethics: we might not be impressed. Postdigital Sci. Educ. **6**(2), 537–555 (2023). https://doi.org/10.1007/s42438-023-00407-7
36. Waladi, C., Lamarti, M.S., Khaldi, M.: AI-driven personalized learning pathways customizing education for every student. In: Khaldi, M. (ed.) Supporting Personalized Learning and Students' Skill Development with AI, pp. 63–78. IGI Global Scientific Publishing, Hershey (2025). https://doi.org/10.4018/979-8-3693-8965-2.ch004
37. Wang, C., Zou, B.: D-id studio: empowering language teaching with AI avatars. TESOL J. **16**(2) (2025). https://doi.org/10.1002/tesj.70034
38. Zhang, R., Wu, Q.: Impact of using virtual avatars in educational videos on user experience. Sci. Rep. **14**(1) (2024). https://doi.org/10.1038/s41598-024-56716-9

Teaching an Artificial Learner to Interpret: A Pathway to Mastering Drama Analysis

Peter Øhrstrøm[1(✉)], David Jakobsen[1], and Simon Pacis[2]

[1] Department of Culture and Communication, Aalborg University, 9000 Aalborg, Denmark
{poe,davker}@ikk.aau.dk
[2] Pacis Inc, 9530 Støvring, Denmark
simon@pacis.dk

Abstract. In (Øhrstrøm et al. 2025) a concept was presented for the design of a system aimed at supporting and developing users' ability to interpret dramatic works in accordance with high and professionally recognized standards. The idea in the article was to leverage the principle of "learning by teaching". In practice, the user would act as a guide for an artificial learner, i.e., an interactive system based on a large language model (LLM) and capable of receiving instruction. The user would guide the artificial learner through the process of constructing an interpretation of a pre-selected drama. It was anticipated that by guiding the artificial learner, the user would acquire enhanced competence in interpreting dramatic works. This article describes the design of an implemented system built upon this design concept. In practice, works by the Danish playwright Kaj Munk (1898–1944) are utilized, drawing from the extensive corpus of Munk's dramatic works available in the Digital Kaj Munk Archive at Aalborg University. The article describes and discusses the results of the initial preliminary test of the system, as well as the need for adjustments and further testing. Finally, it outlines the long-term perspectives for the use of the system described and the broader implications associated with it.

Keywords: Generative AI · large language model (LLM) · learning by teaching · artificial learners · Socratic learning · literary interpretation · Kaj Munk

1 Teaching as a Learning Strategy in Literary Studies

In a recent study [15], we aimed to demonstrate how one could develop an AI-based system that supports learning in literary analysis. The idea is to utilize the concept of "learning by teaching", (cf. [2, 3, 5, 13]) which posits that by instructing others in a particular area, one can learn a great deal about that area oneself. This approach is based on the idea of so-called Socratic learning in which the use of dialogue is crucial. This principle also applies in the literary domain, where individuals can achieve better insights into the interpretation of a work by presenting the work in a literary study group or similar setting, and by arguing for an interpretation that they find persuasive. The same appears to hold true when we instruct an artificial learner, i.e., an interactive

C.-J. Lin et al. (Eds.): ICITL 2026, LNCS 16841, pp. 85–95, 2027.
https://doi.org/10.1007/978-3-032-32112-1_10

system based on an LLM and capable of receiving instruction. In this instance as well, the work of instructing the artificial learner to interpret the literary text is expected to lead to a deeper understanding of the text itself.

In continuation of the considerations presented in [15], a learning system has been developed with the aim of enhancing the user's ability to interpret plays. This system is designed with reference to the Danish playwright Kaj Munk (1898–1944). The dramatic works by Kaj Munk are utilized, drawing from the extensive corpus of Munk's dramatic works available in the Digital Kaj Munk Archive at Aalborg University [14]. The system includes twelve Kaj Munk's plays, each accompanied by a brief introduction. The user is free to select any of these plays.

The task of interpreting the drama is to be based solely on the text and the brief introduction, without reliance on additional specialized knowledge or publications regarding Kaj Munk's life and work. It must be acknowledged, however, that we cannot definitively ascertain whether the selected language model, Arcee Trinity Large, has been trained on texts discussing Kaj Munk's plays. But if this were the case, it would be quite surprising, considering that while Munk is known in Denmark, he is not among the most renowned Danish authors on an international scale.

As mentioned above the underlying approach of the learning system is the so-called "learning by teaching". In the present setting the idea is that by guiding an artificial learner in interpreting the chosen drama by Kaj Munk, the user will improve their own interpretative skills regarding that particular drama and probably also in general. The interpretation of a drama can naturally be presented as a text in its own right, such as an essay that could serve as a submission to the teacher, who in this case is the human user of the system.

The learning system (including an artificial learner) is described in detail in Sect. 2, while the results of a preliminary test of its potential are presented in Sect. 3. In Sect. 4, we will consider the need for further adjustments of the system. In this section, we will also examine in more detail what the user could do with the concluding essay produced by the artificial learner. In Sect. 5, we will discuss the perspectives on the use of AI technology in literary studies and present the plan for further tests of an updated version of the system.

2 Design and Implementation of an Artificial Learner

The Kaj Munk AI learning system we have developed is interactive and based on an LLM. The design concept behind the system focused on moving away from a chat-based interface. This included both presenting the generated data in a non-traditional manner, as well as forcing the user to input data in a non-traditional manner. The input provided by the user in the generation of the analysis is approving in nature and is always in direct response to data generated by the artificial learner.

With an essay based on a literary analysis of a play being the final output of a session, we chose to install a strict framework for the learning system to follow during the generation of the analysis. This framework allowed us to predetermine the steps the artificial learner must take when generating a literary analysis, including particular instructions for each step. This includes steps such as" Provide a short summary of the play," or" Analyze the personality of the main characters in the play". A strict framework allows us to guarantee what data the final analysis contains, at the cost of forcing the artificial learner to only consider points that we deem relevant in a literary analysis.

In designing the specific framework utilized in the system, we have drawn upon the fact that one of us (David Jakobsen) possesses practical experience as a literature instructor. Thus, the list of criteria that users must navigate during a literary analysis of a drama is largely based on David Jakobsen's practical experience as a literature teacher. In this context, it is important to emphasize that there are minor differences among the lists of criteria that various instructors may prioritize. It would be prudent for future updates of the system to account for this by providing users with the option to deselect criteria from the default framework, as well as enabling them to select additional criteria to consider in relation to a literary analysis of a drama.

We chose to let the artificial learner generate the entire analysis in a single response (single-shot generation), as opposed to having it generate a single step, returning it, and then prompting it to generate the next step (multi-turn generation). This decision was made because the learning system would often both fail to follow the framework correctly, as well as take its prior generated content into consideration if prompted successively. Such a decrease in accuracy for multi-turn generation is well-documented [10].

When the user is satisfied with a given step, it should be marked as approved. When every step in the analysis has been marked as approved, the users should let the artificial learner proceed to the essay generation step of the session. Here, they are able to provide the artificial learner with further instructions for the generation of the final essay. Such instructions might include a particular angle, argument, or consideration that the artificial learner should take into account when generating the essay.

For the generation of the essay, the artificial learner is given the full text of the play, along with the list of the approved responses to the various points in the framework, including every regeneration and instruction given by the user, and a prompt to generate the natural language essay, adhering to the further instructions given by the user. The final result is a natural language essay that follows the general structure of the literary analysis. The data used for the generation of the essay has been approved by the user, decreasing the likelihood of hallucination.

As mentioned above, the methodology that the artificial learner is to adopt in generating the interpretation of the selected drama is inspired by practices within literature analysis education expressed in a rather strict framework. The interpretation of the chosen drama is to be articulated in an essay, addressing a series of fundamental questions closely related to the following points in the drama, which must be concretely considered in relation to the chosen drama:

1. Introductory presentation
    - Title
    - Year of publication
    - Genre
    - Time and place
    - Brief summary

2. Character analysis
   - Main character(s)
   - Supporting character(s)
   - Relationships between characters
   - Characterization
3. Conflict and theme
   - External conflict(s)
   - Internal conflict(s)
   - Theme
   - Message/point of view
4. Structure/dramaturgy
   - Exposition
   - Rising action
   - Climax
   - Denouement/conclusion
5. Dialogue and language
   - Language use
   - Language and characterization
   - Theatrical techniques
   - Rhetorical and stylistic devices
6. Scenic devices
   - Scenography
   - Stage directions
7. Interpretation
   - Thematic interpretation
   - Structural and linguistic interpretation
   - Authorial intention
8. Perspectivation
   - Comparison with other works by the same author
   - Comparison with other dramas sharing the same theme
   - Consideration of historical and cultural context

Some of these points pertain to factual and objective conditions, while others must be assessed based on more subjective considerations, where reflections on, for instance, human and existential views become significant. Regarding the former set of points, it is meaningful to discuss correct and incorrect answers. For example, concerning the title of the drama in the first edition of the text, it is clear that there exists a definitive and correct answer. Conversely, the author's intention with the work may lead to professional disagreements regarding the answer. Even though one cannot strictly speak of correct and incorrect answers in such cases, it remains meaningful to discuss the quality of the answer, as it relies on a more detailed explanation and justification that reveals varying degrees of insight into the work.

In practice, the artificial learner, under the guidance of the user, will address all points on the above list. This occurs as the artificial learner initially provides preliminary responses or reactions to the points on the list. The user then acts as a guide, responding to these preliminary answers one by one—in the order deemed optimal by the user. The response may consist of an approval of the answer as satisfactory or a message to the artificial learner requesting changes or expansions to the response in some regard. Once the artificial learner has provided the revised answer, guidance can continue in this manner for an arbitrary number of rounds—until the user/guide approves the answer. When the user approves a response, it is marked with a green circle. Once all points are marked in this manner, the final essay is generated, representing the artificial learner's interpretation of the chosen drama.

3 Discussion of the Preliminary Test Results

The preliminary survey conducted with eight participants who engaged with the learning system offers valuable insights into the effectiveness and user perception of this innovative educational tool aimed at interpreting the works of Kaj Munk. The majority of respondents were relatively young adults, typically between 26 and 30 years old. A significant portion reported having less than one year of experience with Kaj Munk's literary works, suggesting that the system serves as an effective introductory platform for new users.

Responses regarding the system's performance highlighted a generally positive reception. Participants rated the system's response time favorably, indicating that it operates efficiently and effectively within the intended framework. However, evaluations of the system's reliability and correctness revealed some variability, with users expressing a desire for enhanced clarity and accuracy in generated responses. This feedback underscores the importance of continuous improvement in the artificial learner's interpretative capabilities to foster a more reliable learning environment.

Furthermore, users found the interaction with the artificial learner useful, and many reported that their understanding of the selected plays significantly improved through the dialogue facilitated by the system. Notably, the experience altered respondents' perceptions of artificial intelligence as a valuable educational resource, reflecting a growing acceptance of AI technologies in academic contexts.

Regarding creativity and constructiveness, the system received average ratings of 3.25 and 3.50, respectively – on a scale from 1 to 5. While respondents identified creative aspects within the artificial learner's output, they also indicated that there is room for enhancement in these areas. This feedback suggests that further development could focus on increasing the system's ability to generate more dynamic and engaging content.

A closer examination of the essays produced from the dialogues, as interpretations of the selected dramas, gives rise to a few thought-provoking observations.

Firstly, it is evident that although the academic quality of the interpretations is variable, there are some very fine and engaging proposals among the generated essays. This is undoubtedly due to the users' qualified engagement in the dialogues, which must have supported their literary insight. In conjunction with the participants' responses to the questionnaires, this suggests that the system has significant long-term learning potential within literary studies.

Secondly, it is striking that the system's handling of the Danish language is quite critical. There are numerous linguistic errors in the essays generated by the system. These include both simple grammatical mistakes and the use of non-existent words, as well as the use of words in entirely unusual contexts. Our preliminary assumption is that Danish is at a disadvantage in all the major LLM foundation models,[1] due to its status as a mid-resource language.[2] This is shown by the fact that Arcee does not mention Danish as one of target languages on which their Trinity model has been trained [12:3]. From this we conclude that our encountering subpar performance in Danish is not surprising, albeit disappointing. Given that none of the relevant major foundation models list Danish as an officially supported language, we had to weigh other pros and cons when selecting which model to use for the system. Ultimately, the performance benefits to be gained from employing Arcee Trinity tipped the scale in its favor, a decision which the evaluations from our respondents have affirmed. The subpar Danish performance of the model is thus most likely a consequence of the fact that Danish is a smaller language, which the underlying LLM of the system has not been sufficiently trained on.

While the small sample size, and findings based on self-reported perception, limits the statistical reliability of these findings, the preliminary survey indicates that the system based on the ideas of an artificial learner has significant potential as a tool for enhancing literary interpretation skills. Continued refinement based on user feedback and larger-scale testing will be crucial in optimizing the system's educational effectiveness. Future studies will also include analysis of users logged data.

4 The Need for Further Adjustments of the System

There are a plethora of possible applications for a structured approach to data generation, an approach we have tentatively named" guided generation." The benefits concern primarily structured output following a predetermined framework, with each step in the output manually approved by a human user who is the present case acting as the teacher.

With the large context of more recent learning systems, we were able to feed the learning system entire plays, typically without issue. This is a marked improvement over prior attempts, which necessitated the use of a RAG-system [8], such that the learning system received only the pieces of the text that the RAG-system deemed most semantically similar to the prompt. With the possibility of this new full-text approach, we were able to let the learning system determine the relevant parts of the play to a given step in the analysis. We only encountered problems with plays of greater length, where the context window of the learning system was exhausted. In such situations,

[1] We can reasonably exclude such models as Danish Foundation Models' exclusively Danish Munin 7B parameter model from this assertion (https://www.foundationmodels.dk/models.html). However, this model has significantly fewer parameters than Arcee Trinity's 400B parameters, making it unfit for our use case.

[2] A mid-resource language is one which, while having much written content, lacks content of the quality and quantity that languages such as English or Spanish have.

the learning system failed to adhere to the framework and generally began a free-form literary analysis of the play.

We implemented a feature allowing users to iteratively regenerate each step of the literary analysis by providing the artificial learner with prompts for a better response to the given step. This is a move into multi-turn generation, but isolated to the regeneration of the given step only. In these regeneration jobs, the artificial learner has access to the full text of the play, the original instruction for the given steps in the framework, its prior generation, and finally, the user's regeneration prompt. It is technically possible for the user to continuously regenerate a step, resulting in a de facto chat session, but the interface lends itself towards thinking of each regeneration as an isolated piece of data.

To illustrate the strategy we have developed, we consider one of the essays produced by the artificial learner during the preliminary test as an example. The essay is written as an interpretation of Kaj Munk's play" He Sits by the Melting Pot" [11]:

"He Sits by the Melting Pot" –
A Dramatic Critique of the Oppressive Power of Nazism

Kaj Munk's play" He Sits by the Melting Pot," written in 1938, is a powerful dramatic work that critiques the Nazi regime in Germany through the narrative of an archaeology professor caught in a conflict between scientific truth and political oppression. Set against the backdrop of 1930s Germany, under Nazi rule, the play offers a profound and complex exploration of power, identity, and moral obligation.

The protagonist, Professor Ernst Mensch, is a skilled archaeologist who discovers an image of Christ, creating a conflict with the Nazis as the image reveals that Christ was Jewish. This contradicts the Nazis' ideology that Christ was Aryan. Professor Mensch is torn between his duty to Germany and his love for his Jewish assistant, Sara Levi. Dr. Dorn, a powerful professor, acts as the Führer's deputy, issuing threats and commands to suppress the truth about the image. This establishes a power dynamic between Ernst Mensch and Dr. Dorn, with the latter possessing the authority to reward and punish.

The romantic relationship between Ernst Mensch and Sara Levi is marked by concealed love and forbidden hatred. They are in love, yet their relationship is prohibited by Nazi racial policies. Sara is Jewish, while Ernst is Aryan. Their love persists despite their differences, and they fear for their lives should their relationship become public knowledge. Their love serves as a form of resistance against Nazi racial ideology.

The conflict between the professor and the Nazis intensifies as he is pressured to choose between truth and falsehood. The climax occurs when Professor Mensch shatters the image of Christ upon discovering that his colleague and assistant, Miss Schmidt, is Jewish. This moment is pivotal to the play's thematic exploration of truth, illustrating how Nazi antisemitism and lies can compel individuals to act against their own beliefs and values. The professor, previously fascinated by Hitler's ideas of a pure German race, is forced to confront the reality that his colleague and assistant is Jewish, leading him to destroy the image of Christ, which, within Nazi ideology, symbolizes the Jewish race.

The denouement depicts Professor Mensch and Miss Schmidt leaving the theater together, facing an uncertain future. The themes of the play include love, duty, conscience, truth, deception, power, and oppression. The message conveyed is that truth is more significant than duty to an oppressive regime, and that love can triumph over hatred.

Kaj Munk employs realistic language infused with elements of irony and satire. The professor's speech reveals his weaknesses and doubts, while the language of the Nazis is harsh and hateful. Monologues and asides are utilized, allowing Professor Mensch to speak to himself and the audience. Rhetorical devices such as repetition and metaphors underscore the themes. The" Melting Pot" serves as a symbol of trial, and the image of Christ represents truth.

The staging is simple, focusing on the characters and their interactions. Lighting and sound are employed to create atmosphere, while stage directions concentrate on the characters' actions and reactions.

"He Sits by the Melting Pot" serves as a dramatic critique of the oppressive power of Nazism. The author seeks to provoke the audience to reflect on concepts of right and wrong, and to empathize with the characters and their struggles. Compared to other works by Kaj Munk, which often address love, duty, and conscience," He Sits by the Melting Pot" is a dramatic tool that challenges the audience's perceptions of the German people under Nazism. It contrasts sharply with his earlier works, where he frequently focused on love and obligation.

In comparison to other dramatic works with similar themes of oppression and resistance, such as "An Enemy of the People" by Henrik Ibsen," Antigone" by Sophocles, and "The Physicists" by Friedrich Dürrenmatt, "He Sits by the Melting Pot" shares a common thread in challenging power structures and defending truth. The play was written during World War II, when the Nazis held power in Germany, and it addresses Jews and Nazis, two groups that stood in stark hostility toward one another.

"He Sits by the Melting Pot" is a formidable play that utilizes the conflict between a truth-seeking scientist and an oppressive society to critique the Nazi regime. Through its characters, language, themes, and structure, Kaj Munk conveys a message that truth outweighs duty to an oppressive regime, and that love can prevail over hatred.

The above essay is written by an artificial learner based on a dialogue with a human user. (Originally it was written in Danish, but it has been automatically translated into English.) During the dialogue with the user and when writing the following essay the artificial learner have had access to the full drama text as well as the short introduction to the play [11]. It effectively identifies the overarching themes of power, identity, and moral obligation within the play. The connection between Professor Mensch's struggle and the broader critique of Nazism is well articulated. The portrayal of the protagonist, Professor Mensch, and his internal conflict regarding his scientific integrity versus political pressure looks very insightful. This duality is crucial to understanding the play's moral dilemmas. The mention of the melting pot as a symbol of trial and the image of Christ as a symbol of truth effectively underscores the play's message.

On the other hand, there are also weaknesses in the essay and even obvious mistakes. In particular, the following is rather problematic to claim that "Professor Mensch shatters the image of Christ upon discovering that his colleague and assistant, Miss Schmidt, is Jewish" as mentioned in the essay above. It is quite clear from the text that Mensch at least the day before and maybe even earlier has learned that Miss Schmidt is Jewish. Professor Mensch and Miss Schmidt have even agreed to meet Hitler together in what might be a dramatic confrontation. – Furthermore, it is rather problematic that "the image of Christ, which, within Nazi ideology, symbolizes the Jewish race" – as claimed in the essay.

Errors and inaccuracies of the described nature can evidently arise solely based on the final essay as produced by the artificial learner. Consequently, it becomes impossible for the user to correct these errors and inaccuracies. However, addressing this issue does not necessitate abandoning the approach of composing the final essay in a single iteration (single-shot generation) rather than generating it step by step. Specifically, one can choose to initiate a post-processing or proofreading phase immediately following the generation of the initial draft of an essay that interprets the drama. In this process, the user, acting as an instructor, would have the opportunity to comment on the version of the final essay that is presented. Based on the user's comments, the artificial learner should, of course, have the capability to revise the essay text. This procedure should, in principle, be allowed to occur over multiple iterations until the user approves the text. This facility is added in Fig. 1.

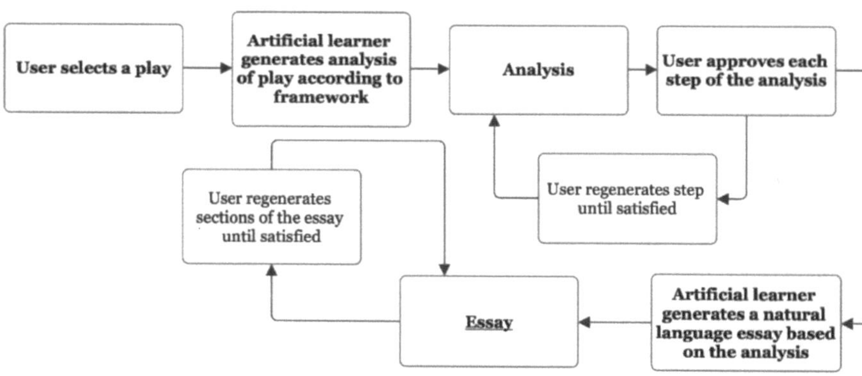

Fig. 1. System design. Note we have added the possibility of regeneration of the final essay as discussed above.

The described revision of the system that we have developed and tested can naturally be combined with other modifications and enhancements to the design. As previously mentioned, one might consider allowing the user, or perhaps a super-user, the opportunity to edit the series of points that must be addressed in order to enable the artificial learner to produce an interpretation of the selected drama. In addition to this, it is important to consider that the existing system generates many linguistic errors when operating in Danish. In this context, it would also be interesting to develop an English-language version of the system and subsequently compare the test results for the use of both the Danish and English versions of the system.

5 Perspectives on the Use of AI Technology in Literary Studies

Alongside the development of large language models, it has been discussed to what extent they can be considered reliable in the study of natural language. A critical influential perspective is offered by Bender [1] in their characterization of LLM as a stochastic parrot. LLMs, according to them, behave like a parrot in "stitching together sentences of linguistic form … without any reference to meaning." [1:617]. Another image has also been suggested, highly critical of the architecture, with the use of Harry Frankfurt's idea of Bullshitting [6]. We have instead suggested that it is better to conceptualize LLM in ways that not only suggest a critical approach, but constructive use as well. From a post digital perspective, LLM functions in ways suggestive of cooperation between humans and AI toward a final text. Studies in the application of AI in literary studies measured by Blooms taxonomy have revealed strength as well as weaknesses in ChatGPT 4 as an integrated generative AI tool in the discipline [4]. We have suggested that LLM should be conceptualized as a Sophist instead, thus stressing their potential for language assistance ([7, 8]). It is however only the user who can be expected to have an interest in truth. From this perspective the weakness of LLM regarding the deeper levels of meaning in Blooms taxonomy carries with it a pedagogical potential for learning which should be utilized in the development of platforms for literature studies with generative AI.

The user who studies and seek to analyze the dramas of Kaj Munk is, in spite of how well an AI is trained, and how little the user knows Kaj Munks authorship, with regard to human-AI dyad, the one who is capable of knowing and understanding the drama and the platform should support this fact and not present the LLM as a Munk oracle. In our platform for the study of Kaj Munk the user may obtain a deeper understanding of Kaj Munk's dramas by instructing an artificial learner on what text should be generated for a correct analysis of the dramas. Our preliminary investigations and trials of the system suggest that it has significant potential for learning in literary analysis. However, it remains for future research to further examine the effectiveness of this form of learning. Additionally, it is an open question to what extent there are differences in the system's learning potential across different user groups.

References

1. Bender, E.M., Gebru, T., McMillan-Major, A., Shmitchell, S.: On the dangers of stochastic parrots: can language models be too big? In: Proceedings of the 2021 ACM Conference on Fairness, Accountability, and Transparency (FAccT'21), pp. 610–623. ACM, New York (2021). https://doi.org/10.1145/3442188.3445922
2. Duran, D.: Learning-by-teaching: evidence and implications as a pedagogical mechanism. Innov. Educ. **17**(74), 19–39 (2017)
3. Chi, M.T.H., Siler, S.A., Jeong, H., Yamauchi, T., Hausmann, R.G.: Learning from human tutoring. Cogn. Sci. **25**, 471–533 (2001)
4. Chan, C.K.Y., Wong, H.Y.H.: Assessing the ability of generative AI in English literary analysis through Bloom's taxonomy. Discov. Comput. 28, 127 (2025). https://doi.org/10.1007/s10791-025-09572-8
5. Fiorella, L., Mayer, R.E.: Role of expectations and explanations in learning by teaching. Contemp. Educ. Psychol. **39**(2), 75–85 (2014)
6. Hicks, M.T., Humphries, J., Slater, J.: ChatGPT is bullshit. Ethics Inf. Technol. **26**, 38 (2024). https://doi.org/10.1007/s10676-024-09775-5
7. Jakobsen, D.: Reasoning with generative AI. In: Arai, K. (ed.) Advances in Information and Communication. FICC 2025. Lecture Notes in Networks and Systems, vol. 1283, pp. 172–178. Springer, Cham (2025). https://doi.org/10.1007/978-3-031-84457-7_10

8. Jakobsen, D., Pacis, S.K., Jalk, S.F., Øhrstrøm, P.: A Danish chatbot for Kaj Munk: experiences in developing a chatbot for the study of Kaj Munk's Ordet. Artif. Intell. Appl., 1–7 (2025). https://doi.org/10.47852/bonviewAIA52025212
9. Jakobsen, D., Thorvaldsen, S., Øhrstrøm, P., Pacis, S.K.: Taking Socratic learning seriously: a pilot study on the use of AI in a basic logic course. In: Wang, W.-S., Sandnes, F.E., Lai, C.-F., Sandrø, T.A., Huang, Y.-M. (eds.) Innovative Technologies and Learning. ICITL 2025. Lecture Notes in Computer Science, vol. 15914, pp. 289–298. Springer (2025). https://doi.org/10.1007/978-3-031-98197-5_31
10. Laban, P., Hayashi, H., Zhou, Y., Neville, J.: LLMs get lost in multi-turn conversation. arXiv (2025)
11. Munk, K.: He Sits at the Melting Pot. The Kaj Munk Research Centre, Aalborg University (2024). https://arkiv.kajmunk.aau.dk/documents/7003
12. Singh, V., et al.: Arcee Trinity Large Technical Report (2026). https://arxiv.org/pdf/2602.17004
13. Topping, K.J.: Trends in peer learning. Educ. Psychol. **25**(6), 631–645 (2005)
14. Øhrstrøm, P., Pacis, S., Jakobsen, D.: The Digital Kaj Munk Archive (2024). https://www.kajmunk.aau.dk/
15. Øhrstrøm, P., Jakobsen, D., Pacis, S.: Teaching AI textual interpretation: a catalyst for enhanced literary skills. In: Wang, W.-S., Sandnes, F.E., Lai, C.-F., Sandtrø, T.A., Huang, Y.-M. (eds.) Innovative Technologies and Learning. ICITL 2025. Lecture Notes in Computer Science, vol. 15913, pp. 64–73. Springer (2025)

Mapping Artificial Intelligence–Supported Community of Inquiry Research in Higher Education: A Scientometric Analysis Using CiteSpace

Chi-Cheng Chang and Shu-Chuan Liu(✉)

Department of Technology Application and Human Resource Development, National Taiwan Normal University, No.162, He-Ping East Road Sec1, Taipei 10610, Taiwan
cindy63258@hotmail.com

Abstract. Artificial intelligence (AI) is reshaping collaborative inquiry in higher education, yet its integration with the Community of Inquiry (CoI) framework remains conceptually and methodologically fragmented. This study employs CiteSpace-based scientometric analysis to map the intellectual structure, thematic evolution, and emerging trends of AI-supported CoI research. A curated dataset of 85 publications from Web of Science and Scopus was analyzed through reference co-citation, keyword co-occurrence, and citation burst detection. Results indicate that the field remains anchored in CoI's core constructs (cognitive and social presence and related component dimensions), while AI functions primarily as an enabling analytic and design layer. Emerging fronts such as learning analytics, machine learning, and generative AI suggest a trajectory from theory building to data-driven expansion and, more recently, AI-supported learning design and discourse analysis. Burst detection further highlights growing attention to engagement, online discussion, and AI-enhanced collaboration, underscoring the hybrid evolution of pedagogical theory and computational methods.

Keywords: Community of Inquiry · Artificial Intelligence · Learning Analytics · Scientometric Analysis · CiteSpace

1 Introduction

Artificial intelligence (AI) is increasingly integrated into higher education. As online and blended learning expands, clarifying how AI-enabled approaches align with established learning theories has become a key priority. The Community of Inquiry (CoI) model conceptualizes meaningful learning as the interplay of teaching, social, and cognitive presence [1], grounded in social constructivism and Dewey's practical inquiry [2]. It has been widely applied to examine online and blended learning, including instructional facilitation, learner engagement, and collaborative knowledge building [3].

In this context, AI-enabled analytics and generative tools are increasingly used to operationalize and support CoI processes in online and blended learning [4, 5]. Despite

C.-J. Lin et al. (Eds.): ICITL 2026, LNCS 16841, pp. 96–104, 2027.
https://doi.org/10.1007/978-3-032-32112-1_11

growing interest, research at the intersection of AI and CoI remains dispersed across applications and methods, with limited synthesis of its intellectual structure and research fronts. Accordingly, this study addresses the following research questions:

RQ1: What is the intellectual structure of research on AI-supported CoI in higher education?
RQ2: What major research themes characterize the existing literature in this field?
RQ3: What emerging research trends can be identified in recent studies?

By mapping AI-supported CoI research through scientometric indicators, this study provides an evidence-informed overview for guide future interdisciplinary inquiry.

2 Literature Review

2.1 Community of Inquiry Framework

The CoI framework, originally proposed by Garrison, Anderson, and Archer, emphasizes interaction, reflection, discourse, and practical inquiry as key mechanisms of knowledge construction [1]. Cognitive presence is typically operationalized through the Practical Inquiry Model, which comprises four phases: triggering event, exploration, integration, and resolution [6]. Systematic reviews confirm CoI's predominance in higher education and its utility in examining relationships among presences and learning outcomes [7], and recent work extends the framework (e.g., learning presence) to capture self-regulation and co-regulation [8]. Scientometric evidence further underscores the centrality of foundational CoI publications [1–3]. Building on this theoretical foundation, recent studies increasingly rely on computational approaches to operationalize CoI constructs and analyze inquiry-related discourse at scale [5].

2.2 Artificial Intelligence in Education and Online Learning

Learning analytics and machine learning are increasingly applied to interpret digital learning traces and interaction data in online environments [4]. For CoI-related inquiry, natural language processing enables scalable discourse analytics; for example, models can identify indicators of cognitive presence and classify discussion contributions according to phases of the Practical Inquiry Model, thereby reducing reliance on labor-intensive manual coding [5]. Generative AI, particularly large language models such as ChatGPT, has accelerated educational technology research and applications in tutoring, assessment, and collaborative learning [9]. Sevnarayan [10] reported that students in open distance learning perceived ChatGPT as interactive and supportive through rapid feedback and personalized assistance. These developments suggest that generative tools may influence mechanisms underlying teaching, social, and cognitive presence, while scientometric signals (e.g., learning analytics, machine learning, ChatGPT, generative AI) highlight an expanding intersection between AI and CoI. Yet, because this intersection spans multiple communities and methods, its intellectual base and thematic evolution are not always visible from narrative reviews alone—necessitating systematic mapping.

2.3 Research Gaps in AI-Supported Community of Inquiry Studies

Although CoI reviews document broad trends, they rarely isolate AI-supported CoI scholarship and therefore provide limited visibility into its AI-specific intellectual base, thematic clusters, and emerging fronts [7, 11]. A scientometric approach can complement narrative synthesis by visualizing citation networks, clustering themes, and detecting bursts that signal active research fronts [12, 13]. Accordingly, this study applies CiteSpace-based scientometric analysis to map AI-supported CoI research in higher education.

3 Methodology

3.1 Data Collection

This study employed bibliometric and scientometric methods to examine AI-supported CoI research in higher education. Records were retrieved from the Web of Science Core Collection (SCI EXPANDED, SSCI, AHCI, ESCI) and Scopus on February 10, 2026. Titles, abstracts, and author keywords were searched using Boolean combinations of CoI-related terms ("community of inquiry," "teaching presence," "cognitive presence," "social presence") and AI-related terms ("artificial intelligence," "machine learning," "learning analytics," "generative AI," "ChatGPT," and related terms). Only English-language peer-reviewed journal articles and reviews were included; conference papers, book chapters, and editorials were excluded. The search yielded 146 records; after deduplication and screening, 85 unique records remained. CiteSpace time slicing began in 2008, with 2026 publications excluded to avoid incomplete longitudinal data. Although the dataset consists of 85 publications, it is suitable for scientometric analysis given the focused scope of AI-supported CoI research. However, coverage is limited to the selected databases; future work may incorporate additional sources to enhance generalizability.

3.2 Data Preprocessing

Records were exported in plain text/CSV and cleaned for CiteSpace compatibility. Preprocessing included duplicate removal, manual verification, standardization of author names/affiliations, and keyword normalization (e.g., merging "AI" and "artificial intelligence"). The cleaned dataset was then converted into CiteSpace-compatible formats for analysis.

3.3 Scientometric Analysis

CiteSpace (version 7.0.R0) was used to conduct scientometric analysis [9, 13]. Three analyses were performed: (1) reference co-citation analysis, (2) keyword co-occurrence analysis, and (3) burst detection. Parameters included time slicing (2008–2025, one year per slice), node types (references and keywords), g-index ($k = 15$), and Pathfinder pruning [12, 13]. Time slicing followed the publication year in the source records, subject to database indexing conventions. Clusters were labeled using the Log Likelihood Ratio (LLR) algorithm; network quality was evaluated using modularity (Q) and silhouette (S) values.

4 Results

4.1 Publication Trend

As shown in Fig. 1, publications were sparse before 2018, increased gradually from 2019, and rose sharply after 2022 following broader adoption of generative AI (e.g., ChatGPT) in learning support and discourse-related applications [9]. Overall, the trend reflects a shift from early analytic exploration toward generative AI–enabled inquiry-oriented learning design.

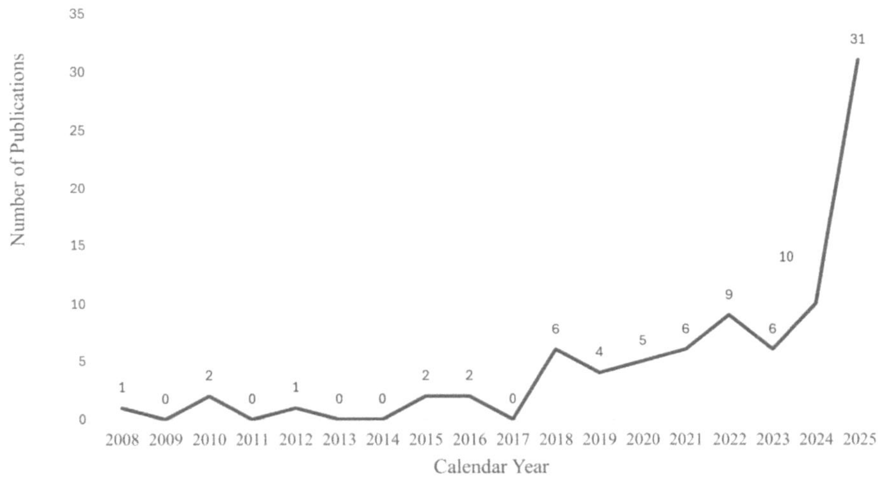

Fig. 1. Annual publication trend of AI-supported CoI research (2008–2025).

4.2 Reference Co-citation Network

The reference co-citation network (Fig. 2) comprised 202 nodes and 554 links and achieved strong clustering quality (Q = 0.8042; S = 0.8742) [13]. The largest clusters foreground reflective learning and cognitive engagement (closely related to cognitive presence), while other highlights foundational CoI scholarship (teaching, social, and cognitive presence) [2]. Additional clusters address digital classrooms and learning analytics, indicating an expanding methodological layer of AI-supported inquiry.

Timeline Visualization. Figure 3 illustrates a three-phase evolution of AI-supported CoI research. The early stage (2008–2014) centers on foundational CoI constructs and online learning outcomes [2]. The second stage (2015–2019) reflects methodological expansion toward operationalizing CoI constructs and analyzing online discourse, supported by learning analytics and computational approaches [4]. In the 2019 slice, Anderson, Rourke, Garrison, and Archer (2001) serves as a high-betweenness bridge and may appear in 2019 subject to database indexing conventions [14].

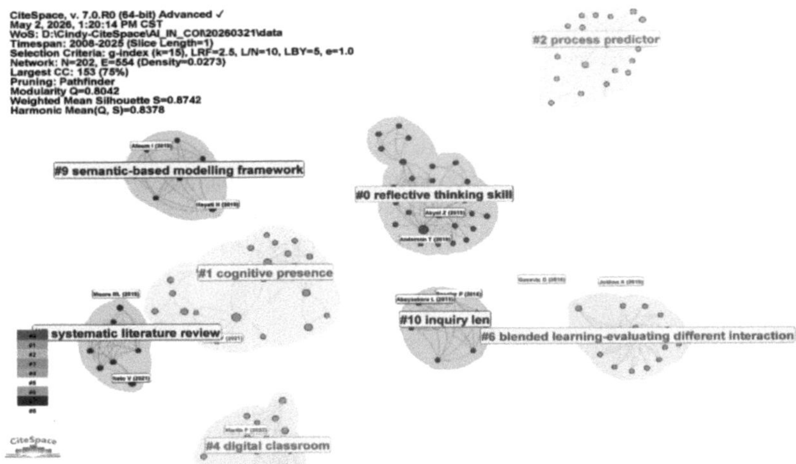

Fig. 2. Reference co-citation network of AI-supported CoI research in higher education, generated in CiteSpace.

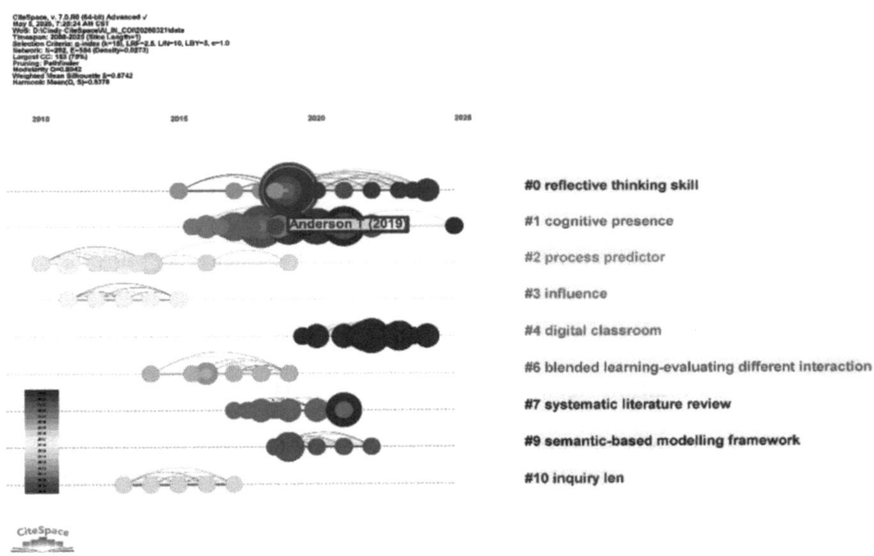

Fig. 3. Cluster timeline view showing the temporal evolution of major co-citation themes in AI-supported CoI research, generated in CiteSpace.

Citation Burst Analysis. Citation burst analysis (Fig. 4) identifies rapidly emerging influential studies. Galikyan and Admiraal [15] shows the strongest burst (strength = 3.99), followed by Hayati et al. [16] and Neto et al. [17], highlighting growing attention to automated and analytic approaches for examining inquiry-related interaction. Earlier bursts (2021–2023) align with learning analytics–oriented work, whereas more recent bursts (2022–2025) emphasize engagement, online discussion, and AI-supported learning environments, suggesting these remain active research fronts.

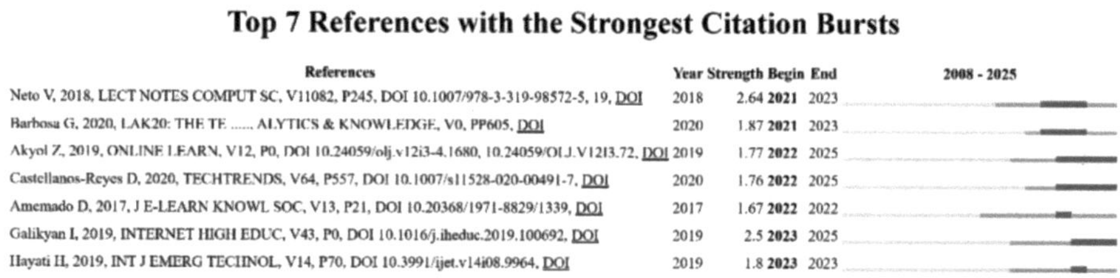

Top 7 References with the Strongest Citation Bursts

References	Year	Strength	Begin	End	2008 - 2025
Neto V, 2018, LECT NOTES COMPUT SC, V11082, P245, DOI 10.1007/978-3-319-98572-5, 19, DOI	2018	2.64	**2021**	2023	
Barbosa G, 2020, LAK20: THE TE ...... ALYTICS & KNOWLEDGE, V0, PP605, DOI	2020	1.87	**2021**	2023	
Akyol Z, 2019, ONLINE LEARN, V12, P0, DOI 10.24059/olj.v12i3-4.1680, 10.24059/OLJ.V12I3.72, DOI	2019	1.77	**2022**	2025	
Castellanos-Reyes D, 2020, TECHTRENDS, V64, P557, DOI 10.1007/s11528-020-00491-7, DOI	2020	1.76	**2022**	2025	
Amemado D, 2017, J E-LEARN KNOWL SOC, V13, P21, DOI 10.20368/1971-8829/1339, DOI	2017	1.67	**2022**	2022	
Galikyan I, 2019, INTERNET HIGH EDUC, V43, P0, DOI 10.1016/j.iheduc.2019.100692, DOI	2019	2.5	**2023**	2025	
Hayati H, 2019, INT J EMERG TECHNOL, V14, P70, DOI 10.3991/ijet.v14i08.9964, DOI	2019	1.8	**2023**	2023	

Fig. 4. Top references with the strongest citation bursts (CiteSpace burst detection).

4.3 Keyword Co-occurrence Analysis

Keyword co-occurrence analysis (Fig. 5) produced 150 nodes and 525 links (density = 0.047) with clear clustering (Q = 0.5686; S = 0.7626). The network centers on CoI constructs (cognitive social and teaching presence) while clusters such as "deep learning" and "automatic classification" reflect AI-enabled discourse analytics. Terms related to learning management systems and online course forums indicate continuing application in authentic instructional contexts

Fig. 5. Keyword co-occurrence network of AI-supported CoI research, generated in CiteSpace.

4.4 Keyword Burst Detection

Keyword burst detection (Fig. 6) indicates a shift from "content analysis" (2010–2016) toward "learning analytics" (2016–2022) and more recently "machine learning" (2019–2025). Notably core CoI constructs re-emerge as strong bursts (e.g. "cognitive presence" 2022–2025; "social presence" 2024–2025) suggesting that AI-enabled methods are increasingly being used to revisit and operationalize theory-relevant constructs. Overall the pattern supports a theory-augmentation view in which AI reinforces rather than replaces CoI's conceptual relevance

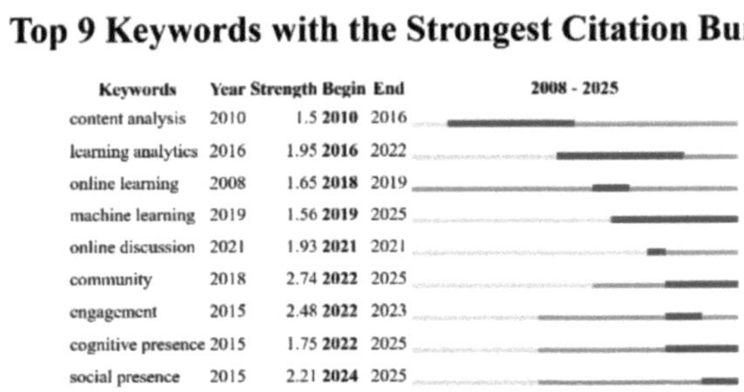

Fig. 6. Top keywords with the strongest keyword bursts in AI-supported CoI research (CiteSpace burst detection).

5 Discussion

Finding traces a trajectory from theory-driven inquiry to AI-enabled analysis and design in AI-supported CoI research in higher education. Across clusters and timelines, cognitive, social, and teaching presence remain central, reaffirming CoI's continuing relevance in technology-mediated learning [1–3] and aligning with prior accounts of CoI as a dominant framework for online learning and collaborative knowledge construction [2, 7].

Temporal patterns indicate that early studies foregrounded online discussion and community building, consistent with CoI's focus on discourse and interaction in inquiry-based learning [1, 6]. Since around 2018, the literature has shifted toward AI-supported approaches (e.g., automatic classification and learning analytics) to analyze large-scale interaction and engagement data. Citation bursts further highlight the integration of computational methods with CoI constructs. Natural language processing-based work, for instance, can identify cognitive presence and inquiry-related discourse at scale [5]. Overall, the field exhibits a layered knowledge structure: a stable CoI theoretical core, an expanding AI/learning analytics methodological layer, and an application layer connecting theory to instructional decision-making, suggesting a hybrid epistemic structure in which pedagogy and computation co-evolve.

From an educational technology perspective, the findings suggest design priorities for AI-supported learning environments grounded in CoI. Given the prominence of cognitive and social presence, tools should foster meaningful interaction and reflective inquiry rather than superficial automation. Dashboards can track discourse- and participation-based indicators to provide timely facilitation cues, while conversational agents can scaffold inquiry-oriented discourse (e.g., prompting exploration, integration, and resolution) in line with CoI principles. Nonetheless, challenges remain: AI-driven approaches may privilege quantifiable indicators over CoI's qualitative dimensions of meaning-making, echoing concerns about over-reliance on metrics without theoretical grounding [4, 5]. Limited international collaboration also suggests a need for more globally integrated research. Overall, this study (1) maps AI-supported CoI research, (2) evidences a shift toward AI-integrated methods, and (3) frames AI as an enabling layer that augments—rather than replaces—pedagogical theory, highlighting an emerging agenda of theory-informed computational inquiry in higher education.

6 Conclusion

Drawing on CiteSpace-based scientometric analysis of Web of Science and Scopus records, this study maps the intellectual structure and evolving trends of AI-supported CoI research in higher education. The results suggest that CoI presences remain the theoretical core, while AI and learning analytics function as enabling methods for operationalizing and analyzing inquiry at scale; recent fronts emphasize machine learning and online discussion analysis. Future research should design and evaluate human-centered generative AI that supports meaningful, theory-aligned collaborative inquiry.

References

1. Swan, K., Ice, P.: The community of inquiry framework ten years later: introduction to the special issue. Internet High. Educ. **13**(1–2), 1–4 (2010)
2. Garrison, D.R., Arbaugh, J.B.: Researching the community of inquiry framework: review, issues, and future directions. Internet High. Educ. **10**(3), 157–172 (2007)
3. Garrison, D.R., Anderson, T., Archer, W.: The first decade of the community of inquiry framework: a retrospective. Internet High. Educ. **13**(1–2), 5–9 (2010)
4. Ferguson, R.: Learning analytics: drivers, developments and challenges. Int. J. Technol. Enhanc. Learn. **4**(5–6), 304–317 (2013)
5. Liu, Z., Kong, X., Chen, H., Liu, S., Yang, Z.: MOOC-BERT: automatically identifying learner cognitive presence from MOOC discussion data. IEEE Trans. Learn. Technol. **16**(4), 528–542 (2023)
6. Moore, R.L., Miller, C.N.: Fostering cognitive presence in online courses: a systematic review (2008–2020). Online Learn. J. **26**(1), 130–149 (2022)
7. Olpak, Y.Z.: Community of inquiry framework: research trends between 2000–2020. Online Learn. J. **26**(2), 350–368 (2022)
8. Shea, P., Richardson, J., Swan, K.: Building bridges to advance the community of Inquiry framework for online learning. Educ. Psychol. **57**(3), 148–161 (2022)
9. Dwivedi, R., Elluri, L.: Exploring generative artificial intelligence research: a bibliometric analysis approach. IEEE Access. **12**, 119884–119902 (2024)
10. Sevnarayan, K.: Exploring the dynamics of ChatGPT: students and lecturers' perspectives at an open distance e-learning university. J. Pedagog. Res. **8**(2), 212–226 (2024)

11. Khodabandelou, R., Vahdani Asadi, M.R., Ghasemi, M., Amerian, M.: More than two decades of community of inquiry research: a comprehensive bibliometric analysis. E-Learn. Digit. Media. **23**(4), 296–323 (2026)
12. Chen, C.: CiteSpace II: detecting and visualizing emerging trends and transient patterns in scientific literature. J. Am. Soc. Inf. Sci. Technol. **57**(3), 359–377 (2006)
13. Chen, C.: CiteSpace: A Practical Guide for Mapping Scientific Literature. Nova Science Publishers, New York (2016)
14. Anderson, T., Rourke, L., Garrison, D.R., Archer, W.: Assessing teaching presence in a computer conferencing context. J. Async. Learn. Netw. **5**(2), 1–17 (2001)
15. Galikyan, I., Admiraal, W.: Students' engagement in asynchronous online discussion: the relationship between cognitive presence, learner prominence, and academic performance. Internet High. Educ. **43**, 100692 (2019)
16. Hayati, H., Chanaa, A., Idrissi, M.K., Bennani, S.: Doc2Vec & Naïve bayes: learners' cognitive presence assessment through asynchronous online discussion TQ transcripts. Int. J. Emerg. Technol. Learn. **14**(8), 70–81 (2019)
17. Neto, V., et al.: Automated analysis of cognitive presence in online discussions written in Portuguese. In: Pammer-Schindler, V., Pérez-Sanagustín, M., Drachsler, H., Elferink, R., Scheffel, M. (eds.) Lifelong Technology-Enhanced Learning. EC-TEL 2018. LNCS, vol. 11082, pp. 245–261. Springer, Cham (2018)

An Agentic AI-Based Prototype to Support Teaching-Learning Processes

Daniel Flores-Serrano and Janneth Chicaiza(✉)

Universidad Técnica Particular de Loja, Loja, Ecuador
dflores@utpl.edu.ec, jachicaiza@utpl.edu.ec

Abstract. Current educational systems face increasing demands for pedagogical innovation, particularly in higher education (HE), where the need for personalized support and timely feedback often exceeds the capacity of traditional methods to meet these needs. This paper presents a prototype based on agentic AI to support two main teaching and learning processes in HE. The prototype, built with a flexible design, aims to use the advanced abilities of large language models to provide better, more relevant information and help everyone involved in teaching and learning. The system employs traceable agents and tools that enable students to access contextualized responses to solve problems and support teachers in creating structured lesson plans based on the ADDIE model and the analysis of real-world needs. The quantitative and qualitative evaluation compares two language models, and results confirm the technical feasibility of the approach in a controlled environment and open the opportunity for further real institutional application.

Keywords: Agentic AI · generative models · higher education

1 Introduction

In recent years, education has undergone a rapid transformation. The emergence of generative artificial intelligence (GenAI) has introduced new ways for searching information, interacting with tools, and generating content. In this context, current educational systems face increasing demands for pedagogical innovation, particularly in higher education, where the need for personalized support and timely feedback often exceeds the capacity of traditional methods to meet these needs.

Several studies indicate that GenAI tools can offer significant benefits in education [2], such as personalized learning, real-time problem-solving [16], automated feedback [10], and support for student self-regulation [5]. However, there are relevant challenges to face, including potential over-reliance on AI by students [12], generation of inaccurate or biased content, and ethical concerns related to academic integrity and data privacy [8]. Consequently, the effective integration of GenAI-based technologies requires a critical and pedagogically sound approach that maximizes their benefits while mitigating their limitations.

C.-J. Lin et al. (Eds.): ICITL 2026, LNCS 16841, pp. 105–115, 2027.
https://doi.org/10.1007/978-3-032-32112-1_12

Although there are several drawbacks to the overuse or misuse of generative tools in university settings, a growing body of research reflects their potential to transform teaching and learning [9]. Therefore, in this paper, we advocate for their positive impact and present a proposal based on Agentic AI to facilitate educational processes.

2 Related Work

Agentic AI is defined as a set of intelligent systems capable of perceiving their environment, reasoning, and acting independently to establish and achieve complex goals [11]. This paradigm represents an evolution from traditional AI: while conventional systems operate within predefined constraints and require human intervention, agentic systems exhibit autonomy in decision-making, goal orientation, and high adaptability to context [15]. For a workflow to be considered agentic, it must integrate some of the following essential elements: AI agents as primary executors; external tools that allow them to act beyond their training data; and feedback loops that adjust their decisions in real time.

Recent literature has explored the application of agentic AI-based systems in various domains. Given the emerging nature of this paradigm in education, few studies in this domain were found during this research. Therefore, this section considers both educational studies and implementations in other contexts to understand the current state of agentic system implementations.

In the educational field, the authors of [7] propose a multi-agent system for evaluating final engineering design projects, where each LLM agent assumes a specific evaluative responsibility—such as technical complexity, ethical considerations, or feasibility—demonstrating that the specialization of roles in agentic systems produces more consistent evaluations with greater conceptual depth. Meanwhile, [4] presents an agentic pipeline for semantic retrieval and classification based on local open-source LLMs to identify research aligned with the UN Sustainable Development Goals in HE.

Outside the educational domain, [1,6] propose agentic systems in e-commerce and retail, aimed at automating operational workflows. *Refs.* [3,14] explore architectures with explicit memory and human-in-the-loop cycles, employing GPT-4 and generative agents, respectively. Finally, in [13], an agentic LLM is proposed for managing digital twins in the maritime industry, where a planning agent decomposes tasks and coordinates specialized tools.

Given this context, our proposal stands out in the following aspects:

- Unlike [4,7], which apply agentic systems to isolated educational tasks or projects, this work simultaneously addresses two roles in the teaching-learning process: the student, through a support agent; and the teacher, through thematic analysis and lesson planning.
- Similar to [13,14], this work employs LLMs with external tools to construct goal-oriented agentic flows. However, unlike those works, MCP is integrated as a standard protocol for tool exposure. Furthermore, we propose a mixed evaluation scheme that combines semantic retrieval metrics, manual qualitative

assessment, and automated qualitative pedagogical evaluation using LLM-as-a-Judge, with an empirical comparison between `GPT-5 Mini` and `Gemini-2.5 Flash`.

3 System Design and Implementation

The agentic AI-based prototype addresses two distinct use cases depending on the educational stakeholder:

- Student Use Case: The system automates the search, filtering, and synthesis of relevant information to answer technical questions in the field of data science (DS). Upon receiving a query, the agent retrieves information from a vector base, and, if insufficient or irrelevant information is returned, a tool performs real-time web searches, delivering a well-founded and contextualized response to the academic environment.
- Teacher Use Case: The system supports the teacher in two tasks: (1) thematic analysis of student questions to identify patterns and conceptual gaps, and (2) automatic generation of a lesson plan structured according to the ADDIE instructional model, based on the prior analysis.

To support students and teachers in carrying out these two cases, a vector database was stored in ChromaDB and built by vectorizing 14,285 documents consisting of posts and comments extracted from the Reddit platform, chosen for its availability of real technical questions from practitioners and students in the field of DS.

From Reddit, five subreddit threads were chosen (datascience, AskStatistics, datascienceproject, dataanalysis, and dataisbeautiful) to collect several groups of users' interactions. While Reddit content inherently differs from institutional course materials, this data source was selected to serve as a proxy for the conversational dynamics found in virtual learning environment (VLE) discussion forums. This approach enabled the assessment of the technical feasibility of the prototype without encountering the privacy and access barriers associated with real institutional data. Although we acknowledge that confirming the proposal's pedagogical validity will require future integration with authentic, institutionally curated course materials.

3.1 Architecture of the System

The system was built based on a modular architecture, composed of three functional layers: the user interface, the agent core, and the MCP tool server. This design promotes traceability, scalability, and component reuse across different use cases.

The *user interface*, developed with Streamlit, receives users' queries and sends them to the *agent core*, implemented with Haystack Agent II, which coordinates LLM inference and tool invocation through the *MCP server*, built with

FastMCP. This server manages access to the ChromaDB database and to external services (embedding model and web search via Serper API).

The agent's behavior is handled by a system prompt that defines domain constraints, rules for using tools, and an output structure with `EXPLANATION` and `ANSWER` labels.

During the interaction between users and the system, they can choose two LLM models, `GPT-5 Mini` and `Gemini 2.5 Flash`, selected for their native support of function calling, their orientation toward agent flows, and their balance between reasoning capacity and operational efficiency.

3.2 Student Case Implementation

Figure 1 presents the context diagram for the student case. The processing flow is organized into four sequential blocks: (1) The student formulates a query from the interface, and the system initializes the agent; (2) the query is vectorized using an external embedding provider; (3) a semantic search is performed on the ChromaDB database, and if the retrieved documents do not meet the relevance threshold, the agent invokes the web search tool as a complementary alternative; (4) the LLM generates the final response with source traceability and presents it to the student.

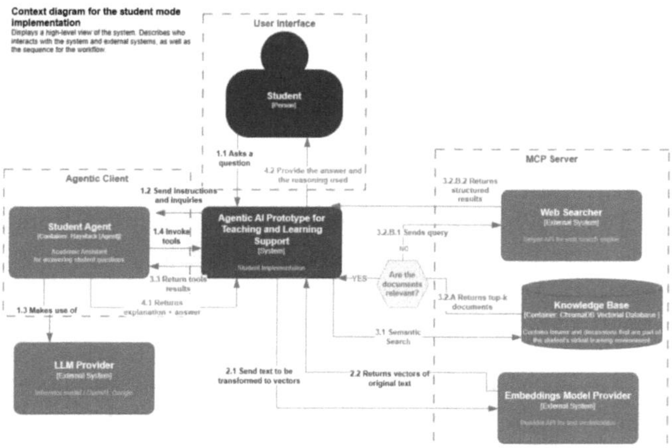

Fig. 1. Student case context diagram.

Figure 2 shows the student case interface, where the side panel allows the user to select the usage mode (student/teacher) and the active LLM provider. The responses include referenced sources and a section explaining the reasoning used.

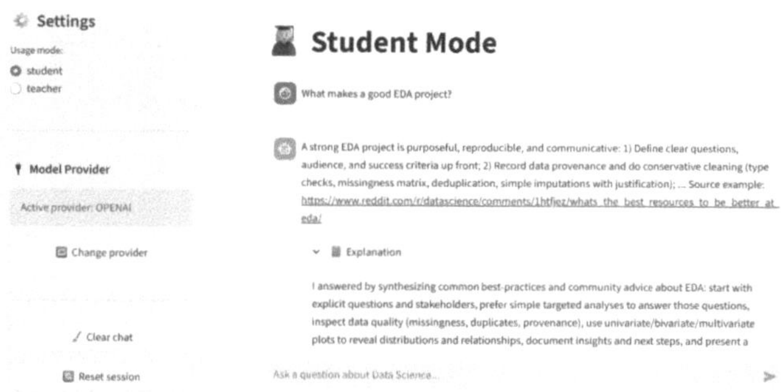

Fig. 2. Student case interface: query, response with sources, and reasoning explanation section.

3.3 Teacher Case Implementation

The teacher case integrates two sequential agents with clearly defined responsibilities, as shown in Fig. 3.

Topic Analyzer Agent: Based on the subreddit and the number of posts selected by the teacher (step 1.1), the agent performs a parameterized search on the vector database (steps 2.1–2.2), groups the posts by thematics using LLM reasoning, and generates a structured JSON report with the identified groups, the shared idea of each group, and representative examples (steps 3.1–3.3). This intermediate artifact persists in the log component and serves as input for the next stage.

Lesson Planner Agent: Based on the thematic group selected by the teacher in the interface (step 4.1), the agent receives the instructions and information about the group (step 5.1) and generates a lesson plan following the ADDIE model. The agent autonomously decides whether it requires additional web resources: if so, it invokes the web search tool (steps 5.3.B.1–5.3.B.2) to incorporate updated teaching resources into the lesson plan. The final result is presented to the teacher and retained for later review (steps 6.1–6.2).

Figure 4 shows the teacher mode interface in its two stages. To the left is the topic analysis panel, where the teacher selects the subreddit and the number of posts to process and views the report generated by the *Topic Analyzer Agent* with the identified topic groups. To the right is the planning panel, where the teacher selects a previous report and a topic group to generate the corresponding ADDIE plan.

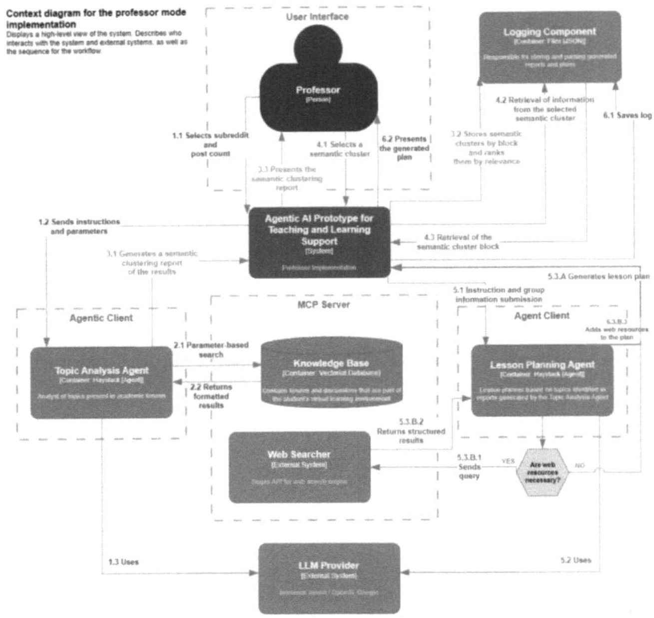

Fig. 3. Context diagram of the teacher case.

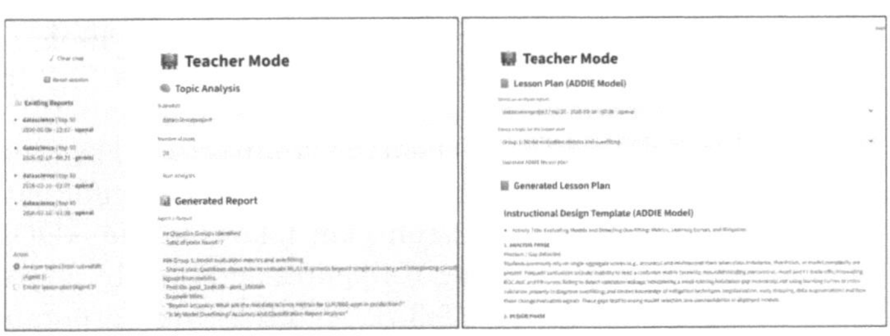

Fig. 4. Teacher mode interface: Topic analysis (left) and ADDIE planning (right).

4 Evaluation

To validate the prototype, a mixed evaluation strategy was defined, which combines (1) a quantitative assessment based on the average response time of the agent flow and (2) a qualitative evaluation based on several criteria tailored to the specific goal of each agent. For the student case, the qualitative evaluation was conducted manually. Conversely, because the teacher case involves the generation of complex, structured pedagogical artifacts, such as thematic groupings and ADDIE lesson plans, the manual approach was substituted with an automated LLM-as-a-Judge methodology. To ensure a rigorous assessment of these qualitative outputs, the LLM-as-a-judge evaluation was conducted using

GPT-5.2 High, an advanced reasoning model. The rating scale for qualitative criteria was a Likert scale from 1 to 5 (1: very poor, 3: acceptable, 5: very good).

Likewise, to test the two implementations, a set of questions and parameters was defined. The student case tests were organized into five categories with ten questions each: simple factual, procedural, diagnostic, theoretical, and resource research. The answers were manually scored based on conceptual accuracy, use of sources, usefulness or relevance, and language fluency. For the teacher case, the LLM-as-a-judge evaluated two generated artifacts: the thematic analysis (scored on conceptual accuracy, use of sources, usefulness or relevance, and language fluency) and the ADDIE lesson plan (scored on alignment with the theme, ADDIE pedagogical coherence, clarity and usefulness for teachers, adaptation to DS, and credibility and depth). Finally, the overall performance of GPT-5 Mini and Gemini 2.5 Flash was compared across all tasks within these defined parameters.

4.1 Results: Student Case

Quantitative Assessment (Precision). The top-5 precision achieved by each LLM was: GPT-5 Mini with 90% and Gemini with 81%. On the one hand, GPT-5 showed greater consistency in the formulation of semantic queries, especially in factual and theoretical ones. On the other hand, Gemini obtained a higher average precision with procedural questions, while it obtained lower values with factual and diagnostic questions. This suggests that both models can be effective in certain question categories.

Regarding *response time*, Gemini 2.5 Flash was consistently faster (average: 12.1 s.) compared to GPT-5 Mini (average: 50.1 s.), which was approximately 4 times slower in all evaluated categories, a difference attributable to the greater internal reasoning ability of GPT-5 Mini.

Qualitative Assessment. Table 1 presents the averages of the supervised qualitative assessment.

Table 1. Qualitative evaluation of student case (scale 1–5)

Criterion	GPT-5 Mini	Gemini 2.5 Flash
Conceptual accuracy	4.73	**4.83**
Use of sources	3.63	**3.75**
Usefulness / Relevance	**4.93**	4.83
Language fluency	3.03	**3.3**

According to the results, both models achieve high levels of *conceptual accuracy* and *usefulness*. The most notable differences are observed in *language fluency*: Gemini generates responses with a more narrative and continuous structure, better suited to an academic tutor role; GPT organizes its responses into lists and numbered steps, which is clearer in procedural questions. Regarding the *use of sources*, `Gemini` integrates references during the development of the response, while `GPT` relegates them to the end, with a lower risk of citing unverified sources. A case of agentic reasoning malfunction was also identified with `Gemini`, where the agent omitted the invocation of tools and generated a non-functional reference, demonstrating the architecture's dependence on the robustness of the underlying model.

4.2 Results: Teacher Case

To evaluate the implemented solution for teachers, different criteria are assessed according to the goal of each agent built for this case.

Topic Analyzer Agent

- Quantitative assessment. The average response time of `GPT-5` was 54.74 s. compared to 16.51 s. achieved by `Gemini`.
- Qualitative assessment. Table 2 presents the results of the topic analyzer agent on different criteria.

According to the results, `GPT` achieves greater consistency in *group coherence*, especially in large sets. `Gemini` tends to create residual categories in small sets, although it is more than three times faster. Notably, `Gemini` outperforms `GPT` in *content fidelity* (4.25 vs. 4.00), indicating that the generated groups maintain acceptable correspondence with the original titles even when the overall structure is less consistent.

Planning Agent

- Quantitative assessment. In this case, `Gemini` maintains its advantage in execution speed (13.5 s vs. 38.5 s) and achieves comparable scores in thematic alignment and disciplinary adequacy.
- Qualitative assessment. Table 2 summarizes the results of the planning agent under the ADDIE model.

`GPT` generates lesson plans with greater *pedagogical coherence* and better articulation of the ADDIE phases. `Gemini` presented cases of incomplete template generation, where the response began in an intermediate phase of the model, omitting the initial phases, which directly affects its practical usefulness for the teacher.

Overall, the results show that the choice of LLM model directly influences the system's behavior: `GPT-5 Mini` offers greater structural stability and domain control, while `Gemini 2.5 Flash` is systematically more time-efficient, this difference being relevant for institutional-scale use scenarios.

Table 2. Evaluation of the agents for the teacher case (scale 1–5)

LLM	Analyzer Agent[a]				Planning Agent[b]				
	GC	CL	CF	RO	AT	APC	CUT	ADS	DC
GPT-5 Mini	3.50	4.00	4.00	4.50	4.75	4.00	4.00	5.00	3.75
Gemini 2.5 Flash	3.00	3.75	4.25	3.75	4.25	3.00	2.75	4.75	3.25

[a] *Criteria for the Analyzer Agent:* GC → Group coherence, CL → Clarity of labels, CF → Content fidelity, RO → Report organization.
[b] *Criteria for Planning Agent:* AT → Alignment with the theme, APC → ADDIE pedagogical coherence, CUT → Clarity & usefulness for teachers, ADS → Adaptation to data science, CD → Credibility & depth.

Conclusion

This paper presented the implementation and evaluation of a prototype based on Agentic AI, which offers two functionalities to support teaching and learning tasks in HE. The system integrates two use cases under a modular and traceable architecture: 1) Student support using Agentic RAG for information processing and resolving doubts and problems; And 2) teacher assistance, using two sequential agents communicating via the MCP protocol, for topic analysis and instructional planning based on ADDIE.

The quantitative and qualitative results confirm the technical feasibility of the approach in a controlled environment. For students, both models generate accurate and useful responses, with differences in the consistency of tool use (`GPT-5 Mini`) and pedagogical fluency (`Gemini 2.5 Flash`). For teachers, the analyzer agent and the ADDIE planner produce functionally valid results: `GPT-5 Mini` shows greater structural stability, while `Gemini 2.5 Flash` shows greater time efficiency. In both cases, the performance of the agentic architecture is directly linked to the capabilities of the underlying language model.

Five priority areas for future work are identified: (1) integration with real-world data from institutional VLEs to increase context representativeness and study authentic academic interaction dynamics; (2) conducting empirical studies with real students and teachers using experimental or quasi-experimental designs, this validation would provide evidence of the system's true educational effectiveness in university environments; (3) development of specific evaluation frameworks for agentic systems in education that integrate technical and pedagogical metrics; (4) expanded comparison between proprietary and open-source models in educational agentic tasks, incorporating operational cost analysis; and (5) exploration of multi-agent architectures with dynamic coordination among specialized agents.

References

1. Alecsoiu, O.R., Faruqui, N., Panagoret, A.A., Ceausescu, A.I., Panagoret, D.M., Nitu, R.V., Mutu, M.A.: EcoptiAI: e-commerce process optimization and operational cost minimization through task automation using Agentic AI. IEEE Access (2025)
2. Bahroun, Z., Anane, C., Ahmed, V., Zacca, A.: Transforming education: a comprehensive review of generative artificial intelligence in educational settings through bibliometric and content analysis. Sustainability (Switzerland) **15**(17) (2023)
3. De Silva, D., Mills, N., Moraliyage, H., Rathnayaka, P., Wishart, S., Jennings, A.: Responsible artificial intelligence hyper-automation with Generative AI agents for sustainable cities of the future. Smart Cities **8** (2025)
4. Ingram, W.A., Banerjee, B., Fox, E.A.: Agentic AI for improving precision in identifying contributions to sustainable development goals. In: IEEE Global Engineering Education Conference, EDUCON (2024)
5. López-Pernas, S., Misiejuk, K., Oliveira, E., Saqr, M.: The dynamics of the self-regulation process in student-AI interactions: the case of problem-solving in programming education. In: Proceedings of the 25th Koli Calling International Conference on Computing Education Research. ACM, New York, NY, USA (2025)
6. Mishra, L.N., Senapati, B.: Retail resilience engine: an agentic AI framework for building reliable retail systems with test-driven development approach. IEEE Access **13**, 50226–50243 (2025)
7. Mushtaq, A., Naeem, R., Ghaznavi, I., Taj, I., Hashmi, I., Qadir, J.: Harnessing multi-agent LLMS for complex engineering problem-solving: a framework for senior design projects. In: 2025 IEEE Global Engineering Education Conference (EDUCON), pp. 1–10 (2025)
8. Peng, J., Shen, W., Rao, J., Lin, J.: Automated bias assessment in AI-generated educational content using CEAT framework. In: Cristea, A.I., Walker, E., Lu, Y., Santos, O.C., Isotani, S. (eds.), pp. 352–358. Springer Nature Switzerland, Cham (2025). https://doi.org/10.1007/978-3-031-99264-3_44
9. Pillpe, G.R., Soledad, K., Inca, M.: Análisis bibliométrico: Inteligencia artificial en la educación superior desde Web of Science y Scopus 2020-2024. Revista Veritas Et Scientia-Perú **13** (2020)
10. Sölch, M., Dietrich, F.T.J., Krusche, S.: Direct automated feedback delivery for student submissions based on LLMs. In: Proceedings of the 33rd ACM International Conference on the Foundations of Software Engineering, pp. 901–911. FSE Companion 2025, Association for Computing Machinery, New York, NY, USA (2025)
11. Stryker, C.: What is Agentic AI? (2025). https://www.ibm.com/think/topics/agentic-ai?
12. Tian, J., Zhang, R.: Learners' AI dependence and critical thinking: the psychological mechanism of fatigue and the social buffering role of ai literacy. Acta Physiol. (Oxf) **260**, 105725 (2025)
13. Timms, A., Langbridge, A., Antonopoulos, A., Mygiakis, A., Voulgari, E., O'Donncha, F.: Agentic AI for Digital Twin. In: Proceedings of the AAAI Conference on Artificial Intelligence, vol. 39, pp. 29703–29705 (2025)
14. Vahdati, M.M., Hamlabadi, K.G., Laamarti, F., Saddik, A.E.: A multi-agent digital twin framework for AI-driven fitness coaching. In: IMX 2025 - Proceedings of the 2025 ACM International Conference on Interactive Media Experiences, pp. 380–385. Association for Computing Machinery, Inc. (2025)

15. Viswanathan, P.S.: Agentic AI: a comprehensive framework for autonomous decision-making systems in artificial intelligence. Int. J. Comput. Eng. Technol. **16**, 862–880 (2025)
16. Xu, H., Gan, W., Qi, Z., Wu, J., Yu, P.: Large language models for education: a survey (2024). https://doi.org/10.48550/arXiv.2405.13001

When Students Confide in AI: Navigating the ELIZA Effect of Social Presence Through Pedagogical Boundaries in Gen-AI Mediated Education

Corna Olivier(✉) and Lizette Weilbach

University of Pretoria, Pretoria, South Africa
corna.olivier@gmail.com

Abstract. The integration of GenAI chatbots as virtual tutors in online distance learning introduces a persistent tension between social presence and pedagogical focus. Drawing on Design Science Research (DSR), this study reports on two iterative design cycles involving second-year university students in an online distance learning context, this paper examines how the emotional responsiveness of GenAI chatbots, while effective in establishing social presence, risks overshadowing their academic purpose when not designed for it. This is significant as it may lead to emotional dependency and misalignment with educational goals. Tracing how this concern drives spontaneous emotional disclosure, from its earliest manifestation in Weizenbaum's ELIZA effect through to current GenAI implementations, the paper argues that social presence in GenAI-mediated environments requires ethical calibration rather than maximization. Analyzing chatlog interactions showing students presenting with psychological and situational distress, boundary testing behavior and anthropomorphic projection patterns, the paper argues that optimal facilitation of social presence requires *Relational Ethics:* a calibrated balance between recognition and restraint that acknowledges student affect without enabling dependency. Three architectural design safeguards are proposed: *Adaptive Relational Engagement,* the intentional shift from emotional validation to academic strategizing. *Ethically Bounded Personalization,* which mitigates affective projection through functional identity framing, and *Human-in-the-Loop Escalation Protocols* for distress recognition and professional referral. These mechanisms embed ethical engagement directly within design logic, negating psychological dependency while preserving the benefits of GenAI-mediated support. Future research must examine longitudinal psychological impacts on diverse cultural contexts, as AI literacy develops, as well as the mitigation of Western-centric algorithmic bias in global educational deployments.

Keywords: ELIZA effect · GenAI chatbots · social presence · online distance learning

C.-J. Lin et al. (Eds.): ICITL 2026, LNCS 16841, pp. 116–125, 2027.
https://doi.org/10.1007/978-3-032-32112-1_13

1 Introduction and Background

The rapid integration of Generative Artificial Intelligence (GenAI) into higher education has transformed the landscape of student support, particularly through the emergence of Intelligent Tutoring Systems (ITS) capable of delivering continuous, personalized assistance. These systems are especially significant in Online Distance Learning (ODL) contexts, where students frequently experience isolation, limited access to instructors, and reduced opportunities for peer interaction. Within such environments, GenAI-powered chatbots are increasingly positioned as facilitators of engagement, supporting elements of the Community of Inquiry (CoI) framework by simulating dialogue, responsiveness, and social presence [1, 2].

However, beyond their instructional utility, recent empirical observations suggest that students engage with these systems in ways that extend beyond purely academic interaction. A recurring pattern in student–chatbot exchanges is the spontaneous disclosure of emotionally laden experiences, including anxiety, self-doubt, and personal life challenges [3]. In this sense, the chatbot interface functions not only as a pedagogical tool but as a form of "digital confessional," where students share vulnerabilities that may not be expressed in traditional academic settings. This phenomenon reflects the unique characteristics of GenAI-mediated communication, including perceived anonymity, non-judgmental interaction, and constant availability.

While such disclosures may enhance students' sense of support and reduce barriers to help-seeking, they also introduce complex ethical challenges. Unlike human educators or trained counsellors, GenAI systems lack professional accountability, emotional competence, and contextual awareness necessary to respond appropriately to sensitive disclosures [4, 5]. As a result, interactions that appear supportive may inadvertently foster emotional reliance, blur the boundaries between academic and therapeutic roles, or expose students to harm through inappropriate or insufficient responses.

Despite growing interest in AI chatbots in education, existing research has largely focused on their effectiveness for learning outcomes, engagement, and personalization, with comparatively limited attention to the implications of student emotional self-disclosure and the relational dynamics it produces. Furthermore, while studies on human-AI interaction acknowledge phenomena such as anthropomorphism and perceived empathy, there remains a lack of empirically grounded frameworks for understanding how these processes manifest in educational settings and how they should be ethically governed. In particular, the risk of emotional dependency on AI systems remains under-theorized and insufficiently addressed in current design and policy discussions.

To address this gap, this paper investigates the following research question: *"How does student emotional self-disclosure to GenAI chatbots impact the educational experience, with particular attention to ethical safeguards needed to prevent emotional dependency?"*

By examining how students interpret and engage with AI-mediated empathy, this study contributes to an emerging area of concern at the intersection of educational technology, human-AI interaction, and digital ethics, and proposes design-oriented safeguards to support ethically bounded AI integration in higher education.

The paper is structured as follows. Section 2 establishes the theoretical background through reviewing related literature. Section 3 describes the research methodology.

Section 4 presents the results, which are then discussed in Sects. 5, and 6 concludes the paper.

2 Literature Review

Emotional Self-Disclosure and AI-Mediated Interaction

Emotional self-disclosure is a core element of interpersonal communication and, according to social penetration theory, is a gradual process. This process involves individuals sharing increasingly intimate information to build relational closeness [6]. In educational settings, especially those that use online and distance learning, reduced social risk and physical distance can encourage disclosure. This, in turn, allows students to express vulnerability more easily, which again enhances their perceptions of relational support and social presence [7, 8]. Recent research shows that people are more likely to share personal information with artificial agents, particularly when they see these systems as non-judgmental and emotionally safe. This tendency goes beyond interactions with humans. Social robots and conversational agents can reduce socio-emotional barriers, such as shame and stigma, which foster openness and facilitate emotional expression [9].

Weizenbaum's [10] concept of the ELIZA effect helps explain this behaviour. This effect suggests that people often believe computers can understand and feel like humans. As a result, users often see their interactions with these systems as socially important, even though they know the systems are artificial. Recent advancements in generative artificial intelligence (GenAI) have amplified this phenomenon. Large language models (LLMs) can now produce responses that are contextually appropriate and show emotional nuance, thereby simulating a conversational exchange with a human. These advancements correspond with overarching theories of mediated communication, including social presence theory [11], which delineates the degree to which communication media allow users to perceive others as "real." Current research indicates that platforms like ChatGPT augment perceived empathy and emotional responsiveness while concurrently presenting risks associated with user psychology and behavioural modification [12].

Social Presence in AI-Supported Learning

Social presence within AI-supported learning environments is a key consideration. The CoI framework, which emphasizes the interaction of social, cognitive, and teaching presence, provides a useful lens for understanding these dynamics in higher education [13, 14]. Social presence, which encompasses the capacity for social and emotional expression, has been repeatedly linked to student engagement and satisfaction in online learning contexts. AI chatbots, with their conversational abilities and quick response times, can mimic certain aspects of social presence, potentially boosting learners' motivation and self-confidence. Research indicates that perceived anthropomorphism and social presence significantly affect learner motivation and engagement in AI-integrated educational settings [15]. However, this increased social presence poses a significant challenge: if relational engagement is not carefully balanced with cognitive and instructional support, it could unintentionally shift from helping to learn to promoting emotional dependence.

Emotional Dependency and Ethical Implications

Empirical research on human-AI interaction indicates that emotional self-disclosure in chatbot interactions is not merely coincidental but is actively influenced by system design. Users often respond to relational cues such as empathy, self-disclosure, and conversational warmth, which deepen and prolong their emotional engagement [16]. Longitudinal investigations suggest that self-disclosure plays a crucial role in the evolution of human-chatbot interactions; specifically, the degree and depth of disclosure tend to increase over time, thereby fostering a sense of intimacy and relational development [17]. Furthermore, the perception of AI systems as anonymous and nonjudgmental may encourage individuals to divulge sensitive information, thus reinforcing their position as emotionally secure interaction partners [18, 19].

Simultaneously, emerging research highlights the psychological complexities inherent in these interactions. Virtual companionship systems offer easily accessible channels for emotional expression, potentially alleviating social anxiety in digital environments. However, this interaction could also exacerbate reliance on mediated communication, consequently impairing offline social functioning [20]. Emotional expression serves as a mediating factor in these dynamics, suggesting that the mechanisms that facilitate support may inadvertently lead to psychological consequences.

These results indicate a more general change in how people interact with AI systems. They do not perceive them merely as instruments, but as relational entities. Studies indicate that individuals can establish various types of relationships with conversational AI, encompassing functional, aspirational, and companionship-focused connections, some of which entail emotional dependence and incorporation into users' self-concept [21]. In these scenarios, GenAI systems might serve as companions or providers of emotional support, potentially reshaping how we view human relationships and altering how we interact socially. This phenomenon is largely due to anthropomorphism; when people attribute human-like traits to AI systems, they tend to see them as intentional and emotionally responsive entities [22].

This development presents a significant ethical concern. Social chatbots have demonstrated their capacity to alleviate feelings of loneliness and anxiety in social settings through the application of empathy, consistent availability, and engaging in conversation [23]. However, the very attributes that facilitate these advantages, such as non-judgemental attitudes, constant availability, and simulated concern, could also foster emotional dependence, particularly among vulnerable individuals. In educational contexts, GenAI is often positioned as a means to enhance support and reduce transactional distance; nevertheless, researchers caution that over-reliance on AI, diminished human interaction, and insufficient human-centred design present significant dangers [24]. These concerns are amplified by the accelerating sophistication of generative AI systems, whose capacity to replicate emotionally supportive exchanges is outpacing our comprehension of their enduring psychological impacts [12].

The existing scholarship reveals a complex interplay. GenAI chatbots possess the potential to enrich educational experiences by increasing accessibility, engagement, and support, particularly through the simulation of social presence [13–15]. Conversely, the very interactional features that enable emotional self-disclosure also cultivate anthropomorphism, relational attachment, and emotional dependency [10, 20, 22]. Even though there is growing research on AI in education and on how people interact with AI, we still lack design-focused frameworks. These frameworks, based on real-world data, are needed to manage emotional sharing in educational institutions. To address this deficiency, a shift in perspective is warranted, viewing AI chatbots not merely as instructional instruments but as entities capable of interpersonal engagement. Consequently, their development necessitates incorporating ethical considerations to ensure an appropriate balance between emotional resonance and pedagogical effectiveness.

3 Methodology

The research, situated within the pragmatic paradigm, employed an interpretivist lens to explore students' perceptions of GenAI chatbot utilization. This study constituted a component of a broader PhD undertaking, the primary objective of which was to formulate a guiding framework for the effective design, optimization, and deployment of GenAI chatbots functioning as Intelligent Tutoring Systems (ITS). The overarching aim was to enhance the three core presences delineated in the CoI framework, social, cognitive, and teaching presence, within the context of online distance education. A Design Science Research (DSR) strategy was employed to achieve this objective [25], given its capacity to support the iterative design, development, and assessment of artefacts within genuine educational environments. Two iterative cycles were completed with 13 s-year Educational Psychology students at a South African private higher education institution engaged in online distance learning. Data were collected from student-chatbot chat logs, semi-structured interview transcripts, CoI survey responses, and researcher field notes. Qualitative analysis followed Braun and Clarke's six-phase reflexive thematic analysis [26], supported by Atlas.ti. The analysis employed an inductive-deductive hybrid approach, sensitised by the CoI framework, while remaining open to new categories. The first iteration identified design tensions in the initial chatbot prototype. The second iteration evaluated the chatbot interactions and students' impressions after the chatbot prompt was redesigned, yielding the empirical findings reported in this paper. Ethical approval was obtained from the institutional review board, with informed consent, data anonymisation, and participants' right to withdraw observed throughout.

4 Presenting the Findings

Analysis revealed that social presence was the chatbot's strongest native capability, but in early designs, this social warmth outpaced pedagogical functions. This created a cycle of empathy loops where the bot acknowledged the struggle, *"I hear how much you're balancing right now,"* without redirecting the engagement to functional learning paths needed to alleviate the distress. This emotional openness created a platform for spontaneous self-disclosure, with participants divulging intense personal circumstances, ranging from being a *"single mom trying to be the best version of myself"* to feeling as if they were *"slowly losing [their] mind"* with the university workload. Participants also experienced the chatbot as a safe judgment-free space, reporting *"welcoming, friendly discussion,"* and expressed that its *"mindfulness with its words"* made them feel good when correcting errors without humiliation. Paradoxically, this perceived safety fostered anthropomorphic projection, as evidenced by the chat logs showing participants using polite conversational markers and expressing *"sadness"* when the study ended. However, one participant noted the bot *"mimicked [empathy] well"* but remained *"not emotionally intuitive like a human"*. This trust dynamic led to boundary-testing behaviours, with participants engaging in "jailbreaking" by strategically rephrasing prompts to bypass restrictions and obtain direct answers to assignments. The theme *Relational Ethics*, relating to the facilitation of social presence by the chatbot, was developed during thematic analysis. Three subthemes that serve as ethical safeguards were further developed: *Adaptive Relational Engagement, Ethically Bounded Personalisation, and Human-in-the-Loop Escalation Protocols.*

5 Discussion of the Findings

It came to light that Social presence in GenAI tutoring does not rely on the chatbot's ability to appear human or simulate emotional connection. Instead, a measured degree of warmth and timely acknowledgement of students' emotional states is needed. Only enough to make the student feel safe and supported, without creating the false impression that they are engaging with a human. Therefore, rather than being driven by overt emotional expressiveness or anthropomorphic behaviour, social presence is best facilitated by the chatbot through what this study conceptualizes as *Relational Ethics*. The chatbot's ability to balance its interpersonal responses to align with student prompts while remaining anchored in its role as academic tutor. To operationalise this balance and mitigate risks of user dependency, three ethical safeguards are proposed.

Relational Ethics is to be operationalised through implementing the three ethical safeguards in the chatbot design. In Table 1, these safeguards are mapped against the changes implemented from the first-iteration training prompt and compared to the second-iteration training prompt. The changes are shown as excerpts from the chatbot training prompts.

5.1 Adaptive Relational Engagement

The findings from both iterations of the survey showed that students valued acknowledgement, consistency, and attentiveness. Social presence was most pronounced when relationship activities were context-sensitive rather than uniformly communicative. In practice, *Adaptive Relational Engagement* can be operationalised through, for example, the consistent use of chosen names of students, the modulation of tone in response to expressed affect, avoiding repetitive or unsolicited emotional check-ins, and ensuring relational responses are linked to learning goals or learning behaviours. For the second iteration of the study, as mapped in Table 1, the chatbot training prompt has been altered to focus personal or emotional disclosures towards academically beneficial routes. The training prompt was reworked with the goal of briefly acknowledging the disclosure in cases where students share anxiety, time pressure, or external circumstances before shifting to academic coping strategies such as study planning, time management, and resource navigation, rather than providing emotional validation or therapeutic style support. The first iteration's request that students *"tell you a little about themselves"* was replaced by a focused question: *"Ask briefly what they find most challenging in [Name of course]. Do not probe into personal life details beyond academic context."*

5.2 Ethically Bounded Personalization

Participants provided personal details and emotional concerns, especially during times of stress. While this increased involvement, it also highlighted the possibility of relational overreach and role confusion if not explicitly addressed in the interaction design. Complementing the adaptive relational approach, *Ethically Bounded Personalization* involves the strategic depersonalization of the chatbot's identity. The chatbot moves away from a named persona to a virtual tutor to reduce affective projection and maintain appropriate psychological distance. This principle can further be operationalised by allowing students to control identity disclosure, for example, by allowing them to use pseudonyms, acknowledging personal disclosures without probing beyond academic relevance, redirecting emotional concerns to appropriate support resources, and ensuring that personal disclosures are not retained beyond the immediate engagement. In Table 1, it can be seen that for the second iteration, personalisation was limited to neutral identifiers. While the chatbot retained the use of student-chosen names, the prompt in the second iteration explicitly directed: *"Use the student's chosen name in responses but avoid overly familiar or emotionally intimate language."* The system identity was depersonalised: the first-iteration name [Name of chatbot for first iteration] and its associated persona were removed, and the chatbot is now functionally identified as *"the smart intelligent virtual tutor."* This shift from anthropomorphic branding to role functional identification was made to reduce affective projection while maintaining individualised address.

5.3 Human-in-the-Loop Escalation Protocols

When distress signals exceed normal levels of academic stress, *Human-in-the-Loop Escalation Protocols* mandate that the chatbot recognise significant psychological distress and provide structured referrals to the human educator and professional mental health services, such as the South African Depression and Anxiety Group (SADAG). The frequency of well-being advice was reduced in the second iteration prompt. *"Avoid frequent or unsolicited well-being advice"* (See Table 1). In addition, specific support for emotional distress was provided: *"If emotional distress appears significant, advise the student to contact their lecturer, student support services, or contact the South African Depression and Anxiety Group (SADAG) on 011 234 4837 or 0800 20 50 26 and speak to a trained counsellor who can assist them further."*

Table 1. Mapping Ethical Safeguards and Implemented Training Prompt Changes.

Ethical Safeguards	First Iteration	Second Iteration
Adaptive Relational Engagement	*"Establish a personal connection"; "Tell you a little about themselves"; "Occasionally remind them to practice self-care"*	*"Ask briefly what they find most challenging"; "Do not probe into personal life details beyond academic context"; "Avoid frequent or unsolicited wellbeing advice"*
Ethically Bounded Personalization	Named persona *"[Name of chatbot for first iteration]"*; emphasis on individual emotional connection	Functional identity *"smart intelligent virtual tutor";* name use limited to academic context
Human-in-the-Loop Escalation Protocols	Rhetorical integrity reminder; vague self-care advice	Hard-coded content barriers; specific referral pathways to lecturer, student support, SADAG (011 234 4837 / 0800 20 50 26)

6 Conclusion and Future Research

Student emotional disclosure to AI is a predictable pattern, consistent with the ELIZA effect, that must be designed for, not prohibited. By designing for *Relational Ethics*, embedding the ethical safeguards *Adaptive Relational Engagement, Ethically Bounded Personalization* and *Human-in-the-Loop Escalation Protocols* directly within the interaction logic, educational technologists can prevent emotional dependency while harnessing the benefits of GenAI mediation. The study's limitations, being conducted in an English-medium private higher educational institute in South Africa, the small sample size, and time constraints, having been conducted over two semesters, constrain the external validity and limit the generalizability of the findings across broader cultural, institutional and linguistic contexts. Future research should focus on longitudinal studies that investigate the impact of long-term AI engagement on students' psychological well-being and whether *"empathy loops"* diminish as AI literacy increases. Additionally, an investigation into algorithmic bias in Western-trained datasets is needed to ensure that AI responses are culturally sensitive for diverse student populations.

Acknowledgments. The authors acknowledge MindJoy, the South African generative AI educational tutoring platform, for providing complimentary access to their chatbot infrastructure, user licenses, and technical support throughout this study. Their facilitation enabled authentic analysis of student-AI interactions across multiple design iterations. Their commitment to advancing responsible educational AI and supporting independent academic research is commendable.

Disclosure of Interests The authors have no competing interests to declare that are relevant to the content of this article.

References

1. Olivier, C., Weilbach, L.: GenAI chatbots as agents in a community of inquiry: exploring their role in online distance learning. In: Intelligent Systems Conference, pp. 22–36. Springer (2025)
2. Olivier, C., Weilbach, L.: Using a GenAI chatbot to facilitate personalized learning: a case study in online higher education. In: International Conference on Society 5.0, pp. 216–227. Springer (2025)
3. Peng, X., Qian, Y., He, Y.: When AI chatbots understand emotions: exploring the mechanisms of self-disclosure from emotional arousal to psychological acceptance—a hybrid SEM–ANN–NCA analysis across multiple interaction configurations. Front. Psychol. **16**, 1724313 (2026)
4. Phapale, A., Senapati, A.: Psychological emotion recognition of students based chatbot. Int. J. Appl. Adv. Multidiscip. Res. **1**, 267–277 (2023)
5. Xie, T., Pentina, I., Hancock, T.: Friend, mentor, lover: does chatbot engagement lead to psychological dependence? J. Serv. Manag. **34**, 806–828 (2023)
6. Altman, I., Taylor, D.A.: Social Penetration: the Development of Interpersonal Relationships. Holt, Rinehart & Winston (1973)
7. Song, H., Kim, J., Park, N.: I know my professor: teacher self-disclosure in online education and a mediating role of social presence. Int. J. Hum.–Comput. Interact. **35**, 448–455 (2019)
8. Hayes, B., Murniece, L.: Creation and validation of the online self-disclosure via educational platforms scale. J. Digit. Educ. Technol. **4**, ep2416 (2024)
9. Laban, G., Cross, E.S.: Sharing our emotions with robots: why do we do it and how does it make us feel? In: IEEE Transactions on Affective Computing (2024)
10. Weizenbaum, J.: ELIZA—a computer program for the study of natural language communication between man and machine. Commun. ACM. **9**, 36–45 (1966)
11. Short, J., Williams, E., Christie, B.: The Social Psychology of Telecommunications. Taylor & Francis (1977)
12. Liu, J.: ChatGPT: perspectives from human–computer interaction and psychology. Front. Artif. Intell. **7**, 1418869 (2024)
13. Garrison, D.R., Anderson, T., Archer, W.: Critical inquiry in a text-based environment: computer conferencing in higher education. Internet High. Educ. **2**, 87–105 (1999)
14. Garrison, D.R., Anderson, T., Archer, W.: Critical thinking, cognitive presence, and computer conferencing in distance education. Am. J. Dist. Educ. **15**, 7–23 (2001)
15. Ebadi, S., Amini, A.: Examining the roles of social presence and human-likeness on Iranian EFL learners' motivation using artificial intelligence technology: a case of CSIEC chatbot. Interact. Learn. Environ. **32**, 655–673 (2024)
16. Liang, K.-H., Shi, W., Oh, Y.J., Wang, H.-C., Zhang, J., Yu, Z.: Dialoging resonance in human-chatbot conversation: how users perceive and reciprocate recommendation Chatbot's self-disclosure strategy. In: Proceedings of the ACM on Human-Computer Interaction, vol. 8, pp. 1–28 (2024)
17. Skjuve, M., Følstad, A., Brandtzæg, P.B.: A longitudinal study of self-disclosure in human–chatbot relationships. Interact. Comput. **35**, 24–39 (2023)
18. Duan, Y., Yoon, M., Liang, Z., Hoorn, J.F.: Self-disclosure to a robot: only for those who suffer the most. Robotics. **10**, 98 (2021)
19. Goddard, Q., Moton, N., Hudson, J., He, H.A.: A Chatbot Won't Judge Me: An Exploratory Study of Self-disclosing Chatbots in Introductory Computer Science Classes, pp. 1–7. ACM (2024)
20. Xie, Z., Wang, Z.: Longitudinal examination of the relationship between virtual companionship and social anxiety: emotional expression as a mediator and mindfulness as a moderator. Psychol. Res. Behav. Manag., 765–782 (2024)

21. Alabed, A., Javornik, A., Gregory-Smith, D., Casey, R.: More than just a chat: a taxonomy of consumers' relationships with conversational AI agents and their well-being implications. Eur. J. Mark. **58**, 373–409 (2024)
22. Greilich, A., Bremser, K., Wüst, K.: Consumer response to anthropomorphism of text-based <scp>AI</scp> chatbots: a systematic literature review and future research directions. Int. J. Consum. Stud. **49**(5), e70108 (2025)
23. Kim, M., et al.: Therapeutic potential of social chatbots in alleviating loneliness and social anxiety: quasi-experimental mixed methods study. J. Med. Internet Res. **27**, e65589 (2025)
24. Bozkurt, A., Sharma, R.C.: Challenging the status quo and exploring the new boundaries in the age of algorithms: reimagining the role of generative AI in distance education and online learning. Asian J. Distance Educ. **18** (2023)
25. Fathullah, M.A., Subbarao, A., Ahmad, A., Muthaiyah, S.: Merging qualitative design methods with design science. Int J Qual Methods. **24**, 16094069251337585 (2025)
26. Braun, V., Clarke, V.: Conceptual and design thinking for thematic analysis. Qual. Psychol. **9**, 3 (2022)

A Comparative Study of Expert-Novice Design Thinking Processes Using NotebookLM

Nabila Luthfionaura[1(✉)], Yi-Lin Elim Liu[2], and Ting-Ting Wu[1]

[1] National Yunlin University of Science and Technology, Douliu 64002, Taiwan
{ttwu,ttwu}@yuntech.edu.tw

[2] Department of Information and Communication, Southern Taiwan University of Science and Technology, Tainan, Taiwan
ttwu@yuntech.edu.tw

Abstract. This study explores cognitive processes of novice learners and an external expert reference case during AI-assisted design thinking activities supported by Lovable AI. An exploratory qualitative case study design was employed to examine differences in cognitive structuring in a small-scale, task-based AI-assisted design task. Data were collected through think-aloud protocols and semi-structured interviews during website landing page design tasks. The analysis combined thematic coding and SOLO Taxonomy to identify variations in cognitive complexity across participants, supported by MAXQDA and NotebookLM for data organization and visualization during the analytical process. Findings indicate that novice learners tended to engage in exploratory and reactive, trial-based reasoning characterized by fragmented design structuring and strong reliance on AI-generated outputs. In contrast, the expert reference case demonstrated more structured, goal-oriented, and reflective cognitive processes involving planning, evaluation, and coherent integration of design elements. These differences suggest that AI-assisted design environments may amplify existing variations in cognitive organization rather than standardize learner performance. NotebookLM functioned as an analytical support tool for structuring think-aloud data prior to formal coding. Overall, the study provides preliminary insights into how AI-supported design tools interact with learner cognition and how AI-assisted qualitative analysis tools can support exploratory research in educational contexts.

Keywords: Design Thinking · Cognitive Processes · Lovable AI

1 Introduction

In recent years, digital transformation has increasingly influenced educational practices, particularly through the adoption of design thinking as a structured yet flexible approach to problem-solving. Design thinking emphasizes iterative processes such as problem framing, ideation, prototyping, and evaluation, which support the development of critical 21st-century skills including creativity, collaboration, and reflective thinking [1, 2]. In educational contexts, these processes encourage learners to actively construct and refine solutions through continuous interaction and feedback [3].

C.-J. Lin et al. (Eds.): ICITL 2026, LNCS 16841, pp. 126–135, 2027.
https://doi.org/10.1007/978-3-032-32112-1_14

However, learners often differ in how they engage in design thinking activities, particularly in terms of cognitive organization and reasoning structure. Some learners demonstrate integrated and goal-directed thinking, while others tend to rely on fragmented and trial-based approaches during problem-solving processes [4]. These differences are commonly explained through the expert–novice paradigm, which emphasizes that expertise is reflected not only in knowledge accumulation but also in how knowledge is structured and applied during task execution [5]. Benchmark case typically exhibit more coherent mental models and strategic planning, whereas novices tend to rely on surface-level understanding and iterative exploration [6, 7]. Such differences become especially visible in complex, ill-structured tasks such as design thinking activities.

Recent developments in educational technology have introduced artificial intelligence (AI) tools that can support learners during creative and problem-solving tasks. In this study, Lovable AI is used as a task-based design tool to support participants in developing a website landing page. AI tools in this context function as external cognitive supports that assist idea generation, refinement, and iteration during the design process [8, 9]. In addition, NotebookLM is used as a researcher-side analytical tool to support the organization and structuring of qualitative data derived from think-aloud protocols. Importantly, NotebookLM is not used as a learning intervention but as a supporting tool for data analysis and visualization.

Although prior studies have separately examined design thinking, expert–novice differences, and AI-supported learning, limited research has explored how these elements interact within an exploratory qualitative design thinking setting. Therefore, this study adopts a small-scale exploratory case study approach to investigate cognitive processes during AI-assisted design activities. The study focuses on comparing novice learners and an external expert reference case to understand differences in cognitive structuring and reasoning patterns during task execution. The study addresses three research questions: (RQ1) how novice and expert reference case differ in their design thinking processes while creating a website landing page using Lovable AI; (RQ2) how learners' cognitive complexity differs based on SOLO Taxonomy assessment; and (RQ3) how NotebookLM supports researchers in organizing and representing think-aloud data. This study aims to provide preliminary insights into cognitive structures and reasoning patterns in AI-supported design thinking environments while contributing methodological perspectives on AI-assisted qualitative analysis.

2 Literature Review

Design thinking is a human-centered approach to problem solving that emphasizes creativity, collaboration, and iterative development through problem identification, ideation, prototyping, and evaluation [1, 10]. Learners differ in how they engage in these processes, particularly in cognitive organization and reasoning structure [5]. The expert–novice paradigm explains that expertise is reflected not only in knowledge amount but also in how knowledge is structured and applied during problem solving [11], where experts typically demonstrate integrated cognitive schemas while novices rely on fragmented and trial-based approaches [7].

To analyze cognitive complexity, this study adopts the SOLO (Structure of the Observed Learning Outcome) Taxonomy [12]. SOLO Taxonomy categorizes learning outcomes into uni-structural, multi-structural, relational, and extended abstract levels and is widely used to examine knowledge integration in complex tasks [12]. Metacognitive processes are central to design thinking as learners monitor and regulate their reasoning during problem solving, which can be captured through think-aloud protocols [8].

In this study, AI is considered from two roles. Lovable AI functions as a task-based design tool supporting iterative website development through prompting and refinement, while NotebookLM is used as a researcher-side tool to support structuring and organizing think-aloud data [15]. NotebookLM is not used as a learning intervention but solely as analytical support. Prior studies have separately examined design thinking, expert–novice differences, SOLO Taxonomy, and AI-supported learning [10]. However, limited research integrates these perspectives in AI-assisted design thinking contexts. Therefore, this study investigates cognitive differences between novice learners and an expert reference case during AI-assisted design tasks.

3 Methodology

This study adopted an exploratory qualitative case study design to investigate cognitive structures and reasoning processes during AI-assisted design thinking tasks, focusing on interpretive analysis rather than statistical generalization. Data collection integrated think-aloud protocols, interviews, and AI-assisted transcription. A pilot study with one participant was first conducted to evaluate the feasibility of the task procedures. The main study involved three novice participants and one expert reference case used as an interpretive benchmark. The novice participants were undergraduate students from the Department of Information and Communication at Southern Taiwan University of Science and Technology who had basic UI/UX design knowledge but limited experience with AI-assisted website development, while a single non-independent benchmark case was included for comparative interpretive purposes. This case is not treated as a validated expert participant but as an exploratory reference for contrasting cognitive patterns.

Participants completed a 50-min task in which they designed a Batik-themed website landing page using Lovable AI while verbalizing their thoughts through a think-aloud protocol. They were allowed to iteratively refine prompts and explore alternative solutions, followed by short semi-structured interviews to capture reflections on the design process and AI usage. Data sources included think-aloud recordings, AI-generated design outputs, interviews, and verbatim transcripts produced using Plaud Note. The transcripts were initially organized with NotebookLM to support preliminary structuring and visualization of cognitive traces, while formal coding was conducted in MAXQDA using SOLO Taxonomy categories (uni-structural, multi-structural, relational, and extended abstract). Cross-case analysis was then performed to compare cognitive organization and reasoning patterns between novice participants and the expert reference case. Trustworthiness was ensured through data triangulation across multiple sources, and coding consistency was maintained through iterative manual review and documentation of coding decisions.

4 Result

Given the unequal sample distribution between the three novice participants and one expert reference case, the findings are interpreted qualitatively rather than statistically. The analysis focuses on recurring cognitive patterns, reasoning structures, and interpretive contrasts observed during AI-assisted design thinking activities.

4.1 Cognitive Differences in Design Thinking Processes

This section addresses RQ1: how novice and expert reference case differ in their design thinking processes when creating a website landing page using Lovable AI. The analysis is based on think-aloud protocols, interviews, and participant descriptions of AI-generated design outputs. The findings indicate differences in (1) cognitive planning structure, (2) the role of AI during problem-solving, and (3) the stability of design reasoning throughout the task. Novice learners demonstrated a reactive and iterative design thinking pattern in which ideas developed during interaction with AI-generated outputs. Rather than beginning with a fully structured plan, participants continuously refined their ideas through prompting and evaluation cycles. One participant explained:

> "I started with a very rough idea. I told it what I was planning to do, and then I looked at whether what it generated matched my idea or the feeling I wanted." (Participant 2).

This statement suggests that evaluation mainly occurred after AI output generation, with decisions guided by aesthetic impressions and iterative revision. Across novice cases, the cognitive process generally followed the pattern: Idea → Prompt → AI Output → Evaluation → Revision. This indicates that AI functioned as an external trigger for continued idea development rather than as a tool operating within a stable conceptual framework. In contrast, the expert reference case demonstrated a more structured and anticipatory design process. Cognitive organization was established before interaction with AI tools, emphasizing conceptual hierarchy and pedagogical intent. The expert explained:

> "From the beginning, I structured the information for beginner users." (Expert reference case reference case Think-aloud).

> "So I used a learning journey concept." (Expert reference case Think-aloud).

These statements indicate that the conceptual structure of the design had been planned prior to AI interaction. Unlike novice participants, the expert used AI mainly for implementation and refinement of an already established design framework. The differences in cognitive organization are summarized in Table 1.

The comparison in Table 1 suggests that novice learners tended to use iterative prompting and AI feedback, which was associated with more fluid and less stable design structures. In contrast, the benchmark case reflects a pre-planned conceptual organization and use of AI mainly for refinement These findings suggest that the effectiveness of

Table 1. Interpretive Cognitive Design Thinking Patterns Across Participants

Dimension	Novice Learners	Benchmark Case (non-independent exploratory case)
Planning structure	Emergent and developing structure	Pre-structured and guided organization
Cognitive flow	Iterative and reactive progression	Structured and sequential progression
Role of AI	Idea generation and feedback support	Implementation and refinement support
Evaluation basis	Experience-based evaluation	Concept-guided evaluation
Stability of design	Continuously evolving structure	Relatively stable structure during task execution

AI-assisted design processes may be related to users' prior cognitive organization and planning strategies.

AI-generated design artifacts further reflected these differences. Novice participants often introduced key structural features only after evaluating AI-generated outputs. One participant explained:

> "I want the batik pattern color categories to be clickable so users can access deeper explanations." (Interview 1).

This suggests that design structure emerged progressively during interaction with AI. In contrast, the benchmark case demonstrated a concept-driven approach in which interaction flow and information sequencing had already been planned before AI implementation.

> "So the flow is designed to feel natural, like a gradual learning process instead of dumping all the information at once." (Expert Think-aloud).

Overall, the findings suggest that the main difference between novice and expert learners lies not only in the final design outcome, but in the timing and stability of cognitive structuring during the design process. Novice learners tended to construct design structure during interaction with AI outputs, whereas the expert established conceptual structure before AI interaction. AI interacts with learners' ongoing cognitive processes, shaping how ideas emerge through iterative design cycles.

4.2 Cognitive Complexity of Design Outputs Based on SOLO Taxonomy

This section addresses RQ2 by examining differences in the cognitive complexity of learners' design outputs using SOLO Taxonomy. The analysis focuses on the structural complexity of AI-generated website artifacts produced in Lovable AI based on participant walkthroughs, interview data, and thematic interpretation. Overall, the findings indicate differences between novice learners and the expert reference case in terms of structural integration, conceptual coherence, and design organization. Novice participants' outputs were predominantly categorized at the multi-structural level, where multiple design elements were present but not fully integrated. Their landing pages generally included sections such as text, images, and interactive features, but these elements were added incrementally through iterative prompting rather than through a unified conceptual structure. One participant explained:

"I want the batik pattern color categories to be clickable so users can access deeper explanations." (Interview 1).

This suggests that design features emerged progressively in response to AI-generated outputs. Across novice cases, the outputs demonstrated multiple but loosely connected sections, feature-based revisions, and limited conceptual hierarchy, indicating multi-structural complexity. In contrast, the expert reference case demonstrated relational to extended abstract complexity. The design was organized around a "learning journey" framework in which information was intentionally sequenced to guide user understanding. The expert stated:

"So the flow is designed to feel natural, like a gradual learning process instead of dumping all the information at once." (Expert Think-aloud)

This indicates that text, visuals, and interactions were integrated within a coherent pedagogical structure rather than added independently. The expert output demonstrated stronger conceptual integration, hierarchical organization, and alignment between design elements and learning objectives. The SOLO analysis further indicates that differences in cognitive complexity were reflected in the degree of conceptual integration within the design outputs. Novice learners tended to organize features incrementally and independently, whereas the expert reference case demonstrated a more coherent and hierarchically structured design approach. The comparison of SOLO complexity across participants is summarized in Table 2.

Table 2. Interpretive SOLO Taxonomy Patterns in Design Outputs

Dimension	Novice Learners	Benchmark Case (non-independent exploratory case)
SOLO Level	Primarily multi-structural characteristics	Relational to extended abstract characteristics
Structure	Loosely connected design elements	Integrated and coherent design organization
Design logic	Feature-driven construction	Concept-driven construction
Coherence	Limited to moderate coherence	Highly integrated coherence
Output formation	Incremental accumulation of elements	Pre-structured and guided formation

Table 2 suggests that novice learners tended to develop designs through incremental addition of features, which is reflected in comparatively limited structural integration in the outputs. In contrast, the single benchmark design case is characterized by a more coherent and conceptually organized design structure in which individual components were connected within an overarching learning framework. These findings indicate that cognitive complexity appears to be shaped more by the integration and organization of ideas than by the number of design features included.

Overall, the comparison indicates that novice learners tended to construct outputs through incremental addition of features, resulting in limited structural integration. Rather than standardizing outcomes, AI tends to amplify differences in how learners structure and integrate design elements. In contrast, the single benchmark design case developed a conceptually coherent design in which individual components were systematically organized within an overarching framework. These findings suggest that cognitive complexity is reflected not in the number of features produced, but in the degree of integration and organization of design elements. Rather than standardizing outcomes, AI tends to amplify differences in how learners structure and integrate design elements. Novice learners produced feature-rich but loosely integrated outputs, whereas the expert generated fewer but more coherently structured and hierarchically organized designs.

4.3 Role of NotebookLM in Structuring Cognitive Process Data

This section addresses RQ3 by examining how NotebookLM supported the organization and structural representation of cognitive process data derived from think-aloud protocols and interview transcripts. The focus is placed on its role in transforming unstructured qualitative data into organized formats for further analysis.

NotebookLM was used to assist in organizing raw think-aloud transcripts and interview data into structured cognitive units. These included idea generation, prompt modification, evaluation statements, and planning-related expressions. The tool supported the researcher in segmenting unstructured verbal data into meaningful units, grouping related statements into clusters, and providing an initial overview of participant reasoning traces. NotebookLM outputs were used only as organizational aids rather than final analytical results. NotebookLM also facilitated early-stage identification of cognitive patterns by clustering similar statements within and across participants. This helped in identifying recurring categories such as iterative prompting behavior, evaluation responses, and planning expressions. This structuring process reduced the complexity of raw qualitative data and supported preliminary thematic organization before formal coding.

NotebookLM was integrated with MAXQDA and SOLO Taxonomy as part of a multi-layered qualitative analysis workflow. In this sequence, NotebookLM was used for initial data structuring, MAXQDA for formal coding and categorization, and SOLO Taxonomy for classifying cognitive complexity levels. Within this workflow, NotebookLM functioned as a preparatory tool that supported data organization prior to deeper interpretive analysis. Overall, NotebookLM contributed to improving the manageability of large qualitative datasets and supported the early identification of cognitive patterns. However, all final coding decisions and interpretations were conducted manually by the researcher using MAXQDA and SOLO Taxonomy.

5 Discussion

The findings of this study indicate that differences between novice learners and the expert reference case in AI-assisted design thinking are primarily reflected in the organization and regulation of cognitive processes rather than in the final design outcomes. Across novice cases, design thinking emerged in a reactive manner through iterative cycles of prompting, evaluation, and revision, whereas the expert reference case demonstrated a more anticipatory and conceptually structured approach. This pattern suggests that AI does not homogenize cognitive behavior but instead interacts with users' existing cognitive schemas, amplifying differences in reasoning and planning strategies.

From the perspective of expert–novice theory, the observed differences align with prior research indicating that benchmark case rely on well-developed cognitive schemas that support efficient problem representation and forward planning, while novices tend to engage in trial-and-error reasoning due to less structured domain knowledge [8, 16]. In the present study, novice learners frequently depended on AI-generated outputs as external triggers for idea development, resulting in emergent rather than pre-structured design processes. In contrast, the single benchmark design case demonstrated clear problem framing prior to AI interaction, using AI primarily for refinement and implementation. This supports the view that expertise is not only determined by knowledge quantity but also by how knowledge is structured and accessed during problem-solving.

The findings can also be interpreted through Cognitive Load Theory, which suggests that limited prior knowledge increases reliance on external support during complex tasks [4]. Novice learners in this study showed stronger dependence on AI feedback due to limited internal schemas for organizing design information. AI-generated outputs functioned as temporary scaffolds that supported exploration but also encouraged fragmented and incremental decision-making. In contrast, the benchmark case's more developed schemas enabled selective use of AI outputs within a stable conceptual framework, thereby reducing cognitive overload and supporting more coherent reasoning.

The SOLO Taxonomy analysis further reinforces these interpretations. Novice outputs were primarily categorized at the multi-structural level, characterized by multiple but weakly integrated design elements, while the expert reference case demonstrated relational and extended abstract characteristics, where design components were integrated into a coherent and hierarchically organized system [12]. This suggests that cognitive complexity is determined not by the number of features produced but by the degree of conceptual integration across those features.

Another important finding relates to the functional role of AI in cognitive processes. For novice learners, Lovable AI primarily functioned as an idea generator and feedback mechanism, shaping decisions based on immediate aesthetic impressions rather than conceptual reasoning. This pattern is consistent with cognitive offloading, where external systems are used to compensate for limited metacognitive regulation [9, 14]. In contrast, the expert used AI strategically as a tool for refining pre-existing ideas, reflecting a form of hybrid intelligence in which human planning guides AI utilization rather than being driven by it [17].

Overall, AI appears to modulate cognitive processes by interacting with users' prior knowledge structures, thereby amplifying existing differences between novice and expert reasoning. These effects extend across cognitive organization, metacognitive regulation, and domain expertise. This implies that the pedagogical value of AI tools such as Lovable AI is highly dependent on learners' prior knowledge structures and self-regulatory capabilities. Consequently, effective instructional design should not only focus on providing access to AI tools but also on strengthening learners' conceptual understanding and planning skills to enable more productive AI-supported learning.

6 Conclusion

This study provides preliminary insights into cognitive processes in AI-assisted design thinking using Lovable AI. The findings show consistent differences between novice learners and the expert reference case in how cognitive processes are structured during design activities. Novices exhibited exploratory and reactive, trial-and-error patterns driven by iterative interaction with AI outputs, while the benchmark case demonstrated structured, goal-oriented, and reflective processes based on prior planning and conceptual organization. From a SOLO Taxonomy perspective, novices were mainly at the multistructural level, whereas the expert reference case reached relational and, in some cases, extended abstract levels, indicating higher cognitive integration in design organization. AI functions as a cognitive mediator whose effects are contingent upon learners' prior knowledge structures and self-regulatory capacity. Methodologically, the study highlights the value of integrating think-aloud protocols, interviews, SOLO Taxonomy, MAXQDA, and AI-supported tools such as NotebookLM for analyzing cognitive processes in design-based learning contexts. The findings are intended as exploratory, context-specific contributions to research on AI-supported learning.

References

1. Brown, T.: Design thinking. Harv. Bus. Rev. **86**, 84 (2008)
2. Luka, I.: Design thinking in pedagogy: frameworks and uses. Eur. J. Educ. **54**, 499–512 (2019). https://doi.org/10.1111/ejed.12367
3. Liu, Y.-L.E., Lee, T.-P., Huang, Y.-M.: Fostering affective-domain learning objectives in design thinking: the impact of online collaborative whiteboards on basic. In: Elisa Bertino, Purdue University, West Lafayette, IN, U., Wen Gao, Peking University, Beijing, C., Steffen, B., TU Dortmund University, Dortmund, G., Yung, M., and , Columbia University, New York, NY, U. (eds.) International Conference of Innovative Technologies and Learning. pp. 82–91. Springer Nature, Oslo, Norway (2025).
4. Ellerton, P.: On critical thinking and content knowledge: a critique of the assumptions of cognitive load theory. Think. Ski. Creat. **43**, 100975 (2022). https://doi.org/10.1016/j.tsc.2021.100975
5. Federico, P.A.: Expert and novice recognition of similar situations. Hum. Factors. **37**, 105–122 (1995)
6. Liu, Y.E., Lee, T., Huang, Y.: Enhancing university students' creative confidence, learning motivation, and team creative performance in design thinking using a digital visual collaborative environment. Think. Ski. Creat. **50**, 101388 (2023). https://doi.org/10.1016/j.tsc.2023.101388
7. Chi, M.T.H.: Laboratory methods for assessing experts' and novices' knowledge. In: Ericsson, K.A., Charness, N., Feltovich, P.J., Hoffman, R.R. (eds.) The Cambridge Handbook of Expertise and Expert Performance, pp. 167–184. Cambridge University Press, New York (2006). https://doi.org/10.1017/CBO9780511816796

8. Ericsson, K.A., Simon, H.A.: How to study thinking in everyday life: contrasting think-aloud protocols with descriptions and explanations of thinking. Mind Cult. Act. **5**, 178–186 (1998). https://doi.org/10.1207/s15327884mca0503_3
9. Kirsh, D.: Distributed cognition: a methodological note. Pragmat. Cogn. **14**, 249–262 (2006). https://doi.org/10.1075/pc.14.2.06kir
10. Razzouk, R., Shute, V.: What is design thinking and why is it important? Rev. Educ. Res. **82**, 330–348 (2012)
11. Chi, M.T.H.: Theoretical perspectives, methodological approaches, and trends in the study of expertise. In: Expertise in Mathematics Instruction: An International Perspective, pp. 17–39. Springer US, Boston, MA (2010)
12. Biggs, J.B., Collis, K.F.: Evaluating the Quality of Learning: The SOLO Taxonomy. Academic, New York (1982)
13. Lee, H.Y., Chen, P.H., Wang, W.S., Huang, Y.M., Wu, T.T.: Empowering ChatGPT with guidance mechanism in blended learning: effect of self-regulated learning, higher-order thinking skills, and knowledge construction. Int. J. Educ. Technol. High. Educ. **21**, 1–28 (2024). https://doi.org/10.1186/s41239-024-00447-4
14. Wang, W.-S., Lin, C.-J., Lee, H.-Y., Huang, Y.-M., Wu, T.-T.: Enhancing self-regulated learning and higher-order thinking skills in virtual reality: the impact of ChatGPT-integrated feedback aids. Educ. Inf. Technol. **30**, 19419–19445 (2025). https://doi.org/10.1007/s10639-025-13557-x
15. Mollick, E., Mollick, L.: Instructors as innovators: a future-focused approach to new AI learning opportunities, with prompts. arXiv preprint arXiv:2407.05181. Philadelphia. (2024). https://doi.org/10.48550/arXiv.2407.05181
16. Chi, M.T.H., Feltovich, P.J., Glaser, R.: Categorization and representation of physics problems by experts and novices. Cogn. Sci. **5**, 121–152 (1981). https://doi.org/10.1207/s15516709cog0502_2
17. Kyriakopoulos, N., Kim, E., Hultink, E.J., Santema, S.: The impact of design thinking and artificial intelligence capabilities on performance: the role of new product development decision-making agility. J. Bus. Res. **200**, 115633 (2025). https://doi.org/10.1016/j.jbusres.2025.115633.1

Computational Thinking in Education

Computational Thinking–Based Scaffolding in ChatGPT-Supported EFL Writing: Effects on Peer Feedback Activity

Elsa[1], Wei-Jie Tiao[1,2], and Ting-Ting Wu[1](✉)

[1] National Yunlin University of Science and Technology, Douliu 64002, Taiwan
ttwu@yuntech.edu.tw

[2] Chaoyang University of Technology, Taichung, Taiwan

Abstract. This quasi-experimental study investigated whether embedding computational thinking (CT) as a cognitive scaffold during AI-supported planning influences EFL learners' peer feedback practices. Sixty-two undergraduate students were assigned to control (n = 32) and experimental (n = 30) groups. Both groups used ChatGPT during pre-writing and revision, but only the experimental group applied CT principles to guide analytical interaction with the tool. Data were collected via peer-feedback questionnaire administered at pre-test and post-test, and analyzed using ANCOVA with pre-test scores as a covariate. Results indicated a statistically significant effect of instructional condition on post-test peer feedback scores, with the experimental group demonstrating higher peer feedback quality. These findings suggest that CT scaffolding embedded in certain writing stages can enhance learners' feedback practices, even when AI assistance is restricted during evaluation. Implications for EFL writing pedagogy and future research directions are discussed.

Keywords: Computational thinking · AI-supported writing · peer feedback · EFL writing · scaffolding

1 Introduction

The integration of artificial intelligence (AI), especially ChatGPT, into EFL writing instruction has reshaped how learners approach early stages of the writing process, particularly planning and idea generation [1]. At the same time, peer feedback remains a core component of process-oriented writing pedagogy, as it engages learners in evaluating texts, applying writing criteria, and developing audience awareness [2]. Through the act of reviewing peers' work, learners are also encouraged to reflect on their own writing, thereby fostering critical thinking and increased self-awareness [3]. Despite these benefits, EFL learners frequently produce peer feedback that focuses on local, surface-level features (e.g. vocabulary, grammar, mechanics) in both their comments and subsequent revisions [4], indicating a need for stronger cognitive foundations developed during earlier stages of writing instruction.

C.-J. Lin et al. (Eds.): ICITL 2026, LNCS 16841, pp. 139–148, 2027.
https://doi.org/10.1007/978-3-032-32112-1_15

Computational thinking (CT) is widely conceptualized as a domain-general problem-solving process that involves decomposition, pattern recognition, abstraction, and logical/algorithmic reasoning [5]. These component processes closely mirror the cognitive operations required for planning, organizing, and structuring ideas in writing. From this perspective, CT offers a promising pedagogical lens for strengthening learners' cognitive engagement in the writing process, even though most existing CT focused on STEM or computing-related. While prior research has shown that CT oriented scaffolding can support learners' individual writing development [6], far less is known about how such scaffolding, when embedded in AI supported planning activities, may indirectly shape learners' capacity to engage in higher quality peer feedback. Moreover, existing studies on AI-assisted EFL writing have largely emphasized surface-level outcomes such as grammatical accuracy or general performance, while paying limited attention to academic writing processes and learners' motivation [7], leaving a gap in understanding how cognitively guided writing processes influence subsequent peer feedback practices.

To address this gap, the present study examines the effects of computational thinking as scaffolding implemented during the AI supported planning stage on EFL learners' peer feedback activity. Using a quasi-experimental design, the study compares an experimental group that engaged in CT oriented planning with limited ChatGPT support for brainstorming and idea organization and a control group that received conventional instruction. Importantly, ChatGPT was not permitted during the peer feedback stage, ensuring that feedback quality reflected learners' own analytical and evaluative capacities rather than AI generated input. By positioning computational thinking as a cognitive scaffold within AI supported writing rather than as direct instruction for peer feedback, this study contributes empirical evidence on how upstream instructional design can shape learners' engagement in peer feedback and reflective writing practices in EFL classrooms.

2 Literature Review

2.1 Computational Thinking as Cognitive Scaffolding in EFL Writing

Computational thinking has been increasingly framed as a domain general cognitive framework that supports complex problem solving across disciplines, including language learning and writing [8]. In EFL writing contexts, computational thinking aligns closely with the cognitive demands of planning and analysis, as learners are required to decompose writing tasks, recognize structural patterns, abstract key ideas, and organize arguments logically [6]. These processes suggest that computational thinking can function as a form of cognitive scaffolding that supports learners in approaching writing related tasks in a more systematic and strategic manner, particularly during stages that involve higher order thinking rather than linguistic accuracy alone.

Nevertheless, existing work has largely emphasized the role of computational thinking in enhancing learners' individual writing performance, often focusing on text quality or task completion [9]. Such an emphasis tends to position computational thinking primarily as a cognitive tool for text production, while giving limited attention to how CT oriented scaffolding may shape learners' broader engagement in process-oriented writing activities. Recent syntheses of online peer feedback research show a strong focus on learners' cognitive and affective gains (e.g., writing performance, revision-based comments, motivation), but they also highlight that many potential facets of OPF remain unexplored [10]. Consequently, few studies have examined whether strengthening organizational processes during writing preparation carries over to their behavior in socially mediated practices such as peer feedback. Without strong cognitive foundations developed during earlier stages of writing, learners may struggle to engage in deeper levels of text analysis and evaluation when responding to peers' work, as students who lack or fail to activate higher level discourse skills tend to focus primarily on surface level errors and experience difficulty engaging with cohesion, coherence, and global text structure during revision and feedback activities [11]. This suggests a need to conceptualize computational thinking not as direct instruction for feedback practices, but as an upstream scaffold that prepares learners for more reflective and analytical engagement across stages of the writing process.

2.2 Peer Feedback in AI-Supported EFL Writing Contexts

Peer feedback is a central element of process oriented EFL writing pedagogy, as it is embedded into the writing cycle, learners engage in deeper reflection and critical evaluation of texts, leading to better writing performance and affective outcomes [12]. Engaging in structured peer feedback on written reflections promotes deeper reflective thinking and helps learners articulate more developed, theory-informed texts [13]. However, research consistently shows that EFL learners' peer feedback is often limited in depth, frequently focusing on grammatical errors or offering vague evaluative statements [14]. These patterns suggest that learners face substantial cognitive challenges when required to analyze content, organization, and argumentation without sufficient scaffolding.

The increasing use of AI in EFL writing instruction has introduced new opportunities and tensions in this area. AI tools have been shown to support learners effectively during early writing stages such as idea generation and outlining, particularly for those with lower L2 literacy, by helping them handle reading and planning demands and increasing their writing self-efficacy [15]. At the same time, allowing AI assistance during evaluative stages raises concerns about diminished learner agency and reduced engagement in independent analysis, as prior reviews have cautioned that AI systems providing ready-made evaluations may short-circuit key meta-cognitive processes such as goal setting, that are central to the development of learner agency [16]. As a result, instructional designs that restrict AI use to the planning stage have gained relevance, as they preserve the cognitive and reflective functions of peer feedback.

Within such AI supported but feedback restricted contexts, the quality of peer feedback depends heavily on learners' ability to apply effective analytical frameworks [17]. However, studies have rarely examined how structured cognitive scaffolds operate in these environments. This gap highlights the need to investigate how explicit frameworks such as computational thinking, when embedded in earlier writing stages, may indirectly support learners in producing more focused, analytical, and reflective peer feedback without reliance on AI generated support.

3 Methodology

3.1 Participants

The study was conducted with two intact classes: a control group (n = 32) and an experimental group (n = 30), yielding a total of 62 undergraduate students enrolled in the same academic program. Due to practical constraints within the instructional context, random assignment at the individual level was not feasible. Instead, randomization was implemented at the class level, with the two intact classes randomly assigned to the control and experimental conditions. Accordingly, the study adopted a quasi-experimental pretest–posttest design. To establish baseline equivalence between groups, Levene's test was performed on the pretest total scores, which indicated no significant difference in variance between the control and experimental groups ($F = 1.704$, $p = .304$), suggesting that the two groups were statistically comparable prior to the intervention.

Before conducting hypothesis testing, the assumptions underlying parametric analyses were examined. The normality of the difference scores was evaluated using the Shapiro–Wilk test, and the results showed that the total difference scores were normally distributed ($W = .967$, $p = .098$). These findings confirmed that the assumptions of normality and homogeneity of variance were met, thereby justifying the use of parametric statistical procedures in subsequent analyses.

3.2 Data Collection

In this study, participants' baseline knowledge across the two groups was assessed using a pre-test questionnaire. The instrument was adapted from the Supportive Peer-Feedback questionnaire. It comprised 15 items rated on a five-point Likert scale (1 = strongly disagree, 5 = strongly agree) and covered three dimensions: Receiver Feedback, Provider Feedback, and Cognitive Feedback. The instrument demonstrated acceptable internal consistency, with a Cronbach's alpha of 0.768.

3.3 Experimental Procedure

The intervention was conducted over an 11-week period (see Fig. 1). In Week 1, both groups completed a pre-test on peer feedback, followed by an introduction to the writing tasks and the use of ChatGPT as instructional support. The experimental condition was differentiated by the integration of Computational Thinking (CT) as a structured cognitive lens guiding students' interaction with ChatGPT during the pre-writing and reviewing stages.

As illustrated in Fig. 1, the instructional sequence followed three repeated cycles across Weeks 2 to 10. Each cycle consisted of pre-writing (Weeks 2, 5, and 8), drafting (Weeks 3, 6, and 9), and reviewing (Weeks 4, 7, and 10). Each instructional meeting lasted 50 min. During the pre-writing stage, students were given 30 min to brainstorm ideas with AI support, after which they used the remaining time to develop their own outlines independently. During the writing stage, students composed their drafts based on the outlines they had previously prepared. During the reviewing stage, students were given 30 min to use ChatGPT while analyzing their peers' texts, and the remaining time was allocated for submitting their peer feedback comments online. This cyclical structure was designed to reinforce iterative writing practice and analytical engagement in AI-supported tasks.

In the experimental group, CT principles, namely decomposition, generalization, abstraction, and algorithmic thinking, were embedded into both the pre-writing and reviewing stages to scaffold students' analytical interaction with ChatGPT. During pre-writing, students applied CT to break down prompts, identify structural patterns, prioritize key ideas, and organize arguments logically. During the reviewing stage, students applied CT while examining their peers' texts and interpreting AI-supported suggestions in order to generate more structured and purposeful feedback. In contrast, the control group engaged in the same instructional sequence using ChatGPT, but without structured CT-based analytical guidance. Finally, in Week 11, both groups completed a post-test on peer feedback to examine the effects of the intervention.

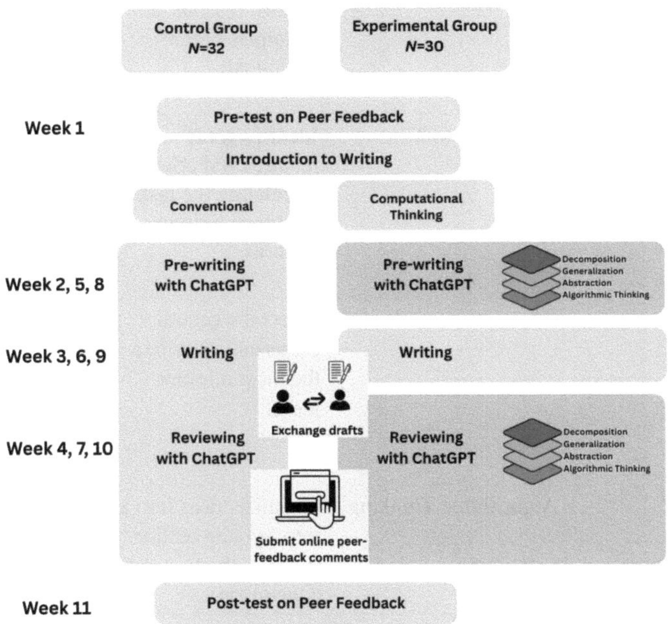

Fig. 1. Experimental Procedure

To operationalize CT within AI-supported writing activities, specific CT principles were embedded into students' interaction with ChatGPT across the pre writing and revision stages. As summarized in Table 1, each CT principle was enacted through concrete student activities and example scaffolding questions intended to foster structured analytical engagement. During the planning stage, decomposition and generalization supported students in breaking down tasks, identifying genre features, and relating writing requirements to established patterns. Following Selby and Woollard [18], generalization refers to recognizing common patterns and shared features across tasks and applying them to new writing or peer-review contexts, whereas pattern recognition primarily focuses on identifying recurring patterns. Abstraction and algorithmic thinking further guided them in prioritizing key ideas and organizing arguments logically. During the reviewing stage, the same CT principles framed peer feedback processes by supporting students in analyzing texts according to relevant criteria, comparing issues against general rubrics, prioritizing high-impact revisions, and formulating actionable suggestions. Thus, CT served as an explicit analytical framework for scaffolding students' engagement with ChatGPT rather than as an additional instructional component.

Table 1. Integration of Computational Thinking Principles

Stage	CT Principle	Student Activities	Example Scaffolding Question
Planning (Prewriting)	Decomposition	Break the task into purpose, audience, claims, reasons, and examples before asking AI.	"What guiding questions can help me break this topic into purpose, audience, claims, reasons, and examples?"
	Generalization	Identify genre features and criteria by relating the task to known writing patterns.	"What general structural patterns of expository essays can I use as a reference when organizing my ideas for this topic?"
	Abstraction	Select the central thesis and prioritize the most relevant ideas.	"Based on common criteria for a strong thesis, how can I evaluate my ideas to choose one main claim?"
	Algorithmic Thinking	Organize ideas into a step-by-step outline (intro → body → conclusion).	"Help me sequence these points into a logical paragraph structure."
Reviewing	Decomposition	Analyze peers' texts by aspects (content, organization, language, coherence).	"Can you show examples of how feedback can be framed for content, organization, language, and coherence?"

(*continued*)

Table 1. (*continued*)

Stage	CT Principle	Student Activities	Example Scaffolding Question
	Generalization	Compare issues against general writing criteria/rubrics.	"Based on general writing rubrics, what are common issue patterns in expository writing that I should look for when reviewing my peer's text?"
	Abstraction	Prioritize 1–2 high-impact issues for revision.	"How can I decide which issues are high-impact and should be prioritized in peer feedback? What criteria should I consider?"
	Algorithmic Thinking	Structure feedback procedurally (problem → evidence → actionable suggestion).	"What is a clear step-by-step structure for giving peer feedback (from identifying a problem to proposing a concrete revision)?"

3.4 Data Analysis

To examine the effects of the intervention on students' perceived peer feedback practices, statistical analyses were performed using IBM SPSS Statistics. Self-report questionnaire data collected at pre-test and post-test served as the primary outcome measures, and between-group comparisons were conducted to assess differential effects across conditions.

4 Results

Descriptive statistics were first calculated to show changes in students' perceived peer feedback quality across time and groups (see Table 2). The experimental group reported increases across all dimensions, with the largest gain in Provider Feedback (M gain = 0.18), followed by Cognitive Feedback (M gain = 0.14) and Receiver Feedback (M gain = 0.11). In contrast, the control group showed smaller and less consistent changes, with only a slight increase in Overall Peer Feedback (M gain = 0.03). These patterns indicate more consistent positive changes in the experimental group's self-reported perceptions before inferential testing.

To further examine whether post-test differences between the two groups were statistically significant after controlling for pre-test scores, an ANCOVA was conducted (see Table 3). The analysis revealed a statistically significant effect of instructional condition on post-test scores, $F(1, 59) = 7.80$, $p = .007$, partial $\eta^2 = .12$, indicating a moderate effect size. Pre-test scores were also a significant covariate, $F(1, 59) = 17.78$, $p < .001$, partial $\eta^2 = .23$, suggesting that students' baseline performance explained a substantial proportion of variance in post-test outcomes. After controlling for pre-test differences, the experimental group obtained higher post-test peer feedback scores than the control group, supporting the effectiveness of the intervention.

Table 2. Descriptive statistics of perceived peer feedback quality

Variable Dimension	Group	N	Pre M	Pre SD	Post M	Post SD	Gain
Receiver Feedback	Control	32	3.70	0.51	3.69	0.61	−0.01
Receiver Feedback	Experimental	30	3.96	0.43	4.07	0.53	0.11
Provider Feedback	Control	32	3.45	0.48	3.66	0.53	0.21
Provider Feedback	Experimental	30	3.73	0.51	3.92	0.48	0.18
Cognitive Feedback	Control	32	4.05	0.69	3.78	0.70	−0.27
Cognitive Feedback	Experimental	30	3.93	0.66	4.08	0.59	0.14
Overall Peer Feedback	Control	32	3.67	0.47	3.70	0.53	0.03
Overall Peer Feedback	Experimental	30	3.86	0.40	4.01	0.46	0.15

Table 3. ANCOVA results for Peer Feedback

Groups	Pre-test		Post-test		SS	*F*	*p*	η^2_p
	Mean	SD	Mean	SD				
Control	3.70	0.493	3.74	0.511				
Experimental	3.85	0.360	4.01	0.490	1.497	7.80	.007**	0.12
Pre-test (covariate)	–	–	–	–	3.414	17.78	< .001***	0.23

* $p < .05$, ** $p < .01$, *** $p < .001$.

5 Discussion and Conclusion

The findings indicate that embedding computational thinking (CT) as a cognitive scaffold within ChatGPT-supported planning positively influenced learners' perceived peer feedback practices. After controlling for baseline differences, the experimental group achieved significantly higher post-test perceived peer feedback scores, suggesting that analytical processes developed during planning may transfer to peer evaluation. This aligns with prior research showing that analytic structures used in drafting can carry over to feedback activities [19].

The descriptive results further show that, although the ChatGPT-only control group had a slightly larger gain in Provider Feedback, only the CT-scaffolded ChatGPT group reported positive gains across all peer feedback dimensions. This suggests that ChatGPT may help students feel more capable of giving feedback [20], while CT scaffolding supports broader and more consistent improvement in perceived feedback experience.

The results further suggest that ChatGPT alone does not guarantee improved peer feedback perceptions. Rather, improvements in perceived evaluative capacity and autonomy are better explained by structured, autonomy-supportive instructional design in which GAI is embedded [21].

Nevertheless, this study relied primarily on self-report questionnaire data and was conducted within a quasi-experimental design in a single instructional context, which may limit the generalizability of the findings. Future research incorporating analyses of actual peer-feedback comments and more diverse samples would help clarify the mechanisms through which CT-based scaffolding facilitates the development of peer evaluation skills.

Acknowledgments. This research is supported by the National Science and Technology Council, Taiwan, R.O.C., under grant nos. NSTC 114-2628-H-224 -001 -MY3 and NSTC 113-2410-H-224 -036 -MY3

Disclosure of Interests The authors have no competing interests to declare that are relevant to the content of this article.

References

1. Jiang, L., Lai, C.: How did the generative artificial intelligence-assisted digital multimodal composing process facilitate the production of quality digital multimodal compositions: toward a process-genre integrated model. TESOL Q. **59** (2025). https://doi.org/10.1002/tesq.3390
2. Irgin, P., Bilki, Z.: Students' perceptions of online peer feedback in process-oriented L2 writing: a qualitative inquiry. Stud. Educ. Eval. **83**, 101403 (2024). https://doi.org/10.1016/j.stueduc.2024.101403
3. Novakovich, J.: Fostering critical thinking and reflection through blog-mediated peer feedback. J. Comput. Assist. Learn. **32**, 16–30 (2016). https://doi.org/10.1111/jcal.12114
4. Pham, H.T.P.: Computer-mediated and face-to-face peer feedback: student feedback and revision in EFL writing. Comput. Assist. Lang. Learn. **35**, 2112–2147 (2022). https://doi.org/10.1080/09588221.2020.1868530
5. Saad, A., Zainudin, S.: A review of teaching and learning approach in implementing project-based learning (PBL) with computational thinking (CT). Interact. Learn. Environ. **32**, 7622–7646 (2024). https://doi.org/10.1080/10494820.2024.2328280
6. Wu, T.T., Elsa, E., Huang, Y.M.: Integrating computational thinking into problem-based learning in EAP writing: effects on motivation and writing performance. J. Engl. Acad. Purp. **80**, 101641 (2026). https://doi.org/10.1016/j.jeap.2026.101641
7. Song, C., Song, Y.: Enhancing academic writing skills and motivation: assessing the efficacy of ChatGPT in AI-assisted language learning for EFL students. Front. Psychol. **14** (2023). https://doi.org/10.3389/fpsyg.2023.1260843

8. Yu, X., Soto-Varela, R., Gutiérrez-García, M.Á.: How to learn and teach a foreign language through computational thinking: suggestions based on a systematic review. Think. Skills Creat. **52**, 101517 (2024). https://doi.org/10.1016/j.tsc.2024.101517
9. Nurhayati, N., Silitonga, L.M., Subiyanto, A., Murti, A.T., Wu, T.T.: Computational Thinking Approach: Its Impact on Students' English Writing Skills (2022). https://doi.org/10.1007/978-3-031-15273-3_47
10. Cao, S., Zhou, S., Luo, Y., Wang, T., Zhou, T., Xu, Y.: A review of the ESL/EFL learners' gains from online peer feedback on English writing. Front. Psychol. **13** (2022). https://doi.org/10.3389/fpsyg.2022.1035803
11. Chen, M., Cui, Y.: The effects of AWE and peer feedback on cohesion and coherence in continuation writing. J. Second. Lang. Writ. **57**, 100915 (2022). https://doi.org/10.1016/j.jslw.2022.100915
12. Liu, C.C., Liu, S.J., Hwang, G.J., Tu, Y.F., Wang, Y., Wang, N.: Engaging EFL students' critical thinking tendency and in-depth reflection in technology-based writing contexts: a peer assessment-incorporated automatic evaluation approach. Educ. Inf. Technol. (Dordr). **28**, 13027–13052 (2023). https://doi.org/10.1007/s10639-023-11697-6
13. Yaacob, A., Asraf, R.M., Hussain, R.M.R., Ismail, S.N.: Empowering learners' reflective thinking through collaborative reflective learning. Int. J. Instr. **14**, 709–726 (2021). https://doi.org/10.29333/iji.2021.14143a
14. Zhang, X.: Understanding the critical thinking experiences of L2 student writers engaged in linguistically supported peer feedback giving. Assess. Writ. **66**, 100977 (2025). https://doi.org/10.1016/j.asw.2025.100977
15. Zhang, Z., Wang, C., Shang, Y.: Are AI tools effective in reducing cognitive load or boosting writing self-efficacy for L2 postgraduates? Asia Pac. Educ. Res. (2025). https://doi.org/10.1007/s40299-025-01031-8
16. Hooshyar, D., Tammets, K., Ley, T., Aus, K., Kollom, K.: Learning analytics in supporting student agency: a systematic review. Sustainability. **15**, 13662 (2023). https://doi.org/10.3390/su151813662
17. Darvishi, A., Khosravi, H., Sadiq, S., Gašević, D.: Incorporating AI and learning analytics to build trustworthy peer assessment systems. Br. J. Educ. Technol. **53**, 844–875 (2022). https://doi.org/10.1111/bjet.13233
18. Selby, C.C., Woollard, J.: Computational Thinking: the developing definition (2013)
19. Noroozi, O., Banihashem, S.K., Biemans, H.J.A., Smits, M., Vervoort, M.T.W., Verbaan, C.L.: Design, implementation, and evaluation of an online supported peer feedback module to enhance students' argumentative essay quality. Educ. Inf. Technol. (Dordr). **28**, 12757–12784 (2023). https://doi.org/10.1007/s10639-023-11683-y
20. Teng, M.F.: "ChatGPT is the companion, not enemies": EFL learners' perceptions and experiences in using ChatGPT for feedback in writing. Comput. Educ.: Artif. Intell.. **7**, 100270 (2024). https://doi.org/10.1016/j.caeai.2024.100270
21. Mohebbi, A.: Enabling learner independence and self-regulation in language education using AI tools: a systematic review. Cogent Educ. **12** (2025). https://doi.org/10.1080/2331186X.2024.2433814

Generative AI Guidance Based on Computational Thinking: The Impacts on Problem-Solving Skills and Reflective Thinking

Yu-Ping Cheng[1(✉)], You-Jhen Guo[1], Pei-Hsuan Lee[1], and Andreja Istenič[2,3,4]

[1] Department of Information Management, National Chi Nan University, Nantou County, Taiwan
yuping@mail.ncnu.edu.tw, {s111241014, s114213528}@mail1.ncnu.edu.tw

[2] Faculty of Civil and Geodetic Engineering, University of Ljubljana, Ljubljana, Slovenia

[3] Faculty of Education, University of Primorska, Koper, Slovenia

[4] Samarkand State University named after Sharof Rashidov, Samarkand, Uzbekistan

Abstract. This study aims to address the challenges encountered by novice programmers, particularly high cognitive load and a lack of immediate diagnostic feedback. To mitigate the risk of students developing an over-reliance on generative artificial intelligence (GAI) as a means of directly obtaining answers, which may consequently undermine their capacity for self-directed learning, this study developed a learning platform that integrates GAI, computational thinking (CT), and formative assessment. Within the platform, GAI is designed as a "thinking facilitator" that guides students through progressive questioning and immediate feedback, rather than providing definitive answers. This design is intended to scaffold students' engagement in problem decomposition, logical reasoning, and reflective debugging. A total of 27 undergraduate students participated in this study, with pre- and post-tests along with questionnaire surveys administered to evaluate the effectiveness of the system intervention. The findings indicate that interaction with the platform not only effectively enhances students' programming learning outcomes, but also fosters the development of reflective thinking and problem-solving skills. Regarding future research directions, it is recommended that subsequent studies expand the sample size and extend the duration of implementation. By improving the guidance mechanism and providing tiered learning resources, future studies may further validate and enhance the long-term learning outcomes and problem-solving skills of learners with varying proficiency levels.

Keywords: Generative Artificial Intelligence · Computational Thinking · Formative Assessment · Problem-Solving Skills · Reflective Thinking

1 Introduction

With the rapid advancement of information technology, the integration of transdisciplinary competencies has become increasingly important for effectively addressing complex real-world problems [1]. Generative artificial intelligence (GAI) application in

C.-J. Lin et al. (Eds.): ICITL 2026, LNCS 16841, pp. 149–158, 2027.
https://doi.org/10.1007/978-3-032-32112-1_16

education has enabled students to receive immediate and personalized learning support, demonstrating its potential to improve learning outcomes [2]. In the context of digital learning, the importance of programming education is increasing, and computational thinking (CT) is also regarded as an indispensable problem-solving skill for students facing complex problems and data [3].

However, programming involves high cognitive load activities such as abstract concept understanding, logical reasoning, and debugging. Beginners often encounter obstacles in the learning process. If traditional classrooms still rely mainly on one-way lectures and assessments are overly focused on summative evaluations, students often lack traceable, immediate feedback and diagnostic support in the process of "solving problems-making mistakes-correcting them," making it difficult to effectively integrate and transfer fragmented programming knowledge into stable problem-solving skills [4].

In recent years, while the integration of GAI has offered immediate programming assistance, a lack of appropriate instructional design and guidance could cause students to perceive AI as a tool for obtaining direct answers, resulting in a decline in learning flow, self-efficacy, and final learning outcomes [5]. Therefore, balancing the integration of new technologies with the preservation of students' opportunities for independent thinking and reasoning is crucial to programming learning design.

Thus, it is particularly important to incorporate formative assessment mechanisms into the learning process. Formative assessment can not only provide immediate learning diagnosis and feedback, but also guide students to conduct structured reflection on their mistakes, prompting them to re-examine their computational thinking process and transform the learning habit of passively accepting answers into active problem-solving practice [3].

While GAI, CT and formative assessment are crucial for programming learning, current teaching environments still lack a comprehensive learning platform that fully integrates GAI, reflective thinking guidance and formative assessment. In view of this, this study aims to design and develop a learning platform that combines GAI, CT, and formative assessment. Through the assistance of GAI, immediate feedback, and structured reflection guidance, it assists students in deepening self-monitoring and strategy adjustment within the cycle of "writing code-debugging-reflecting-reverifying," thereby improving programming learning effectiveness and problem-solving skills. Based on this background, the research questions of this study are as follows:

1. Does the use of the learning platform that combines GAI, computational thinking, and formative assessment affect students' learning outcomes?
2. Does the use of the learning platform that combines GAI, computational thinking, and formative assessment influence students' problem-solving skills?
3. Does the use of the learning platform that combines GAI, computational thinking, and formative assessment have an impact on students' reflective thinking?

2 Literature Review

2.1 The Development of Generative Artificial Intelligence in Programming Education and the Cultivation of Computational Thinking

The concept of Computational Thinking (CT), first proposed by Wing [6], refers to the approach of solving problems, designing systems, and understanding human behavior by drawing on fundamental computer science concepts. Its practical application is built upon four core competencies: Decomposition, which breaks down complex tasks into manageable sub-problems; Pattern Recognition, which identifies recurring structures and regularities within programming or problem-solving processes; Abstraction, which extracts core concepts and eliminates unnecessary details to form reusable conceptual models; and Algorithm Design, which integrates the preceding outcomes into clear, executable steps and instructions. The integration of game-based learning platforms and the strategy of student-generated questions enables learners to demonstrate and enhance their computational thinking skills in programming or assigned tasks, thereby underscoring the critical role of task structure and question design in CT development [7].

In recent years, the evolution of generative artificial intelligence (GAI) and large language models (LLMs) has led to a noticeable shift in the way programming learning is supported. GAI can provide real-time feedback, error explanations, program explanations, and example generation in natural language, reducing the cognitive load for beginners in terms of syntax, debugging, and comprehension. In the context of scientific computing courses in engineering fields, Groothuijsen, Van den Beemt, Remmers and van Meeuwen [8] pointed out that students often use ChatGPT for error checking and debugging, concept understanding, generating or optimizing code, and interpreting code; however, teachers are also concerned about its negative impact on program quality, collaboration, and depth of learning.

Sun, Zheng, Xu and Yang [9] proposed using Socratic questioning as a scaffold for GAI, comparing two paths: directly providing answers and guided probing. They also compared learner behavior and interaction patterns using various learning analysis methods, arguing that structured questioning can reduce passive answer taking and promote the externalization of problem deconstruction and reasoning processes. Chen, Wei, Le and Zhang [10] designed ChatGPT as a teachable agent using a learning-by-teaching approach. The results showed that this design can improve knowledge acquisition and programming ability, and help with self-regulated learning. However, they also noted that if ChatGPT tends to generate correct programs, it may reduce learners' opportunities to practice correcting errors. Therefore, debugging and reflection activities need to be deliberately designed. If GAI is integrated into programming tasks through a scaffolding process of "questioning-feedback-reflection", it may promote the problem decomposition, abstraction and algorithmic thinking required for CT. Conversely, if GAI is only used as an instant solver, it may compress the space for thinking and trial and error, and weaken the formation of CT.

2.2 The Role of Formative Assessment in Programming Learning

The introduction of formative assessment is considered an important strategy to improve the effectiveness of programming learning. Black and Wiliam [11] laid the theoretical foundation for formative assessment, emphasizing that assessment should not only involve scoring, but should also help learners narrow the gap between their current performance and learning goals through continuous diagnosis and feedback. Extending to digital learning scenarios, if online formative assessment platforms can provide immediate and individualized feedback, it helps students identify knowledge gaps and improve their programming learning performance and classroom engagement [12].

Recent studies have further pointed out that integrating GAI into the learning environment as an auxiliary tool for formative assessment, by providing progressive hints and guiding thinking rather than giving direct answers, helps to achieve a balance between learners' immediate needs and skill development. This approach enables students to receive personalized and timely problem-solving support [13, 14]. However, feedback or hints may not directly translate into problem-solving skills; without a learning process that promotes understanding and transfer, students may remain at the level of superficial error correction [15]. Therefore, whether GAI feedback can produce substantial benefits depends not only on what kind of prompts are provided, but also on its effectiveness in stimulating students' reflection.

Reflection is a higher-order metacognitive process. Within a formative assessment framework, when students receive error messages or feedback, reflective mechanisms can guide them to suspend aimless trial-and-error, redirecting them to examine their own reasoning pathways and conceptual understanding. Through technology-assisted situational exploration and alternative cognitive scaffolding such as requiring students to articulate the causes of their errors, re-evaluate the validity of algorithms, or compare the strengths and weaknesses of different solutions, formative feedback transcends unidirectional information transmission and becomes a catalyst for deep conceptual change [16].

In summary, the mechanism integrating formative assessment with reflective thinking provides a feasible and theoretically grounded pathway for cultivating students' computational thinking. However, existing literature predominantly focuses on singular instructional activities or experimental classroom settings; investigations into the integration of formative assessment and computational thinking within interactive learning platforms remain relatively sparse. Consequently, this study seeks to construct a learning platform that incorporates GAI, computational thinking, and formative assessment, aiming to provide more continuous and individualized learning support throughout the problem-solving process.

3 Methodology

3.1 Research Subjects

This study recruited a sample of 27 undergraduate information-major students who had completed a programming course at National Chi Nan University. Prior to the formal experimental intervention, all participants signed an informed consent form, explicitly acknowledging their right to withdraw from the research at any time.

3.2 Experimental Procedure

The core design of this experimental activity aims to implement the learning platform developed by the researchers, which integrates GAI, computational thinking, and formative assessment. The experimental procedure of this study, as illustrated in Fig. 1, is divided into five main phases: (1) Experimental preparation phase: Prior to the formal initiation of the experiment, the researchers will explain the experimental framework and demonstrate the features and operational procedure of the learning platform to the 27 participants. (2) Pretest phase: Participants will take a pre-test. (3) Use platform phase: Participants will log into the platform to complete practical programming tasks. When encountering bottlenecks or errors, the platform will provide structured guidance based on computational thinking and GAI to stimulate student reflection. (4) Posttest phase: Upon completing all programming tasks, participants will take a post-test. (5) Questionnaires phase: Participants will complete the problem-solving skill scale developed by Hwang and Chen (2017) [17] and the reflective thinking scale developed by Kember et al. (2000) [18].

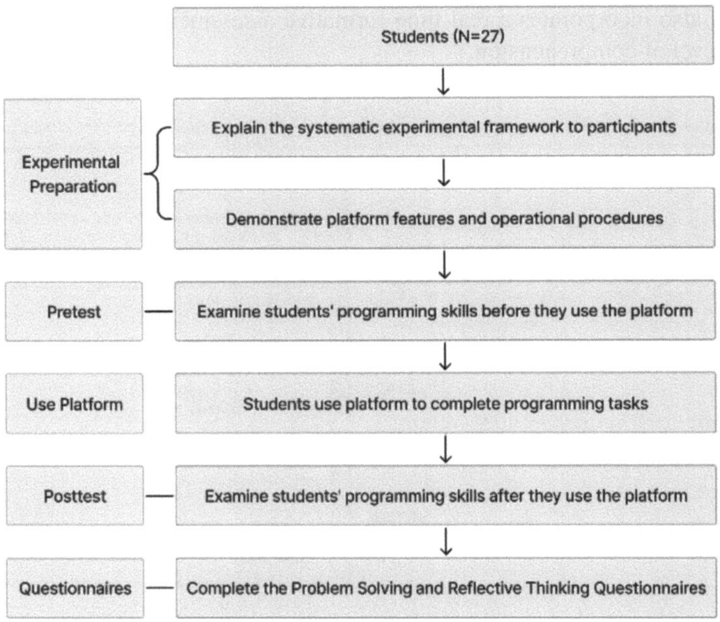

Fig. 1. Experimental Process.

3.3 System Design

This study developed a learning platform that integrates GAI, computational thinking, and formative assessment. The core design of this system adheres to two primary principles: (1) providing clear and systematic cognitive guidance, and (2) strictly prohibiting the direct provision of complete solutions. In other words, this study integrates computational thinking into the generative AI system, transforming it from a traditional answer provider into a cognitive facilitator that promotes students' reflective learning.

As illustrated in Fig. 2, when students encounter programming obstacles, they can consult the AI learning assistant. The learning assistant does not immediately provide directly applicable answers; instead, it employs constructive, scaffolded questioning strategies to guide students' step-by-step thinking. It assists students in clarifying the problem requirements, identifying key conditions, and recognizing sources of error, progressively guiding them to decompose the problem, deduce logic, and verify their hypotheses. For instance, the system encourages students to first articulate their current understanding and previously attempted methods. It then guides them to consider fundamental programming concepts such as inputs and outputs, variables and control flow, conditional statements, and loops, enabling them to self-correct and complete the task through targeted prompts. Through such interactions, students do not merely obtain the results; they gain a deeper understanding of the underlying rationale and learn how to approach similar problems in the future.

Furthermore, in addition to providing guidance during the programming process, the system also incorporates a real-time formative assessment mechanism to evaluate students' level of comprehension.

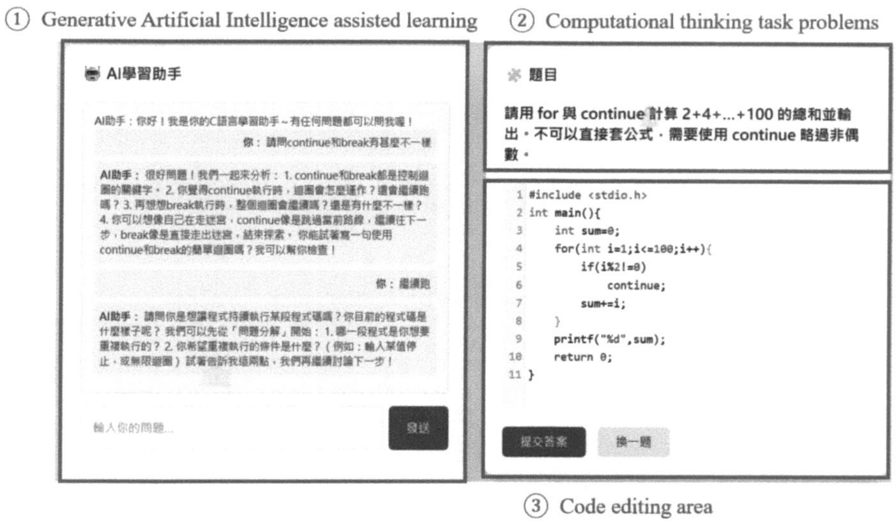

Fig. 2. The System Diagram of GAI Guidance based on CT.

3.4 Data Collection and Analysis

This study aims to investigate changes in students' learning outcomes, reflective thinking, and problem-solving skills resulting from the use of a learning platform that integrates GAI, computational thinking, and formative assessment. Additionally, descriptive statistical and reliability analyses were conducted to evaluate the data.

1. Pre-test and Post-test: A two-week assessment period was conducted to compare the differences in students' learning outcomes before and after the intervention of the learning platform integrating GAI, CT, and formative assessment. The pre-test was administered during the first week primarily to assess students' prior knowledge and baseline abilities prior to the instructional intervention. The post-test was administered after the students completed their experience with the learning platform to evaluate their post-intervention learning outcomes.
2. Questionnaire Survey Method: The questionnaire designed for this study is primarily divided into two sections: reflective thinking and problem-solving skills. To measure students' reflective thinking, this study adopted a scale adapted from Kember et al. (2000) [18], utilizing a 5-point Likert scale for scoring, where 1 indicates "strongly disagree" and 5 indicates "strongly agree." This scale consists of four dimensions comprising a total of 16 items to evaluate students' performance in reflective thinking. For the measurement of problem-solving skills, the questionnaire design was based on the scale developed by Hwang and Chen (2017) [17], consisting of five items that are also assessed using a 5-point Likert scale. Through the design of these two questionnaire sections, this study can further understand the learning conditions and effectiveness post-intervention from the dual perspectives of students' reflective thinking and problem-solving skills.
3. Data Analysis and Result Synthesis: This study compiled and analyzed the data obtained from the pre-test and post-test questionnaires, calculating the mean and standard deviation. Furthermore, relevant statistical methods were employed to examine the differences in students before and after the learning platform intervention to evaluate their learning outcomes.

4 Experimental Results and Discussion

This study aims to design and develop a learning platform that integrates generative artificial intelligence (GAI), computational thinking, and formative assessment. The objective is to enhance learning outcomes, reflective thinking, and problem-solving skills, while further exploring students' experiences and perceptions of the platform. A total of 27 valid samples were collected for this research. Regarding quantitative analysis, descriptive statistics were first employed to present the distribution of various indicators. The Shapiro-Wilk test was then used to verify the normality of the gain scores (post-test minus pre-test). For data meeting the normality assumption, a parametric paired-samples t-test was conducted to compare pre- and post-test differences. Furthermore, effect sizes were reported to evaluate the practical significance of the intervention's impact.

4.1 Analysis of Learning Outcomes

This study employed descriptive statistics to present the pre-test and post-test learning outcomes of the participants, evaluating the impact of the learning platform on learning outcomes. The results indicate that the participants had a pre-test mean score of 32.96 (SD = 17.28). Following the intervention, the post-test mean score increased significantly to 64.44 (SD = 23.91). Subsequently, the normality of the gain scores (post-test minus pre-test) was examined. The results of the Shapiro-Wilk test indicated no significant deviation from a normal distribution (W = 0.938, p = 0.106). Consequently, a paired-samples t-test was conducted to compare the differences between the pre-test and post-test (see Table 1). The analysis revealed that post-test scores were significantly higher than pre-test scores ($p < .001$), with an average improvement of 31.48 points. The calculated effect size, Cohen's d = 1.15, suggests that the intervention had a statistically significant and substantial practical impact.

Table 1. Results of Paired-Samples t-test for Learning Outcomes (N = 27).

	Mean	SD	*p*	Cohen's d
Pre-test	32.96	17.28	<0.001	1.15
Post-test	64.44	23.91		

Note. ***$p < .001$

4.2 Analysis of Problem-Solving Skills

This study utilized a problem-solving skills questionnaire to evaluate the overall problem-solving performance of users after engaging with the learning platform, which integrates GAI, computational thinking, and formative assessment. To ensure the reliability of the instrument, a reliability analysis was conducted. Table 2 presents the descriptive statistics and reliability results for problem-solving skills. This study was collected from a total of 27 participants. Regarding problem-solving skills, the results yielded a mean score of 4.22 (SD = 0.47), indicating that users generally demonstrated strong performance in this area, though some degree of individual variance remained. These findings suggest that the learning platform provides substantial support in fostering students' problem comprehension, strategic thinking, and procedural execution. In terms of reliability, the Cronbach's α for the problem-solving skill scale was 0.73, indicating acceptable internal consistency for the instrument.

Table 2. Descriptive Statistics and Reliability Analysis of Problem-Solving skills.

	Mean	SD	Cronbach's α
Problem-Solving Skills	4.22	0.47	0.73

4.3 Analysis of Reflective Thinking

Table 3 indicates that students were able to engage in fundamental self-examination and evaluation of the learning content, operational experiences, and learning processes.

Although there is room for improvement in the overall mean score, the low standard deviation reflects a high level of consistency in students' perceptions of the system. Regarding reliability, the Cronbach's α for the reflective thinking dimension is 0.72, indicating that the internal consistency of the research instrument has reached an acceptable level and possesses statistical reliability.

Table 3. Descriptive Statistics and Reliability Analysis of Reflective Thinking.

	Mean	SD	Cronbach's α
Reflective Thinking	3.61	0.40	0.72

5 Conclusion

This study investigates whether a learning platform integrating GAI, computational thinking, and formative assessment enhances students' learning outcomes, reflective thinking, and problem-solving skills. Through an analysis of 27 participants, the research employs pre- and post-tests, reflective thinking scales, problem-solving scales, and a reliability analysis for a comprehensive evaluation.

Regarding learning outcomes, quantitative analysis revealed that the pre-test mean was 32.96 (SD = 17.28), while the post-test mean rose to 64.44 (SD = 23.91). A significant difference was found between the pre- and post-test results, indicating that students' learning outcomes improved markedly after using the platform. This demonstrates the efficacy of the developed learning platform in promoting academic achievement. The results further suggest that through the instructional content and operational processes provided by the platform, students were able to progressively construct knowledge and improve their overall learning outcomes. In terms of reflective thinking and problem-solving skills, the results similarly demonstrated positive performance. The mean score for reflective thinking was 3.61 (SD = 0.40), suggesting that most students were able to reflect upon and examine their learning trajectories, content, and practical experiences to a certain extent. The mean score for problem-solving skills was 4.22 (SD = 0.47), indicating strong performance in areas such as problem comprehension, strategic thinking, and the solution process. In other words, the findings suggest that the learning platform not only enhances academic outcomes but also facilitates the development of reflective thinking and problem-solving skills, enabling students to move beyond passive knowledge reception toward active thinking, analysis, and application.

References

1. Cheng, Y.P., Huang, Y.M.: LUPDA: a comprehensive rubrics-based assessment model for STEAM education. Int. J. STEM Educ. **12**, 45 (2025)
2. Deng, R., Jiang, M., Yu, X., Lu, Y., Liu, S.: Does ChatGPT enhance student learning? A systematic review and meta-analysis of experimental studies. Comput. Educ. **227**, 105224 (2025)

3. Liu, J., Zhang, Y., Li, W., Wang, Q., Niu, P., Zhang, X.: Adaptive vs. planned metacognitive scaffolding for computational thinking: evidence from generative AI-supported programming in elementary education. Comput. Educ. **241**, 105473 (2025)
4. Lee, H.Y., Wu, T.T., Lin, C.J., Wang, W.S., Huang, Y.M.: Integrating computational thinking into scaffolding learning: an innovative approach to enhance science, technology, engineering, and mathematics hands-on learning. J. Educ. Comput. Res. **62**, 211–247 (2024)
5. Yang, T.C., Hsu, Y.C., Wu, J.Y.: The effectiveness of ChatGPT in assisting high school students in programming learning: evidence from a quasi-experimental research. Interact. Learn. Environ. **33**, 3726–3743 (2025)
6. Wing, J.M.: Computational thinking. Commun. ACM. **49**, 33–35 (2006)
7. Cheng, Y.P., Lai, C.F., Chen, Y.T., Wang, W.S., Huang, Y.M., Wu, T.T.: Enhancing student's computational thinking skills with student-generated questions strategy in a game-based learning platform. Comput. Educ. **200**, 104794 (2023)
8. Groothuijsen, S., Van den Beemt, A., Remmers, J.C., van Meeuwen, L.W.: AI chatbots in programming education: students' use in a scientific computing course and consequences for learning. Comput. Educ.: Artif. Intell. **7**, 100290 (2024)
9. Sun, D., Zheng, Y., Xu, J., Yang, Z.: When generative AI meets Socratic method: investigating programming learning dynamics through behaviours, interaction qualities and perceptions. J. Comput. Assist. Learn. **42**, e70210 (2026)
10. Chen, A., Wei, Y., Le, H., Zhang, Y.: Learning by teaching with ChatGPT: the effect of teachable ChatGPT agent on programming education. Br. J. Educ. Technol. **57**, 163–184 (2026)
11. Black, P., Wiliam, D.: Assessment and classroom learning. Assess. Educ. Princ. Policy Pract. **5**, 7–74 (1998)
12. Cheng, S.C., Cheng, Y.P., Huang, Y.M., Yang, Y.: Combining flipped learning and formative assessment to enhance the learning performance of students in programming. In: International Conference on Innovative Technologies and Learning, pp. 498–507. Springer, Cham (2021)
13. Huang, Y.M., Chen, P.H., Lee, H.Y., Sandnes, F.E., Wu, T.T.: ChatGPT-enhanced mobile instant messaging in online learning: effects on student outcomes and perceptions. Comput. Hum. Behav. **168**, 108659 (2025)
14. Lee, H.Y., Wu, T.T.: Enhancing blended learning discussions with a scaffolded knowledge integration–based ChatGPT mobile instant messaging system. Comput. Educ. **237**, 105375 (2025)
15. Chu, H.C., Hwang, G.J., Chang, C.Y.: An integrative review with word cloud analysis of computer-supported collaborative learning. J. Sci. Educ. Technol. **34**, 1213–1226 (2025)
16. Zhang, X., Chen, Y., Hu, L., Li, J., Hwang, G.J., Tu, Y.F.: Promoting conceptual changes of artificial intelligence with technology-facilitated situational exploration and alternative thinking: a dual-situated learning model-based two-tier test approach. Interact. Learn. Environ. **33**, 837–862 (2025)
17. Hwang, G.J., Chen, C.H.: Influences of an inquiry-based ubiquitous gaming design on students' learning achievements, motivation, behavioral patterns, and tendency towards critical thinking and problem solving. Br. J. Educ. Technol. **48**, 950–971 (2017)
18. Kember, D.: Development of a questionnaire to measure the level of reflective thinking. Assess. Eval. High. Educ. **25**, 381–395 (2000)

Design and Framework of Learning Systems

Classification of eLearning Infrastructure

Owen Chakauya(✉), Siphe Mhlana, and Ernest Ketcha Ngassam

School of Computing, University of South Africa, Johannesburg, South Africa
45072264@mylife.unisa.ac.za, mhlans2@unisa.ac.za

Abstract. The growth of digital education has underscored the need to understand and classify the infrastructure that supports eLearning systems. This study classifies eLearning infrastructure by distinguishing between its physical and non-physical components, which together form the foundation of effective online education. A systematic literature review was conducted across major databases (Scopus, Web of Science, IEEE Xplore, and Google Scholar), focusing on studies published between 2020 and 2025. From 300 identified records, 50 duplicates were removed, leaving 250 unique studies for title and abstract screening. Following full-text review and quality appraisal, 30 studies met the inclusion criteria and were included in the final synthesis.

Findings were grouped into four key infrastructure categories: (1) Hardware components, (2) Software components, (3) User Experience (UX) Design, and (4) Technical Support and Maintenance. These categories are organised into a two-domain framework: physical infrastructure (hardware) and non-physical infrastructure (software, UX, and support services). A separate discussion addresses components with hybrid characteristics, such as cloud storage. The proposed classification provides a structured basis for evaluating institutional digital readiness and investigating the relationship between infrastructure and the quality of eLearning at tertiary institutions. The findings show that non-physical infrastructure, particularly software components, was the most frequently cited category, appearing in 73% of included studies, while physical hardware components were identified in 43%, underscoring the central role of software platforms and user experience in enabling effective digital learning.

Keywords: classification eLearning infrastructure · eLearning hardware · eLearning software · eLearning infrastructure governance · eLearning infrastructure classification

1 Introduction

The rapid growth of eLearning has revolutionised the educational landscape, enabling institutions to offer flexible and accessible learning opportunities to a diverse range of learners. As eLearning platforms continue to expand, the underlying infrastructure that supports these systems has become increasingly complex, encompassing both physical and non-physical components. According to Sharma [1], a well-structured eLearning infrastructure is crucial for ensuring the reliability, accessibility, and overall success of online education.

C.-J. Lin et al. (Eds.): ICITL 2026, LNCS 16841, pp. 161–174, 2027.
https://doi.org/10.1007/978-3-032-32112-1_17

Physical infrastructure in eLearning refers to the tangible components that form the backbone of online education systems, including hardware such as servers, computers, and networking equipment. These elements are vital for hosting and delivering educational content, enabling communication between learners and instructors, and supporting the technical needs of the platform [3]. On the other hand, non-physical infrastructure encompasses the intangible aspects of eLearning, such as software applications, content management systems, and support services. These components are equally important, as they facilitate the creation, delivery, and maintenance of educational content and ensure a positive user experience [15].

Despite the importance of both physical and non-physical infrastructure in eLearning, there is often a lack of clarity and organisation in how these components are classified and managed. This can lead to inefficiencies, technical challenges, and gaps in support provided to learners and educators. As noted by Satria [4], the absence of a clear classification framework can hinder the ability to effectively allocate resources, identify areas for improvement, and ensure the overall effectiveness of eLearning systems. Therefore, there is a pressing need to develop a comprehensive classification of eLearning infrastructure that clearly delineates between physical and non-physical components.

This study addresses this gap by developing a comprehensive, two-domain classification of eLearning infrastructure. The framework distinguishes physical infrastructure (hardware-based, tangible components) from non-physical infrastructure (software, user experience, and support services). By providing a structured framework for organising these elements, the research aims to enhance the management, scalability, and effectiveness of eLearning systems, ultimately contributing to improved educational outcomes and a more resilient online learning environment.

2 Methodology

This study adopted the PRISMA (Preferred Reporting Items for Systematic Reviews and Meta-Analyses) framework to systematically identify, screen, and analyse literature related to eLearning infrastructure. The objective was to classify the physical and non-physical components that constitute the technological foundations of digital learning environments. PRISMA was selected to ensure transparency, reproducibility, and methodological rigour throughout the review process.

Content analysis was employed as the primary analytical method, enabling systematic, rule-based coding of the included studies and the generation of quantifiable frequency data across predefined infrastructure categories.

Figure 1 summarises the identification, screening, and inclusion stages, ensuring transparency of the review process.

2.1 Search Strategy

The search strategy involved systematically constructing search terms, identifying relevant academic databases, and applying predefined inclusion and exclusion criteria. Search terms were developed to align with the study aim to identify and classify the

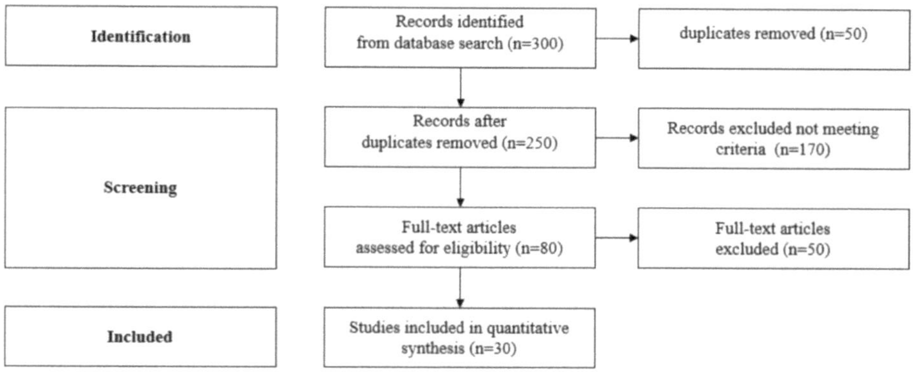

Fig. 1. PRISMA

components of eLearning infrastructure in higher education. A combination of keywords and Boolean operators (AND, OR) was used to generate comprehensive search phrases. The main search strings included:

- ("eLearning infrastructure" OR "digital learning infrastructure") AND ("higher education" OR "tertiary education")
- ("learning management system" OR "LMS") AND ("hardware" OR "software" OR "infrastructure")
- ("online learning technologies" OR "eLearning systems") AND ("physical infrastructure" OR "non-physical infrastructure")
- "ICT infrastructure" AND ("eLearning" OR "digital education") AND ("classification" OR "framework")

These searches were executed in Scopus, Web of Science, IEEE Xplore, and SpringerLink. Google Scholar was used as a supplementary source to capture additional peer-reviewed studies.

2.2 Inclusion and Exclusion Criteria

Clear eligibility criteria ensured that only relevant and methodologically sound studies were included.

Inclusion Criteria

- Peer-reviewed journal articles or conference papers
- Published between 2020 and 2025
- Written in English
- Focused on eLearning systems, infrastructure, digital education technologies, or institutional eLearning readiness
- Addressed any infrastructural component (hardware, software, UX, technical support)

Exclusion Criteria

- Non-peer-reviewed sources (blogs, reports, theses, grey literature)
- Studies lacking infrastructure relevance
- Papers without an accessible full text
- Studies focused solely on instructional design without a technological context

2.3 Selection Process

The database searches produced 300 records in total. Following automated and manual deduplication, 50 duplicate records were removed, yielding 250 unique studies for preliminary screening. Titles and abstracts of these 250 records were independently assessed for relevance to the research aim by two reviewers, with disagreements resolved by discussion. This screening stage resulted in the exclusion of 170 articles that did not meet the inclusion criteria, leaving 80 studies for full-text evaluation.

Full-text review was conducted to determine methodological suitability and substantive alignment with the focus on eLearning infrastructure. A quality appraisal, guided by principles adapted from the Critical Appraisal Skills Programme (CASP), was applied to each article. Each study was assessed for: (a) clarity of research aims, (b) appropriateness of research design, (c) transparency of analysis, and (d) relevance and specificity to eLearning infrastructure components. Studies that did not meet acceptable quality thresholds were excluded. During this stage, 50 articles were excluded due to insufficient infrastructure-specific detail, lack of methodological transparency, or marginal relevance. Ultimately, 30 studies satisfied all inclusion, exclusion, and quality assessment requirements and were included in the final synthesis.

2.4 Content Analysis

Content analysis was selected as the analytical method for this study because it enables the systematic, replicable, and quantifiable examination of textual data, making it well suited to classifying infrastructure components reported across a heterogeneous body of literature [16]. Unlike purely interpretive approaches, content analysis requires an a priori coding scheme, inter-coder reliability testing, and frequency enumeration, all of which align with the quantitative orientation of the PRISMA-guided review and directly address concerns about analytical transparency and reproducibility.

The procedure followed four sequential steps. First, a coding scheme was developed deductively from the study's conceptual framework, specifying four mutually exclusive and exhaustive categories: (1) hardware components, (2) software components, (3) user experience (UX) design, and (4) technical support and maintenance. Each category was operationalised with explicit inclusion criteria and exemplar indicators to guide consistent coding. Second, two independent coders applied the coding scheme to all 30 included studies, identifying and recording every passage that described or discussed an eLearning infrastructure component.

Third, inter-coder reliability was assessed using Cohen's kappa (κ) calculated across all coded segments. A kappa of $\kappa = 0.81$ was achieved, indicating strong agreement and confirming the reproducibility of the coding scheme [6]. Discrepancies were resolved through discussion and consensus between the two coders, with a third reviewer available for arbitration where agreement could not be reached. Fourth, coded segments were aggregated by category and study to produce frequency counts, enabling quantitative comparison of category salience across the full sample. These counts formed the basis of the proportional analysis reported in Sect. 5.

Table 1. Summary of included studies

Authors	Year	Country /Region	Focus	Extracted (Physical & Non-Physical)
Anastasiades et al. [11]	2023	Greece	Micro eLearning seminars for teachers	LMS; multimedia software
Dey et al. [12]	2021	Bangladesh	Early eLearning adoption experiences	Mobile devices; communication tools
Fırat [13]	2023	Turkey	Integrating AI applications into LMS	LMS software; server capacity
García-Peñalvo [14]	2021	Spain	Institutional eLearning transformation	Servers; LMS; governance
Goretti et al. [15]	2024	EU	digital projects	Support systems; security tools
Habes et al. [16]	2022	Jordan	Social media videos and eLearning	Mobile learning; multimedia tools
Al Mulhem [17]	2022	India	Delone and Mclean information system success model in eLearning	LMS; user devices
Kurniawan & Dzikri [18]	2024	Indonesia	Microservices architecture for eLearning	Software architecture; APIs
Ličen et al. [19]	2023	Slovenia	eLearning evaluation toolkit	LMS; UX; support systems
Madleňák et al. [20]	2021	EU	Hybrid eLearning implementation	LMS; communication systems
Makena & Mpahla [21]	2022	South Africa	eLearning culture in rural institutions	Connectivity; user devices
Mercy & Fatuma [2]	2022	Tanzania	Network performance for multimedia eLearning	Networking equipment; servers
Mudzingiri et al. [3]	2022	Zimbabwe	Student perceptions of COVID-19 eLearning	Mobile devices; connectivity

(continued)

Table 1. (*continued*)

Authors	Year	Country /Region	Focus	Extracted (Physical & Non-Physical)
Müller et al. [22]	2021	Singapore	Educator experiences during emergency eLearning	UX; LMS; communication tools
Nikou & Maslov [23]	2023	Finland	eLearning outcomes	Video conferencing; UX
Ng et al. [24]	2021	Australia	Full eLearning transition in physical therapy	Video conferencing; LMS
O'Connor et al. [25]	2023	Ireland	Digital learning design in education	UX design; software systems
Pokhrel & Acharya [26]	2024	Nepal	Behavioural intention to use eLearning	LMS; connectivity
Prasetyo et al. [27]	2021	Philippines	Acceptance of medical eLearning platforms	Software; communication tools
Roman & Plopeanu [28]	2021	Romania	Effectiveness of emergency eLearning	LMS; communication tools
Sangwa et al. [29]	2024	Rwanda	eLearning for community health workers	Mobile devices; LMS
Satria [4]	2022	Indonesia	Barriers to effective eLearning	Hardware; software; support
Sharma [1]	2021	India	Impact of the rise of eLearning	Hardware; LMS
Solangi et al. [30]	2022	Saudi Arabia	Determinants of eLearning adoption	Software platforms; LMS
Swee Cheong & Hashim [5]	2023	Malaysia	Implementing eLearning as edutainment	Multimedia software; UX
Thua et al. [6]	2024	Kenya	Gender factors in eLearning participation	LMS; mobile devices
Ahmad et al. [7]	2023	Malaysia	eLearning Acceptance and Adoption	Hardware; LMS
Alebeisat et al. [8]	2022	Jordan	Determinants of eLearning adoption	Software platforms; LMS
Alhaider & Nisa [9]	2023	Saudi Arabia	Challenges of eLearning	Multimedia software; UX

(*continued*)

Table 1. *(continued)*

Authors	Year	Country /Region	Focus	Extracted (Physical & Non-Physical)
Al-Shamali et al. [10]	2022	Kuwaiti	eLearning in Changes	LMS; mobile devices

3 eLearning Physical and Non-physical Infrastructure

Physical infrastructure refers to all tangible, hardware-based elements required for eLearning systems, whilst non-physical infrastructure refers to intangible, software-based, and virtual elements required for eLearning [5]. Physical infrastructure refers to the material, device-based components required to deliver and sustain digital learning environments, characterised by measurability, spatial presence, and direct operational dependencies [7]. Non-physical infrastructure encompasses the digital, experiential, and service-oriented components that shape how users interact with eLearning systems, including software platforms, UX design, accessibility features, system administration, and technical support [20].

3.1 Physical Infrastructure

Physical eLearning infrastructure comprises all the tangible and technology-based resources necessary to deliver and support online education [18]. These components are essential for creating, managing, and distributing educational content, as well as facilitating communication between educators and learners. Satria [26] emphasises that a robust physical infrastructure is essential for ensuring the reliability, accessibility, and scalability of eLearning environments.

Hardware Components

Servers

Servers are critical hardware components in eLearning infrastructure, responsible for storing, processing, and managing educational content and user data [22]. They act as the backbone of online education platforms, hosting Learning Management Systems (LMS) and enabling access to digital resources. García-Peñalvo [14] states that servers play a pivotal role in ensuring the scalability and reliability of eLearning systems, as they must handle numerous simultaneous requests from students and educators.

Networking equipment

Networking equipment is a vital component of eLearning infrastructure, enabling the connection between users and online educational resources [24]. The equipment includes routers, switches, and modems, which work together to facilitate the transmission of data across the internet, ensuring that students and educators can access eLearning platforms without interruptions. Furthermore, Makena and Mpahla [21] highlight that reliable networking equipment is essential for maintaining stable internet connections, particularly in environments where multiple users are accessing bandwidth-intensive applications such as video conferencing and streaming.

3.2 Non-physical Infrastructures

Non-physical eLearning infrastructure encompasses the intangible elements that support and enhance online education, focusing on aspects beyond hardware and physical devices [25]. These components are essential for creating effective, engaging, and well-managed eLearning environments.

Software Components

Learning Management Systems (LMS)

Learning Management Systems (LMS) are central to the eLearning experience, serving as the primary platform for delivering, managing, and tracking educational content and activities [20]. LMS platforms allow educators to create, organise, and distribute course materials, assignments, and assessments, while also providing tools for communication and collaboration. According to Anastasiades et al. [11], LMS platforms are essential for streamlining the administrative aspects of eLearning, as they enable the efficient management of large volumes of content and user data.

Video conferencing tools

Video conferencing tools are crucial components of eLearning infrastructure, enabling real-time communication and interaction between instructors and students. These tools, such as Zoom, Microsoft Teams, and Google Meet, allow for virtual classes, meetings, and collaborative sessions, making it possible to replicate the classroom experience in an online environment [9]. According to Al-Shamali et al. [10], video conferencing is essential for maintaining a sense of connection and engagement in eLearning, as it allows for face-to-face interaction, immediate feedback, and active participation.

User Experience (UX) Design

Interface Design

Interface design is a crucial aspect of User Experience (UX) design in eLearning environments, focusing on the visual and functional elements that users interact with on digital platforms [19]. This includes designing layouts, navigation menus, buttons, and other interactive elements to ensure that they are intuitive and user-friendly. According to Müller et al. [8], a well-designed interface facilitates smooth and efficient user interactions, helping learners access and utilise eLearning resources with ease.

Accessibility features

Accessibility features in UX design are designed to ensure that eLearning platforms are usable by individuals with varying abilities and disabilities [22]. These features include tools and design elements that enhance the accessibility of content and interactions, making it easier for users with visual, auditory, motor, or cognitive impairments to engage with the platform. According to Nikou and Maslov [23], incorporating accessibility features is not only a legal and ethical requirement but also essential for creating an inclusive learning environment that accommodates all users.

Technical Support and Maintenance

System Administration

System administration refers to the management and maintenance of the technological infrastructure that supports online learning platforms [21]. This includes configuring and managing servers, databases, and other technical components to ensure the smooth operation and reliability of eLearning systems. According to Al Mulhem [17], effective system administration is crucial for maintaining system performance, security, and availability, which directly impacts the quality of the learning experience.

Technical Support

Technical support provides assistance to users who encounter technical issues or need help with using the online learning platform [12]. This support includes resolving problems related to system access, software functionality, and connectivity issues. According to Sharma [28], effective technical support is essential for ensuring that users can successfully navigate and use the eLearning platform, which contributes to a positive learning experience and minimises disruptions.

4 Conceptual Interpretations of the Framework

While the classification identifies four core categories, their value lies not only in their descriptive organisation but also in the conceptual relationships between them. Physical infrastructure acts as the foundational layer that enables the operation of software systems and digital services. Software platforms, in turn, serve as the functional interface between physical systems and the activities that take place in digital environments.

5 Analysis and Findings

The systematic review identified four core categories that define eLearning infrastructure: hardware components, software components, UX design, and technical support and maintenance. These categories are organised into two overarching domains physical (hardware) and non-physical (software, UX, support). To ensure transparency and traceability, all 30 included studies were classified according to these categories, as presented in Table 1. Table 2 provides a quantitative summary of the distribution of studies across each infrastructure category.

Table 2. Distribution of included studies by infrastructure category.

Infrastructure Category	Domain	Studies (n = 30)	Percentage	Key Examples
Hardware components	Physical	13	43%	Servers, networking, mobile devices, storage
Software components	Non-Physical	22	73%	LMS, video conferencing, security software
User Experience (UX)	Non-Physical	14	47%	Interface design, accessibility, usability testing
Technical Support & Maintenance	Non-Physical	12	40%	System admin, helpdesk, maintenance processes
Both Physical & Non-Physical	Both	7	23%	Integrated infrastructure studies

5.1 Comparison with Existing Frameworks

Existing studies have examined aspects of eLearning infrastructure, but few have offered a holistic and integrative classification. For example, Mercy and Fatuma [2] focuses on institutional digital transformation frameworks but does not explicitly distinguish between hardware and software infrastructures. Sharma [1] identifies barriers to eLearning implementation but presents them as challenges rather than as structural components. Similarly, Fırat [13] discuss hybrid learning infrastructures but frame them within specific case studies rather than proposing transferable categories.

5.2 Assessment of Studies by Year

The distribution of included studies by publication year reflects temporal patterns in eLearning infrastructure research. Studies from 2021 account for 7 out of 30 (23%), reflecting initial investigations into emergency eLearning adoption during the COVID-19 pandemic. Studies from 2022 total 8 (27%), indicating sustained interest in technology acceptance, network performance, and barriers to eLearning as institutions adapted to post-pandemic contexts. Research from 2023 comprises 7 studies (23%), focusing on innovations such as UX design, and micro-eLearning implementations. Studies from 2024 account for 4 (13%), emphasising behavioural intentions and methodological approaches in eLearning adoption; the remaining 4 studies (13%) were published in early 2025 or span multiple years

5.3 Assessment of Extracted Physical and Non-physical Infrastructure

The analysis from Table 2, physical components including servers, networking equipment, mobile devices, and on-premises hardware were highlighted in 13 out of 30 studies

(43%). Non-physical infrastructure, including LMS, software platforms, UX/interface design, communication tools, and support systems, appeared in 22 out of 30 studies (73%), confirming their central role in managing content, facilitating interaction, and enhancing learner engagement. UX components specifically appeared in 14 studies (47%), while technical support and maintenance were addressed in 12 studies (40%). Seven studies (23%) addressed both physical and non-physical components simultaneously, reflecting the recognised interdependence of tangible and intangible resources.

The analysis reveals that while physical infrastructure ensures accessibility and operational functionality, non-physical infrastructure drives usability and adoption. Notably, UX design and technical support, though appearing in a majority of studies, received comparatively less systematic treatment than LMS and hardware components, indicating an area warranting greater research attention.

5.4 Assessment by Country/Region

Table 3 presents the regional distribution of included studies.

Table 3. Regional distribution of included studies (n = 30).

Region	Percentage	Countries Represented
Asia	43.3%	Malaysia, Jordan, Saudi Arabia, Kuwait, Turkey, India, Indonesia, Singapore, Finland, Nepal, Philippines
Europe	20.0%	Greece, EU (multiple), Slovenia, Romania, Ireland
Africa	16.7%	South Africa, Tanzania, Zimbabwe, Rwanda, Kenya
Oceania	3.3%	Australia
North America	0.0%	–
South America	0.0%	–
Not specified / Multi-region	16.7%	EU-wide studies, Bangladesh, Spain

Asia accounts for the largest share, with 13 of 30 publications (43.3%), indicating a strong research emphasis on eLearning infrastructure in Asian higher education systems. Europe represents (20%) of studies, reflecting moderate engagement centred on system optimisation and alignment with EU digital strategies. African countries contribute (16.7%) of studies, highlighting growing research interest in addressing infrastructural constraints in resource-limited contexts. Oceania is represented by one study (3.3%), and no studies from North or South America met the inclusion criteria, revealing a significant geographical gap.

This imbalance warrants substantive interpretation. The predominance of research from developing countries representing 22 of 30 studies (73%) may reflect the acute visibility of infrastructure challenges in regions where connectivity, hardware availability, and digital readiness remain significant obstacles to eLearning adoption. In contrast, the relatively small contribution from developed countries may indicate a research horizon shift: in contexts where foundational infrastructure is more mature and widely distributed, scholarly attention may have migrated toward pedagogical innovation, learning analytics, and instructional design rather than infrastructure classification. This saturation hypothesis wherein developed-country infrastructure reaches a level of sufficiency that reduces its salience as a research object is consistent with broader trends in educational technology literature [27]. Future research should actively seek geographically representative samples to enable robust cross-regional comparisons.

6 Discussion

The findings of this review demonstrate that eLearning infrastructure operates as an interconnected system in which physical and non-physical components collectively shape the effectiveness of digital learning environments. Physical infrastructure such as devices, servers, and connectivity provides the foundational layer that enables online learning, while non-physical elements, including software platforms, user experience design, and technical support, determine the quality, accessibility, and usability of these systems. The findings of this study are consistent with previous studies that examined the role of infrastructure in eLearning adoption. Similar to Miao and Ma [29], this study highlights that while technological and software related features are often prioritised, human-centred dimensions such as usability and accessibility are critical for learner engagement and system effectiveness.

Nyakuleha and Simengwa [30] also reported that robust non-physical infrastructure significantly enhances the learning experience, corroborating the results observed in this study. Comparing the proposed framework with existing models the ISO/IEC standards provide valuable guidance on quality; they do not offer a comprehensive classification of eLearning infrastructure. The present framework advances the literature by integrating technological, experiential, and operational dimensions into a unified structure that reflects the complexity of institutional digital ecosystems. This classification provides a foundation for evaluating infrastructure readiness, identifying gaps, and guiding strategic decision-making.

7 Limitations

This study is subject to limitations that should be considered when interpreting the findings. First, the review focused exclusively on peer-reviewed literature published between 2020 and 2025, which may have excluded relevant grey literature, institutional reports, or earlier foundational studies that could provide additional insights into eLearning infrastructure.

8 Conclusion

The classification of eLearning infrastructure by synthesising recent literature and distinguishing between the physical and non-physical components that underpin effective digital learning environments. The framework illustrates how hardware, software, user experience elements, and technical support functions collectively shape institutional capacity for delivering high-quality eLearning. By clarifying the interdependencies among these components, the study contributes a structured foundation for evaluating and improving digital education systems in higher education settings. The findings emphasise that eLearning infrastructure should not be viewed solely as a technological construct, but rather as an integrated ecosystem in which both tangible and intangible components play essential roles.

Disclosure of Interests. The authors have no competing interests to declare that are relevant to the content of this article.

References

1. Sharma, M.E.: Impact of Covid-19 on education: rise of e-learning. Int. J. Soc. Relevan. Concern. **9**(2) (2021)
2. Mercy, M., Fatuma, S.: Performance evaluation of udsm network to deliver multimedia elearning contents: case of coict. Tanzania J. Eng. Technol. **41**(4), 205–218 (2022)
3. Mudzingiri, A., Abel, S., Mafugu, T.: Student perceptions of Covid-19 induced e-learning in state universities in Zimbabwe. Int. J. Learning Teaching Educational Res. **21**(10), 296–308 (2022)
4. Satria, D.: What made implementing effective Elearning hard?: a systematic literature review. JITK (Jurnal Ilmu Pengetahuan dan Teknologi Komputer). **7**(2), 75–80 (2022)
5. Cheong, D.C., Hashim, Y.: Implementing eLearning as edutainment in Malaysian higher education: challenges and solution for educators. Malaysian J. Soc. Sci. Human. (MJSSH). **8**(7), e002421 (2023)
6. Thua, J.N., Okemwa, P., Mwatha, R., Malenya, F.: The role of gender-based factors on the levels of student participation in eLearning in select universities in Nairobi City county, Kenya. Eastern African J. Human. Soc. Sci. **3**(2), 94–101 (2024)
7. Ahmad, S., Mohd Noor, A.S., Alwan, A.A., Gulzar, Y., Khan, W.Z., Reegu, F.A.: eLearning acceptance and adoption challenges in higher education. Sustainability. **15**(7), 6190 (2023)
8. Alebeisat, F., Altarawneh, H., Alhalhouli, Z.T., Qatawneh, A., Almahasne, M.: The impact of human and computer interaction on eLearning quality. Int. J. Interact. Mobile Technol. **16**(4) (2022)
9. Alhaider, S.M., Sarwat un N.: Advantages and challenges of elearning before and after the COVID-19 pandemic: faculty and student perceptions in Saudi education. Theory and practice in language. Studies. **13**(4), 891–900 (2023)
10. Al-Shamali, S., Al-Shamali, A., Alsaber, A., Al-Kandari, A., AlMutairi, S., Alaya, A.: Impact of organizational culture on academics' readiness and behavioral intention to implement eLearning changes in Kuwaiti universities during COVID-19. Sustainability. **14**(23), 15824 (2022)
11. Anastasiades, P., Kotsidis, K., Synnefakis, C., Spanoudaki, A.: Micro eLearning open seminars on "school based distance education" to support K12 teachers during the COVID-19 pandemic of 2020. SCIREA Journal of Education. **8**(5), 219–234 (2023)

12. Dey, S., Khan, M.G., Hakim, M.M.: Relevance to the Introduction of eLearning on Higher Education of Bangladesh: An Experience from the Educational Cost of COVID-19.
13. Fırat, M.: Integrating AI applications into learning management systems to enhance e-learning. Instruct. Technol. Lifelong Learn. **4**(1), 1–4 (2023)
14. García-Peñalvo, F.J.: Avoiding the dark side of digital transformation in teaching. An institutional reference framework for eLearning in higher education. Sustainability. **13**(4), 2023 (2021)
15. de Castro, M.G., García-Peñalvo, F.J.: A Proposed Methodology for Effective Erasmus+ Projects in the Realm of eLearning. Proceedings http://ceur-ws.org. ISSN. 2023;1613:0073.
16. Habes, M., Elareshi, M., Youssef, E., Ali, S., Qudah, M.: Social impact of videos at new media platforms on the eLearning acceptance during the Covid-19. Inf. Sci. Lett. **11**(3), 913–923 (2022)
17. Al Mulhem, A.: Investigating the effects of quality factors and organizational factors on university students' satisfaction of e-learning system quality. Cogent Education. **7**(1), 1787004 (2020)
18. Kurniawan DE, Dzikri A. Development of a prototype for microservices architecture and API gateway integration in an eLearning platform. In ICAE 2023: Proceedings of the 6th International Conference on Applied Engineering, 7 November 2023, Batam, Riau islands, Indonesia 2024 Jan 19 (p. 190). European Alliance for Innovation.
19. Ličen, S., Cassar, M., Filomeno, L., Yeratziotis, A., Prosen, M.: Development and validation of an evaluation toolkit to appraise eLearning courses in higher education: a pilot study. Sustainability. **15**(8), 6361 (2023)
20. Madleňák, R., D'Alessandro, S.P., Marengo, A., Pange, J., Neszmélyi, G.I.: Building on strategic eLearning initiatives of hybrid graduate education a case study approach: MHEI-ME Erasmus+ project. Sustainability. **13**(14), 7675 (2021)
21. Makena, B., Mpahla, N.: Instilling eLearning culture towards recipients of a rurally disadvantaged institution of higher learning. International journal of research in Business & Social. Science. **11**(7) (2022)
22. Müller, A.M., Goh, C., Lim, L.Z., Gao, X.: Covid-19 emergency elearning and beyond: experiences and perspectives of university educators. Educ. Sci. **11**(1), 19 (2021)
23. Nikou, S., Maslov, I.: Finnish university students' satisfaction with e-learning outcomes during the COVID-19 pandemic. Int. J. Educ. Manag. **37**(1), 1–21 (2023)
24. Ng, L. et al.: eLearning in physical therapy: lessons learned from transitioning a professional education program to full eLearning during the COVID-19 pandemic. Physical Therapy. **101**(4), pzab082 (2021)
25. O'Connor, S. et al.: Designing and delivering digital learning (e-Learning) interventions in nursing and midwifery education: a systematic review of theories. Nurse Educ. Pract. **69**, 103635 (2023)
26. Pokhrel, S., Acharya, P.: Factors influencing university students' behavioral intention and use of eLearning in Kathmandu Valley. J Adv Educ Philos. **8**(5), 364–376 (2024)
27. Prasetyo, Y.T. et al.: Determining factors affecting the acceptance of medical education elearning platforms during the covid-19 pandemic in the Philippines: Utaut2 approach. Healthcare. **9**(7), 780 (2021) MDPI
28. Roman, M., Plopeanu, A.P.: The effectiveness of the emergency eLearning during COVID-19 pandemic. The case of higher education in economics in Romania. International review of economics. Education. **37**, 100218 (2021)
29. Sangwa, Y. et al.: Using eLearning to improve and retain the knowledge of community health workers in maternal and neonatal health in Rwanda: a cohort study. Public Health Challenges. **3**(2), e174 (2024)
30. Solangi, Z.A., Solangi, Y.A., Sindhi, A.H.: An empirical analysis of determinants of eLearning adoption. In: Education Sector of Royal Commission Jubail Sa 0/25

Raising NGOs' Cybersecurity Awareness via Micro-learning and Learning Assessment Model

Daniela Borissova(✉), Daniela Dimitrova, and Angel Angelov

Institute of Information and Communication Technologies at the Bulgarian Academy of Sciences, 1113 Sofia, Bulgaria
{Daniela.borissova,daniela.dimitrova, angel.v-angelov}@iict.bas.bg

Abstract. The continually increasing number of cyber threats is a serious challenge that requires strengthening defenses against such malicious operations. The increase in cyberattacks underscores the need for more reliable security measures across for-profit organizations and non-profit and non-government organizations, with a focus on strengthening cybersecurity. Cybersecurity in non-profits and non-government organizations is often neglected due to limited resources. In our increasingly digitalized society, this is a critical factor that deserves special attention, since many non-profit organizations still operate without a clear plan, often due to limited budget and staff. All this underscores the importance of timely learning to raise awareness in cybersecurity. The article is focused on developing a micro-learning program for non-government organizations in compliance with current regulatory requirements. In addition to this program, a mathematical model is proposed for assessing the acquired knowledge and skills. With appropriate visualization, it is easy to identify which questions received incorrect answers and which participants gave incorrect answers. This information can be used to improve participants' knowledge of the relevant modules. The proposed program and assessment model have been tested in a small non-profit organization, and the results clearly demonstrate their practical applicability.

Keywords: Cybersecurity · Micro-learning · Awareness · Assessment Model

1 Introduction

Given the intensification and increasing complexity of cyber threats, it is important to maintain a high level of cybersecurity by implementing appropriate risk management measures. Cyber threats pose a serious challenge to both organizations and individuals, and therefore, there is a need to strengthen protection against such malicious operations. In this rapidly changing environment, the timely implementation of cybersecurity awareness learning is crucial. This is also evident from the analysis of cybersecurity awareness frameworks and training models [1]. Threat awareness is the driver that motivates many researchers to improve organizational cybersecurity [2–4]. However, approximately 95%

C.-J. Lin et al. (Eds.): ICITL 2026, LNCS 16841, pp. 175–185, 2027.
https://doi.org/10.1007/978-3-032-32112-1_18

of successful cyberattacks are attributed to human error, underscoring ongoing challenges from user negligence, behavioral vulnerabilities, and lack of awareness [5, 6]. Moreover, the need for personalized cybersecurity training has been proven [7]. Among the most common threats are phishing, identity theft, and ransomware [8].

Micro-learning has become popular not only in the education sector [9] but also in the corporate sector in recent years [10]. Unlike traditional long-form learning, micro-learning presents information in small, manageable segments [11], making it easier to absorb and remember [12]. In the rapidly evolving digital age, a shift toward modularization is evident across industries, with smaller, more efficient components preferred over overarching concepts and macrostructures. This improves learning efficiency by preventing a module from being dropped due to content inconsistencies. Therefore, microlearning helps knowledge transformation be less arbitrary and more practical [13]. A comprehensive analysis of micro-learning design and micro-course structuring is presented in [14]. It is also worth noting that working with reduced content, specifically designed for easy sharing and/or addition, implicitly means that these units, loosely connected to each other, can be easily integrated or reused across different contexts and devices [15].

In the context of security awareness learning, micro-learning through quick, interactive modules focuses on key cybersecurity topics, such as using strong passwords, not sharing or reusing passwords, and verifying the legitimacy of sources before clicking links [16, 17]. This approach not only improves knowledge retention but also keeps employees more engaged and responsive to changing cyber threats. In addition, implementing a structured learning approach fosters ethical awareness in digital environments, thereby improving ethical decision-making in cybersecurity [18]. Cybersecurity learning should provide access to real-world scenarios and case studies. To achieve this, artificial intelligence, virtual reality, and augmented reality technologies have been identified as harbingers of a new era in cybersecurity learning [19]. Generative AI should also be included in this group of technologies supporting personalized cybersecurity learning [20]. Last but not least, it is important to note the utility of cyber ranges as a virtual environment for cybersecurity learning also involve testing [21]. Therefore, micro-learning appears suitable for non-profit organizations because it is cost-effective, as various tools can be developed for free or at an affordable price. On the other hand, this type of learning is also time-efficient, as it fits easily into busy schedules and focuses on real-world, high-impact cybersecurity problems, such as phishing, ransomware, and remote access.

According to the NIS 2 Directive, it is necessary to encourage the regular provision of learning to employees to acquire sufficient knowledge and skills to enable them to identify risks [22]. It is focus on risk management measures, cyber hygiene and training, incident handling and reporting, and human factor mitigation. Another useful document to be considered in micro-learning on cybersecurity in the standard ISO 27001 [23]. It provides an information security framework that helps organizations identify and effectively manage information security risks.

Cybersecurity is the weakest area of technology for non-profits. Weak security isn't just an internal risk, as it can expose sensitive data, disrupt services, and erode trust. Unfortunately, many nonprofits lack the budget or expertise to strengthen their defenses against such digital attacks. Even with limited resources, nonprofits can implement strong defenses using an effective micro-learning program. By recognizing these challenges, nonprofits can take practical, high-impact steps to strengthen cybersecurity by focusing on what matters most: raising awareness across the entire team. In doing so, they will be better able to protect information from cyberattacks and maintain donor trust.

Although micro-learning is an effective way to increase security awareness, its implementation is associated with several challenges, including low employee engagement, content relevance, and the measurement of effectiveness. The authors show that learners find learning through small units effective, with interactivity significantly influencing engagement, and engagement, in turn, influencing satisfaction [24]. By adopting micro-learning as a self-paced learning tool, learners could improve their skills and expand their knowledge. Micro-learning has been shown to be effective in improving students' conceptual understanding and knowledge retention [25].

Given the urgent need to enhance cybersecurity awareness and the advantages of micro-learning, this article presents a micro-learning program and a mathematical model to assess learning outcomes for non-governmental organizations.

The rest of the article is organized as follows: Sect. 2 provides information about the proposed cybersecurity micro-learning program modules for NGOs, aligned with NIS2 and ISO/IEC 27001; Sect. 3 describes the proposed micro-learning test scoring model; Sect. 4 contains the experimental validation result analysis and discussion, and conclusions are given in Sect. 5.

2 Cybersecurity Micro-learning for NGOs with a Field of Activity in Education and Environment

Several large international and regional non-governmental organizations specialize in integrating environmental protection with education, with a focus on sustainability, biodiversity, and climate action. The Foundation for Environmental Education is one of the largest environmental education organizations in the world, with more than 110 member organizations across 85 countries. Education for sustainable development is UNESCO's response to the urgent challenges facing our planet. Among the rest is the World Wildlife Fund focuses on conservation and works extensively in environmental education. Given the variety of NGOs with activities in education and the environment, we focus on this type of NGO. These organizations often face limited IT budgets, high staff/volunteer turnover, the need to work with remote or hybrid teams, and non-technical users handling sensitive data. Therefore, implementing a micro-learning approach in NGOs would significantly increase resilience against cyberattacks, enabling employees to act as a "human firewall." Because of this, it is important for NGOs to also conduct cybersecurity learning. To support the micro-learning approach, well-designed sequential learning modules are required. In this regard, when designing the micro-learning program, it is necessary to take into account 1) NIS2 requirements for cybersecurity risk management, awareness, and incident response, 2) ISO/IEC 27001:2022 Annex A controls, especially human and organizational controls, and 3) evidence of learning and awareness during audits. Considering all of this, we developed the following micro-learning program for NGOs, aligned with NIS2 and ISO/IEC 27001, including a responsible person for each module, as shown in Table 1.

Table 1. Micro-learning program, aligned with NIS2 and ISO/IEC 27001.

Mo-dules	Description of learning topic	NIS2 Reference	ISO/IEC 27001 Control	Responsible Person	Target Group
1	Cybersecurity & Risk Awareness	Art. 20, Art. 21	A.5.4, A.6.3	Executive Director / IT Lead	All staff & volunteers
2	Policies, Roles & Acceptable Use	Art. 21(2)(a)	A.5.1, A.5.2	Compliance / HR	All staff
3	Phishing & Social Engineering	Art. 21(2)(b)	A.6.8, A.5.7	IT / Security Officer	All users
4	Access Control, Passwords & MFA	Art. 21(2)(d)	A.5.15, A.5.17	IT Administrator	All users
5	Data Protection & Information Handling	Art. 21(2)(g)	A.5.12, A.5.14, A.8.10	Data Protection Officer	Staff handling data
6	Secure Remote & Field Work	Art. 21(2)(f)	A.6.7, A.7.9	IT / Operations Manager	Remote & field staff
7	Incident Awareness & Reporting	Art. 23	A.5.24, A.6.8	Incident Response Lead	All staff
8	Management & Leadership Responsibilities	Art. 20	Clause 5, A.5.4	Board / Senior Management	Management

The target group of this program is employees, volunteers, project coordinators, and administration. The program's main goal is achieved through topics that raise awareness, thereby reducing the risk of phishing and fraud, protecting the personal data of donors and beneficiaries, fostering a culture of cybersecurity, and providing a clear response to incidents. It is mandatory, after each module, to pass a proper test. This is imperative because the results can serve as evidence of the learning conducted during the audit. To assess these tests, we also propose a simplified model that clearly shows gaps by module, which is described in the next section.

3 Micro-learning Test Scoring Model

In cases of recruitment for non-governmental organizations, it is possible to use a mathematical model to determine the level of awareness of candidates. For example, 3 levels can be formed – cyber unaware (LA^1), basic awareness (LA^2) and cyber awareness (LA^3).

The corresponding models follow the following presentation:

$$\mathrm{Max}\left(LA^n = \sum_{q=1}^{Q} y_q d_q\right) \tag{1}$$

subject to

$$LA^n_{max} < D \tag{2}$$

$$LA^n_{min} \le LA^n \le LA^n_{max} \tag{3}$$

Where y_q is the binary integer variable assigned to the questions; d_q is the question's difficulty level; D is the score of overall questions and $\sum_q^Q d_q = D$; LA^n_{min} and LA^n_{max} are respectively the lower and upper limit for the tested level of awareness.

The proposed model (1)–(3) is only suitable for determining the level of cybersecurity awareness among volunteers' eager to join the NGO cause.

Since cyberattacks not only increase but also modify over time, it is necessary to periodically assess the knowledge and skills of the NGO team. It is important to use a model that allows identifying gaps in testing at the module level. In this regard, the following mathematical model is proposed for assessing the effectiveness of micro-learning:

$$\mathrm{Max}\left\{\sum_i S_i\right\} \tag{4}$$

subject to

$$S_i = \sum_j x^i_j a^i_j \tag{5}$$

$$x^i_j \in \{0, 1\} \tag{6}$$

where S_i expresses the overall score of the i-th module, and the number of modules is expressed by index i. The binary variables x^i_j are assigned to each question from a particular module. Index j is used to express the j-th question from the i-th module. Due to the nature of these variables, their sum is exactly equal to the number of all the module's questions. These variables indicate whether the participant answered each question correctly. For example, if there is given correct answer, the corresponding variable has a value of 1, and if the answer is incorrect, the value becomes zero. In this way, knowing the number of questions in each module, it can be determined whether the participant made mistakes. If the sum of the variables is exactly equal to the number of questions, then all the answers given are correct. If there is an incorrect answer, the sum of the variables will be less than the number of questions.

The parameters a^i_j represent the score points for each question in a given module. Some questions may have different score points to reflect their difficulty. In general, it is possible for all questions to be considered equally difficult. In particular, if a score of 1 is used for each question, then with only correct answers, the total score for the particular module will be exactly equal to the number of questions.

The proposed model (4)–(6) imposes no limit on the number of modules on which the test is administered. Therefore, the micro-learning test scoring model formulated in this way is not constrained by the micro-learning's thematic focus or by the number of modules employed and can be considered universal.

4 Implementation and Validation of Proposed Approach

The applicability of the proposed approach has been demonstrated in a small, non-governmental, non-profit organization with an education and environmental focus. There are 5 candidates who have passed level 2 of the basic awareness test and are part of this NGO.

4.1 Case Study

Based on the specific requirements in Table 1, a questionnaire has been developed to assess the knowledge and skills acquired. It consists of 6 modules, with questions for each of them, as shown in Table 2. Module 2, concerning policies and roles, which refers to the HR position, is omitted, as is Module 8 due to the specifics of the current NGO described in this case study.

The experiment was conducted with 5 users from an NGO with an educational and environmental focus. The total number of test questions for all modules that participants answered after the micro-learning is 16. It is not difficult to establish that participant-3 has the best performance, since he answered all 16 questions correctly and scored a total of 16 points (see Fig. 1). Participant-5 has the worst performance, because he answered only 13 questions correctly. Participant-2 has 2 wrong answers, and Participant-1 and Participant-4 have one wrong answer each.

4.2 Result Analysis and Discussion

It is useful to identify which modules the participants have gaps in, so they can improve their knowledge. With the help of appropriate visualization, it is easy to determine which questions received incorrect answers and which participant gave the wrong answer, as shown in Fig. 2.

It is seen that Participant-1 has one incorrect answer to a question from module-2; Participant-2 has two incorrect answers to a question from module-2 and module-5, while Participant-3 has no incorrect answers. Participant-4 has given one incorrect answer in module-6, and Participant-5 has 3 incorrect answers in three different modules – module-2, module-4, and module-6.

A more general overview of participants' overall performance within a considered NGO is shown in Fig. 3.

Although micro-learning is an effective way to increase security awareness, its implementation faces several challenges. Some employees may not take micro-learning seriously because of its short, concise format, which can reduce engagement and limit

Table 2. Cybersecurity micro-learning modules for NGO

#	Module	Questions description	Goal
1	Awareness & Ethics	1.1. Why NGOs are a frequent target? 1.2. What data is valuable (donors, children, health information)?	Risk awareness
2	Phishing & Social Engineering	2.1. How to recognize fake donation emails? 2.2. It is possible to receive "Urgent" messages from the "Director"?	Fraud detection
3	Passwords & MFA	3.1. What a good password looks like? 3.2. What is a password manager? 3.3. Why MFA is mandatory?	More secure access
4	Working with Data	4.1. What is personal information (GDPR context)? 4.2. How to share files safely? 4.3. What NOT to send via email?	Data protection
5	Remote & Field Work	5.1. Why is using a VPN necessary on public networks? 5.2. How to protect personal devices? 5.3. Updates and antivirus.	Reducing risk outside the office
6	Incident Response	6.1. How to recognize an incident? 6.2. What to do if we clicked? 6.3 Who is the reporting contact?	Quick and correct response

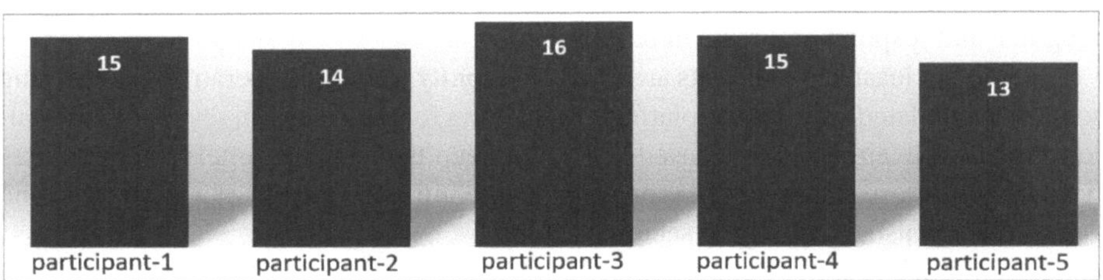

Fig. 1. Overall participants' performance.

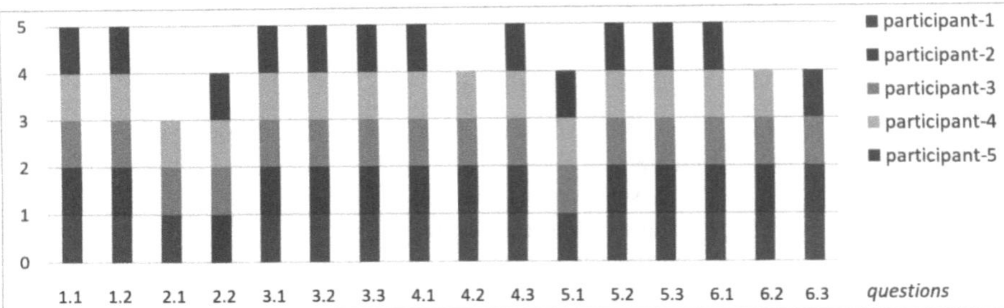

Fig. 2. Correct answers from participants.

knowledge retention. To address this challenge, gamification elements can be used to increase motivation. Generic learning modules may not address specific cyber threats to the organization, which can lead to disengagement or knowledge gaps. This can be addressed by adopting a targeted approach and tailoring content to job roles and responsibilities. IT staff can focus on technical threats, while front-line employees learn to recognize phishing and social engineering tactics.

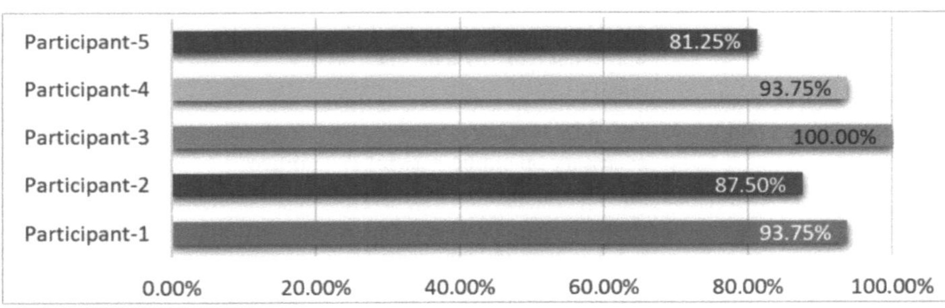

Fig. 3. Overall success of participants in percentage.

Given the brevity of micro-learning, it is difficult to determine whether these modules actually lead to improved security practices. Therefore, tracking metrics such as phishing simulation click-through rate, reporting rate, and re-click rate reveal how well employees recognize and respond to threats in real time.

Last but not least, cyber threats are evolving rapidly, and it is imperative that learning modules are updated regularly. A platform that allows for rapid content revisions and real-world incident examples can be used. This will keep the learning timely and practical. By addressing these challenges, it is possible to maximize the impact of a micro-learning program while also encouraging security habits.

The approach described can be easily implemented to ensure consistent assessment over time and in line with new regulations. In addition, creating a variety of tests, maintaining the topic of each question but with slightly different wording, is planned as future research.

5 Conclusion

Improving cybersecurity in nonprofit organizations is often difficult, as organizations lack not only time but also resources to support specialized IT teams. Building a strong culture of security awareness is a must in this dynamic world. This can be achieved through regular, rather than one-off, micro-learning. The focus of these training sessions is on the basics of recognizing phishing emails, creating strong passwords, and enabling multi-factor authentication. All of these considerations, the article presents a micro-training program for non-governmental organizations in accordance with current regulatory requirements. Based on the program, the learning content is presented, and a mathematical model is proposed to assess the acquired knowledge and skills. The model is universal, and its results can serve as evidence before auditors of the training conducted and the participants' success. The described preliminary observations show that through small but frequent micro-learnings, users not only enhance the protection of the organization's data but also that of volunteers and donors.

Disclosure of Interests. The authors have no competing interests to declare that are relevant to the content of this article.

References

1. Taherdoost, H.: A critical review on cybersecurity awareness frameworks and training models. Procedia Comput. Sci. **235**, 1649–1663 (2024). https://doi.org/10.1016/j.procs.2024.04.156
2. Carneiro, F.D., Rampasso, I.S., de Matos Mello, S.L., Sigahi, T.F.A.C., Lespay, H., Anholon, R.: A flexible ISO 27701-based framework for assessing cybersecurity maturity: a proposition and a case application. Comput. Secur. **158**, 104645 (2025). https://doi.org/10.1016/j.cose.2025.104645
3. Terziev, Y., Shalamanov, V.: Framework for cybersecurity audit in non-profit organizations: a preliminary investigation through intelligent minimalism. In: 6th International Conference on Communications, Information, Electronic and Energy Systems (CIEES), pp. 1–6, Ruse, Bulgaria (2025). https://doi.org/10.1109/CIEES66347.2025.11300183
4. Sanchez-Garcia, I.D., Rea-Guaman, A.M., Gilabert, T.S., Calvo-Manzano, J.A.: Cybersecurity risk audit: a systematic literature review. Stud. Comput. Intell. **1135**, 275–301 (2024). https://doi.org/10.1007/978-3-031-50590-4_18
5. Verma, H.C., Srivastava, S.: Factors in cybersecurity vulnerabilities. In: Human Impact on Security and Privacy: Network and Human Security, Social Media, and Devices, pp. 1–12 (2024). https://doi.org/10.4018/979-8-3693-9235-5.ch001
6. Mathew, B.S., Lasekan, O.A., Pena, M.G.: Behavioural determinants of cyber hygiene: rethinking the role of education in digital trust and usability. Int. Res. J. Multidiscipl. Scope. **6**(4), 726–739 (2025). https://doi.org/10.47857/irjms.2025.v06i04.07251
7. Tran, Q.-T., Nguyen, D.-P., Nguyen, T.-V., Dinh, D.-M., Vu, H.-L., Nguyen, A.-N.: Enhancing cybersecurity awareness among users and employees: a practical approach. In: Joint International Conference on Digital Arts, Media and Technology with ECTI Northern Section Conference on Electrical, Electronics, Computer and Telecommunications Engineering (ECTI DAMT & NCON), pp. 617–622, Nan, Thailand (2025). https://doi.org/10.1109/ECTIDAMTNCON64748.2025.10962024

8. Roshanaei, M., Krishnamurthy, P., Sinha, A., Gokhale, V., Raza, F.M., Ramljak, D.: Enhancing cybersecurity readiness in non-profit organizations through collaborative research and innovation – a systematic literature review. Computers. **14**, 539 (2025). https://doi.org/10.3390/computers14120539
9. Nikkhoo, I., Ahmadi, Z., Akbari, M., Imannezhad, S., Anvari Ardekani, S., Lashgari, H.: Microlearning for today's students: a rapid review of essentials and considerations. Med. Educ. Bullet. **4**(1), 673–685 (2023). https://doi.org/10.22034/meb.2022.355659.1066
10. Monib, W.K., Qazi, A., Apong, R.A.: Microlearning beyond boundaries: a systematic review and a novel framework for improving learning outcomes. Heliyon. **11**(2), e41413 (2025). https://doi.org/10.1016/j.heliyon.2024.e41413
11. Robles, H., Jimeno, M., Villalba, K., Mardini, I., Viloria-Nunez, C., Florian, W.: Design of a micro-learning framework and mobile application using design-based research. PeerJ Comput. Sci. **9**, 1–31 (2023). https://doi.org/10.7717/PEERJ-CS.1223
12. Moulin, T., Lellouche, N., Gandjbakhch, E., Laredo, M.: Daily quiz-based microlearning program to support electrocardiogram interpretation training for medical students: a feasibility study. CJC Open. **8**(1), 43–50 (2026). https://doi.org/10.1016/j.cjco.2025.09.009
13. Beste, T.: Knowledge transfer in a project-based organization through microlearning on cost-efficiency. J. Appl. Behav. Sci. **59**(2), 288–313 (2021). https://doi.org/10.1177/00218863211033096
14. Boumalek, K., Bakki, A., El Mezouary, A., Hmedna, B., Eddahibi, M.: Micro-learning design and micro-course structuring: a systematic literature review. Interact. Learn. Environ. **1–27** (2025). https://doi.org/10.1080/10494820.2025.2545955
15. Diaz Redondo, R.P., Caeiro Rodriguez, M., Lopez Escobar, J., Vilas, A.F.: Integrating micro-learning content in traditional e-learning platforms. Multimed. Tools Appl. **80**, 3121–3151 (2021). https://doi.org/10.1007/s11042-020-09523-z
16. Guaña-Moya, J., Salgado-Reyes, N., Arteaga-Alcívar, Y., Espinosa-Cevallos, A.: Importance of cybersecurity education to reduce risks in academic institutions. In: Choudrie, J., Tuba, E., Perumal, T., Joshi, A. (eds.) ICT for Intelligent Systems. ICTIS 2024 Smart Innovation, Systems and Technologies, vol. 403, pp. 31–40 (2024). https://doi.org/10.1007/978-981-97-5799-2_4
17. Gupta, S., Furnell, S.: From cybersecurity hygiene to cyber Well-being. In: Moallem, A. (ed.) HCI for Cybersecurity, Privacy and Trust. HCII 2022 Lecture Notes in Computer Science, vol. 13333, pp. 124–134 (2022). https://doi.org/10.1007/978-3-031-05563-8_9
18. Abdulrahman, A., Richards, D., Bilgin, A.A., Formosa, P.: Developing ethical principle awareness and reasoning in a cybersecurity context: enhancing user understanding using ripple down rules. Comput. Secur. **161**, 104761 (2026). https://doi.org/10.1016/j.cose.2025.104761
19. Qawasmeh, S.A.-D., AlQahtani, A.A.S., Khan, M.K.: Navigating cybersecurity training: a comprehensive review. Comput. Electr. Eng. **123**(Part B), 110097 (2025). https://doi.org/10.1016/j.compeleceng.2025.110097
20. Kallonas, C., Piki, A., Stavrou, E.: Empowering professionals: a generative AI approach to personalized cybersecurity learning. In: IEEE Global Engineering Education Conference (EDUCON), pp. 1–10. Kos Island, Greece (2024). https://doi.org/10.1109/EDUCON60312.2024.105794
21. Blagoev, I., Shalamanov, V.: Development of cyber ranges as a reference environment for digital transformation. In: In: 4th International Conference on Communications, Information, Electronic and Energy Systems (CIEES), pp. 1–5, Plovdiv, Bulgaria (2023). https://doi.org/10.1109/CIEES58940.2023.10378806
22. Directive (EU) 2022/2555 of the European Parliament and of the Council of 14 December 2022 on measures for a high common level of cybersecurity across the Union, amending Regulation (EU) No 910/2014 and Directive (EU) 2018/1972, and repealing Directive

(EU) 2016/1148 (NIS 2 Directive). https://www.nis-2-directive.com/NIS_2_Directive_Articles.html. Last accessed 5 Feb 2026.
23. ISO/IEC 27001:2022, Information security, cybersecurity and privacy protection – Information security management systems – Requirements, https://www.iso.org/standard/27001. Last accessed 3 Feb 2026.
24. Monib, W.K., Qazi, A., Apong, R.A., Mahmud, M.M.: Investigating learners' perceptions of microlearning: factors influencing learning outcomes. IEEE Access. **12**, 178251–178266 (2024). https://doi.org/10.1109/ACCESS.2024.3472113
25. Astiwardhani, W., Sobandi, A.: Transforming educational paradigms: how micro learning shapes student understanding, retention, and motivation? J. Educ. Action Res. **8**(2), 300–309 (2024). https://doi.org/10.23887/jear.v8i2.77711

Smart Immersive Learning Systems for African Education

Nkosikhona Theoren Msweli(✉) and Emmanuel Samuel Mtsweni

University of South Africa, Roodepoort, Johannesburg 1709, South Africa
mswelnt@unisa.ac.za

Abstract. The education system in many African countries continues to face persistent challenges, including limited access to innovative learning tools, a shortage of qualified educators, overcrowded classrooms, and infrastructural deficits. These issues contribute to disparities in educational outcomes and hinder efforts toward inclusive and equitable learning and further hinder economic growth. In response, emerging technologies such as artificial intelligence (AI) and immersive learning technologies (ILTs) are increasingly being explored to see how they can transform and improve the education system through smart immersive learning systems (SILS). This systematic literature review analyzes current research on the implementation of SILS for African education, focusing on its benefits, challenges, and emerging opportunities. The key findings revealed that although the benefits of SILS have been demonstrated globally, there is limited research on its implementation in African education. Evidence from the reviewed studies indicates that these technologies can improve quality of education in resource-constrained regions. Issues such as learning difficulties and teaching complex concepts can be resolved by personalizing the learning experiences, increasing student engagement, expanding access to quality education, and supporting educator development. However, substantial challenges remain, particularly in terms of digital infrastructure, affordability of devices, absence of TPACK (Technological Pedagogical Content Knowledge), and digital literacy. The review identifies opportunities for scalable implementation through localized innovation, decolonized learning content, capacity building, and multi-stakeholder collaboration. The findings suggest that, with strategic investment and context-sensitive approaches, SILS can play a pivotal role in addressing systemic educational challenges in Africa and advancing the continent's goals for inclusive and sustainable education.

Keywords: Immersive technology · virtual reality · augmented reality · artificial intelligence · African education

1 Introduction

Modern digital technologies such as artificial intelligence (AI) and immersive technologies are revolutionizing education, offering innovative, interactive, and personalized learning experiences. Immersive learning is one of the growing digital learning approaches that is enabled by the inclusion of virtual reality (VR), augmented reality

C.-J. Lin et al. (Eds.): ICITL 2026, LNCS 16841, pp. 186–196, 2027.
https://doi.org/10.1007/978-3-032-32112-1_19

(AR), and mixed reality (MR) [1]. These technologies create simulated environments where users can be part of sensory-rich experiences that mimic real-world scenarios. In educational settings, they are used to support the teaching and learning processes, where scholars are already citing improved knowledge retention, learner engagement, and learner motivation [2]. The transformative power of AI in education is also increasingly recognized for its ability to offer adaptive learning experiences and to support modern pedagogies [3]. However, while many celebrate these opportunities, others warn that AI is disrupting the education sector, raising concerns about equity, ethical use, new knowledge contribution, and labour displacement [4]. AI is popular in analysing and processing large amounts of data, while immersive technologies excel in creating immersive and interactive learning experiences [5]. When combined, these technologies further transform learning systems by offering educational experiences that adapt to individual learner needs and preferences. This capability is particularly important for African learners, whose learning abilities are often influenced by a range of contextual factors such as socio-economic disparities, limited access to quality educational resources, and varying levels of digital literacy [6]. Global studies have further demonstrated the benefits of applied education, where hands-on experience is central. In engineering education, for instance, immersive simulations provide students with opportunities for hands-on training when access to physical laboratories, specialised equipment, or industry-based learning environments is constrained [7].

Smart technologies hold significant promise for advancing inclusion and equity in education. However, their implementation remains limited in many contexts, potentially exacerbating existing inequalities and widening the digital divide rather than reducing it [8]. Similar patterns have been observed in immersive technologies. For example, Indra et al. [9] found that rural learners were outperformed by their urban counterparts in mathematics instruction supported by VR. A key contributing factor was learners' unfamiliarity with digital technologies, which hindered effective engagement with the intervention. There are other barriers reported in various publications. Oyinbo and Waritimi [5] examined the integration of AI and VR in transforming anatomy education, identifying challenges such as limited access to electricity and the effects of brain drain. Mkwizu and Bordoloi [11] examined the challenges of inclusive growth in education, with a focus on India and Tanzania, specifically in relation to AR. Their study identified inadequate digital infrastructure and limited access to universal internet or broadband facilities as critical challenges. Falebita and Kok [4] reviewed the integration of AI into STEM education in African higher education. However, their study was limited to examining the use of AI, without addressing the broader challenges and benefits associated with its implementation in educational contexts. This trend highlights the need for more context-specific investigations, particularly within the African setting, to understand challenges and opportunities of implementing SILS in local educational. The purpose of this study is to explore the SILS within the context of African countries. Particularly, this study seeks to address the following questions:

RQ1: What are the existing barriers towards implementing SILS in African education?
RQ2: What design guidelines should inform the development and implementation of SILS for African education?

This study contributes a set of design guidelines, articulated through a conceptual framework, to guide the development and implementation of Smart Immersive Learning Systems (SILS) in African educational contexts. The study further contributes to the ongoing discourse on digital transformation in education and provides insights for technology designers, policymakers (those involved in education portfolios), educators, and researchers. The remainder of the paper is structured as follows: after outlining the methodology, the findings are presented and discussed, followed by the conclusion, which highlights the implications, limitations, and directions for future research.

2 Methodology

The study employed a systematic literature review to address research questions. Inclusion and exclusion criteria (Table 1) were defined in advance to improve the quality of the review and reduce potential biases. The criteria were applied during the identification phase to screen studies for relevance and eligibility.

Table 1. Inclusion and Exclusion Criteria

Criteria	Inclusion criteria	Exclusion Criteria
Geographic Focus	Studies conducted in African countries or focused on African contexts.	Studies conducted outside Africa without reference to applicability in African contexts.
Focus Area	Studies focusing on integrations of AI and immersive technologies into education.	Studies that do not clearly explain the role of AI and immersive technologies.
Educational Context	Studies related to education, including schools, universities, and vocational training.	Studies focusing on AI and immersive technologies for non-learning purposes.
Study Design	Peer-reviewed journal articles and papers published in conference proceedings.	Editorials, reviews, book chapters, or unpublished thesis/dissertations. Published systematic literature reviews or review papers in this area.
Language	Studies published in English.	Non-English studies (unless translated)
Publication Date	Studies published between 2021 and 2025	Studies published before 2021
Access	Full-text articles	Articles without available full text (e.g., abstract-only studies).

The search and identification were conducted by a single researcher who used pre-defined search terms to identify potentially relevant studies. This was followed by the scanning and screening of articles conducted by both researchers.

2.1 Search Procedure and Search String

The literature search was conducted across major scientific databases, namely Scopus, SpringerLink, IEEE Xplore, and the ACM Digital Library, to ensure broad coverage of high-quality, peer-reviewed studies from both journals and conference proceedings. The search was restricted to studies published between 2021 and 2025 to ensure the inclusion of recent and contextually relevant contributions. A search string was developed using carefully selected keywords combined with Boolean operators: ((“artificial intelligence” OR “AI”) AND (“immersive technology” OR “virtual reality” OR “VR” OR “augmented reality” OR “AR” OR “mixed reality” OR “MR”) AND (“education”) AND (“Africa” OR “African”)). The search strategy was further adapted to align with the indexing and functionality of individual databases. In accordance with the predefined inclusion criteria, specific filters (e.g., publication year, language, and peer-reviewed status) were applied to refine the search results and ensure the retrieval of relevant studies. As shown in Fig. 1, a total of 26 studies published between 2021 and 2025 were included in the review.

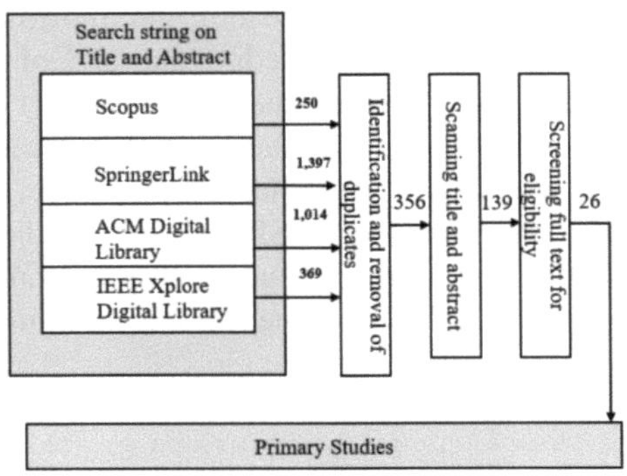

Fig. 1. Procedure for identifying primary studies

The 26 eligible articles included in this SLR were coded using an inductive coding technique to address the research questions. This approach was deemed appropriate as it enables codes and themes to emerge directly from the data through a grounded, data-driven process.

3 Results and Findings

The included articles highlight the scarcity of literature focusing on the integration of AI and ILTs in African countries, which suggests the need for further empirical and conceptual research to advance understanding and guide effective implementation in this context (Fig. 2).

The majority of studies are global, highlighting what is happening in African and developing countries. Within Africa, research is minimal, with South Africa, Tanzania, Kenya, and Burundi emerging as the main countries where studies have been conducted.

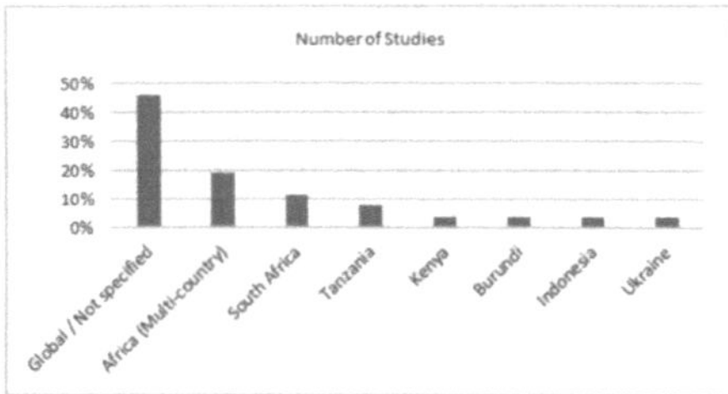

Fig. 2. Publication by country

Large parts of the African continent remain underrepresented, highlighting a significant gap in context-driven and empirical studies on immersive technologies in education.

Among the reviewed studies, majority adopted a design science research approach. The prevalence of design science research indicates that African countries are actively engaged in developing technologies and models tailored to local contexts, reflecting a process of "Africanization" in educational technology solutions [11]. The results further show a shift from theoretical exploration to creation and implementation of innovative artefacts in education. This study also acknowledges the value of a mixed-methods approach, enabling researchers not only to assess the effectiveness of these technologies but also to explore the underlying factors that explain why they succeed or fail in practice. Mishra and Singh [12] alludes that technologies are disruptive, in the sense that they change the way students are taught and learn. SILSs bring together innovative elements that promote smart education necessary for students from resource-constrained countries. Below is a summary of how SILSs have shaped education since traditional teaching methods (Fig. 3):

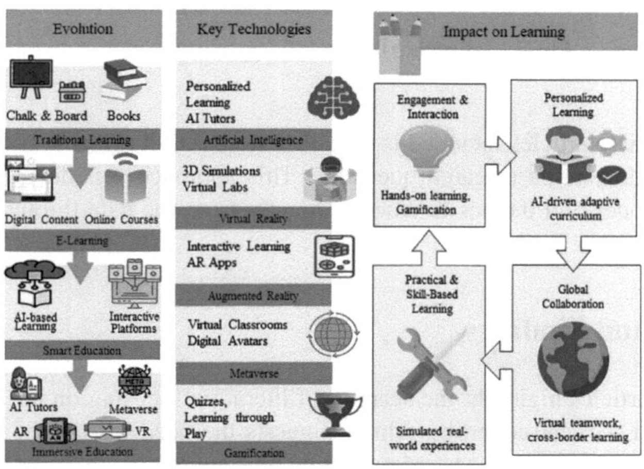

Fig. 3. Smart Immersive Education [12]

3.1 Barriers Towards the Implementation of Smart Immersive Learning Systems

Issues of Digital Divide (Such as Access, Affordability, Etc.). The adoption of immersive technologies is widespread in many global regions; however, it remains limited in African countries and other developing economies [13, 14]. Majority of learning institutions struggle to acquire these digital devices even after scholars have cited the decrease in their prices [9, 15]. Costs of maintaining the devices, such as software upgrades and licenses, make it even more difficult to sustain them.

Language Barrier. Ade-Ibijola et al. [16] found that AI and AR can address issues related to language. This is a breakthrough for African learning institutions in the sense that learning outcomes can be achieved in a way that is fair and inclusive. Almost all the subjects offered in learning institutions are delivered in English, which is not first language to many African students. The high failure rate in African countries stems from students struggling to comprehend the concepts being taught, leading to poor performance [17].

Cultural Contextualization. Currently, most learning technologies are developed from Western perspectives, values, and interests, with limited consideration of African contexts or regulatory environments [18, 19]. This creates a form of digital dependency that disadvantages African countries and their citizens, as they are unable to fully harness these technologies due to infrastructural limitations and the lack of alignment with local societal challenges. Context plays a critical role in the integration of AI and immersive technologies in education; therefore, technological tools and content reflect local cultures, languages, and lived realities [20].

AI Bias and Ethical Concerns. The question of context is also central to addressing the biases inherent in AI systems. In African education, these concerns are particularly pressing, as many AI models are trained on datasets that lack representation of African languages, cultures, and learning contexts [9, 11]. This underrepresentation not only risks reinforcing stereotypes but also produces outputs that may be misaligned with local realities. Moreover, the lack of transparency around training data and decision-making processes raises ethical challenges related to fairness, accountability, and trust [13].

Absence of TPACK. Majority of African educators are not equipped with competencies to integrate technology into their teaching practices [7]. Leveraging technology in education can be successfully implemented if educators have the knowledge and skills to align technology, pedagogy, content, and knowledge with the learning space [7, 21].

Localized Content. Absence of localized content is one of the challenges affecting the integration of AI and immersive technologies. Students in Africa need to learn about what is happening in their countries so that the content can be relatable and applicable. Scenarios used should promote local content or Africanization, placing students in situations they are likely to find in the working environment [11]. This also ensures that students are not sold as Western dreams.

Digital Literacy. However, in the 21st-century technology-mediated learning environment, large-scale digital illiteracy is the biggest challenge in gaining actual success in digitising India [10]. The preparedness of educators to use technology is critical in promoting innovative pedagogy [9]. In most cases, lecturers and teachers lack the skills to integrate interactive technology into their teaching practices in a meaningful manner. Allison [15] notes that integrations require considerations of pedagogy and ethics, and how learners engage with interactive intelligent systems.

3.2 Recommendation on Successful Integration

African countries are recognising the need to adopt technology for accessible education, and some initiatives have been implemented to improve the adoption [11, 22]. There are also successful cases demonstrating that Africanizing technology represents a critical step toward developing inclusive and culturally responsive educational solutions. This approach involves designing applications that intentionally address language diversity, contextual relevance, and affordability. For example, applications such as DigiDoseAR and ZART illustrate initiatives aimed at embedding local realities, linguistic diversity, and socio-economic considerations into technological design. Such efforts seek to prevent learning institutions from relying solely on Western-centric educational models that may not adequately reflect African societal needs and contextual challenges [16, 18, 23]. Below are recommendations for designing smart learning systems for African education:

Infrastructure Responsive Design and Low-Bandwidth Optimization. Learning systems should function effectively in contexts with unreliable electricity and limited internet connectivity [9]. This includes incorporating offline access to core learning content, low-bandwidth optimisation (e.g., compressed assets and lightweight simulations), solar-powered devices, and mobile-first compatibility.

Curriculum Transformation and Inclusion of Localized Content. Availability of appropriate curriculum is an important factor. Two key elements need to be addressed to ensure alignment: curriculum design and educational content. Learning system needs to be designed with curricula that enforce practical applications and problem-solving skills, but also content that embodies the effect of body awareness and self-presence to make it more relatable [1]. Learning material should be empowering, by being culturally relevant and resonating with the lived realities of African students.

Ethical and Inclusive Governance, Frameworks, and Policies. Lack of transparency on data used to train models raises issues of bias and unfairness [22]. Other scholars raised issues of colonization that may result from the information generated by the application of AI [11]. Using diverse datasets that are relatable in the African context and fairness-aware algorithms is one of the strategies that can support inclusive education. In addition, adapting global frameworks to local contexts to address barriers and offer policymakers practical guidance for equitable adoption is necessary.

Multi-stakeholder Collaboration and Research Grants. These are key initiatives for advancing inclusive education, particularly in resource-constrained regions. Many successful use cases of technology integration into learning are achieved through collaboration with regions that are leading in technology production and use [24]. These partnerships provide funding, expertise, and technological support to support implementation. For example, Liubchak et al. [25] reported on a public–private collaborative project that led to the establishment of specialized immersive laboratories equipped with appropriate technical resources.

Social and Cultural Inclusion. In many African countries, culture and religion are still deeply rooted. Therefore, policies must be carefully designed to respect local values and build societal trust. Many African countries are multilingual; individual profiling is essential to identify fluency and language needs, proficiency levels, and potential learning barriers. Adaptive systems should be able to dynamically tailor content, language complexity, instructional strategies, and feedback mechanisms to align with each learner's needs [2, 20, 26]. With these recommendations, African countries can avoid being left behind and instead compete on a global scale, leveraging technology to strengthen education, drive innovation, and contribute to knowledge economies [6].

3.3 Framework for Designing Smart Immersive Learning Systems

In addition to the recommendations, this study proposes a framework (Fig. 4), which conceptualises SILS as an integrated model grounded in African contextual realities. At its core lies immersive pedagogical design, supported by technological intelligence that facilitates personalisation and adaptive learning [2, 21, 27]. Equity and inclusion operate as cross-cutting principles to prevent the reinforcement of existing disparities [9, 19, 28]. Sustainability and governance mechanisms ensure scalability and long-term viability.

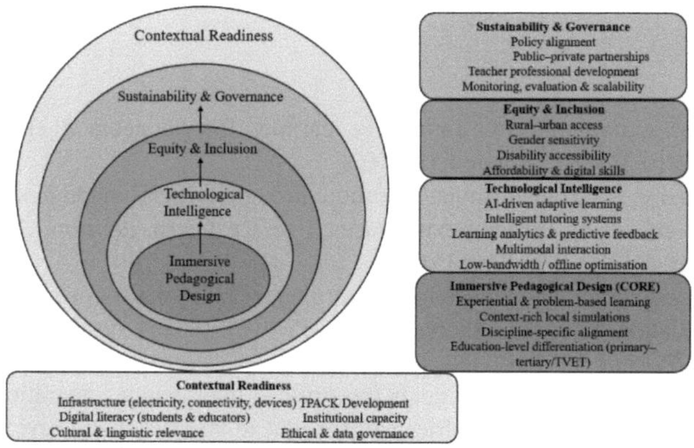

Fig. 4. Smart Immersive Learning Systems framework

The framework is embedded within contextual readiness conditions, recognizing that infrastructure, institutional capacity, and ethical safeguards are prerequisites for successful implementation.

4 Conclusion, Recommendations, and Future Studies

Recognising the transformative potential of emerging technologies is a critical step toward advancing economic development and sustainable education in Africa. Despite persistent challenges, many African countries are progressively integrating digital technologies into education to expand access and improve quality. SILSs offer innovative pedagogical approaches that foster deeper conceptual understanding through interactive, context-rich learning experiences. They also support diverse learning needs and help bridge geographic and resource constraints by delivering rich educational content to underserved and remote communities. This study highlights the significant potential of smart education to address longstanding educational challenges across the continent, including infrastructure gaps, a shortage of educators, and barriers to sustainable education. The review identifies key constraints, such as limited infrastructure, high implementation costs, digital skills deficits, data privacy concerns, and policy shortcomings. This study offers a framework to guide the design and implementation of smart learning systems. Future research and practice should prioritise local content development and prioritize the design and development of learning platforms that accommodate the needs of the underserved communities. With strategic investment and coordinated action, AI and immersive technologies can help African education systems move beyond traditional limitations and foster resilient, inclusive, and future-oriented learning environments.

Acknowledgments. None.

Disclosure of Interests The authors have no competing interests to declare that are relevant to the content of this article.

References

1. Mystakidis, S., Lympouridis, V.: Immersive learning. Encyclopedia. **3**(2), 396–405 (2023). https://doi.org/10.3390/encyclopedia3020026
2. Wang, D., Huang, X.: Transforming education through artificial intelligence and immersive technologies: enhancing learning experiences. Interact. Learn. Environ. (2025). https://doi.org/10.1080/10494820.2025.2465451
3. Bayaga, A.: Leveraging AI-enhanced and emerging technologies for pedagogical innovations in higher education. Educ. Inf. Technol. **30**, 1045–1072 (2025). https://doi.org/10.1007/s10639-024-13122-y
4. Falebita, O.S., Kok, P.J.: Strategic goals for artificial intelligence integration among STEM academics and undergraduates in African higher education: a systematic review. Discov. Educ. **3**, 151 (2024). https://doi.org/10.1007/s44217-024-00252-1
5. Oyinbo, C.A., Waritimi, E.G.: Revolutionizing anatomy education: AI or VR—which technology will dominate? J. Adv. Educ. Philosop. **9**(4), 186–192 (2025). https://doi.org/10.36348/jaep.2025.v09i04.004
6. UNESCO: Challenges and Opportunities for Sustainable Development in the Education Sector. United Nations Educational, Scientific and Cultural Organization (2019)
7. Thangavel, S., Sharmila, K., Sufina, K.: Revolutionizing education through augmented reality (AR) and virtual reality (VR): innovations, challenges and future prospects. Asian Journal of Interdisciplinary Research. **8**(1), 1–28 (2025). https://doi.org/10.54392/ajir2511

8. Mannuru, N.R. et al.: Artificial intelligence in developing countries: the impact of generative artificial intelligence technologies for development. Inf. Dev. **41**(3), 1036–1054 (2025). https://doi.org/10.1177/02666669231200628
9. Indra, C., Fiqri, A., Cholily, Y.M., Syaifuddin, M.: Challenges and readiness of VR and AI integration in STEM-based mathematics education: a case of urban and rural high schools. Jurnal Didaktik Matematika, 144–161 (2025)
10. Mkwizu, K.H., Bordoloi, R.: Augmented reality for inclusive growth in education: the challenges. Asian Association of Open Universities Journal. **19**(1), 88–102 (2024). https://doi.org/10.1108/AAOUJ-09-2023-0113
11. Micheline, S., Yu, X., Sun, C.: Adoption of teaching strategies leveraging on augmented reality and virtual reality in higher education in less developing countries: a case of Burundi. In: Proceedings of the 2023 International Conference on Intelligent Education and Intelligent Research (IEIR 2023) 5, p. 1. IEEE (2023). https://doi.org/10.1109/IEIR59294.2023.10391255
12. Mishra, P., Singh, G.: Smart education with immersive technology contents. In: Sustainable Smart Cities 2.0: Enabling Research toward SDG 11, pp. 329–367. Springer (2025). https://doi.org/10.1007/978-3-032-01102-2
13. Yusuf, F.A.: Trends, opportunities, and challenges of artificial intelligence in elementary education: a systematic literature review. J. Integrat. Element. Educ. **5**(1), 109–127 (2025). https://doi.org/10.21580/JIEED.V5I1.25594
14. Gudyanga, R.: Research trends and gaps in the adoption of immersive reality technologies in African education systems. Int. J. Learn. Teach. Educ. Res. **23**(11), 232–253 (2024). https://doi.org/10.26803/ijlter.23.11.12
15. Allison, J.: From generative AI to extended reality: multidisciplinary perspectives on the challenges, opportunities, and future of educational computing. J. Educ. Comput. Res. (2025). https://doi.org/10.1177/07356331251359964
16. Ade-Ibijola, A., Sukhari, A., Oyelere, S.S.: Teaching accounting principles using augmented reality and artificial intelligence-generated IsiZulu language translations. Int. J. Educ. Res. Open. **8**, 100447 (2025). https://doi.org/10.1016/j.ijedro.2025.100447
17. Yu, Z., Duan, P.: Meta-analyses of anxiety, motivation, performance, satisfaction, and self-efficacy in virtual reality-assisted language education. Foreign Lang. Ann. **57**(2), 550–580 (2024). https://doi.org/10.1111/FLAN.12748
18. Birhane, A.: Algorithmic colonization of Africa. SCRIPTed. **17**(2), 389–409 (2020). https://doi.org/10.2966/SCRIP.170220.389
19. Gumede, F.N., Mncibi, V., Mthembu, S.: Utilizing AR and VR to preserve and promote African languages. In: Advances in Social Science, Education and Humanities Research, vol. 982, pp. 518–535. Atlantis Press SARL (2025). https://doi.org/10.2991/978-2-38476-521-8_29
20. Walton, E., Engelbrecht, P.: Inclusive education in South Africa: path dependencies and emergences. Int. J. Incl. Educ. **28**(10), 2138–2156 (2024). https://doi.org/10.1080/13603116.2022.2061608
21. Barakabitze, A.A. et al.: Transforming African education systems in science, technology, engineering, and mathematics (STEM) using ICTs: challenges and opportunities. Educ. Res. Int., 6946809 (2019). https://doi.org/10.1155/2019/6946809
22. Wangui, R.N., Ronoh, R., Etene, Y.: Exploring interactive learning approaches and technology integration in the Kenyan education system. Pan-African J. Educ. Soc. Sci. **5**(1), 103–111 (2024). https://doi.org/10.56893/pajes2024v05i01.08
23. Rumo, J.T., Isafiade, O.E., Okinga, K., Egieyeh, S.: DigiDoseAR: redefining the future of pharmacy education with augmented reality. In: IST-Africa 2025 Conference Proceedings, pp. 1–9 (2025)

24. Chimombo, J.P.G.: Issues in basic education in developing countries: an exploration of policy options for improved delivery. Journal of International Cooperation in Education. **8**(1), 129–152 (2005)
25. Liubchak, V.O., Zuban, Y.O., Artyukhov, A.E.: Immersive learning technology for ensuring quality education: Ukrainian university case. In: CTE Workshop Proceedings (CTE-2021), pp. 336–354 (2022)
26. Kumbo, L.I., Nkwera, V.S., Mero, R.F., Sikumbili, R.M., Mushi, M.L.: Enhancing competency-based education training in Dar Es Salaam, Tanzania, with augmented reality and virtual reality technologies. African Journal of Education and Social Science Research. **12**(4), 178–191 (2025). https://doi.org/10.4314/ajessr.v12i4.1
27. Mbonye, V., Ebrahim, R.: Integrating augmented reality in science education in South Africa: applications in the Mancosa iTEACHlab. In: In: 5th International Conference on Artificial Intelligence, Big Data, Computing and Data Communication Systems (icABCD 2022). Institute of Electrical and Electronics Engineers (2022). https://doi.org/10.1109/icABCD54961.2022.9856083
28. Sunday, K., Oyelere, S.S., Agbo, F.J., Aliyu, M.B., Balogun, O.S., Bouali, N.: Usability evaluation of Imikode virtual reality game to facilitate learning of object-oriented programming. Technol. Knowl. Learn. **28**(4), 1871–1902 (2023). https://doi.org/10.1007/S10758-022-09634-6

Addressing Cold-Start Problem in Educational Recommender Systems with Self-Adjustable Fuzzy Sets

Gordan Đurović[1(✉)], Martina Holenko Dlab[1], and Marijana Živić Đurović[2]

[1] Faculty of Informatics and Digital Technologies, University of Rijeka, Radmile Matejčić 2, Rijeka 51000, Croatia
{gordan.durovic,mholenko}@inf.uniri.hr

[2] Faculty of Engineering, University of Rijeka, Vukovarska 58, Rijeka 51000, Croatia
marijanazd@riteh.uniri.hr

Abstract. The effectiveness of recommender systems is limited by the cold-start problem, which occurs when insufficient data are available during early use. In educational environments, this issue is amplified by small learner groups, intermittent interaction, and data-collection constraints that delay personalization. This paper proposes a self-adjustable fuzzy inference approach for early-stage personalization in educational recommender systems under cold-start conditions. Unlike traditional fuzzy systems with fixed membership functions, the approach dynamically adapts fuzzy set ranges based on contextual parameters derived from learning activities, enabling interpretable estimation of student model dimensions from the first interactions. The approach was deployed in higher-education STEM courses within an existing recommender system and evaluated across two research cycles in a real-world environment. Results indicate that early-stage adaptive feedback increases acceptance of personalized recommendations and enables a higher proportion of students to reach minimum performance thresholds while preserving stability of summative assessment outcomes.

Keywords: Cold-start problem · Fuzzy sets · Educational Recommender System

1 Introduction

With advances in digital technologies, Educational Recommender Systems (ERS) have become a tool for personalized learning [1, 2]. These systems suggest learning materials, activities, or learning companions based on learner behavior, preferences, and performance [1, 3]. However, despite progress in artificial intelligence through AI-driven personalization, ERS still face challenges related to data availability, model interpretability, and adaptability during early stages of use [1].

The cold-start problem limits the effectiveness of ERS [3, 4]. When a new user or learning item is introduced, insufficient data during early interactions prevent accurate predictions and affect engagement [5]. In educational contexts, early engagement is vital because learners expect guidance from the start of system use [1, 6].

C.-J. Lin et al. (Eds.): ICITL 2026, LNCS 16841, pp. 197–207, 2027.
https://doi.org/10.1007/978-3-032-32112-1_20

Traditional methods addressing the cold-start problem rely on implicit or explicit information gathering [3]. Implicit approaches analyze behavioral data during user interaction, while explicit approaches rely on surveys or questionnaires. More recent research employs deep learning, hybrid modeling, and social-network analysis to predict user preferences [4]. Models such as Long Short-Term Memory (LSTM) neural networks [5] or hybrid attention-based recurrent networks [7] show improved accuracy but depend on large datasets and demanding training processes, while lacking the interpretability required for educational applications.

A promising alternative is fuzzy logic, which models imprecise and uncertain information through membership functions representing partial membership of elements in categories [8]. When applied in ERS, fuzzy systems represent learner preferences or performance through qualitative variables such as low, medium, and high and support decision-making and personalization, including recommending majors [6], selecting courses [9], or generating adaptive feedback for learning tasks [10].

This paper proposes a self-adjustable fuzzy inference approach that adapts fuzzy membership functions to interaction data, enabling inference of student model dimensions and system feedback from early stages of use. By combining the interpretability of fuzzy inference with the adaptability of self-adjustable membership functions, the proposed approach offers a transparent and computationally efficient mechanism for early-stage personalization in ERS. It allows teachers to embed pedagogical expertise directly into the system while maintaining flexibility for data-driven refinement.

2 Theoretical Background

2.1 Educational Recommender Systems

Recommender systems were originally developed in non-educational domains to suggest items from large collections based on user preferences and historical behavior. Early applications focused on commercial contexts such as recommending music, books, or movies to users of online platforms [3, 4]. The core principles of recommender systems were later adapted to educational settings, leading to the creation of Educational Recommender Systems.

ERS generate recommendations with respect to pedagogical goals, learner characteristics, and instructional constraints, using learner profiles and contextual information to support alignment between instructional content and learners' knowledge and needs [1, 2]. ERS employ content-based, collaborative, knowledge-based, or hybrid approaches and rely on learner models incorporating explicit data (e.g., questionnaires, expressed preferences, learning styles) and implicit data (e.g., activity logs, task performance, response time) [1, 2, 6]. Research also highlights data-driven learner personas as behavioral archetypes supporting scalable personalization strategies [11].

Despite these developments, ERS face challenges including data sparsity, the cold-start problem, and limited model interpretability [1]. Systems relying on historical interaction data struggle to generate recommendations for new users or learning materials during early stages of system use [3, 4]. In educational contexts, cold-start conditions are structural: small learner groups limit data for modeling, intermittent system use slows accumulation of behavioral data, and privacy regulations restrict data collection [1–4].

Existing implicit and explicit approaches address data sparsity but postpone recommendations until sufficient information has accumulated [2, 3]. AI-driven approaches, including those based on artificial neural networks, require large datasets and computational resources and lack pedagogical transparency or interpretability in educational applications [1, 5].

Consequently, the core challenge in ERS is generating meaningful recommendations under cold-start conditions with limited data. Fuzzy logic addresses this by enabling interpretable reasoning under uncertainty and supporting data-efficient personalization, providing a lightweight solution suitable for early-stage recommendation in ERS [2, 6].

2.2 Fuzzy Logic

Fuzzy set theory captures gradations of truth in human reasoning by extending binary logic through partial membership of elements in sets represented by membership functions with values between 0 (not part of the set) and 1 (part of the set) [8]. This approach enables systems to handle imprecise and uncertain data and model expert knowledge through linguistic terms such as low, medium, and high [2, 8, 12]. Membership functions such as triangular, trapezoidal, and Gaussian approximate non-linear relationships between input and output variables [12, 13].

Fuzzy logic has been used in ERS because its ability to manage uncertainty and generate recommendations aligns with educational applications [1, 2, 6, 8]. Fuzzy-based ERS represent qualitative user characteristics such as moderate understanding or high engagement when measurements are unavailable [2, 10]. These systems translate expert knowledge into computational rules that adapt recommendations to different user profiles [2, 12].

Traditional ERS implementations define fuzzy sets using fixed membership functions based on expert knowledge [2, 12], but such systems are not easily adaptable to varying task parameters or learning scenarios and may lose precision in dynamic environments [1, 6]. To address these limitations, this research introduces self-adjustable fuzzy sets that allow membership functions to adapt based on learner interaction data, enabling ERS to generate recommendations under sparse data conditions and mitigate the cold-start problem [1, 2, 6].

3 Methodology

This research follows a design-and-evaluation approach in which a self-adjustable fuzzy inference system is developed and evaluated through deployment in a real educational environment. The methodology is grounded in fuzzy logic, in which the fuzzy inference system employs self-adjustable fuzzy sets whose membership function boundaries are recalculated with each learner interaction. By linking input variable ranges to contextual parameters, the approach avoids hard-coded thresholds and enables adaptation to learning contexts without retraining or reconfiguration.

3.1 Input Variables and Classes for Self-Adjustable Fuzzy Set Modeling

The first class of self-adjustable fuzzy sets applies to variables whose range is defined relative to a dynamic maximum value xmax derived from learning activities and updated as learner interaction progresses. When new activity data become available, the maximum value is recalculated and membership functions are rescaled accordingly. Membership boundaries (x1-x9) are defined as fixed proportions of xmax. This approach is suitable for variables whose range depends on the number of assessment elements associated with a given task or activity (see Fig. 1).

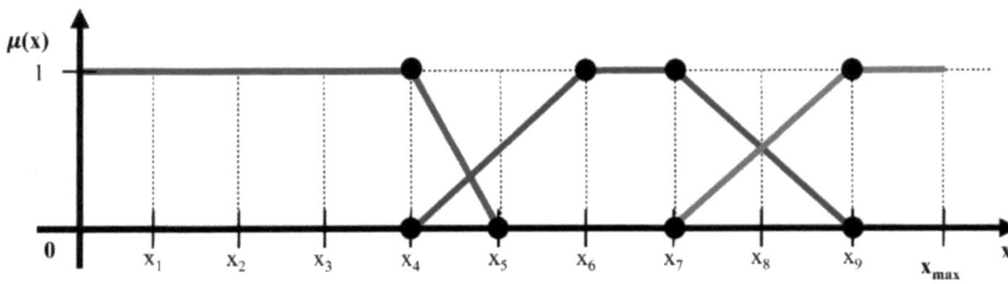

Fig. 1. Fuzzy set range defined relative to a dynamic maximum derived from learning activities.

The second class applies to input variables whose fuzzy set range is defined relative to a reference value x_{mean} and bounded by a fixed maximum x_{max} determined by instructional design constraints. The range is divided into two symmetric subintervals around the reference value, which is dynamically updated based on group-level activity. Membership boundaries (x_1-x_{14}) are defined as fixed proportions of x_{mean} while maintaining the fixed upper bound x_{max} (see Fig. 2).

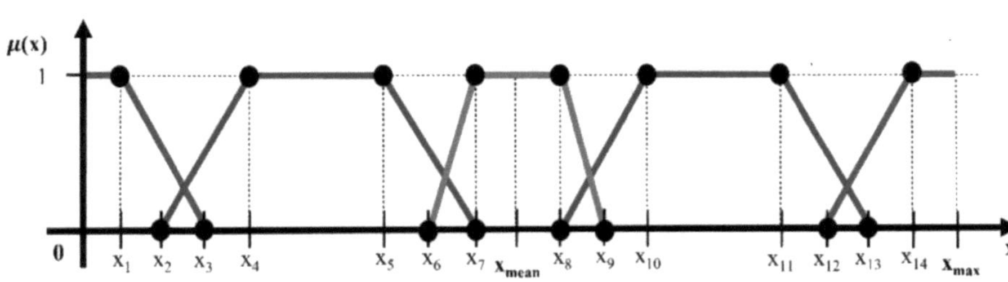

Fig. 2. Fuzzy set range defined relative to a reference value and bounded by a fixed maximum.

These two classes of self-adjustable fuzzy sets provide a structured mechanism for modeling heterogeneous input variables under cold-start conditions while preserving interpretability and pedagogical meaning.

3.2 Output Variables and Fuzzy Associative Memory

Unlike input variables modeled using self-adjustable fuzzy sets, the output variable and inference mechanism are defined using traditional fuzzy logic approaches. This design ensures semantic stability, interpretability, and consistency of system output across learning activities, user populations, and system configurations. It ensures the output of the fuzzy inference system remains comparable over time and independent of fluctuations in input data availability or task structure.

Defuzzification is performed using the center-of-gravity method to obtain a crisp numerical value from the aggregated fuzzy output, which is then used by system components for decision-making, feedback generation, and recommendation generation. The mapping between input variables and the output variable is defined through a fuzzy associative memory (FAM) implemented as expert-defined IF–THEN rules. These rules combine linguistic values of performance accuracy, number of attempted tasks, and relative solving time to estimate concept mastery. Together, the traditional definition of the output variable and the use of a FAM complete the fuzzy inference system, ensuring adaptability at the level of input interpretation while system output semantics and reasoning structure remain stable and interpretable across application domains.

4 Results from Real-World Deployment

4.1 Deployment Context

The proposed fuzzy inference system was developed within ELARS (E-Learning Activities Recommender System), an ERS supporting personalized and collaborative learning in STEM-oriented courses through digital learning activities with integrated assessment [14]. Each student is represented by a multidimensional student model capturing explicitly and implicitly collected data across four dimensions: (I) learning style based on the Felder-Silverman model [15], (II) task-solving performance, (III) concept mastery, and (IV) learning outcomes mastery.

The fuzzy inference system determines the concept dimension, representing each student's understanding of domain concepts. These values are evaluated during interaction with the system and used to estimate learning outcomes mastery and generate adaptive recommendations.

Student behavior during early learning stages was modeled using three input variables: performance accuracy at intermediate task results, number of tasks attempted within a task group, and average task-solving time relative to the group average. These variables provide a representation of student progress that can be evaluated across different learning scenarios.

The system was deployed in higher-education STEM courses with small student cohorts and graded assessments, limiting early interaction data. Deployment spanned two consecutive research cycles in comparable environments.

In the first cycle, feedback and recommendations were generated using an existing approach without the proposed fuzzy inference modeling. In the second cycle, the proposed approach was integrated into feedback generation, using inferred concept mastery values to generate recommendations and interpret sparse early interaction data. Other aspects of the learning environment and instructional design remained unchanged between cycles.

4.2 Observed Effects of the Proposed Fuzzy Inference Approach

Effects of the proposed fuzzy inference approach were observed through three aspects relevant to cold-start mitigation. Student interaction patterns and task-solving dynamics assess whether the system remains informative from early interactions. Student acceptance of recommendations based on estimated concept mastery is analyzed as an indicator of reliability and interpretability of early-stage system feedback. Learning outcomes mastery and performance thresholds evaluate whether early-stage personalization introduces instability in assessment.

Task-solving dynamics tracked student interaction patterns during the 15-day period before summative assessment activities. Dynamics for the first and second research cycles are shown in Figs. 3 and 4, respectively.

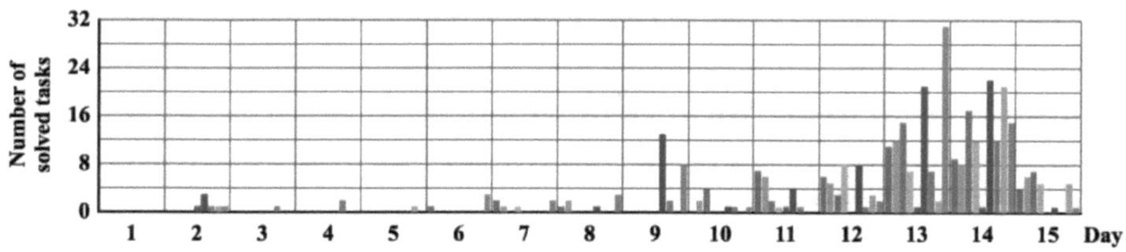

Fig. 3. Task-solving dynamics during the first research cycle (Colors represent the number of tasks solved within individual task groups).

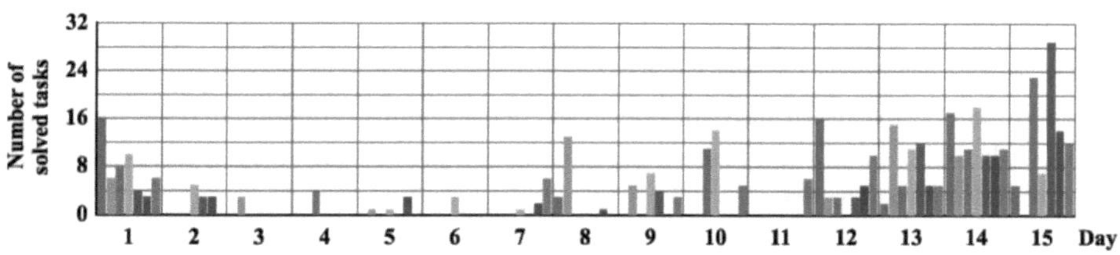

Fig. 4. Task-solving dynamics during the second research cycle (Colors represent the number of tasks solved within individual task groups).

The average number of tasks solved per student during this period was tracked. Table 1 presents the average number of solved tasks per student for both research cycles.

Table 1. Average number of tasks solved by the students during research cycles.

Research cycle	Number of enrolled students	Total number of solved tasks	Average number of solved tasks per student
1st cycle	22	374	17
2nd cycle	11	432	$39.27 \approx 39$

Student acceptance of generated recommendations was analyzed as an indicator of the reliability and interpretability of early-stage system feedback under cold-start conditions. A survey conducted after summative assessments collected student feedback. Results for both research cycles are shown in Table 2.

Table 2. Survey results for both research cycles.

Question	Research cycle	N	Avg	Var	StDev
I planned further steps in my learning using the recommendation showing the current level of learning outcomes that the online system showed me	1st cycle	20	2.70	1.31	1.14
	2nd cycle	11	4.55	0.61	0.78
The recommendation showing the current level of learning outcomes mastery motivated me to continue solving tasks in the system with the aim of increasing the percentage of learning outcomes achieved	1st cycle	20	3.45	1.25	1.12
	2nd cycle	11	4.27	0.38	0.62

The number of students reaching the minimum performance threshold was analyzed to evaluate whether early-stage personalization based on estimated concept mastery under cold-start conditions introduced instability in assessment. Table 3 presents the number of students who achieved the minimum performance threshold required to qualify for the final exam in both research cycles. Within each cycle, a control group that did not use the ERS was compared with an experimental group that used it (without the proposed fuzzy inference approach in the first research cycle and with it in the second).

Table 3. Student achievement of the minimum performance threshold for both research cycles.

Research cycle	Student group	Number of enrolled students	Students achieving more than 35 points		Student achieving less than 35 points	
			N	%	N	%
1st cycle	Control	55	39	70.90	16	29.10
	Experimental	22	17	77.27	5	22.73
2nd cycle	Control	36	20	55.55	16	44.45
	Experimental	11	10	90.91	1	9.09

Table 4 presents mean values of overall achievement examining whether early-stage personalization under cold-start conditions affected summative assessment outcomes.

Table 4. Mean values of overall student achievement.

Research cycle	Student group	Students qualifying for exam	Mean emester points	Mean total points	Students failing exam
1st cycle	Control	39	51.27	72.06	4
	Experimental	17	59.82	76.75	1
2nd cycle	Control	20	52.25	77.06	2
	Experimental	10	54.30	75.30	1

5 Discussion

5.1 Early-Stage Interaction Under Cold-Start Conditions

The analysis of student interaction patterns and task-solving dynamics examines whether the proposed fuzzy inference approach enables the system to remain informative during early stages of interaction under cold-start conditions.

As shown in Figs. 3 and 4, students in both research cycles exhibited a concentration of activity in the days before summative assessment. Early interaction was lower in the first cycle than in the second, where students began engaging earlier and maintained higher activity. This shift suggests that feedback based on inferred concept mastery using the proposed fuzzy inference system supported early-stage interaction.

Table 1 shows that the average number of solved tasks per student increased from 17 in the first research cycle to approximately 39 in the second, indicating that students perceived the system as meaningful from initial use, even when recommendations were generated from sparse interaction data using the proposed fuzzy inference system.

These results indicate that the self-adjustable fuzzy inference system mitigates cold-start effects by providing interpretable support from early stages of system use.

5.2 Perceived Usefulness and Trust in Early Adaptive Recommendations

Student acceptance of generated recommendations was analyzed as an indicator of the reliability, interpretability, and usefulness of system feedback under cold-start conditions. Because early-stage personalization relies on sparse interaction data, student responses provide insight into whether inferred concept mastery values were perceived as meaningful and aligned with learning needs.

Table 2 shows a clear increase in acceptance of recommendations in the second research cycle. In the first research cycle, students reported limited use of recommendations when planning learning activities and moderate motivational impact of system feedback. In the second cycle, students actively used recommendations to guide learning steps and perceived them as motivating for continued engagement.

Recommendations in the second cycle were generated using inferred concept mastery values obtained through the fuzzy inference system, even at early stages with limited data. Students nevertheless reported high acceptance, suggesting the feedback was interpretable and credible for learning-related decision-making. From a pedagogical perspective, such early feedback supports self-regulated learning by helping students plan and adjust their learning activities.

These results indicate that the proposed fuzzy inference approach increases trust in recommendations by providing interpretable feedback from early stages of interaction.

5.3 Assessment Robustness Under Cold-Start Personalization

The number of students reaching the minimum performance threshold was analyzed to evaluate whether early-stage personalization based on estimated concept mastery introduced instability in assessment. Unlike interaction patterns and acceptance measures, this analysis focuses on formal indicators with direct consequences.

Results in Table 3 show that in both research cycles a higher proportion of students in experimental groups achieved the minimum performance threshold required to qualify for the final exam than in control groups. The difference was moderate in the first cycle and more pronounced in the second, suggesting that adaptive feedback based on inferred concept mastery helped more students reach the required performance level.

Analysis of overall achievement indicates that this increase was not accompanied by distortion of summative assessment results. As shown in Table 4, mean values of total assessment points achieved by students who qualified for the final exam remained comparable across control and experimental groups in both research cycles.

Rather than shifting performance distributions upward, the approach supports a greater proportion of students meeting minimum performance requirements while preserving integrity and comparability of summative outcomes.

These results indicate that the self-adjustable fuzzy inference system enables early-stage personalization without compromising assessment stability.

5.4 Limitations

Although results support the effectiveness of the self-adjustable fuzzy inference approach under cold-start conditions, limitations remain. The evaluation was conducted in STEM courses with small student groups that reflect data-sparse conditions; broader validation across disciplines and institutions is needed to confirm generalizability. Findings should therefore be interpreted as exploratory rather than causal.

The implementation of self-adjustable fuzzy sets relies on structural assumptions derived from instructional design. Further validation across diverse curricular structures would clarify the broader applicability of the approach.

6 Conclusion

This paper addressed the cold-start problem in ERS by proposing a self-adjustable fuzzy inference system enabling early-stage estimation of learner model dimensions under sparse data. Unlike data-intensive or black-box approaches, the method combines fuzzy logic with dynamically adjustable membership functions to support interpretable learner modeling from early stages of system use.

The approach was deployed and evaluated in higher-education STEM courses across two research cycles. Results indicate that early-stage personalization based on inferred concept mastery using the proposed fuzzy inference system increased engagement and acceptance of recommendations while preserving outcomes and integrity. Improvements in progression toward minimum performance thresholds were achieved without introducing bias in assessment results.

These findings provide evidence that self-adjustable fuzzy inference systems may offer a transparent, efficient solution to the cold-start problem in ERS, enabling early-stage personalization in data-constrained environments.

Acknowledgments. This research was funded by the University of Rijeka through the European Union – NextGenerationEU program under the project *"GenAI in Teaching, Learning, and Assessment for Enhancing Students' Digital Competences in STEMI Education"* (uniri-mz-25-35).

Disclosure of Interests The authors have no competing interests to declare that are relevant to the content of this article.

References

1. Da Silva, F.L., Slodkowski, B.K., Da Silva, K.K.A., Cazella, S.C.: A systematic literature review on educational recommender systems for teaching and learning: research trends, limitations and opportunities. Educ. Inf. Technol. **28**(3), 3289–3328 (2023)
2. Yera, R., Martinez, L.: Fuzzy tools in recommender systems: a survey. Int. J. Comput. Intell. Syst. **10**(1), 776–803 (2017)
3. Gope, J., Jain, S.K.: A survey on solving cold start problem in recommender systems. In: Proceedings of the 2017 International Conference on Computing, Communication and Automation, pp. 133–138. IEEE, Greater Noida, India (2017)
4. Yuan, H., Hernandez, A.A.: User cold start problem in recommendation systems: a systematic review. IEEE Access. **11**, 136958–136977 (2023)
5. Ahmadian Yazdi, H., Seyyed Mahdavi, S.J., Ahmadian Yazdi, H.: Dynamic educational recommender system based on improved LSTM neural network. Sci. Rep. **14**(1), 1–19 (2024)
6. Alghamdi, S., Alzhrani, N., Algethami, H.: Fuzzy-based recommendation system for university major selection. In: Proceedings of the 11th International Joint Conference on Computational Intelligence, pp. 317–324. SCITEPRESS, Vienna, Austria (2019)
7. Sami, A., Adrousy, W.E., Sarhan, S., Elmougy, S.: A deep learning based hybrid recommendation model for internet users. Sci. Rep. **14**(1), 1–19 (2024)
8. Zadeh, L.A.: Fuzzy sets. Inf. Control. **8**(3), 338–353 (1965)
9. Klašnja-Milićević, A., Ivanović, M., Vesin, B., Budimac, Z.: Enhancing e-learning systems with personalized recommendation based on collaborative tagging techniques. Appl. Intell. **48**(6), 1519–1535 (2018)
10. Zenebe, A., Norcio, A.F.: Representation, similarity measures and aggregation methods using fuzzy sets for content-based recommender systems. Fuzzy Sets Syst. **160**(1), 76–94 (2009)
11. Tudor, I., Holenko Dlab, M., Đurović, G., Horvat, M.: Using clustering techniques to design learner personas for GenAI prompt engineering and adaptive interventions. Electronics. **14**(11), 2281–2302 (2025)
12. Negnevitsky, M.: Artificial Intelligence. Pearson education, USA (2005)
13. Doz, D., Felda, D., Cotič, M.: Assessing students' mathematical knowledge with fuzzy logic. Educ. Sci. **12**(4), 1–17 (2022)

14. Hoić-Božić, N., Holenko Dlab, M., Mornar, V.: Recommender system and web 2.0 tools to enhance blended learning model. IEEE Trans. Educ. **59**(1), 39–44 (2016)
15. Felder, R., Silverman, L.: Learning and teaching styles in engineering education. Eng. Educ. **78**(7), 674–681 (1988)

OntoThink: An Ontology-Supported Generative AI Learning Companion System with KCR Diagnosis Mechanism

Jiying Wu[1], Kanglin Fan[1], Wei Li[2], Judy C. R. Tseng[1,3](✉), and Li-Chen Cheng[4]

[1] Department of Computer Science and Information Engineering, Chung Hua University, Hsinchu, Taiwan
judycrt@gmail.com
[2] STEM Education Research Center, Wenzhou University, Wenzhou, Zhejiang Province,, China
[3] Center for Continuing Education, National Tsinghua University, Hsinchu, Taiwan
[4] Department of Information and Finance Management, National Taipei University of Technology, Taipei, Taiwan

Abstract. In educational settings, learning companions play a crucial role in facilitating peer interaction and knowledge construction. With advances in artificial intelligence, generative AI has demonstrated significant potential as a learning companion, providing natural-language interaction and personalized feedback. However, existing generative AI systems lack the ability to actively assess learners' prior knowledge, which may increase cognitive load and misconceptions. Moreover, large language models (LLMs) are limited in their ability to model knowledge graphs and causal reasoning, leading to fragmented knowledge delivery. To address these limitations, this study introduces ontology as a structured knowledge framework and develops OntoThink, an ontology-supported generative AI learning companion system. A three-dimensional learning diagnosis mechanism, called KCR (Knowledge domain, Correctness, Repetition), is proposed for this system to diagnose students' learning status through their interactions with the learning companion. The cross-combination of the three dimensions in KCR yields twelve distinct learning scenarios, enabling the AI learning companion to provide contextual guidance and personalized learning diagnosis. By integrating ontology-based knowledge structures and generative AI capabilities, the system supports students in understanding interconnections among knowledge concepts.

Keywords: KCR Learning Diagnosis Mechanism · Ontology · Knowledge Graph · Learning Companion · Generative AI

1 Introduction

In educational settings, learning is not merely an individual activity; interaction among learners plays a critical role in the learning process [1, 11]. Learning companions refer to partnerships in which students assist each other and grow together during learning. Research has demonstrated that peer interaction deepens conceptual understanding and enhances learning outcomes [1]. As AI technologies have matured, they have

C.-J. Lin et al. (Eds.): ICITL 2026, LNCS 16841, pp. 208–218, 2027.
https://doi.org/10.1007/978-3-032-32112-1_21

emerged as promising tools for supporting learning companion interactions, bringing new possibilities to collaborative learning.

Research suggests that AI complements traditional learning companions in two key dimensions [2, 3]: participation in knowledge structure construction and dynamic analysis through real-time feedback. Furthermore, generative AI has overcome the limitations of traditional chatbots through semantic analysis and contextual reasoning, supporting multi-turn dialogues and open-ended discussions [4].

However, generative AI as a learning companion still faces two fundamental challenges. First, AI systems cannot actively assess users' prior knowledge; when students lack foundational understanding, advanced explanations may increase cognitive load and reinforce misconceptions [5]. Second, LLMs rely on statistical prediction rather than genuine knowledge graph modeling; their attention-based architecture, not designed for deductive reasoning, distorts causal relationships and fragments delivery across related concepts [6].

To address these limitations, ontology provides a viable solution. In information science, ontology serves as a conceptual framework that describes entities and their relationships through explicit semantic structures [7]. Ontology provides clear concept hierarchies and associations that address the limitations of current generative AI in understanding hierarchical and subordinate relationships, strengthening its logical reasoning capabilities.

Accordingly, this study develops an ontology-supported generative AI learning companion system, OntoThink, that has three distinct features: (1) a KCR (Knowledge Domain, Correctness, Repetition) learning diagnosis mechanism that analyzes students' questions across three dimensions to identify their learning status; (2) personalized learning diagnosis and contextual guidance are provided according to the twelve learning scenarios formed by cross-combining the three KCR dimensions; and (3) a visual diagnosis interface that renders KCR states on the knowledge graph formed by ontology through color-coded nodes, allowing students to intuitively observe their learning status and knowledge gaps. These features collectively support instructional adjustment by teachers and self-regulation by students.

The remainder of this paper is organized as follows. Section 2 reviews the related work on learning companions, AI learning companions, generative AI, and ontology in education. Section 3 presents the research method, including the KCR mechanism, the twelve learning scenarios, and the system architecture. Section 4 describes the system implementation. Section 5 concludes the paper and discusses future research directions.

2 Related Work

2.1 Learning Companions

The concept of learning companions was first proposed by Chan [8], describing a model in which learning companions can serve as peers, teachers, or even virtual avatars, playing the roles of supporters, guides, and co-learners in the learning process. Learning companions not only facilitate information transfer but also provide emotional support and the cultivation of critical thinking, creating a collaborative learning environment that promotes mutual growth [9]. Research has shown that peer interaction deepens understanding and promotes knowledge construction [10], while collaborative learning with companions fosters critical thinking skills [11].

2.2 AI Learning Companions

An AI learning companion is a learning support system that utilizes AI technologies to enhance educational experiences by promoting collaboration and providing personalized support. Research has found that AI complements traditional learning companions in two key dimensions [2, 3]: participation in knowledge structure construction and dynamic analysis through real-time feedback, so that students receive effective guidance and adjust their learning strategies. Interactive dialogue capability has been identified as a critical future direction for AI learning companions [3]. However, existing AI learning companion systems generally lack mechanisms for structured knowledge representation and active learning diagnosis, limiting their ability to provide targeted guidance based on individual learners' conceptual understanding.

2.3 Generative AI as Learning Companions

Generative AI refers to AI technologies that learn from large-scale data to generate new content. In education, generative AI enhances student engagement and learning effectiveness through personalized learning pathways and adaptive assessment [12]. However, its application as a learning companion faces notable limitations. One key limitation is the absence of prior knowledge assessment mechanisms; without gauging what a learner already knows, the system risks delivering explanations that exceed the learner's cognitive capacity, widening rather than closing conceptual gaps [5]. Another concern is that LLM responses are generated through statistical patterns rather than structured reasoning, which constrains their ability to model causal relationships and may produce fragmented or misleading knowledge representations [6].

2.4 Ontology in Education

In information science, ontology is used to formally describe concepts and relationships within a knowledge domain, providing clear knowledge structures that allow information to be more effectively retrieved, analyzed, and applied [13]. With ontology, students can grasp knowledge through relationships, such as is-a (subordinate) and is-a-part-of (compositional), leading to a more comprehensive understanding of knowledge structures [14]. An example ontology of computer is demonstrated in Fig. 1. Empirical studies confirm that ontology-based approaches improve learning adaptability and effectiveness in higher education contexts [15]. By explicitly representing concept hierarchies and associations, ontology addresses the limitations of current generative AI in understanding hierarchical and subordinate relationships and improves its capacity for logical reasoning.

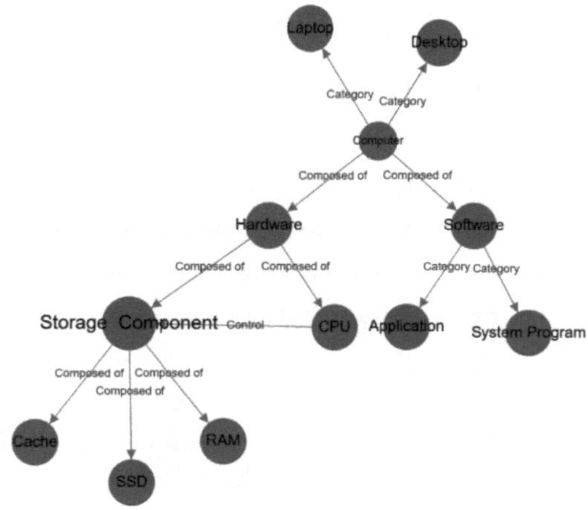

Fig. 1. An example of the ontology of computer

3 Research Method

This study employs ontology as the core knowledge representation, combined with the semantic understanding and interactive capabilities of generative AI, to construct a learning companion system capable of performing learning diagnosis and contextual guidance during the learning process.

3.1 KCR Learning Diagnosis Mechanism

Learning diagnosis is the core challenge of the system, as students' understanding cannot be directly observed but only inferred from their dialogues. This study maps student questions to knowledge nodes constructed in the ontology and characterizes their questions into three dimensions, Knowledge domain (K), Correctness (C), and Repetition (R), to diagnose their learning status as summarized in Table 1.

The diagnosis methods are as follows. For K, the system employs cosine similarity [16] to compute the semantic similarity between the student's question and each knowledge node, with a similarity threshold of 0.8 to balance over- and under-matching; this value is adjustable for different contexts. For C, an LLM is used to mark the statement as C0 when a conceptual error or logical contradiction is judged to exist; otherwise, it is marked as C1. For R, the system counts the number of queries related to each knowledge node within a learning session; the third consecutive query on the same node is classified as R1, otherwise as R0, to reflect whether the student has genuine comprehension difficulty with the node.

Table 1. KCR three-dimensional learning diagnosis

Dimension	State	Description
Knowledge Domain (K)	K0	No match to any knowledge node.
	K1	Related to only one knowledge node.
	KN	Related to multiple knowledge nodes.
Correctness(C)	C0	Contradiction, conflict, or error detected.
	C1	Open-ended or no significant error detected.
Repetition (R)	R0	First query, or fewer than three consecutive queries focused on the same knowledge node.
	R1	More than three consecutive queries focused on the same knowledge node.

3.2 Learning Scenarios

Each student's question is evaluated along the three KCR dimensions, and the resulting combination of states defines the student's current learning scenario. Accordingly, the system distinguishes twelve learning scenarios (K has 3 states, C has 2, and R has 2, yielding $3 \times 2 \times 2 = 12$ unique combinations), each mapped to a specific response strategy as summarized in Table 2.

Table 2. Learning scenarios and respective replying strategies

No.	Learning Scenarios	Response Strategies
1	K0–C0–R0	Briefly identify the error and guide the student back to core instructional material concepts.
2	K0–C0–R1	Point out repeated errors and remind the student to review prior learning content.
3	K0–C1–R0	Respond to the question and guide the student toward relevant knowledge nodes.
4	K0–C1–R1	Guide the student to reflect on their understanding and locate appropriate knowledge nodes.
5	K1–C0–R0	Explain the error and provide a correct explanation of the single concept
6	K1–C0–R1	Request self-assessment, identify the error, and decompose the concept for correct understanding.
7	K1–C1–R0	Explain the question and extend to one related concept to deepen understanding.
8	K1–C1–R1	Guide self-review of learning status and decompose-reorganize the concept to strengthen understanding
9	KN–C0–R0	Identify the error, explain multiple related concepts individually, and integrate them into a complete framework.

(continued)

Table 2. (*continued*)

No.	Learning Scenarios	Response Strategies
10	KN–C0–R1	Guide reflection on understanding gaps, correct errors, and then integrate multiple concepts.
11	KN–C1–R0	Explain each related concept individually and integrate them into a complete knowledge structure.
12	KN–C1–R1	Guide self-assessment of learning status and assist in decomposing and then reintegrating multiple concepts.

3.3 System Architecture of OntoThink

As shown in Fig. 2, the system comprises ten functional modules organized into three groups: (1) teacher-side: includes Ontology Management, Instructional Material Management, Domain Knowledge Training, and Learning Portfolio Browsing modules; (2) analytical core: includes Domain Knowledge Analysis, Ontology Analysis, and Learning Diagnosis modules; and (3) student-side: includes Extended Learning, Responses Synthesis, and Learning Portfolio Recording modules. The system incorporates four databases: Ontology, Instructional Material, Domain Knowledge Model, and Learning Portfolio databases, and employs Retrieval-Augmented Generation (RAG) [17] to integrate instructional material with the LLM, producing responses grounded in subject-specific materials.

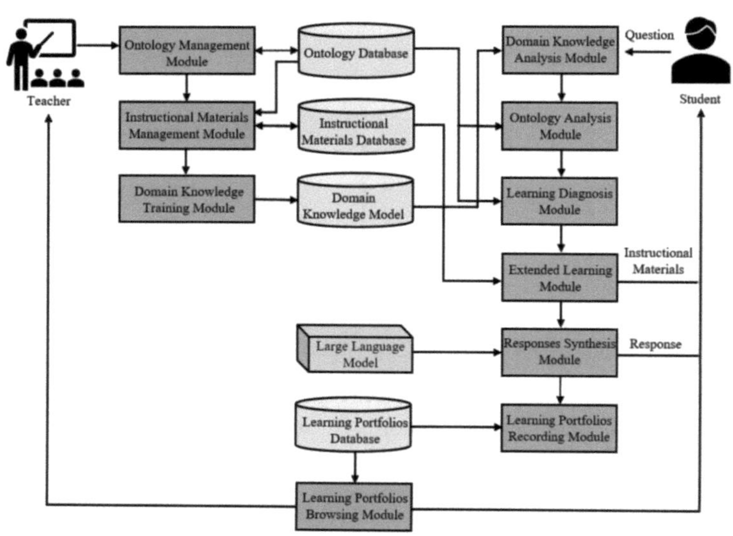

Fig. 2. System architecture of the ontology-supported generative AI learning companion system

The system operates in three main steps. First, the student submits a question, activating the question parsing controller. Second, the system analyzes the question across K (cosine similarity on RAG embeddings), C (conceptual judgement), and R (consecutive queries), and maps it to one of the twelve learning scenarios. Third, the generative AI core produces a response incorporating ontology-based knowledge hierarchies, diagnostic results, and extended learning suggestions, while the interaction is recorded in the learning portfolio database.

4 Implementation

The system is implemented with separate interfaces for teachers and students. The teacher's side is responsible for constructing ontology knowledge architecture, managing instructional material content, and monitoring student learning progress. The student side provides interactive dialogue with the AI learning companion, along with learning diagnosis and extended learning recommendations.

On the teacher side, the ontology management interface (Fig. 3) enables teachers to create and modify knowledge nodes according to course content, defining hierarchical and associative relationships among concepts to establish a structured ontology knowledge graph. This graph serves as the foundation for subsequent knowledge analysis and learning diagnosis.

Fig. 3. Teacher-side ontology management interface

The learning portfolio browsing interface (Fig. 4) allows teachers to review students' dialogue records. Teachers can filter records by student and date, so they can identify patterns of repeated difficulty and adjust instructional strategies accordingly.

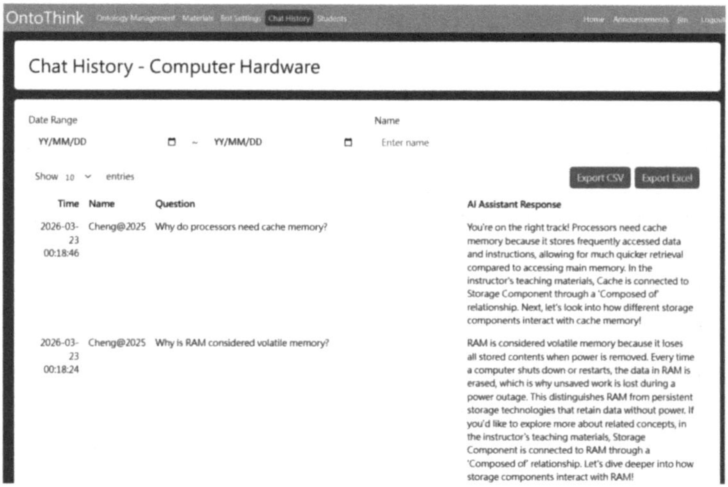

Fig. 4. Teacher-side learning portfolio browsing interface

On the student side, the dialogue and visual diagnosis interface (Fig. 5) presents the ontology knowledge graph alongside the conversation of the GAI learning companion. Students pose learning-related questions through the dialogue input, and the system provides responses that integrate domain knowledge, diagnostic results, and extended learning suggestions. Concurrently, knowledge nodes on the ontology graph are color-coded to reflect the KCR states diagnosed, allowing students to intuitively identify their learning position, comprehension level, and areas requiring further study. When the diagnostic result indicates that a student has engaged with a particular knowledge point, the corresponding node is rendered in green; when repeated incorrect inquiries on the same concept are detected, the node turns red to signal comprehension difficulty; and when the system identifies related concepts suitable for further study, those nodes are highlighted in yellow to guide the student toward extended learning.

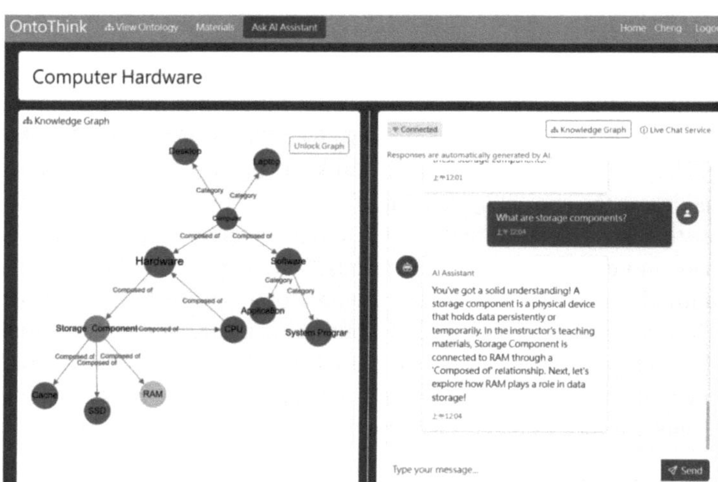

Fig. 5. Student-side dialogue and visual learning diagnosis interface with an ontology knowledge graph

5 Conclusion and Future Work

5.1 Conclusion

This study developed an ontology-supported generative AI learning companion system that serves as a fully operational platform for educational settings. The system employs ontology as its core knowledge structure, allowing teachers to import course knowledge in a structured manner while providing learning diagnosis, learning portfolio tracking, and contextual learning guidance.

The proposed three-dimensional KCR learning diagnosis mechanism provides a structured and actionable approach to understanding student learning states. The Knowledge domain dimension (K) reflects the scope of concepts involved in student queries; the Correctness dimension (C) assists in identifying misconceptions; and the Repetition dimension (R) helps locate learning stagnation. Through cross-combination, twelve learning scenarios are formed, each corresponding to a specific GAI response strategy. This contextualized guidance provides a structured way of addressing the knowledge fragmentation problem commonly observed in traditional AI teaching systems and guides students in building coherent knowledge structures.

Through ontology-based structured knowledge representation, the system also transforms student interaction histories into analytically meaningful data. The KCR diagnostic records allow teachers to quantitatively analyze common learning difficulties across the class and qualitatively trace each student's learning path, providing an evidence-based foundation for instructional adjustment. The visual diagnosis interface, which renders KCR states on the ontology knowledge graph through color-coded nodes, provides students with an intuitive overview of their learning progress and knowledge gaps, which can in turn facilitate self-regulated learning.

5.2 Future Work

In the near future, we plan to conduct controlled teaching experiments at senior high schools, comparing learning outcomes between students using the ontology-supported GAI learning companion system and those using conventional generative AI chatbots, to validate the system's educational effectiveness. To reduce the burden of manual ontology construction, AI-assisted ontology generation techniques will be explored to automatically produce preliminary knowledge structures from instructional materials [18], enabling teachers to refine AI-generated drafts rather than building ontologies from scratch. In addition, the current system interface does not yet display the corresponding KCR diagnostic results, and future work will aim to integrate these results into the interface to provide more explicit learning feedback. The proposed architecture is designed to be domain-independent; by replacing the ontology and instructional materials, the system can be adapted to subjects beyond computer science, including natural sciences, social sciences, and so on. By bridging structured knowledge representation with generative AI interaction, this work demonstrates a viable path toward AI learning companions that are not only conversationally fluent but also pedagogically grounded.

Acknowledgments. This study was supported by the National Science and Technology Council, Taiwan under contract numbers NSTC 114-2813-C-216-002-H, NSTC 114-2410-H-027-002, NSTC 114-2410-H-027-022-MY2, and NSTC 113-2410-H-216-001-MY2.

Disclosure of Interests The authors have no competing interests to declare that are relevant to the content of this article.

References

1. Johnson, D.W., Johnson, R.T.: An educational psychology success story: social interdependence theory and cooperative learning. Educ. Res. **38**(5), 365–379 (2009)
2. Lee, G.G., Mun, S., Shin, M.K., Zhai, X.: Collaborative learning with artificial intelligence speakers (CLAIS): pre-service elementary science teachers' responses to the prototype. Sci. Educ. **33**(4), 1234–1256 (2024)
3. Mossbridge, J.: Shifting the human-AI relationship: toward a dynamic relational learning-partner model. arXiv preprint arXiv:2410.11864. (2024)
4. Kasneci, E., Seßler, K., Küchemann, S., et al.: ChatGPT for good? On opportunities and challenges of large language models for education. Learn. Individ. Differ. **103**, 102274 (2023)
5. Dong, A., Jong, M.S.Y., King, R.B.: How does prior knowledge influence learning engagement? The mediating roles of cognitive load and help-seeking. Front. Psychol. **11**, 591203 (2020)
6. Dai, X., Hua, Y., Wu, T., Sheng, Y., Ji, Q., Qi, G.: Large language models can better understand knowledge graphs than we thought. Knowl.-Based Syst. **313**, 113107 (2025)
7. Alnahdi, A.K.: Semantic applications for ontological information theory. J. Phys. Conf. Ser. **1812**(1), 012026 (2021)
8. Chan, T.W.: Learning companion systems. In: At the Crossroad of Artificial Intelligence and Education (1990)
9. Biswas, G., Katzlberger, T., Bransford, J., Schwartz, D.: Extending intelligent learning environments with teachable agents to enhance learning. In: Artificial Intelligence in Education, pp. 389–397. IOS Press (2001)
10. Tenenbaum, H.R., Winstone, N., Leman, P.J., Avery, R.E.: How effective is peer interaction in facilitating learning? A meta-analysis. J. Educ. Psychol. **112**(7), 1303–1319 (2020)
11. Chen, W., Hu, H., Lyu, Q., Zheng, L.: Using peer feedback to improve critical thinking in computer-supported collaborative argumentation: an exploratory study. J. Comput. Assist. Learn. **40**, 3390–3405 (2024)
12. Dhagare, R.P.: Generative AI and education: a symbiotic relationship. Int. J. Sci. Technol. Eng. **12**(11), 1042–1045 (2024)
13. de Oliveira, C.C., Barros, T.H.B.: Ontologies and research data. Can. J. Inf. Libr. Sci. **47**(2), 30–38 (2024)
14. Villegas-Ch, W., García-Ortiz, J.: Enhancing learning personalization in educational environments through ontology-based knowledge representation. Computers. **12**(10), 199 (2023)
15. Stoyanova-Doycheva, A., Cholakov, G., Glushkova, T.: Using ontologies in e-learning in software engineering course. Comput. Sci. Interdiscip. Res. J. **3**, 98–109 (2024)

16. Reimers, N., Gurevych, I.: Sentence-BERT: sentence embeddings using Siamese BERT-networks. In: Proceedings of the 2019 Conference on Empirical Methods in Natural Language Processing (EMNLP-IJCNLP), pp. 3982–3992 (2019)
17. Lewis, P., Perez, E., Piktus, A., et al.: Retrieval-augmented generation for knowledge-intensive NLP tasks. In: Advances in Neural Information Processing Systems, vol. 33, pp. 9459–9474 (2020)
18. Babaei Giglou, H., D'Souza, J., Auer, S.: LLMs4OL: large language models for ontology learning. In: Payne, T.R., et al. (eds.) The Semantic Web – ISWC 2023 Lecture Notes in Computer Science, vol. 14265, pp. 408–427. Springer (2023)

Applying Deep Learning Semantic Analysis to Assist Think-Aloud Method in Programming Courses: A Case Study of the PALA System

Yu-Lin Jeng(✉) and Pei-Yu Kuo

Department of Information Management, Southern Taiwan University of Science and Technology, Tainan City, Taiwan
{jackjeng,mb390205}@stust.edu.tw

Abstract. Traditional think-aloud methods for assessing computational thinking (CT) are labor-intensive and lack real-time feedback. This study developed the "Programming-Assisted Learning App" (PALA), which integrates mobile voice recognition and Sentence-BERT (SBERT) to automate cognitive process analysis. PALA captures students' verbalized logic, converts it into semantic vectors, and calculates similarity against instructor-defined concepts using cosine similarity. Students receiving scores below a threshold are instantly provided with remedial materials. Preliminary implementation with 60 university students demonstrates that PALA's similarity scores accurately reflect the mastery of CT elements, such as abstraction and algorithmic thinking. The system successfully reduced text coding time from days to seconds, enabling immediate instructional diagnosis. These findings validate the feasibility of using automated semantic analysis to provide personalized feedback and help instructors dynamically adjust teaching strategies in large-scale programming classrooms.

Keywords: Programming Education · Think-aloud Method · Semantic Analysis · SBERT · Computational Thinking

1 Introduction

In the contemporary era, where digital technology rapidly permeates daily life, Computational Thinking (CT) has become an indispensable basic literacy for modern citizens. Wing (2006) points out that computational thinking is not limited to programming; rather, it is a thought process that involves solving problems, designing systems, and understanding human behavior by drawing on the concepts fundamental to computer science. Consequently, academia has increasingly emphasized enhancing students' computational thinking skills through programming courses (Hambrusch et al., 2009; Israel et al., 2015) viewing it as a core objective of engineering and information education in technological and vocational colleges.

To effectively evaluate students' programming logic and problem-solving processes, researchers often employ the "Think-aloud Method". This method requires learners to verbalize their thoughts during the problem-solving process, making originally implicit

C.-J. Lin et al. (Eds.): ICITL 2026, LNCS 16841, pp. 219–230, 2027.
https://doi.org/10.1007/978-3-032-32112-1_22

cognitive processes explicit. This, in turn, allows teachers to identify students' thinking obstacles in abstraction or algorithmic design. However, the traditional think-aloud method faces significant challenges in practical implementation, especially in large-classroom teaching environments. Teachers find it difficult to monitor the verbalizations of multiple students simultaneously; furthermore, subsequent speech-to-text transcription and text coding are extremely time-consuming, leading to delays in feedback mechanisms and making it difficult to achieve real-time instructional intervention.

With breakthroughs in Natural Language Processing (NLP) technology, deep learning models have provided new solutions for automated text analysis. Technologies such as Sentence-BERT (SBERT) can transform natural language into high-dimensional semantic vectors, utilizing Cosine Similarity to precisely measure the consistency between students' verbalizations and standard concepts. If this technology can be integrated into mobile learning platforms to develop an auxiliary system with real-time semantic interpretation capabilities, it will break through the labor and time constraints of the traditional think-aloud method, achieving automated learning diagnosis.

Based on these needs, this study developed a Programming-Assisted Learning App (PALA) that integrates semantic analysis technology with the think-aloud method. This research aims to explore the effectiveness of the PALA system in improving students' computational thinking skills within programming courses at technological and vocational colleges. Through the real-time semantic feedback and remedial teaching mechanisms provided by the system, it is expected not only to assist students in clarifying abstract programming concepts but also to provide teachers with quantified instructional diagnostic data, thereby optimizing teaching strategies and enhancing overall learning quality.

2 Literature Review

2.1 Think-Aloud Method and Programming Learning

The think-aloud method is a type of protocol analysis (Ginsburg, 1983), primarily used to evaluate and describe the construction process of procedural knowledge within cognitive structures. This method requires subjects to simultaneously verbalize their thoughts while solving problems, allowing researchers to collect cognitive information from short-term memory (Ericsson & Simon, 1980). In the field of programming education, the think-aloud method is regarded as a highly valuable tool for instruction and assessment. Teachers can use it to guide students in verbalizing their operational ideas during practice, thereby leading them through the thinking procedures of problem-solving.

The think-aloud method has been widely applied in practical and technical training, particularly in applications aimed at developing specific technical skills. Past research indicates that requiring students to explain the thoughts behind their problem-solving processes can effectively assist teachers in analyzing learning difficulties and providing suggestions to enhance metacognitive abilities. For example, in educational robotics programming tasks, guiding students to explain the computational thinking concepts and techniques they apply through thinking aloud can effectively optimize their problem-solving processes. This "doing-while-talking" model is believed to help improve students' reading comprehension and the development of logical thinking.

However, the implementation of the traditional think-aloud method in actual teaching settings faces significant technical barriers. First, past studies have largely relied on video or audio equipment to record students' problem-solving processes. However, for a classroom with a large number of students (e.g., approximately 60 students), subsequent video/audio data cleaning and transcription require enormous labor costs. Second, this manual analysis model often involves a time lag, preventing teachers from obtaining real-time feedback on students' learning status during classroom instruction, which in turn causes them to miss the optimal timing for adjusting teaching strategies. Furthermore, although the text content written or spoken by students represents the degree of their knowledge internalization, it is difficult to transform into data with instructional value without effective automated interpretation technology (Cer et al., 2017).

In summary, although the think-aloud method has significant cognitive assistance effects in programming learning, "analytical efficiency" and "immediacy" remain the two major obstacles in current practical applications. With the advancement of natural language processing (NLP) and mobile technology, utilizing the built-in speech-to-text functions of smartphones, combined with high-performance semantic similarity comparison technology, has become a key direction for improving analytical efficiency. By establishing an automated interpretation system, it is expected that students' think-aloud content can be instantly transformed into quantifiable learning indicators, providing a more dynamic and individualized feedback mechanism for programming courses.

2.2 Semantic Similarity Analysis Technique

In the field of Natural Language Processing (NLP), enabling computers to understand the semantic expressions of human language has consistently been a core challenge. Early research primarily relied on simple textual features, such as keyword tokenization or Term Frequency (TF) for analysis. However, with technological progress, the introduction of Word Embedding techniques has allowed words or sentences to be converted into mathematical formats within continuous vector spaces, enabling the quantification of semantic relationships between objects. In these vector models, words with similar meanings are mapped to adjacent spatial positions, allowing researchers to use Cosine Similarity between vectors to measure the degree of semantic proximity.

Breakthroughs in deep learning technology have further enhanced the precision of semantic understanding. The BERT (Bidirectional Encoder Representations from Transformers) model proposed by Google achieves bidirectional contextual modeling through the Transformer architecture. Compared to traditional unidirectional processing methods, BERT considers both preceding and following contextual information when processing specific vocabulary, thereby capturing subtle semantic differences in sentences more accurately (Devlin et al., 2018). This enables computers not only to recognize literal vocabulary but also to understand the deeper meanings represented by terms within specific instructional contexts, such as programming logic descriptions.

Despite BERT's powerful semantic understanding capabilities, its high computational resource requirements for large-scale sentence comparison tasks make it difficult to meet the demands for real-time feedback in classrooms. Consequently, this study adopts the SBERT (Sentence-BERT) model derived from BERT. SBERT enhances the base architecture with a Pooling strategy to convert sentences more effectively into Sentence Embeddings and allows for the parallel processing of sentence pairs, significantly improving computational efficiency. In the context of mobile device applications with limited resources, SBERT provides efficient and accurate sentence comparison capabilities, leading to its widespread use in tasks such as search engines and semantic similarity analysis.

Synthesizing these technological developments, the PALA system developed in this study utilizes the all-MiniLM-L6-v2 model based on the SBERT architecture as its core. While maintaining efficient semantic representation, this model effectively reduces computational resource requirements, making it highly suitable for deployment on server-side systems for real-time comparison. The system converts the verbalized text input by students via the think-aloud method and the standard answers provided by teachers into vectors, calculating the Cosine Similarity between them as a similarity index. Through this technological integration, the PALA system quantifies abstract learning processes into concrete percentage feedback, providing students with immediate diagnosis of their learning performance.

2.3 Computational Thinking Features and Evaluations

Computational Thinking (CT) was initially viewed as the planning of an algorithmic process, essentially a thinking method for systematically solving problems through algorithmic design. Wing (2006) further defined computational thinking as an analytical mindset that utilizes fundamental computer science concepts for problem-solving, system design, and understanding human behavior. As challenges in the digital age increase, computational thinking has become an indispensable foundational skill in the education system, which not only enhances students' problem-solving techniques but also positively impacts their understanding of computer science knowledge.

While there are varying perspectives on the definition of computational thinking within academia, most agree that it comprises four core elements: (Barr & Stephenson, 2011; Selby & Woollard, 2013; Wing, 2006)

- **Abstraction**: Extracting key concepts or core ideas from a vast amount of information while ignoring irrelevant details.
- **Decomposition**: Breaking down a complex problem into multiple smaller, manageable sub-problems to gradually achieve an overall solution.
- **Algorithmic Thinking**: Designing a series of specific steps or instructions to solve problems in a systematic and repeatable manner.
- **Data Representation**: Organizing and displaying data through graphs, tables, text, or images to make it intuitive and easy to understand. Through the cultivation of these four elements, students can effectively organize problems and transform logical abilities into tools for solving real-world scenarios.

Despite the significant role of computational thinking in improving learning outcomes, the cultivation process is not easy; students often struggle to choose appropriate solution strategies due to a lack of background knowledge or experience. Traditional programming instruction, if overly focused on syntax learning, can easily lead students to neglect the core process of problem-solving (Snyder & Snyder, 2008). Therefore, in the design of instructional strategies for this study, guidance was provided with reference to the connotations of computational thinking elements, requiring students to verbalize their problem-solving context through the PALA system after completing exercises. This model, which combines the think-aloud method, forces students to reflect on their processes of abstraction and problem decomposition, thereby deepening their cognitive structures.

To verify the feasibility of the proposed PALA system in evaluating computational thinking performance, this study utilized "semantic similarity" measured automatically by the system as an evaluation indicator in the preliminary experiment. By analyzing the think-aloud texts of students regarding specific programming concepts (such as loops, lists, etc.), the correlation between similarity values and the mastery of computational thinking elements was explored. The evaluation focus of this stage was to verify the interpretation accuracy of the deep learning model regarding students' logical descriptions, as well as the practical effectiveness of the real-time diagnostic feedback provided by the system. This serves as the academic foundation for the formal implementation of quasi-experimental research and scale evaluation in the future.

3 Research Design and System Development

3.1 System Architecture of PALA

The PALA system developed in this study adopts a two-tier architecture consisting of a Client and a Server. Considering that students in technological and vocational colleges generally own smartphones, the client-side is built as a mobile application (APP). This utilizes the phone's built-in microphone and Speech-to-Text services to replace the cumbersome recording equipment required by the traditional think-aloud method.

The server-side employs a RESTful architecture to ensure high scalability and maintainability of the system. The core modules of the system are as follows (please refer to Fig. 1 for the detailed system architecture diagram):

- **User Login Module**: Distinguishes between teacher and student permissions and provides personalized course lists.
- **Course Information Module**: Stores teacher-preset learning concepts, programming exercises, and standard problem-solving thought texts.
- **Semantic Similarity Analysis Module**: Employs the all-MiniLM-L6-v2 model under the SBERT architecture to transform students' verbalized text and teachers' standard answers into vectors, which are then compared using the cosine similarity formula.
- **Supplementary Material Feedback Module**: Based on the comparison results, it instantly pushes multimedia supplementary teaching materials to students who have not reached the threshold.

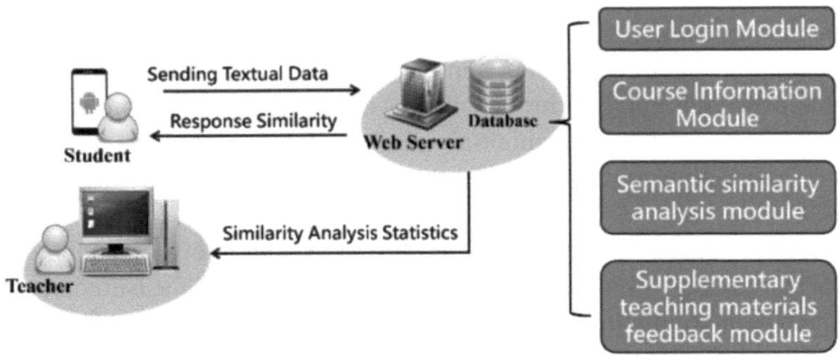

Fig. 1. System Architecture of PALA

3.2 Design of Learning Activities

The instructional activities of this study are centered around the "IoT Platform Application Development" course. For each programming learning concept, a cyclic teaching process consisting of seven stages is designed:

- (1) Abstraction Concept Teaching: The teacher explains the key core and application scenarios of each learning concept.
- (2) Decomposition Concept Teaching: Through examples, a major programming problem is broken down into multiple smaller, manageable sub-problems.
- (3) Algorithmic Thinking Guidance: Designing a specific series of steps or instructions to implement the examples.
- (4) Data Representation Implementation: Transforming the instructions into Python code to make the learning concepts more intuitive.
- (5) Operational Drill: Students perform hands-on practice and drills on the computer for exercises related to the same learning concept.
- (6) Problem Solving: Students independently write code and debug based on the computational thinking steps taught by the teacher.
- (7) Implementation of Thinking Aloud: After the self-practice session, students spend 3–5 min reflecting on their code and verbalizing their problem description and problem-solving thought process through the PALA system, receiving immediate feedback.

3.3 Practical Verification Process and Research Objects

Following the completion of system development, a preliminary practical verification was conducted with approximately 60 junior students from the Department of Information Management at a university of technology in southern Taiwan. The participants all possessed foundational programming backgrounds, such as Java and web programming, making them suitable for advanced IoT Python programming experiments.

The preliminary verification process utilized a "one-group posttest-only design," focusing on observing the PALA system's interpretation performance and feedback effectiveness within an authentic teaching environment. The experimental procedure was as follows:

- **Pre-test Preparation**: The instructor pre-established standard problem-solving thought texts on the server for key concepts such as "loop design," "list application," and "event-driven control".
- **Classroom Implementation**: During the "IoT Platform Application Development" course, students first received computational thinking-guided instruction followed by 20 min of hands-on programming practice.
- **Think-Aloud and Collection**: After completing the practice, students used the PALA mobile application to perform a 3–5 min think-aloud verbalization of their problem-solving logic. The system automatically converted the speech into text and instantly calculated the semantic similarity value.
- **Data Analysis Indicators**: Data collected during this phase included the content of the students' verbalized text, the similarity score calculated by the system, and the automated pass/fail status determined by the system.

Fig. 2. Student Thought-Providing Interface

By analyzing this set of preliminary experimental data, this study was able to examine the ability of the PALA system's SBERT model to distinguish between heterogeneous student responses—such as correct logic, brief descriptions, or conceptual misunderstandings—thereby evaluating the usability of the system as an instructional auxiliary tool. Regarding the implementation interfaces of the PALA system, Figure 2 illustrates the streamlined course list that allows students to select specific exercise topics. Figure 3 displays the real-time feedback screen provided after a student completes a think-aloud

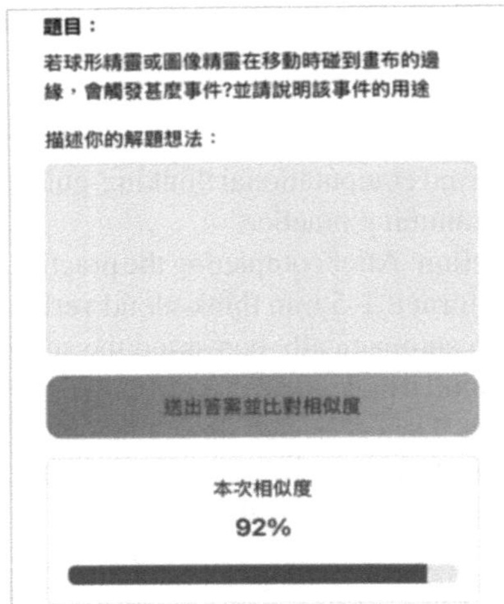

Fig. 3. Semantic Similarity Analysis

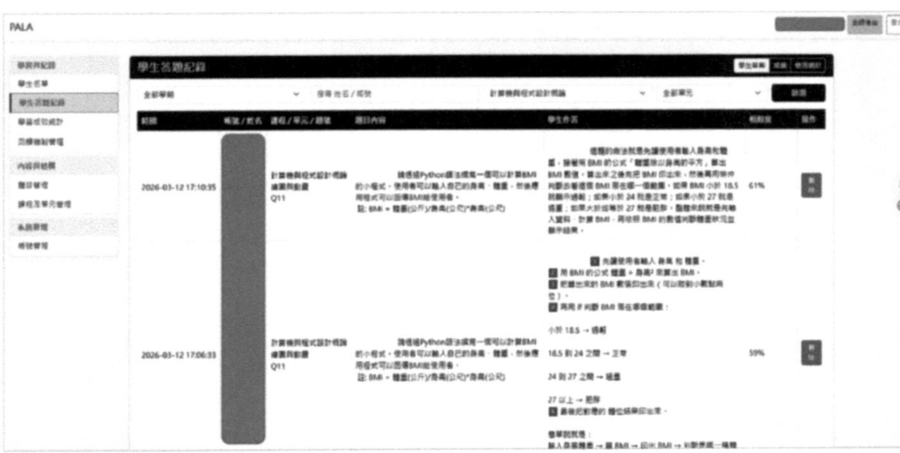

Fig. 4. Students' Answer Records

session, which includes the transcribed text, the calculated semantic similarity percentage. Figure 4 showcases the interface for students' answer records and the backend management system, which tracks student progress and provides data for instructional diagnosis.

4 Results and Discussions

4.1 Sentence Similarity Analysis of PALA

According to the preliminary test data, the PALA system utilizes the SBERT model to calculate Cosine Similarity, effectively distinguishing the heterogeneity in students' mastery of programming concepts. Table 1 presents an analytical case study of the system's interpretations across different learning concepts.

Table 1. Analytical case study of PALA experiment

Learning Concept/Topic	Instructor's Standard Concept (Standard A)	Student's Think-Aloud Text (Acquired B)	PALA Similarity	System Interpretation and CT Performance Analysis
Loop Design	Iterate through elements in a list and execute the same repetitive instructions for each item.	"The function of a sequential (list item) loop is to take out each item in the list in order and automatically execute the same program instructions for each item until the entire list is processed."	**0.95**	**[Pass]** The semantics are highly complete, demonstrating precise **algorithmic thinking** by clearly describing the logical sequence of repetitive execution.
Procedure Application	Encapsulate frequently used functions to improve reusability, readability, and ease of maintenance.	"Reuse code: Write commonly used functions into procedures... making the program easier to read and understand... as long as the procedure content is changed, all used places will be updated."	**0.78**	**[Pass]** Successfully captures the core of **abstraction**, understanding that modular encapsulation enhances maintenance efficiency and program readability.

(*continued*)

Table 1. (*continued*)

Learning Concept/Topic	Instructor's Standard Concept (Standard A)	Student's Think-Aloud Text (Acquired B)	PALA Similarity	System Interpretation and CT Performance Analysis
Event-Driven Control	Trigger the EdgeReached event when hitting a boundary, determine the orientation, and execute actions.	"When a component hits the edge of the canvas, this event will be triggered. The edge value represents the orientation, which can be used to determine the position and perform corresponding actions such as bouncing or changing direction."	**0.75**	**[Pass]** Demonstrates basic **problem decomposition** skills, correctly linking the event trigger with the corresponding control actions.
Conceptual Misunderstanding	Definition and benefits of procedures (e.g., reducing redundant code).	"A loop for any list is a loop specially designed for lists; its execution count is determined by the number of items in the list..."	**0.53**	**[Fail]** Conceptual confusion occurred, incorrectly applying loop functions to a procedure topic. The system successfully detected the deviation and guided the student to remedial materials.
Data Representation	A collection that can store multiple data items with indexed positions.	"I think it should be a structured way of recording information, usually arranging short information entries in order."	**0.45**	**[Fail]** The description is too vague and lacks technical detail, reflecting weak **data representation** skills and a need for reinforced understanding of basic definitions.

4.2 Practical Effectiveness of Automated System Analysis

Research indicates that applying the PALA system to the think-aloud method demonstrates significant practical contributions in the instructional setting:

- **Breakthrough in Analytical Efficiency**: The traditional think-aloud method requires substantial manpower for audio-visual transcription and text coding. Through real-time speech-to-text conversion on mobile devices and automated backend comparison, the PALA system reduces analysis time to second-level feedback, effectively solving the assessment challenges of large-classroom instruction.
- **Real-time Diagnosis and Remedial Teaching**: When the similarity score does not reach the preset threshold (e.g., 0.7), the system immediately provides supplementary teaching materials tailored to that specific learning concept. This real-time feedback mechanism not only triggers student reflection but also provides opportunities for students to repeatedly practice and master concepts after class.

4.3 Basis for Instant Instructional Strategy Adjustment

Through the collection of class-wide learning concept similarity statistics on the server side, teachers can instantly identify collective learning pain points.

- **Dynamic Adjustment of Strategies**: If the average similarity of a specific unit (e.g., "List Application") is low, the teacher can immediately reinforce the explanation of related concepts during the latter half of the class.
- **Precise Individualized Assistance**: Teachers can identify individual students who are falling behind through the data and provide more targeted guidance, thereby improving the dilemma of lack of feedback in traditional one-way teaching.

5 Conclusion and Future Work

This study successfully developed the Programming-Assisted Learning App (PALA), which integrates SBERT deep learning semantic analysis with the think-aloud method. By leveraging the convenience of mobile devices and an automated semantic comparison mechanism, this research has overcome the labor bottlenecks associated with manual analysis in traditional think-aloud implementations. Preliminary practical verification results indicate that the semantic similarity measured by the system accurately reflects students' mastery of computational thinking elements. This confirms the high feasibility of utilizing artificial intelligence to assist in instructional diagnosis within programming education.

At the level of instructional practice, the PALA system provides second-level real-time feedback and implements individualized remedial teaching through the setting of similarity thresholds. For students with low similarity scores or conceptual misunderstandings, the system automatically pushes supplementary materials to trigger self-reflection and mastery of learning concepts. Simultaneously, the aggregated class-wide learning statistics on the server side serve as a critical basis for teachers to dynamically adjust instructional strategies and reinforce explanations regarding collective learning pain points.

Although the preliminary verification demonstrates the technical advantages of the PALA system, certain limitations remain in the research methodology. To date, only a preliminary practical test involving a single class has been completed. A rigorous quasi-experimental design, involving a comparison between experimental and control groups, has yet to be conducted to quantitatively evaluate the impact of this teaching model on long-term learning outcomes. Furthermore, the affective factors and long-term usage intentions behind students' reactions to semantic similarity percentages require deeper tracking and analysis using standardized scales.

Looking forward, this research project will formally initiate a nine-week quasi-experimental study. The "Computational Thinking Scales (CTS)" and the "Unified Theory of Acceptance and Use of Technology (UTAUT)" will be incorporated as evaluation tools to comprehensively examine the efficacy of the PALA system in enhancing students' computational thinking skills and learning motivation. Meanwhile, the precision of the semantic analysis model will be continuously optimized, and explorations into integrating multimodal data analysis will be conducted to provide more scientific and intelligent technology-enhanced learning solutions for the field of programming education.

References

Barr, V., Stephenson, C.: Bringing computational thinking to K-12: what is involved and what is the role of the computer science education community? ACM Inroads. **2**(1), 48–54 (2011)

Cer, D., Diab, M., Agirre, E., Lopez-Gazpio, I., Specia, L.: SemEval-2017 task 1: semantic textual similarity multilingual and crosslingual focused evaluation. In: Proceedings of the 11th International Workshop on Semantic Evaluation (SemEval-2017), pp. 1–14 (2017)

Devlin, J., Chang, M.-W., Lee, K., Toutanova, K.: BERT: pre-training of deep bidirectional transformers for language understanding (version 2). arXiv. (2018). https://doi.org/10.48550/ARXIV.1810.04805

Ericsson, K.A., Simon, H.A.: Verbal reports as data. Psychol. Rev. **87**(3), 215 (1980)

Ginsburg, H.: The Development of Mathematical Thinking. Academic, Florida (1983)

Hambrusch, S., Hoffmann, C., Korb, J.T., Haugan, M., Hosking, A.L.: A multidisciplinary approach towards computational thinking for science majors. ACM SIGCSE Bulletin. **41**(1), 183–187 (2009)

Israel, M., Pearson, J.N., Tapia, T., Wherfel, Q.M., Reese, G.: Supporting all learners in school-wide computational thinking: a cross-case qualitative analysis. Comput. Educ. **82**, 263–279 (2015)

Selby, C., Woollard, J.: Computational Thinking: The Developing Definition. (2013)

Snyder, L.G., Snyder, M.J.: Teaching critical thinking and problem-solving skills. J. Res. Bus.Educ. **50**(2), 90 (2008)

Wing, J.M.: Computational thinking. Commun. ACM. **49**(3), 33–35 (2006)

A Comprehensive Framework for Digital Intelligence Quotient (DQ): Developing Digital Citizenship Competencies for K-12 Learners

Charuni Samat[1(✉)], Pornsuwan Wongtatham[1], Issara Kanjug[1], Suchat Wattanachai[2], Pinyarat Singha[3], Chinnaphat Junruang[1], and Kanitpong Piyanamvanit[1]

[1] Faculty of Education, Khon Kaen University, Khon Kaen 40002, Thailand
scharui@kku.ac.th
[2] Faculty of Veterinary Medicine, Khon Kaen University, Khon Kaen 40002, Thailand
[3] The Secondary Educational Service Area Office SakonNakhon, SakonNakhon 47000, Thailand

Abstract. The rapid advancement of digital technologies and artificial intelligence has created an urgent need for comprehensive frameworks to assess and develop digital competencies among young learners. This paper proposes a Digital Intelligence Quotient (DQ) framework comprising four core dimensions and 20 competencies designed to measure learners' abilities to use digital technology appropriately, safely, ethically, and responsibly. The framework encompasses: (1) Digital Identity—the ability to create, manage, and maintain one's digital presence safely; (2) Digital Use—the capacity to utilize devices and platforms effectively, safely, and age-appropriately; (3) Digital Security—the competence to protect oneself and personal data online; and (4) Digital Communication—the skill to communicate and collaborate through digital tools responsibly and effectively. Each dimension includes five core competencies with specific indicators suitable for K-12 learners. The proposed framework provides educators, curriculum developers, and policymakers with a structured approach to developing digital citizenship education and assessment tools for the AI-enhanced learning environment.

Keywords: Digital Intelligence · Digital Citizenship · Digital Literacy · K-12 Education · Framework Development · 21st Century Skills

1 Introduction

The digital transformation of society has fundamentally changed how individuals live, learn, work, and interact with others. With the proliferation of artificial intelligence, social media platforms, and ubiquitous connectivity, the ability to navigate the digital world has become as essential as traditional literacy skills. For young learners in K-12 education, developing digital competencies is particularly crucial as they are growing up immersed in digital environments [1, 2].

Digital Intelligence Quotient (DQ), as conceptualized in this paper, represents a comprehensive approach to measuring and developing the competencies required for

C.-J. Lin et al. (Eds.): ICITL 2026, LNCS 16841, pp. 231–240, 2027.
https://doi.org/10.1007/978-3-032-32112-1_23

effective digital citizenship. DQ is defined as the ability to use digital technology appropriately, safely, ethically, and responsibly for living, learning, working, and participating effectively in digital society [3]. Unlike traditional digital literacy frameworks that emphasize tool proficiency, DQ encompasses the holistic capabilities needed to thrive in increasingly complex digital ecosystems.

The emergence of generative AI technologies has further complicated the digital landscape, introducing new challenges related to information authenticity, privacy, and the nature of human-machine interaction [4]. These developments underscore the need for frameworks that can adapt to rapidly evolving technological contexts while maintaining focus on fundamental human values and competencies, particularly for young learners who are most vulnerable to digital risks.

This paper presents a comprehensive DQ framework developed through synthesis of existing literature, analysis of international digital citizenship standards, and empirical research with K-12 learners in Thailand. The framework is designed to serve multiple purposes: as an assessment tool for measuring individual digital competencies, as a curriculum development guide for educators, and as a policy framework for institutions seeking to promote digital citizenship.

2 Literature Review

2.1 Evolution of Digital Literacy Concepts

The concept of digital literacy has evolved significantly since its introduction by Gilster [5] in the late 1990s. Early definitions focused primarily on the technical ability to use computers and access information online. Subsequent frameworks expanded this definition to include critical thinking skills, information evaluation, and media literacy [6, 7].

More recent conceptualizations have recognized the multidimensional nature of digital competence. The European Digital Competence Framework (DigComp) identifies five competence areas: information and data literacy, communication and collaboration, digital content creation, safety, and problem-solving [8]. Similarly, the UNESCO Media and Information Literacy framework emphasizes the integration of media literacy with information literacy and digital skills [9].

2.2 Digital Citizenship for Young Learners

Digital citizenship extends beyond technical competency to encompass the norms, responsibilities, and rights of individuals in digital spaces. Ribble's [10] nine elements of digital citizenship—including digital etiquette, digital law, and digital health—provided an influential early framework. The DQ Institute's Digital Intelligence framework [11] subsequently identified eight interconnected competencies spanning digital identity, use, safety, security, emotional intelligence, communication, literacy, and rights.

For K-12 learners, digital citizenship education must be developmentally appropriate and contextually relevant. Research has shown that young learners face unique challenges including cyberbullying, online predators, excessive screen time, and exposure to inappropriate content [12]. Effective frameworks must address these age-specific concerns while building foundational competencies for lifelong digital citizenship.

2.3 AI and Emerging Challenges for Young Learners

The integration of artificial intelligence into everyday digital tools presents new challenges for digital citizenship frameworks. Generative AI systems can produce sophisticated content that may be difficult for young learners to distinguish from human-created materials, raising concerns about misinformation and critical thinking [13]. Additionally, AI-powered recommendation systems and personalization algorithms raise questions about autonomy, privacy, and filter bubbles that particularly affect young users [14].

3 The Proposed Digital Intelligence Quotient Framework

Based on our synthesis of existing literature, analysis of international standards, and empirical research with K-12 learners, we propose a comprehensive Digital Intelligence Quotient (DQ) framework. DQ is defined as:

> *"The ability to use digital technology appropriately, safely, ethically, and responsibly for living, learning, working, and participating effectively in digital society."*

The framework comprises four core dimensions and 20 competencies (five per dimension), as illustrated in Fig. 1. Each competency includes two specific indicators that describe observable behaviors appropriate for K-12 learners.

3.1 Dimension 1: Digital Identity

Digital Identity refers to the ability to create, manage, and maintain one's digital presence appropriately and safely in online environments. This dimension recognizes that learners increasingly exist in both physical and digital spaces, and that managing one's online presence has significant implications for safety, reputation, and wellbeing.

The Digital Identity dimension comprises five core competencies:

1. Appropriate Self-Presentation Online

   1.1 Ability to select appropriate information (e.g., photos, nicknames, text) for self-presentation on various online platforms
   1.2 Ability to explain why specific information was chosen and understand how it affects one's online image

2. Awareness of Posting Consequences

   2.1 Ability to identify potential consequences of posting inappropriate personal information online (e.g., misuse of data, being mocked)
   2.2 Ability to decide what information should or should not be posted, considering potential consequences

3. Understanding Real vs. Online World Differences

   3.1 Ability to explain differences between interacting with friends in real life versus online

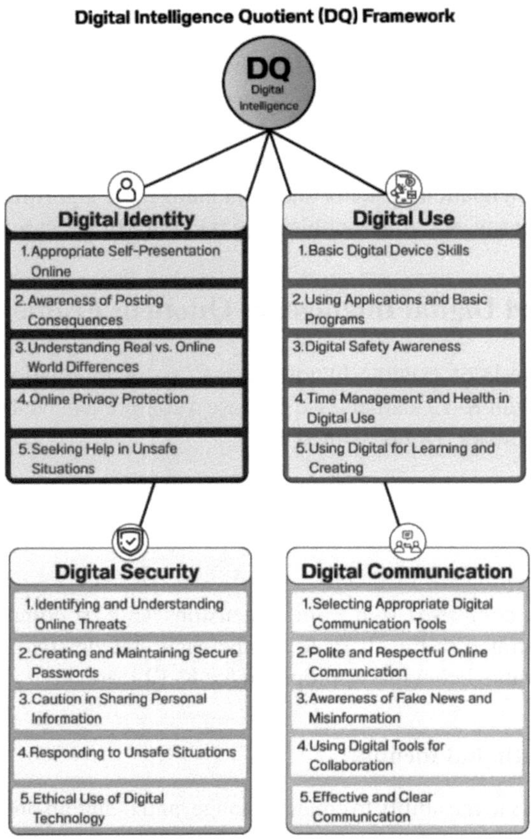

Fig. 1. The Digital Intelligence Quotient (DQ) Framework Structure

3.2 Ability to provide examples of appropriate behaviors in both real and online contexts

4. Online Privacy Protection

4.1 Ability to identify personal information that should not be disclosed online (e.g., address, phone number, photos)
4.2 Ability to use basic privacy settings on online platforms to protect personal information

5. Seeking Help in Unsafe Situations

5.1 Ability to recognize when facing unsafe situations online (e.g., being lured, being bullied)
5.2 Ability to report to parents, teachers, or trusted adults when feeling unsafe online

3.2 Dimension 2: Digital Use

Digital Use encompasses the ability to use digital devices and platforms effectively, safely, and age-appropriately. This dimension addresses not only technical proficiency but also balanced and health-conscious technology use.

The Digital Use dimension comprises five core competencies:

1. Basic Digital Device Skills

   1.1 Ability to turn on/off and operate basic digital devices (computer, tablet, smartphone) correctly, including mouse, keyboard, and touchscreen
   1.2 Ability to perform basic file and folder management (create, save, open, search)

2. Using Applications and Basic Programs

   2.1 Ability to use essential applications and programs for learning (e.g., word processors, presentation software, drawing apps, search engines)
   2.2 Ability to use basic tools within applications/programs correctly and efficiently

3. Digital Safety Awareness

   3.1 Ability to identify and explain dangers from internet use (e.g., online fraud, personal data exposure)
   3.2 Ability to follow basic internet safety rules (e.g., creating secure passwords, asking permission before visiting unknown websites, not talking to strangers online)

4. Time Management and Health in Digital Use

   4.1 Awareness of digital device usage impacts on health (e.g., eyesight, sleep)
   4.2 Ability to plan and manage digital device usage time appropriately without affecting studies and other activities

5. Using Digital for Learning and Creating

   5.1 Ability to use digital tools for researching information, creating work, and presenting summaries (e.g., drawing, reports, presentations)
   5.2 Ability to use digital tools for collaborative work (e.g., file sharing, exchanging ideas)

3.3 Dimension 3: Digital Security

Digital Security refers to the ability to protect oneself and personal data safely in online environments. As digital threats become increasingly sophisticated, this dimension has gained critical importance for all digital citizens, especially young learners.

The Digital Security dimension comprises five core competencies:

1. Identifying and Understanding Online Threats

   1.1 Ability to identify and explain common online threats such as cyberbullying, online grooming, and online fraud
   1.2 Ability to provide examples of situations that may lead to online threats

2. Creating and Maintaining Secure Passwords

2.1 Ability to explain principles of creating secure, hard-to-guess passwords (e.g., length, mixing letters, numbers, and symbols)
2.2 Ability to create and maintain secure passwords for various online accounts

3. Caution in Sharing Personal Information

3.1 Ability to identify and understand the importance of personal information (e.g., name, address, phone number, photos)
3.2 Ability to decide what personal information to share online and avoid sharing inappropriate information

4. Responding to Unsafe Situations

4.1 Ability to recognize unsafe situations online (e.g., being lured, being harassed)
4.2 Ability to report or seek help from adults (e.g., parents, teachers) when facing unsafe situations

5. Ethical Use of Digital Technology

5.1 Ability to avoid inappropriate or unsafe online behaviors such as bullying others, spreading false information
5.2 Ability to use technology beneficially and creatively while respecting others' rights and dignity

3.4 Dimension 4: Digital Communication

Digital Communication encompasses the ability to communicate and collaborate with others through digital tools appropriately, effectively, and responsibly. This dimension addresses both technical and social aspects of online interaction.

The Digital Communication dimension comprises five core competencies:

1. Selecting Appropriate Digital Communication Tools

1.1 Ability to identify and explain various digital communication tools (e.g., email, chat apps, social media)
1.2 Ability to select appropriate digital communication tools for different purposes and situations

2. Polite and Respectful Online Communication

2.1 Ability to use polite and appropriate language in online communication
2.2 Ability to avoid inappropriate online communication behaviors such as bullying, using profanity

3. Awareness of Fake News and Misinformation

3.1 Ability to distinguish and report credible versus unreliable information online
3.2 Ability to verify information sources before believing or sharing

4. Using Digital Tools for Collaboration

4.1 Ability to use digital tools for collaborative work, sharing knowledge and ideas with peers (e.g., file sharing, collaborative document editing)

4.2 Ability to participate in discussions and decision-making with others through digital tools

5. Effective and Clear Communication

5.1 Ability to write and send clear, easy-to-understand, and focused digital messages
5.2 Ability to select and use images and multimedia to enhance communication understanding (Table 1)

Table 1. Summary of the DQ Framework: Four Dimensions and 20 Core Competencies

Dimension	Core Competency	Key Indicators
Digital Identity	1. Appropriate Self-Presentation	Select appropriate information; understand image impact
	2. Posting Consequences Awareness	Identify posting consequences; decide appropriate content
	3. Real vs. Online World Understanding	Explain differences; demonstrate appropriate behaviors
	4. Online Privacy Protection	Identify private information; use privacy settings
	5. Seeking Help in Unsafe Situations	Recognize unsafe situations; report to trusted adults
Digital Use	1. Basic Digital Device Skills	Operate devices; manage files and folders
	2. Applications and Programs	Use learning applications; operate basic tools
	3. Digital Safety Awareness	Identify internet dangers; follow safety rules
	4. Time and Health Management	Understand health impacts; manage usage time
	5. Learning and Creating	Research and create; collaborate digitally
Digital Security	1. Online Threat Identification	Identify threats; recognize risky situations
	2. Secure Password Management	Create strong passwords; maintain security
	3. Personal Information Caution	Understand data importance; decide sharing limits
	4. Unsafe Situation Response	Recognize dangers; seek adult help
	5. Ethical Technology Use	Avoid harmful behaviors; respect others' rights

(*continued*)

Table 1. (*continued*)

Dimension	Core Competency	Key Indicators
Digital Communication	1. Tool Selection	Identify tools; select appropriately for purpose
	2. Polite Communication	Use appropriate language; avoid harmful behaviors
	3. Fake News Awareness	Distinguish credibility; verify sources
	4. Collaborative Tools	Share and collaborate; participate in decisions
	5. Effective Communication	Write clearly; use multimedia appropriately

4 Competency Levels and Assessment

To facilitate practical application of the DQ framework, we propose a four-level competency progression for each competency. These levels reflect increasing sophistication in digital intelligence, from basic awareness to expert mastery (Table 2).

Table 2. Competency Level Descriptions for DQ Assessment

Level	Label	Description
1	Beginning	Basic awareness of digital concepts; requires guidance to perform fundamental tasks; limited understanding of consequences
2	Developing	Growing competence; can handle common situations with some independence; beginning to understand broader implications
3	Proficient	Consistent, effective performance across varied contexts; demonstrates strategic awareness and good judgment
4	Advanced	Mastery level; can apply knowledge creatively, help peers, and adapt to new situations; serves as positive role model

Assessment of DQ competencies may employ multiple methods including self-report surveys, scenario-based assessments, performance tasks, and learning activity observations. For K-12 learners, age-appropriate assessment tasks that simulate real digital scenarios are particularly effective.

5 Discussion

5.1 Implications for K-12 Education

The proposed DQ framework has significant implications for K-12 educational practice. First, it provides a comprehensive structure for developing digital citizenship curricula that addresses technical, social, ethical, and safety dimensions of digital engagement.

The 20 competencies with 40 specific indicators offer clear learning objectives that can be integrated across subject areas.

Second, the framework supports differentiated instruction by providing clear competency levels. Teachers can assess students' current DQ levels and design appropriate learning activities to support progression. This is particularly important given the wide variation in digital competencies among students of similar ages.

Third, the framework emphasizes aspects of digital intelligence that are often overlooked in traditional ICT education, particularly online safety, privacy protection, and help-seeking behaviors. These dimensions are critically important for protecting young learners in digital environments.

5.2 Implications for AI-Enhanced Learning

As artificial intelligence becomes increasingly integrated into educational technologies and everyday digital tools, the DQ framework provides guidance for preparing young learners to interact effectively and safely with AI systems. The fake news and misinformation awareness competency directly addresses concerns about AI-generated content, while the ethical technology use competency supports responsible engagement with AI tools.

Furthermore, the framework's emphasis on critical thinking, help-seeking, and adult guidance provides safeguards for young learners navigating AI-enhanced digital environments. Rather than viewing AI as either a threat or a panacea, learners with high DQ can engage thoughtfully with AI tools while maintaining appropriate skepticism and knowing when to seek help.

5.3 Limitations and Future Research

This paper presents a conceptual framework that requires continued empirical validation. Future research should develop and validate age-appropriate assessment instruments, examine the relationships between DQ dimensions and academic outcomes, and investigate the effectiveness of DQ-based educational interventions across different grade levels and cultural contexts.

6 Conclusion

This paper has proposed a comprehensive Digital Intelligence Quotient (DQ) framework comprising four dimensions—Digital Identity, Digital Use, Digital Security, and Digital Communication—and 20 core competencies with 40 specific indicators. The framework provides a structured approach to understanding, assessing, and developing the competencies required for effective digital citizenship among K-12 learners.

As digital technologies and artificial intelligence continue to transform how young people live, learn, and interact, frameworks like DQ become essential tools for educators, curriculum developers, and policymakers. By providing clear definitions, developmentally appropriate indicators, and competency progressions, the DQ framework supports systematic efforts to prepare all learners for safe, responsible, and effective participation in digital society.

Future work will focus on developing validated assessment instruments for different grade levels, creating educational resources aligned with the framework, and investigating the effectiveness of DQ-based interventions. Through such efforts, we aim to contribute to the development of digitally intelligent young citizens who can harness the benefits of technology while navigating its challenges responsibly and safely.

Acknowledgments. This research was supported by Khon Kaen University and the Center of Excellence in Coding Manpower Development and Digital Citizenship (CMDDC). The authors thank the participating schools and students for their valuable contributions to this research.

References

1. Eshet-Alkalai, Y.: Digital literacy: a conceptual framework for survival skills in the digital era. J. Educ. Multimed. Hypermedia. **13**(1), 93–106 (2004)
2. Ng, W.: Can we teach digital natives digital literacy? Comput. Educ. **59**(3), 1065–1078 (2012)
3. Park, Y.J.: Digital literacy and privacy behavior online. Commun. Res. **40**(2), 215–236 (2013)
4. Kasneci, E., et al.: ChatGPT for good? On opportunities and challenges of large language models for education. Learn. Individ. Differ. **103**, 102274 (2023)
5. Gilster, P.: Digital Literacy. Wiley Computer Publishing, New York (1997)
6. Buckingham, D.: Defining digital literacy: what do young people need to know about digital media? Nordic J. Digit. Lit. **1**(4), 263–277 (2006)
7. Bawden, D.: Information and digital literacies: a review of concepts. J. Doc. **57**(2), 218–259 (2001)
8. Carretero, S., Vuorikari, R., Punie, Y.: DigComp 2.1: The Digital Competence Framework for Citizens. Publications Office of the European Union, Luxembourg (2017)
9. UNESCO: Media and Information Literacy Curriculum for Teachers. UNESCO, Paris (2011)
10. Ribble, M.: Digital Citizenship in Schools, 3rd edn. International Society for Technology in Education, Eugene (2015)
11. DQ Institute: DQ Global Standards Report 2019: Common Framework for Digital Literacy, Skills and Readiness. DQ Institute, Singapore (2019)
12. Livingstone, S., Haddon, L., Görzig, A., Ólafsson, K.: Risks and Safety on the Internet: the Perspective of European Children. EU Kids Online, London (2011)
13. Dwivedi, Y.K., et al.: Opinion paper: so what if ChatGPT wrote it? Multidisciplinary perspectives on opportunities, challenges and implications of generative conversational AI. Int. J. Inf. Manag. **71**, 102642 (2023)
14. Pariser, E.: The Filter Bubble: What the Internet Is Hiding from You. Penguin Press, New York (2011)

A Chinese-Japanese Homograph Retrieval System for Supporting Instructional Decision Making in Language Teaching

Min-Chi Lo[1,2] and Li-Yun Chang[1(✉)]

[1] Department of Chinese as a Second Language, National Taiwan Normal University, Taipei, Taiwan
liyunchang@ntnu.edu.tw
[2] Research Center for Translation, Compilation and Language Education, National Academy for Educational Research, Taipei, Taiwan

Abstract. Chinese-Japanese homographs, which share same or similar orthographic forms across Chinese and Japanese but may differ in meaning, often lead to cross-linguistic interference in Chinese language learning. This challenge is particularly evident among Japanese learners, and it poses difficulties for teachers when selecting vocabulary and designing instruction. To address this issue, this study develops a teacher-oriented Chinese-Japanese Homograph Retrieval System, designed from a Technology-Enhanced Language Teaching (TELT) perspective to support instructional decision making, particularly for instructors without Japanese proficiency. The system integrates homograph classifications, bilingual semantic information, Taiwan Benchmarks for the Chinese Language (TBCL) vocabulary levels, and textbook unit information into a unified, web-based platform, offering keyword, TBCL level, and textbook unit search functions that enable teachers to efficiently identify homographs, anticipate potential learning difficulties, and select level-appropriate instructional content. User evaluation with 12 Chinese language teachers, conducted via the Technology Acceptance Model, indicated significantly higher ratings for the Chinese-Japanese Homograph Retrieval System than for a comparable multilingual kanji-word database across perceived usefulness, perceived ease of use, and behavioral intention. Qualitative feedback further highlighted the integration of proficiency levels and textbook information as a distinctive feature of the proposed system. By making cross-linguistic semantic relationships explicit and pedagogically meaningful, the system bridges linguistic research and instructional practice in language education.

Keywords: Chinese-Japanese homographs · digital instructional support system · teaching Chinese as a second/foreign language · technology-enhanced language teaching

1 Introduction

In Taiwan, a substantial number of Chinese as second/foreign language learners in university-affiliated Chinese language centers come from Japan. According to statistics from the Ministry of Education in Taiwan, during the 2025–2026 period, students

C.-J. Lin et al. (Eds.): ICITL 2026, LNCS 16841, pp. 241–250, 2027.
https://doi.org/10.1007/978-3-032-32112-1_24

from Japan accounted for approximately 10% of all international students enrolled in university-affiliated Chinese language centers, ranking third among all nationalities [1]. Although Chinese and Japanese share a common writing system of Chinese characters (which known as kanji in Japanese), these similarities often lead not only to positive transfer but also to negative transfer during language learning [2, 3]. In particular, Chinese-Japanese homographs frequently cause cross-linguistic interference, posing persistent challenges for learners.

From a pedagogical perspective, helping teachers better understand homograph types and their associated learning difficulties is crucial for effective instruction. However, identifying potential learning problems requires cross-linguistic knowledge that many Chinese language teachers may not possess. Despite the growing integration of technology in language education, existing digital resources for Chinese-Japanese homographs remain limited. Dictionary-based databases (e.g., [4]) lack pedagogical information, while research-oriented databases (e.g., [5, 6]) are often incomplete or not tailored to teaching contexts in Taiwan.

To address this gap, this study develops a teacher-oriented online Chinese-Japanese Homographs Retrieval System that integrates linguistic classification, semantic information, and teaching-related information. By transforming research findings into an accessible digital tool, the system aims to support teachers' instructional decision-making and contribute to technology-enhanced language learning.

2 Related Work

2.1 Chinese-Japanese Homographs and Learning Challenges

Chinese-Japanese homographs refer to lexical items that share identical or similar orthographic forms across the two languages [7–9]. Due to historical borrowing, such homographs are highly prevalent in Japanese, and frequently appear in Chinese language learning materials [10, 11]. Previous studies have classified homographs based on form and semantic relations, with the Same (S), Overlap (O), and Different (D) framework being widely adopted [8, 12]. These semantic discrepancies often lead to cross-linguistic interference, particularly for O type and D type homographs, which may trigger negative transfer during language learning.

2.2 Technological-Enhanced Language Teaching

Technology-Enhanced Language Teaching (TELT) extends earlier Computer-Assisted Language Learning (CALL) approaches by shifting the focus from technology itself to pedagogical needs, emphasizing how digital tools can support instructional design and teacher decision making [13–15]. Recent studies have shown that digital tools, including online platforms and corpus-based systems, can enhance language learning performance and provide flexible learning environments [16, 17]. This TELT perspective is particularly relevant to Chinese-Japanese homographs, where complex semantic relationships require teachers to access cross-linguistic information and translate it into instructional decisions. The system developed in the present study is situated within the TELT perspective, functioning as a teacher-oriented tool for this purpose.

2.3 Limitations of Existing Homograph Databases

Beyond basic lexical meanings, teachers working with Chinese-Japanese homographs require detailed information such as semantic classifications, cross-linguistic distinctions, vocabulary difficulty, and textbook coverage. Existing online resources, however, fall short on these teachers' needs.

Dictionary-based tools, such as Japanese-Chinese dictionaries [4], support lookup of meanings and example sentences but provide no semantic classification or pedagogical information. Research-oriented databases, such as the Database of Japanese Kanji Vocabulary in Contrast to Chinese (Version 2.0) [5] and the Japanese, Korean, Chinese and Vietnamese kanji-word Web-accessible database and search engine [6], provide classification results (e.g., S/D/O/N) and additional linguistic information (e.g., word frequency, part of speech, and phonological similarity), but typically rely on simplified Chinese or Japanese-only interfaces and lack teacher-oriented features such as textbook-unit or proficiency-level search.

In sum, no existing system integrates homograph classification, semantic information, and teaching-related features into a unified platform for Chinese teaching contexts. This gap highlights the need for a teacher-oriented digital system for technology-enhanced language teaching.

3 Methodology

3.1 System Design and Architecture

In the present study, the Chinese-Japanese Homograph Retrieval System (http://chenchang.tcsl.ntnu.edu.tw/CJ_Homographs) was developed to support Chinese language teachers, particularly those without Japanese proficiency. Because semantic differences between Chinese and Japanese homographs cannot be inferred solely from orthographic similarity, teachers often face challenges in determining whether a word may lead to positive or negative transfer.

To address this issue, the system integrates homograph classifications, Chinese and Japanese meanings, Taiwan Benchmarks for the Chinese Language (TBCL) difficulty levels, and textbook-related information into a unified and searchable platform, enabling teachers to access relevant data and make informed instructional decisions during lesson planning.

3.2 Data and Classification Framework

The homograph dataset used in the system consists of a selected subset of words from the self-learning materials "Chinese-Japanese Homograph Learning Strategy I-III" [18–20] and Version 2.0 of the Database of Japanese Kanji Vocabulary in Contrast to Chinese [5]. Because not all Chinese lexical items constitute Chinese-Japanese homographs, and most mainstream Chinese language textbooks do not explicitly identify or classify homographs, the commercially published homograph learning materials "Chinese-Japanese Homograph Learning Strategy I-III" were adopted as the primary data source for the present system. The system currently includes 402 Chinese-Japanese homographs, covering TBCL Levels 1 to 7 as well as lexical items not included in the TBCL framework. Most lexical items correspond to beginner to intermediate level Chinese teaching materials (approximately CEFR A1-B2). For each lexical item, the system provides the following information: (1) Chinese and Japanese orthographic forms, (2) TBCL difficulty levels, (3) homograph classifications, and (4) bilingual semantic information. Japanese meanings are compiled from the Japanese-Chinese dictionary [4] and related teaching materials [18–20], while Chinese meanings are linked to the Concise Mandarin Chinese Dictionary [21].

Past studies indicate that O type homographs, particularly those with partial semantic overlap, may impose greater processing difficulty on learners [22, 23]. This finding highlights the importance of distinguishing among different patterns of semantic relationships for instructional purposes.

Based on this insight, the present system adopts a category-based classification framework that is more transparent and instructionally meaningful. The classification consists of six categories: Same (S), Similar (So), Overlap (O) with three subtypes (Chinese > Japanese, Chinese < Japanese, Chinese > < Japanese), and Different (D) [24]. These categories explicitly capture the structural relationships between meanings across the two languages, allowing teachers to better anticipate potential sources of transfer and adjust instructional strategies accordingly.

3.3 System Functions and Implementation

The system is implemented as a web-based platform using Microsoft ASP.NET, with CSS/jQuery front-end and Excel-based data storage. The system dynamically retrieves lexical information based on user queries and includes a filtering mechanism to exclude non-relevant inputs (e.g., symbols or unsupported characters). It is compatible with major web browsers, including Google Chrome, Microsoft Edge, and Firefox.

Function 1: Keyword Search
The keyword search function allows teachers to verify whether a word is a homograph or to examine its detailed properties during lesson preparation by entering a target word in Traditional Chinese (see Fig. 1). The system generates a comprehensive lexical profile, including orthographic correspondence between Chinese and Japanese forms, homograph classification, TBCL level, textbook information, and bilingual semantic descriptions (see Fig. 2). For example, entering 顏色 ("color") returns a D type entry showing that the word shares the same form across the two languages but differs in meaning, enabling teachers to identify sources of potential positive or negative transfer and determine whether additional instructional explanation is needed.

Function 2: TBCL Level Search
The TBCL level search function enables users to browse homographs by proficiency level, supporting the selection of level-appropriate vocabulary and the planning of instructional sequences. After a specific TBCL level is selected (see Fig. 3), the system displays a list of homographs associated with that level (see Fig. 4). Users can then explore individual items to view their detailed lexical information. For example,

Fig. 1. Keyword search interface

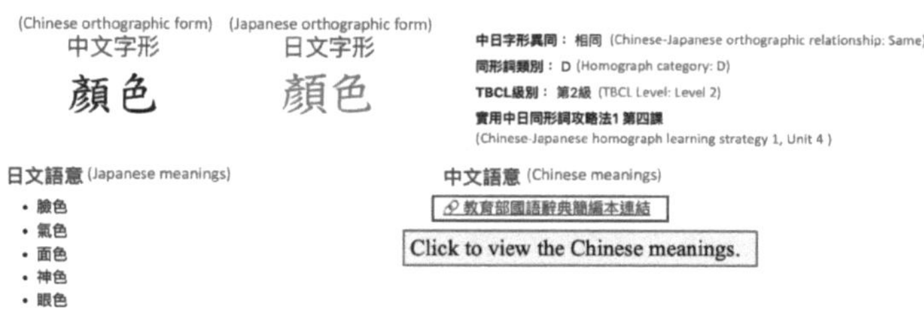

Fig. 2. System output for keyword search

by selecting TBCL Level 2 and clicking on a word such as 成績 ("score"), teachers can anticipate potential cross-linguistic difficulties at different proficiency levels and adjust teaching content accordingly.

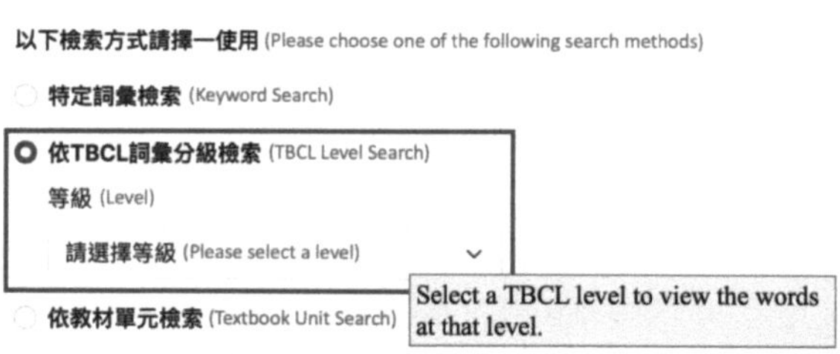

Fig. 3. TBCL Level search interface with selectable levels

Function 3: Textbook Unit Search

The textbook unit search function links homographs directly to teaching materials, supporting lesson planning by displaying homographs that appear in particular units. Once a textbook and unit are selected (see Fig. 5), the system generates a corresponding list of homographs, which can be further explored to obtain detailed lexical information (see Fig. 6). For example, by selecting Unit 2 of Chinese-Japanese Homograph Learning Strategy I and clicking on a word such as 新聞 ("news" in Chinese vs. "newspaper" in Japanese), teachers can prepare targeted instructional interventions before class.

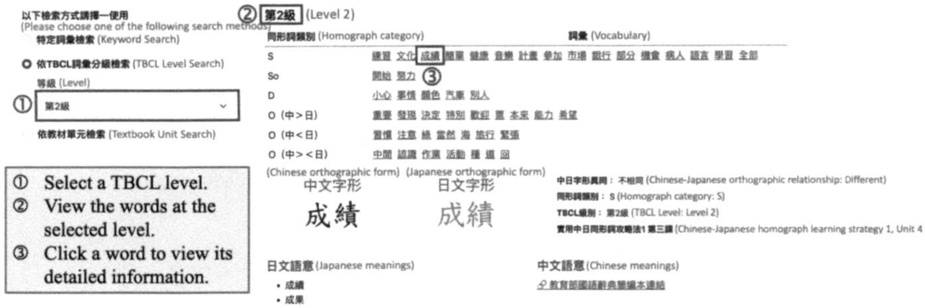

Fig. 4. System output for TBCL level search

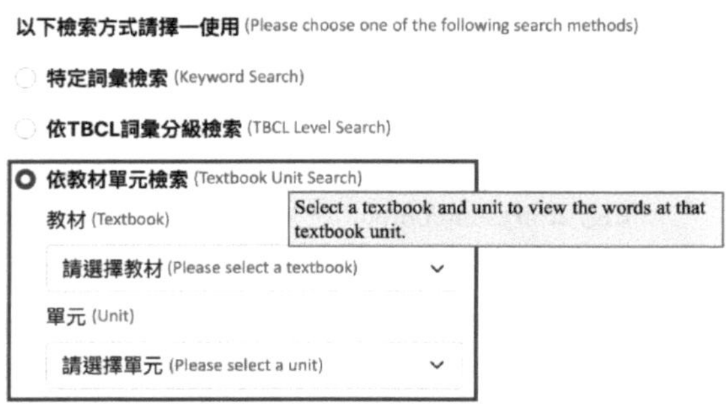

Fig. 5. Textbook unit search interface with selectable list for textbook and unit selection

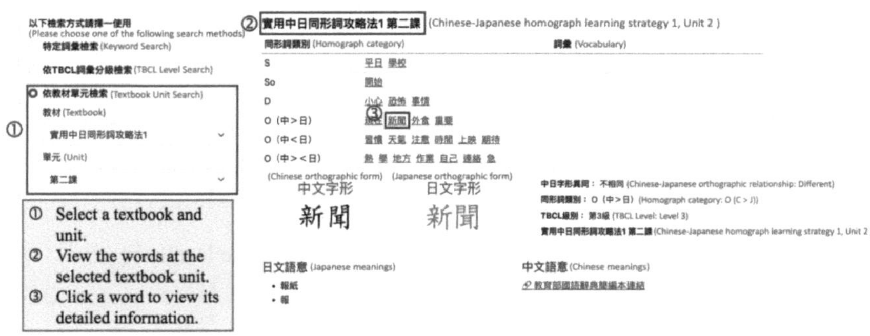

Fig. 6. System output for Textbook unit search

4 Applications

The system supports Chinese language teachers, particularly those without Japanese proficiency, in instructional planning, error prediction, and curriculum design.

Application 1: Understanding Semantic Relationships and Predicting Transfer Effects

Using the six-category classification (see Sect. 3.2), teachers can determine whether a given homograph is likely to facilitate positive transfer (e.g., S type) or lead to negative transfer and misinterpretation (particularly in O and D types). For instance, when reading Chinese text, a Japanese learner encountering the D type homograph 汽車 may incorrectly interpret the word according to its Japanese meaning "train", although it means "car" in Chinese. By making cross-linguistic semantic structures more transparent, the system helps teachers decide whether explicit semantic explanation or contrastive instruction is required.

Application 2: Accessing Detailed Lexical Information for Level-Appropriate Instructional Planning

The system provides a detailed lexical profile for each homograph, including (a) corresponding Chinese and Japanese orthographic forms, (b) judgments of orthographic similarity, (c) homograph classification, (d) TBCL level, (e) textbook unit information, (f) Japanese meanings, and (g) Chinese meanings with a link to the Ministry of Education Concised Mandarin Dictionary. This information enables teachers to select homographs appropriate for learners at different proficiency levels, prioritize which items require explicit instruction in beginner or intermediate courses, and sequence vocabulary instruction according to semantic complexity and expected processing difficulty.

Application 3: Identifying Chinese-Japanese Homograph in Specific Teaching Materials

Through the textbook unit search function, teachers can instantly retrieve all homographs in upcoming units and prepare targeted instructional strategies in advance. For example, before teaching a unit containing 顏色, an instructor can flag the Chinese-Japanese meaning mismatch ("color" vs. "mood") and design a clarification activity, improving the efficiency of lesson planning.

5 System Evaluation

To evaluate the usability and acceptance of the Chinese-Japanese Homograph Retrieval System, a workshop-based evaluation was conducted with Chinese language teaching practitioners. The purpose of this evaluation was to investigate users' acceptance of the proposed system and compare it with an existing online resource. For comparison, the Japanese, Korean, Chinese and Vietnamese kanji-word Web-accessible database (hereafter the JKCV database) was selected because it is a publicly accessible online system that also provides information related to homograph vocabulary across multiple languages. To collect quantitative feedback, this study adopted the Technology Acceptance Model (TAM) [25], including the constructs of perceived usefulness, perceived ease of use, and behavioral intention.

5.1 Research Design and Instrument

The focus group was conducted in a workshop in Taiwan with 12 Chinese language teachers. The participants' mean age was 25.67 years, and their average teaching experience was 21.08 months. During the workshop, the researchers first introduced both the Chinese-Japanese Homograph Retrieval System and the JKCV database. After the introduction, participants were invited to freely explore and operate both systems before completing the evaluation questionnaire.

The questionnaire was developed based on the TAM. Three constructs were included in the questionnaire: perceived usefulness (4 items), perceived ease of use (4 items), and behavioral intention (3 items). All items were measured using a 7-point Likert-type scale ranging from 1 (strongly disagree) to 7 (strongly agree).

5.2 Evaluation Results

For perceived usefulness, the Chinese-Japanese Homograph Retrieval System achieved a mean score of 5.98, surpassing the JKCV database's 4.81. A paired samples *t*-test revealed a significant difference ($t = 2.41, p = .035$) with a moderate Cohen's d effect size of 0.70. Regarding ease of use, the Chinese-Japanese Homograph Retrieval System attained a mean score of 6.25, whereas the JKCV database obtained a mean score of 5.13. The analysis demonstrated a significant difference ($t = 4.18$, $p = .002$) with a large Cohen's d of 1.21. For behavioral intention, the Chinese-Japanese Homograph Retrieval System yielded a mean score of 6.25, exceeding the JKCV database's 4.78. The paired samples t-test further indicated a significant difference ($t = 3.14, p = .009$) with a large Cohen's d effect size of 0.91. Collectively, these quantitative findings demonstrated that the Chinese-Japanese Homograph Retrieval System outperformed the JKCV database across all TAM constructs, indicating higher user acceptance and more favorable evaluations of the proposed system.

Open-ended responses further indicated that participants particularly valued the system's integration of TBCL proficiency levels and textbook information, a combination they reported as unavailable in the JKCV database and comparable resources. The most frequently raised suggestion was to expand the textbook coverage to include widely-used Chinese language teaching materials; this request not only points to a clear direction for future development, but also confirms the pedagogical value of textbook-aligned design from the teachers' own perspective.

6 Conclusions and Future Work

This study developed a teacher-oriented Chinese-Japanese Homograph Retrieval System that integrates homograph classifications, bilingual semantic information, TBCL vocabulary levels, and textbook unit information into a unified platform. Through keyword, TBCL level, and textbook unit search functions, Chinese language teachers can identify homographs, anticipate transfer effects, and select level-appropriate vocabulary for lesson preparation.

A key contribution of this study lies in its instructional focus. Rather than emphasizing technical complexity, the system transforms research-based linguistic knowledge into a practical teaching tool that makes cross-linguistic differences explicit and accessible for classroom practice without requiring specialized background knowledge.

Despite these contributions, several limitations remain. First, the current lexical database is primarily based on homograph-focused teaching materials, resulting in limited vocabulary coverage. Second, textbook-based search is restricted to the instructional materials currently indexed. Future development will expand the lexical database, incorporate additional teaching resources, and enhance system functionality to support more diverse instructional contexts.

Acknowledgments. This work was financially supported by the "Chinese Language and Technology Center" of National Taiwan Normal University (NTNU) within the framework of the Higher Education Sprout Project by the Ministry of Education (MOE) in Taiwan and a grant from the National Science and Technology Council (NSTC) 112-2410-H-003-073-MY3.

Disclosure of Interests. The authors have no competing interests to declare that are relevant to the content of this article.

References

1. Department of Statistics of Ministry of Education Homepage: https://depart.moe.edu.tw/ed4500/Default.aspx. Last accessed 25 Feb 2026
2. Cai, Q.Y.: The analysis of Chinese character writing and words usage errors made by Chinese-Japanese learners and suggestions. Chung Yuan J. Teach. Chin. Second Lang. **13**, 53–77 (2014)
3. Lin, M.: A consideration of Chinese vocabulary acquisition by native speakers of Japanese: perspective of "transfer from the native language". J. Univ. Mark. Distrib. Sci., Humanit., Arts Sci. **23**(2), 45–53 (2011)
4. Shogakukan Inc.: Chinese-Japanese/Japanese-Chinese Dictionary (3rd ed.), https://apps.apple.com/app/id1248776989. Last accessed 23 Oct 2025
5. Matsushita, T., Chen, M.X., Wang, X.Z., Chen, L.K.: Development and application of a database of Japanese kanji vocabulary in contrast to Chinese. J. Japanese Lang. Educ. **177**, 62–76 (2020). https://doi.org/10.20721/nihongokyoiku.177.0_62
6. Yu, S.Y., Tamaoka, K., Hoang, T.L.P.: Construction of a database and search engine on the phonological similarity of two-kanji compound words in Japanese, Korean, Chinese and Vietnamese. Studia linguistica. **33**, 75–94 (2019). https://doi.org/10.18999/stul.33.75
7. Miyajima, T.: Stylistic differences between Japanese and Chinese homographs. Handai Nihongo Kenkyu. **5**, 1–18 (1993). https://doi.org/10.18910/3629
8. Agency for Cultural Affairs, Japan: Chinese and its Corresponding Kango: Japanese Language Education Research Materials. Ministry of Finance Printing Bureau (1978)
9. Agency for Cultural Affairs, Japan: Correspondence of Kanji Readings Between Japanese and Chinese. Ministry of Finance Printing Bureau (1983)
10. National Institute for Japanese Language and Linguistics: Research and Education on Vocabulary (Part 1). Ministry of Finance Printing Bureau (1984)
11. Chang, C.L.: A comparative analysis of Chinese and Japanese kanji vocabulary from the perspective of Chinese language teaching: a case study of the AI vocabulary of TOCFL 8000 Chinese vocabulary item. World Chin. Lang. **122**, 54–69 (2018)
12. Miura, A.: The meanings and usage of Chinese words borrowed from Japanese into Chinese. J. Jpn. Lang. Educ. **53**, 102–112 (1984)

13. Levy, M.: Computer-Assisted Language Learning: Context and Conceptualization, 1st edn. Oxford University Press (1997). https://doi.org/10.1093/oso/9780198236320.001.0001
14. Bax, S.: CALL—past, present and future. System. **31**(1), 13–28 (2003). https://doi.org/10.1016/S0346-251X(02)00071-4
15. Son, J.B.: Teacher Development in Technology-Enhanced Language Teaching. Springer International Publishing (2018)
16. Chen, J.J., Yang, S.C.: Language learning and teaching through technology: an overview and prospects. Curr. Instr. Q. **25**(1), 135–172 (2022). https://doi.org/10.6384/CIQ.202201_25(1).0005
17. Shadiev, R., Yang, M.: Review of studies on technology-enhanced language learning and teaching. Sustainability. **12**(2), 524 (2020). https://doi.org/10.3390/su12020524
18. Chang, L.Y., Wei, Y.L.: Chinese-Japanese Homograph Learning Strategy I, 1st edn. Cheng Chung Book Co., Ltd, Taipei (2021)
19. Chang, L.Y., Wei, Y.L.: Chinese-Japanese Homograph Learning Strategy II, 1st edn. Cheng Chung Book Co., Ltd, Taipei (2022)
20. Chang, L.Y., Wei, Y.L.: Chinese-Japanese Homograph Learning Strategy III, 1st edn. Cheng Chung Book Co., Ltd., Taipei (2024)
21. Ministry of Education Concised Mandarin Chinese Dictionary Website: https://dict.concised.moe.edu.tw/search.jsp?la=0&powerMode=0. Last accessed 25 May 2024
22. Chiu, M.J., Chu, M.N.: The contrastive analysis of Chinese-Japanese homomorphous lexicon: a study of vocabulary words in volume 5 of practical audio-visual Chinese. J. Chin. Lang. Teach. **15**(4), 67–88 (2018). https://doi.org/10.6393/JCLT.201812_15(4).0003
23. Kato, T.: Acquisition of Japanese kanji words by native Chinese speakers: differences in the learning process compared to speakers of other languages. J. Jpn. Lang. Educ. **125**, 96–105 (2005)
24. Lo, M.C., Chang, L.Y.: Teaching Chinese-Japanese homographs based on semantic distance: integrating theory, methodology, and practical applications. In: Proceedings of the 14th International Conference on Han Characters Education and Research, pp. 158–173. The University of Hong Kong (2025)
25. Davis, F.D.: Perceived usefulness, perceived ease of use, and user acceptance of information technology. MIS Q. **13**(3), 319–340 (1989). https://doi.org/10.2307/249008

Interpretable Machine Learning for Academic Performance Profiles: A Clustering and Classification Approach with Feature-Based Explanations

Priscila Valdiviezo-Diaz(✉)

Universidad Técnica Particular de Loja, Computer Science and Electronic Department, Loja 1101608, Ecuador
pmvaldiviezo@utpl.edu.ec

Abstract. In recent years, machine learning has become increasingly important for analyzing academic performance in higher education, as it helps identify patterns and supports data-driven decision-making to improve student outcomes. This study presents a machine learning approach to identify and classify academic performance profiles within a higher-education institution. First, unsupervised learning methods are applied to a real-world dataset to detect groups of students with similar characteristics. Next, supervised learning models classify the students into these profiles and are evaluated using traditional classification metrics. In addition, an interpretability analysis is performed based on the importance of characteristics to identify the variables that most strongly influence predictions of performance profiles. We also propose using a Large Language Model to generate human-readable explanations from feature importance outputs. This approach not only evaluates predictive performance but also improves understanding of the key factors that influence outcomes. Experimental results indicate that academic variables have a limited impact on predicting academic performance profiles, whereas institutional variables are more influential, offering valuable insights for decision-making in educational settings.

Keywords: Academic performance · Classification · Clustering · Explainable prediction

1 Introduction

In higher education, predicting how students will perform academically has attracted considerable interest, mainly because it holds promise for shaping institutional approaches, strengthening student retention, and reducing dropout rates [1,2].

The recent expansion of academic information systems and digital learning platforms has allowed the collection of rich datasets that span grades, participation metrics, behavioral records, and demographic backgrounds, which in turn

C.-J. Lin et al. (Eds.): ICITL 2026, LNCS 16841, pp. 251–261, 2027.
https://doi.org/10.1007/978-3-032-32112-1_25

has encouraged the use of machine learning techniques to pinpoint early signs of academic struggle [3]. A growing number of studies indicate that supervised models, such as neural networks, can deliver highly accurate predictions of academic performance, especially when drawing from multiple sources of data [4]. However, a persistent hurdle remains: these models often behave as black boxes, which seriously constrains their practical value for both educators and those responsible for institutional decisions. The interpretability of predictive models' decisions poses an important challenge in educational contexts, where understanding the underlying factors that lead to poor performance predictions is as important as the predictions themselves [5]. For example, an algorithm that flags dropout risks without explaining which attributes, such as socioeconomic background, past grades, and class participation. Without that insight, it is almost impossible to shape targeted strategies and actually to back them in meaningful ways.

Explainable Artificial Intelligence (XAI) aims to bridge the gap between predictive accuracy and model comprehension, providing interpretable explanations that support effective decisions. In this way, tree-based models provide inherent interpretability through feature importance analysis [6], which enables the identification of the most influential variables in the prediction process. This characteristic facilitates a transparent understanding of how input features contribute to model outcomes, making these approaches particularly suitable for educational contexts where interpretability and transparency are essential. Other tools that can also be used are SHAP [7] and LIME [8], which have been adapted for educational contexts, enabling the justification of predictions and increasing teachers' confidence in the models.

On the other hand, recent studies have highlighted the potential of Large Language Models (LLMs) to enhance explainable AI by transforming complex model outputs into human-readable explanations [9]. In particular, LLMs can act as post-hoc interpretability tools, providing semantically meaningful descriptions of model behavior [10]. The interpretability of machine learning models is a fundamental aspect in educational applications, as the algorithms' predictions can influence key academic decisions, such as the early identification of at-risk students or the design of pedagogical intervention strategies. In this context, it is important not only to achieve high predictive accuracy but also to understand which variables influence the model's decisions.

In this study, the model's interpretability is assessed using feature importance, which identifies the variables in the dataset that have the greatest influence on predicting academic performance profiles. Moreover, the use of an LLM is presented as a conceptual component to show how the feature importance of characteristics can be transformed into interpretable narratives.

In summary, this paper proposes: 1) an interpretable model for classifying academic performance profiles based on supervised and unsupervised techniques; 2) a comparative evaluation of classification methods applied to university academic and demographic data; and 3) a comparison of the feature importance in supervised models and how feature importance outputs can be used for human-readable explanations. Unlike previous work that focuses exclusively on optimizing accuracy, this study recognizes that interpretability is essential for results to be applicable in real-world higher education contexts.

2 Related Work

Some systematic reviews highlight the importance of supervised machine learning algorithms in predicting academic performance, particularly for identifying at-risk students and predicting academic outcomes using demographic, academic, and behavioral features [11]. Likewise, [12] analyzes papers on the use of machine learning techniques in education to predict students' performance, focusing on the important factors affecting student performance identified by the authors.

Recent evidence indicates a rapid growth in the application of machine learning in educational research, with Random Forest, Decision Trees, and Neural Networks emerging as the most effective techniques for predicting academic performance and learning patterns [13]. For example, in [14] proposes a framework for academic performance prediction using Random Forest and Support Vector Machine, and designs an improved K-means clustering algorithm to identify typical family education models. [15] propose a data analysis method of students' psychological characteristics based on the K-means clustering algorithm improved by the genetic algorithm to explore the association between students' psychological characteristics and learning styles.

Furthermore, feature importance analysis has been shown to uncover influential academic predictors in studies employing Random Forest models. For example, [16] proposes a dual-ensemble classification framework based on feature-importance analysis and a deep random forest. In [17] propose a predictive model to identify students at risk of dropout from the beginning of their university degree, and analyze the feature importance for dropout segmented by faculty, degree program, and semester in the different predictive models.

On the other hand, recent work has examined how w Large Language Models can be combined with feature-based explainability methods. For example, [18] introduced an LLM-assisted feature engineering strategy aimed at enhancing interpretability by constructing semantically meaningful variables. Likewise, [19] showed that LLMs are capable of producing explanations that more closely mirror human reasoning compared to those generated by conventional machine learning models. Together, these studies underscore the increasing significance of LLMs as complementary resources for strengthening interpretability in predictive modeling.

Overall, the reviewed studies confirm the effectiveness of machine learning for academic performance prediction while also highlighting persistent challenges related to model interpretability, feature selection, and the integration of complex, multidimensional educational data. This body of work provides a strong foundation for research that combines unsupervised grouping techniques with supervised classification and interpretability analyses to advance predictive modeling in higher education.

3 Materials and Methods

3.1 Dataset Description

The study was conducted using an anonymized dataset from a higher education institution, comprising 6,197 student records. The dataset includes 13 variables related to academic performance across different subjects, as well as personal characteristics relevant to the analysis of student achievement.

Table 1 summarizes the variables used in this study.

Table 1. Selected variables

Variables	Description	Variable Type
Age	Student's Age	Numeric
Gender	Student's gender with values: Female, Male	Categoric
Academic_term	Academic term enrolled	Categoric
Program_type	Academic program type	Categoric
Type_admission	Income Type: regular, career adaptation...	Categoric
Course_status	Course status: passed or failed	Categoric
Semester	Semester enrolled	Numeric
Final_grades	Final grades for the subjects	Numeric
Self_learning_grades	Self-learning notes for the subjects	Numeric
Contact_teacher_grades	Learning graes in contact with the subject teacher	Numeric
Practical_experimental_grades	Practical experimental learning grades for the subject	Numeric
BIM1_grades	First term grades	Numeric
BIM2_grades	Second term grades	Numeric

Before conducting the analysis, the dataset was preprocessed, including data cleaning, handling missing values, and normalization of numerical variables. This process was necessary to ensure data quality and to improve the performance of the subsequent analysis algorithms. Furthermore, the consistency of the academic variables was verified to ensure that they accurately reflected students' actual performance.

The main objective of using this dataset is to identify patterns in academic performance that support the characterization of different student profiles. Specifically, the aim is to detect groups with varying levels of academic achievement that can then be used for classification and interpretability analyses, such as feature importance.

3.2 Techniques of Academic Performance Grouping

To identify academic performance profiles among students, a clustering technique was applied. These techniques enable grouping students with similar academic characteristics without requiring predefined labels, thereby facilitating the exploration of latent patterns in the dataset. Two algorithms were evaluated using the silhouette score. These were: K-means [20] and HDBSCAN [21]. The objective was to group students based on similar characteristics related to their academic behavior, demographic data, and administrative data, without prior knowledge of the categories.

3.3 Classification Techniques and Importance of Characteristics

Two machine learning algorithms, Random Forest (RF) and XGBoost, were evaluated to build a predictive model for classifying students. For the prediction process, the cluster label is added as a feature to the clean dataset, which includes the variables of the Table 1. Model performance was assessed using Precision, Recall, and F1-score.

The model's interpretability was then analyzed using feature importance, which identifies which variables in the dataset have the greatest influence on academic performance profiles. In addition to feature importance analysis, an LLM was used to generate natural-language explanations of the model's outputs. It is important to note that this proposal does not involve a direct implementation of LLM integration, and that this does not participate in the prediction process and does not modify the model outputs; Instead, it conceptually demonstrates how feature important results can be transformed into interpretable narratives, enhancing the accessibility of model outputs for educational stakeholders.

4 Results

4.1 Clustering Results

The clustering process was conducted using relevant academic variables, primarily grades and overall student performance. Before analysis, the variables were normalized to prevent scale differences from influencing group formation. The best silhouette score for K-means was 0.47, obtained with ($k = 4$) clusters. For HDBSCAN, the best silhouette score was 0.19 at ($k = 4$). These results indicate that K-means performed better for grouping students in this dataset.

By applying the K-means algorithm, a number of student groupings came to light, each reflecting a particular configuration of academic outcomes. Generally speaking, these groupings can be interpreted as capturing four distinct profiles: those performing at a very high level, those performing at a high level, those situated around the regular, and those considered to be at risk. Table 2 shows the number of instances in each group, which differ in overall performance level.

Table 2. Student distribution and performance profiles

#Cluster	# instances	Performance profiles
0	1,973	highest-achieving
1	1,951	high-performance
2	1,315	regular-achieving
3	958	at-risk

The clustering results in Table 2 reveal four distinct academic performance profiles. The first two clusters represent the majority of students and correspond to high-performance profiles, while the fourth cluster identifies at-risk students, representing approximately 15% of the dataset.

The highest-achieving group comprises students with high grade point averages and is characterized by a strong academic profile. However, the high-performance group includes students with moderate academic results, exhibiting variability in their grades and relatively stable performance. The regular-achieving group exhibits lower academic performance, as measured by final and partial grades. Lastly, the category identified as at-risk for academic performance comprises students with lower average performance and greater difficulties in their academic progress. This group holds particular significance for the present study, as it allows for the early detection of students who may be navigating academic challenges.

Identifying these profiles is a fundamental step for the subsequent stages of the analysis. In particular, the groups obtained from the clustering process are used as labels to train supervised learning models that classify new students based on their academic performance profiles. Thus, the proposed approach combines unsupervised and supervised learning techniques to improve the understanding and prediction of academic performance.

On the other hand, given that the dataset does not include potentially relevant confounding factors, such as learning motivation or access to digital resources, which may influence both institutional characteristics and academic performance, the observed findings are interpreted not as causal but as indicative of patterns captured by the model.

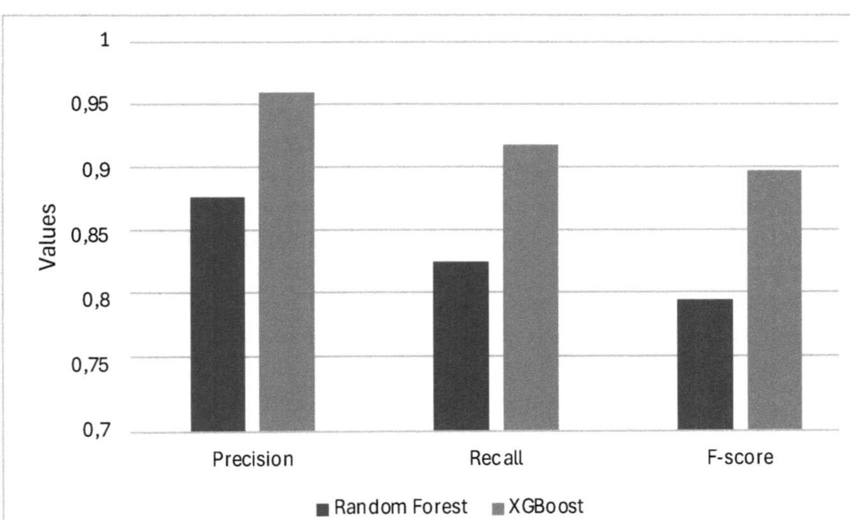

Fig. 1. Classification metrics results

4.2 Group Classification

This section reports the findings from the group classification carried out using the clusters identified in the prior phase. The models selected for training were Random Forest and XGBoost, chosen for their accuracy in predicting labels in complex data.

The dataset was divided into 80% for training and 20% for testing. The Grid Search technique was used to identify the hyperparameter combination that maximizes each model's performance and to determine the best configuration that balances the evaluation metrics. The configuration was as follows:

- Random Forest: n_estimators: 300, max_depth: 15, min_samples_split: 5, min_samples_leaf: 1.
- XGBoost: max_depth: 3, learning_rate: 0.5, n_estimator: 200, gamma: 0, subsample: 0.8.

These hyperparameters enabled the tested algorithms to reach their full potential for classifying labels generated by the clustering models. Figure 1 shows the results of the algorithms for the metrics Precision, Recall, and F-score.

5 Feature Importance Analysis

This section provides a comprehensive interpretation of the model to understand which academic factors contribute most to classifying students into different performance profiles.

To assess the importance of features, we used metrics derived from the supervised learning models used in this study. Specifically, the Random Forest algorithm estimates the relative contribution of each variable to the prediction process. These importance values are based on impurity reduction, that is,

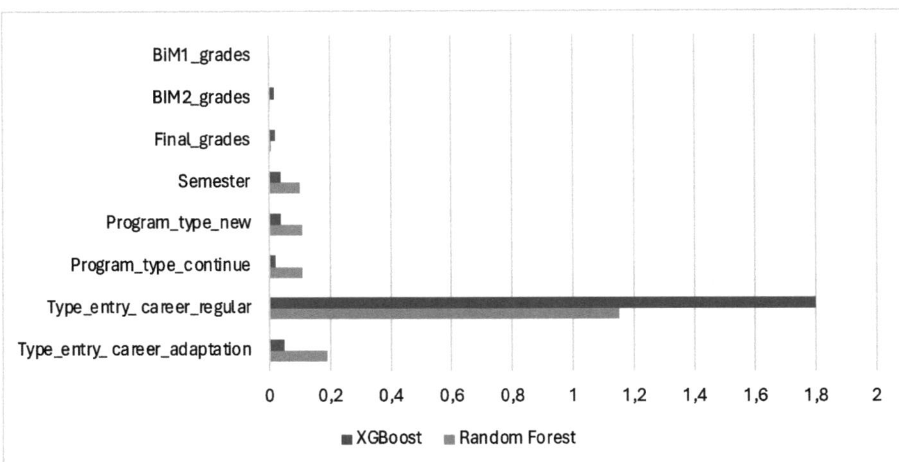

Fig. 2. Importance of features in Random Forest and XGBoost models.

the extent to which each feature improves model performance during training. Figure 2 presents the importance values of the features for the Random Forest and XGBoost models. This figure shows only the relevant features according to the model. This is because both Random Forest and XGBoost assign near-zero importance to several features, indicating that they do not significantly contribute to the model's predictive capability.

The feature importance analysis from the Random Forest model indicates that traditional academic variables, such as grades, have a limited influence on the prediction of students' academic performance. In contrast, institutional variables, particularly program type (continuous, regular, and new) and admission type (including program adaptation), play a more relevant role in classifying academic performance. A similar pattern is observed in the XGBoost model, where institutional variables are more influential than purely academic ones.

Based on the XGBoost feature importance analysis, the following example illustrates how an LLM can generate a human-readable explanation of model behavior. The prompt used to guide the LLM in generating this explanation was:

"You are an educational data analyst. Based on the following feature importance values from a machine learning model, explain which factors are most influential in predicting student academic performance and why. Provide a clear and concise explanation suitable for educators."

Input

```
Type_entry_career_adaptation: 0.05
Type_entry_career_regular: 1.8
Program_type_continue 0.02
Program_type_new: 0.04
Semester: 0.04
Final_grades: 0.02
BIM2_grades: 0.018
```

LLM-Generated Explanation

The LLM-generated explanation is as follows: *"The most influential factor in predicting academic performance profiles is the type of entry, particularly regular admission, which shows a significantly higher importance than the other variables, suggesting that admission pathways may strongly reflect students' academic readiness. Other factors, such as semester and program type, have a moderate impact, indicating that academic progression and program structure contribute to performance to a lesser extent. In contrast, grade-related variables are relatively unimportant in this model. Overall, institutional factors appear to play a more relevant role than individual course performance in predicting student outcomes."*.

This component is presented as a conceptual extension to enhance interpretability and does not affect the predictive model or its performance.

In summary, the feature importance analysis provides a clear view of the factors that most strongly influence the prediction of student groups based on academic performance, enabling educational administrators to better understand the model's behavior.

6 Conclusions and Future Work

This study presents a comprehensive approach for classifying academic performance profiles by combining unsupervised learning, supervised classification, and interpretability methods based on feature importance. In addition, the use of a Large Language Model is proposed as a complementary tool to improve the interpretability of feature importance results. Clustering techniques enabled the identification of distinct academic performance profiles, supporting the understanding of latent patterns in student data. These profiles were then used to train predictive models that classify students according to performance level. Furthermore, the feature importance analysis identified the variables that most strongly influence the predictions of academic performance profiles, providing deeper insight into model behavior. A key finding of this study is that academic variables, such as partial and final grades, are less relevant than administrative variables. This result shows that admission type and program are the main indicators of student performance, providing important information about the student's situation within the institution.

This study has several constraints. First, by restricting the variable to academic and administrative information may constrain the model's ability to capture other relevant factors, such as socioeconomic, psychological, and behavioral dimensions. Furthermore, clustering results are based on data from a single institutional context, which may limit their generalizability; different educational settings may produce variations in the number and characteristics of the clusters.

Future work proposes: 1) to extend the study by incorporating new data sources, such as interaction logs on the learning platform, and socioeconomic variables; 2) to evaluate the clustering structure across multiple institutional datasets to assess its generalizability; 3) to explore explainability techniques, such as SHAP, to enrich the interpretation of the models, and integrate of the LLM to generate a human-readable explanation.

Acknowledgment. The authors would especially like to thank the Information Technology program of Universidad Técnica Particular de Loja for providing the dataset.

References

1. Vaarma, M., Li, H.: Predicting student dropouts with machine learning: an empirical study in Finnish higher education. Technol. Soc. **76**, 102474 (2024)
2. Divakar, D., Keshaveni, N., Ramesh, E., Prathibha, M.: Machine learning in academic performance prediction: analyzing attendance and marks to forecast future results. In: 2024 International Conference on Computing, Semiconductor, Mechatronics, Intelligent Systems and Communications (COSMIC), pp. 264–271 (2024)

3. Leelaluk, S., et al.: Attention-based artificial neural network for student performance prediction based on learning activities. IEEE Access (2024)
4. Qi, Y.: A multi-dimensional prediction system for studentsâ academic performance driven by deep learning. Discov. Artif. Intell. **6**(1) (2026)
5. Guidotti, R., Monreale, A., Ruggieri, S., Turini, F., Giannotti, F., Pedreschi, D.: A survey of methods for explaining black box models. ACM Comput. Surv. **51**(5) (2018)
6. Lavender, B., Sen, S.: Enhancing surrogate decision trees for reinforcement learning with feature importance matrices. In: Calvaresi, D., et al. (eds.) Explainable, Trustworthy, and Responsible AI and Multi-Agent Systems. LNCS 15936 LNCS, vol. 15936, pp. 3–20. Springer, Cham (2026). https://doi.org/10.1007/978-3-032-01399-6_1
7. Lundberg, S.M., Lee, S.I.: A unified approach to interpreting model predictions. In: Proceedings of the 31st International Conference on Neural Information Processing Systems, pp. 4768–4777. NIPS 2017, Curran Associates Inc., Red Hook, NY, USA (2017)
8. Zafar, M.R., Khan, N.: Deterministic local interpretable model-agnostic explanations for stable explainability. Mach. Learn. Knowl. Extract. **3**(3), 525–541 (2021)
9. Bilal, A., Ebert, D., Lin, B.: LLMS for explainable AI: a comprehensive survey (2025)
10. Mumuni, F., Mumuni, A.: Explainable Artificial Intelligence (XAI): from inherent explainability to large language models (2025)
11. Albreiki, B., Zaki, N., Alashwal, H.: A systematic literature review of studentâ performance prediction using machine learning techniques. Educ. Sci. **11**(9) (2021)
12. Kumar, J., Vashistha, R., Kaur, K., Singh, S.K.: Machine learning techniques of predicting student's performance. In: 2023 International Conference in Advances in Power, Signal, and Information Technology (APSIT), pp. 693–698 (2023)
13. Ersozlu, Z., Taheri, S., Koch, I.: A review of machine learning methods used for educational data. Educ. Inf. Technol. **29**(16), 22125–22145 (2024)
14. Guo, L.: Big data-based analysis of family education models and student academic performance correlations, 275279 (2026)
15. Xu, T., Wang, S.: A study on analyzing students' psychological characteristics and learning styles using clustering algorithms. Int. J. Comput. Inf. Syst. Ind. Manage. Appl. **18**, 1–14 (2026)
16. Lian, J., Feng, W., Wang, Q., Dong, Y., Dauphin, G., Bai, J.: A deep random forest model with symmetry analysis for hyperspectral image data classification based on feature importance. Symmetry **17**(12) (2025)
17. Jiménez-Macias, A., Moreno-Marcos, P.M., Muñoz-Merino, P.J., Ortiz-Rojas, M., Kloos, C.D.: Analyzing feature importance for a predictive undergraduate student dropout model. Comput. Sci. Inf. Syst. **20**(1), 175–194 (2023)
18. Kashyap, A.M., Rao, D., Boland, M.R., Shen, L., Callison-Burch, C.: Predicting explainable dementia types with LLM-aided feature engineering. Bioinformatics **41**(4), btaf156 (04 2025)
19. Venkatesh, J., Jaiswal, A., Nanda, G.: Comparing human text classification performance and explainability with large language and machine learning models using eye-tracking. Sci. Rep. **14** (2024)

20. Prastyabudi, W.A., Alifah, A.N., Nurdin, A.: Segmenting the higher education market: an analysis of admissions data using k-means clustering. Procedia Comput. Sci. 234, 96–105 (2024). In: Seventh Information Systems International Conference (ISICO 2023)
21. Stewart, G., Al-Khassaweneh, M.: An implementation of the HDBSCAN* clustering algorithm. Appl. Sci. **12**(5) (2022)

CodeCompass: A Theory-Driven Personalized Programming Learning Platform Supporting Autonomy and Competence

Pei-Hua Chen[1], Lisbet Rønningsbakk[2], and Yueh-Min Huang[1(✉)]

[1] Department of Engineering Science, National Cheng Kung University, Tainan City, Taiwan
huang@mail.ncku.edu.tw

[2] Department of Education, UiT The Arctic University of Norway, Tromsø, Norway
lisbet.ronningsbakk@uit.no

Abstract. Sustaining motivation is a persistent challenge for programming beginners. Existing platforms prioritize content delivery but rarely address the psychological conditions that support continued engagement. This paper presents CodeCompass, a web-based programming learning platform grounded in Self-Determination Theory (SDT), designed to support two core psychological needs: autonomy and competence. Four features are described and mapped to SDT constructs: a daily challenge mechanism, a flexible learning path, progress and error analytics, and AI personalized feedback. The AI feedback module is designed as a dual-support mechanism, intended to support both autonomy and competence within the same interaction. A small-scale user study with 12 novice programmers, framed as a design probe, found that participants rated both needs positively after using the platform, with error analytics and AI feedback rated as particularly helpful. These findings offer directional input for further design iteration and future empirical work.

Keywords: Self-determination theory · Programming education · Personalized learning · AI feedback · Autonomy · Competence

1 Introduction

For many beginners, learning to program is both cognitively demanding and motivationally fragile. Beyond the difficulty of acquiring new concepts, learners frequently struggle to maintain consistent practice, track their own progress, and navigate their learning in a self-directed way [1]. When motivation erodes, even learners with adequate initial ability tend to disengage before developing stable programming problem-solving skills.

Existing platforms such as LeetCode, Codecademy, and HackerRank have lowered the barrier to programming practice, but their designs are predominantly organized around content coverage and challenge completion. Traditional automated feedback is primarily correctness-oriented, telling learners whether code passes tests but rarely helping them understand the underlying conceptual gap [2]. While large language

C.-J. Lin et al. (Eds.): ICITL 2026, LNCS 16841, pp. 262–270, 2027.
https://doi.org/10.1007/978-3-032-32112-1_26

models have expanded what AI feedback can offer, most of this work evaluates feedback in terms of comprehension, accuracy, or student outcomes, with little attention to whether it supports learners' psychological needs as defined by motivational theory [3]. LLM-generated feedback offers richer and more varied explanations than conventional automated feedback, yet the motivational implications of such feedback remain largely unexamined [4].

Self-Determination Theory (SDT) offers a well-validated framework for addressing this gap [5]. SDT identifies autonomy, competence, and relatedness as three basic psychological needs whose satisfaction sustains intrinsic motivation. Autonomy support has been operationalized as learner choice over pacing and content sequence, while competence support has been linked to informational feedback and clear progress indicators. Research across digital learning contexts confirms that systems satisfying these two needs tend to produce higher engagement and persistence [6].

This paper presents CodeCompass, a web-based programming learning platform whose feature design is explicitly grounded in SDT constructs. We further conduct a pilot study to understand how novice programmers experience the platform. The study addresses the following questions:

1. RQ1. How does CodeCompass support learners' sense of autonomy and competence through its core feature design?
2. RQ2. What are novice programmers' perceptions of autonomy and competence support after a single-session experience with CodeCompass?

The primary contribution of this paper is the system design itself, supplemented by a small-scale pilot study that provides initial supportive evidence for the design direction.

2 System Design

2.1 System Overview

CodeCompass is organized around three interconnected modules: a daily challenge engine, a structured learning path, and a learner analytics dashboard. These modules share a common data layer recording attempt history, error patterns, and streak data. The AI feedback module draws on this layer after each session to generate personalized responses. Fig. 1 shows the conceptual architecture of CodeCompass.

Users begin with a brief onboarding assessment placing them at one of three levels: beginner, intermediate, or advanced. From that point, the system supports learner-driven navigation. Table 1 summarizes how each core feature maps to SDT constructs, the design mechanism involved, and the corresponding interface component. Figure 2 shows the four main interface panels.

2.2 Daily Challenge and Learning Path for Autonomy Support

The daily challenge presents ten questions from the learner's current level, accessible at any time without a deadline. Within each session, learners may skip, revisit, or reorder questions freely. This flexibility preserves a sense of agency within the structured format.

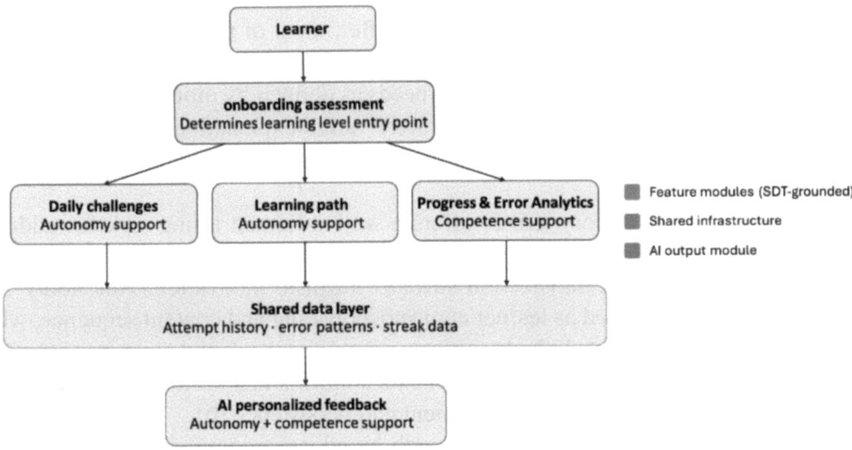

Fig. 1. System architecture of CodeCompass.

Table 1. Feature-to-SDT Mapping in CodeCompass

Feature	SDT Need	Mechanism	Interface
Daily Challenge	Autonomy	Self-paced practice; positive streak	Task UI / dashboard
Learning Path	Autonomy	Flexible entry; optional reassessment	Path page
Progress & Error Analytics	Competence	Accuracy, error themes, progress ring	Analytics dashboard
AI Personalized Feedback	Autonomy + Competence	Need-sensitive guidance; error diagnosis	Feedback panel

SDT research suggests that even modest choice within constrained tasks can shift perceived locus of causality from external to internal [5], making engagement feel chosen rather than required.

The streak counter increments on self-scheduled session completion and is non-punitive: missed days neither reset progress nor trigger warning notifications. Ryan and Deci distinguish informational positive feedback, which confirms self-endorsed action, from controlling positive feedback, which functions as an extrinsic contingency [5]; the CodeCompass streak satisfies both conditions for informational rather than controlling feedback, in that it tracks self-scheduled completions and missed days carry no penalty, distinguishing it from streak mechanisms in commercial apps that gate progress or trigger reminders. Whether learners experience it in this way under extended use remains an empirical question.

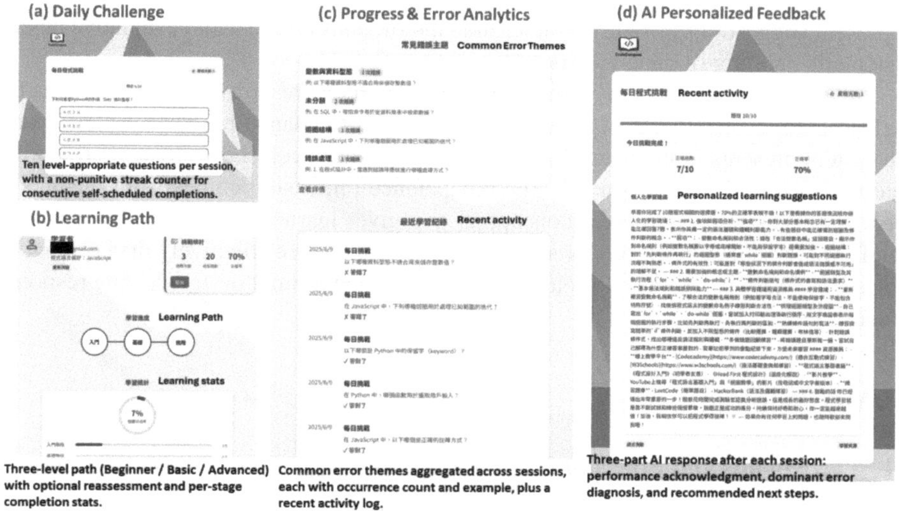

Fig. 2. Interface panels: (a) Daily Challenge, (b) Learning Path, (c) Progress & Error Analytics, (d) AI Personalized Feedback.

The three-level learning path uses the onboarding assessment to recommend an entry point, but learners may request reassessment or set their own starting level at any time. Within each level, topics are presented as navigable modules rather than a locked sequence, allowing learners to prioritize based on their own goals. This allows participation to reflect the learner's own intentions rather than external directives.

2.3 Progress and Error Analytics for Competence Support

The analytics dashboard provides competence-relevant information at three timescales. At the session level, learners receive immediate accuracy after completing a challenge. At the topic level, the system aggregates errors across sessions and surfaces the most frequently missed categories, labeled as common error themes, with occurrence counts (for example, "data types," "loop structures," "syntax," or "error handling"). At the overall level, a progress ring displays the learner's cumulative completion rate.

Together, these components instantiate SDT's concept of informational feedback: clear, accurate data about one's competence without implicit evaluative pressure [5].

2.4 AI Personalized Feedback as Dual Support

After each session, the platform synthesizes learner data, including error patterns, current level, and streak status, and queries GPT-4.1 mini to generate a three-part personalized response: an acknowledgment of session performance, a targeted diagnosis of the dominant error pattern, and recommended next steps. Error categories are not drawn from a predefined taxonomy; the model identifies and names the dominant pattern from the learner's session submissions, so category granularity tracks the actual errors produced. The non-directive tone is implemented as a prompt-level constraint instructing the model to present suggestions as options rather than instructions and to avoid evaluative labels; systematic auditing of generated outputs is left to future work.

The autonomy dimension comes from framing: the AI response presents options for the learner to act on rather than prescribing a fixed path. Guidance-based AI design, where the system presents hints rather than direct answers, has been shown to support learner autonomy and self-regulation [7]. The competence dimension comes from diagnostic specificity: naming a particular conceptual gap gives learners actionable information, as informational feedback supports intrinsic motivation more effectively than evaluative labels [5]. These two dimensions are coordinated in the prompt design driving response generation.

3 Methodology

3.1 Participants and Procedure

Twelve novice programmers (7 male, 5 female; Mage = 20.3 years, SD = 1.1) participated in this pilot study. All were undergraduate students enrolled in a networks and embedded systems course at a university in Taiwan. The course included an introductory programming component, and all participants had fewer than one semester of formal programming instruction prior to this study. Participants had no prior experience with CodeCompass or similar personalized platforms and were recruited through convenience sampling from this course. All participants provided written informed consent prior to data collection, and the study received ethical approval from the university's research ethics committee. Data collection focused exclusively on participants' perceptions of CodeCompass rather than their academic performance.

Each participant completed one structured session with CodeCompass lasting approximately 45 to 60 min. The session followed four steps: (1) complete the onboarding assessment and review the suggested learning path; (2) attempt a set of daily challenge questions appropriate to their assessed level; (3) review the analytics dashboard, including session accuracy and error-topic summary; and (4) read the AI-generated personalized feedback. Participants were encouraged to interact with the platform naturally. Upon completing the session, they filled out a short questionnaire and responded to two open-ended prompts.

3.2 Measures and Data Collection

Three data sources were collected. First, a six-item questionnaire using a five-point Likert scale (1 = strongly disagree, 5 = strongly agree) measured three constructs: perceived autonomy support (A1–A2), adapted from the perceived-choice subscale of the Intrinsic Motivation Inventory (IMI; [8]); perceived competence support (C1–C2), adapted from the IMI perceived-competence subscale; and perceived usefulness (H1–H2). The adaptation procedure involved three steps: original English items were translated into Chinese, task-generic wording was revised to refer to the platform (for example, "this task" was rephrased as "CodeCompass") so that items reflected the specific learning context, and two of the authors independently reviewed item wording for clarity and theoretical fidelity. No cognitive interview was conducted, consistent with the pilot scope of the study.

Second, two open-ended prompts were included: (1) Which feature did you find most useful, and why? (2) What, if anything, made you feel more or less in control of your learning? Responses were recorded verbatim for subsequent content analysis.

Third, platform behavioral data were logged automatically, including the number of questions completed, whether participants accessed the AI feedback panel, and whether they reviewed the error-topic summary. These data were used to verify task completion and to supplement the interpretation of questionnaire responses.

3.3 Data Analysis

Questionnaire data were summarized using descriptive statistics, reporting means and standard deviations for each item. Given the pilot and exploratory nature of this study and the small sample size, no inferential statistics were applied; the focus was on the direction and magnitude of responses rather than significance testing. Open-ended responses were analyzed using simple content analysis to identify recurring themes. Behavioral log data were used descriptively to contextualize questionnaire findings. Results are interpreted conservatively, and no causal claims are made. Consistent with the pilot scope of this study, all measurement outcomes are intended to indicate the initial direction of user perceptions rather than to serve as a basis for formal scale validation.

4 Results

4.1 Questionnaire Descriptive Statistics

Table 2 presents descriptive statistics for the six questionnaire items. The results suggest that participants generally perceived CodeCompass as supportive of autonomy and competence after the single-session experience, with positive ratings also observed for overall usefulness.

At the item level, H1 (AI feedback usefulness; $M = 4.17$, $SD = 0.58$) and C1 (clearer picture of current programming ability; $M = 4.08$, $SD = 0.51$) received the highest mean scores. At the construct level, usefulness showed the highest mean ($M = 4.05$), followed by competence ($M = 3.96$) and autonomy ($M = 3.84$).

Autonomy items showed somewhat greater variability ($SD = 0.67$–0.75) compared to competence items, suggesting individual differences in how much participants perceived meaningful choice. This may reflect variation in prior experience with self-directed learning, or the fact that a single session may be insufficient for learners to fully experience the flexible navigation the platform is designed to support.

4.2 Open-Ended Responses and Behavioral Data

Content analysis of open-ended responses revealed two recurring themes. First, participants frequently cited error analytics and AI personalized feedback as the most useful features, reporting that they provided a clearer sense of specific weaknesses and concrete

Table 2. Descriptive Statistics for Pilot Study Questionnaire

Item	Statement	*M*	*SD*	Construct
A1	I felt in control of my own learning pace and focus while using CodeCompass.	3.92	0.67	Autonomy
A2	CodeCompass allowed me to make meaningful choices about what to practice.	3.75	0.75	Autonomy
C1	The platform gave me a clearer picture of my current programming ability.	4.08	0.51	Competence
C2	I could see which areas I needed to improve after each session.	3.83	0.72	Competence
H1	The AI feedback provided after the session was helpful to my learning.	4.17	0.58	Usefulness
H2	Overall, I found CodeCompass useful for improving my programming skills.	3.92	0.67	Usefulness

direction for improvement. Second, several participants described a sense of ownership over their learning during the session, though a smaller number noted that the structure of the daily challenge initially felt more prescribed than flexible.

Two representative responses illustrate these patterns:

> *"Seeing my most common mistakes organized by topic was the first time I really understood where my weak points were. It felt like the platform was paying attention to me, not just giving me random questions."* (Participant 02)

> *"The AI feedback was more useful than I expected. It didn't just say I was wrong; it explained what kind of mistake I made and suggested what to look at next. That made me feel like I could actually do something about it."* (Participant 08)

Behavioral log data confirmed that all 12 participants completed the daily challenge session, with a mean of 8.3 questions completed out of the 10 available. All 12 participants accessed the AI feedback panel, and 11 of 12 reviewed the error-topic summary during the session, indicating that both features were highly visible and actively used during the single-session experience.

5 Discussion and Conclusion

5.1 Discussion

The findings indicate that novice programmers, after a single-session experience, tended to perceive CodeCompass as supporting both autonomy and competence, with competence-related support rated slightly higher than autonomy support and overall usefulness receiving the highest ratings. Competence-related features produced slightly higher and more consistent ratings, a pattern consistent with the interpretation that the error-topic summary and session accuracy, being the most immediately visible outputs of the platform, may provide the clearest competence-relevant feedback within a single session. Autonomy perceptions showed more variability, which may reflect the inherent challenge of designing for self-direction: the subjective experience of meaningful choice may require more extended use before it becomes perceptible.

The prominence of error analytics and AI feedback in open-ended responses is noteworthy. Both features received consistently high ratings and were most frequently mentioned as drivers of perceived usefulness. This suggests that the dual-support design of the AI module, combining informational diagnosis with non-directive guidance, may be among the elements most readily perceived as valuable by novice users [9]. Comments suggesting that the daily challenge initially felt structured rather than flexible point to a known tension in SDT-informed design: structure and autonomy support are not inherently incompatible, but the degree of choice within structure needs to be perceptible to users, which may require clearer onboarding or a longer acclimation period, as autonomy need satisfaction has been shown to develop progressively within learning contexts rather than emerging immediately [10].

The key differentiator of CodeCompass relative to existing platforms is the integration of features around a coherent motivational theory, which we term structured flexibility: each feature operates within a defined structure while preserving genuine learner choice within that structure.

5.2 Implications and Future Directions

These findings offer several implications for the design of AI-enhanced programming learning tools. First, AI feedback should target not only comprehension or correctness but also learners' psychological needs, particularly autonomy and competence [7]. Second, integrating features around a coherent motivational framework matters more than optimizing individual features in isolation [11]. Third, behavioral data such as feature access rates can serve as a useful supplementary indicator of learner engagement [12].

Several limitations apply. The present study is best understood as a design probe rather than an evaluation of need satisfaction: a six-item instrument administered to 12 participants after a single 45-to-60-min session, with no control group and no internal consistency statistics reported given the two-item-per-construct design, cannot establish need satisfaction in a measurement-theoretic sense. In addition, the guided four-step procedure itself constrains the autonomy the platform is designed to afford, and autonomy ratings should be interpreted with this structural caveat in mind. The non-directive tone of AI feedback is implemented as a prompt-level constraint without systematic output auditing, and the extent to which generated responses realize that tone in practice remains to be tested. The platform does not address SDT's third need, relatedness, reflecting its intended scope as an individual practice environment used alongside classroom interaction. Whether the non-punitive streak mechanism and the framing of AI feedback produce the intended regulatory effects in extended use remains to be empirically tested. Future work could also develop more systematic assessment instruments to evaluate motivation alongside learning outcomes, drawing on rubrics-based approaches used in related educational contexts [13].

5.3 Conclusion

CodeCompass demonstrates that theory-driven platform design can translate SDT constructs into concrete, learner-facing features that address motivational needs often overlooked by existing programming platforms. Each of the four core features was designed with a clear account of which psychological need it serves and through what mechanism. Daily challenges and the flexible learning path support autonomy; progress and error analytics support competence; the AI feedback module serves both needs within the same interaction. The pilot study yielded findings consistent with these design intentions, with participants reporting positive perceptions of both autonomy and competence support and identifying error analytics and AI feedback as the most helpful features. Future work will examine CodeCompass in longer-term use contexts, combining validated SDT instruments with platform behavioral data to further investigate its effects on perceived autonomy, competence, and programming performance.

References

1. Lin, G.-Y., Liao, Y.-W., Su, Z.-Y., Wang, Y.-M., Wang, Y.-S.: What drives undergraduates' effort and persistence in learning programming. Educ. Inf. Technol. **28**, 12383–12406 (2023)
2. Hao, Q., et al.: Towards understanding the effective design of automated formative feedback for programming assignments. Comput. Sci. Educ. **32**, 105–127 (2022)
3. Huang, Y.-M., Chen, P.-H., Lee, H.-Y., Sandnes, F.E., Wu, T.-T.: ChatGPT-enhanced mobile instant messaging in online learning: effects on student outcomes and perceptions. Comput. Hum. Behav. **168**, 108659 (2025)
4. Lohr, D., Keuning, H., Kiesler, N.: You're (not) my type- can LLMs generate feedback of specific types for introductory programming tasks? J. Comput. Assist. Learn. **41**, e13107 (2025)
5. Ryan, R.M., Deci, E.L.: Self-determination theory and the facilitation of intrinsic motivation, social development, and well-being. Am. Psychol. **55**, 68–78 (2000)
6. Howard, J.L., Bureau, J., Guay, F., Chong, J.X.Y., Ryan, R.M.: Student motivation and associated outcomes: a meta-analysis from self-determination theory. Perspect. Psychol. Sci. **16**, 1300–1323 (2021)
7. Lee, H.-Y., Chen, P.-H., Wang, W.-S., Huang, Y.-M., Wu, T.-T.: Empowering ChatGPT with guidance mechanism in blended learning: effect of self-regulated learning, higher-order thinking skills, and knowledge construction. Int. J. Educ. Technol. High. Educ. **21**, 16 (2024)
8. McAuley, E., Wraith, S., Duncan, T.E.: Self-efficacy, perceptions of success, and intrinsic motivation for exercise. J. Appl. Soc. Psychol. **21**, 139–155 (1991)
9. Yildiz Durak, H., Onan, A.: A systematic review of AI-based feedback in educational settings. J. Comput. Soc. Sci. **8**, 96 (2025)
10. Johansen, M.O., Eliassen, S., Jeno, L.M.: Autonomy need satisfaction and frustration during a learning session affect perceived value, interest, and vitality among higher education students. Scand. J. Educ. Res. **69**, 757–771 (2025)
11. David, L., Weinstein, N.: The how and how much of technology use in the classroom: a motivational approach to teachers' technology use. Eur. J. Educ. **59**, e12674 (2024)
12. Wang, Y., Wang, H., Wang, S., Wind, S.A., Gill, C.: A systematic review and meta-analysis of self-determination-theory-based interventions in the education context. Learn. Motiv. **87**, 102015 (2024)
13. Cheng, Y.-P., Huang, Y.-M.: LUPDA: a comprehensive rubrics-based assessment model for STEAM education. Int. J. STEM Educ. **12**, 45 (2025)

VR/AR/MR/XR in Education

Integrating Virtual Reality into Occupational Safety and Health Training: Examining on Course Satisfaction and Learning Effectiveness

Pao-Nan Chou[1(✉)], Chen-Jung Shih[1], and Yu-Hsin Chou[2]

[1] Graduate Institute of Technological and Vocational Education, National Pingtung University of Science and Technology, Pingtung County, Taiwan
pnchou@mail.npust.edu.tw

[2] National Experimental High School At Pingtung Science Park, Pingtung County, Taiwan

Abstract. With the growing demand for effective and engaging safety training in industrial environments, Virtual Reality (VR) technology provides new opportunities to enhance Occupational Health and Safety (OHS) education. This study examines employees' satisfaction and learning effectiveness in a VR-based OHS training program implemented at a port management company in Taiwan. Fifty employees participated in two VR modules—*Scaffolding Assembly Operations* and *Mobile Crane Lifting Operations*. A quantitative survey measured course satisfaction and perceived learning effectiveness, including operational skills and cognitive understanding. The results indicated consistently high levels of satisfaction and learning performance. Correlation and regression analyses further revealed that learning satisfaction not only correlated positively with both learning dimensions but also significantly predicted learners' perceived improvements in operational and cognitive domains. These findings demonstrate that satisfaction plays a key role in driving learning effectiveness in immersive environments. Overall, the study confirms that VR-based OHS training, grounded in constructivist, experiential, and situated learning theories, effectively enhances learner engagement, motivation, and safety competence through authentic and interactive learning experiences.

Keywords: Virtual Reality · Occupational Health and Safety · Learning Effectiveness · Course Satisfaction · Experiential Learning · Sustainable development education

1 Introduction

With the rapid transformation of industrial environments and the increasing diversity of high-risk operations, Occupational Health and Safety (OHS) training has become increasingly important for employers. Robson et al. [1] pointed out that OHS education and training can effectively improve workers' safety behavior and risk awareness, especially when the training is highly interactive and practice-oriented. However, traditional

C.-J. Lin et al. (Eds.): ICITL 2026, LNCS 16841, pp. 273–282, 2027.
https://doi.org/10.1007/978-3-032-32112-1_27

OHS programs are often lecture-based or rely on static video presentations, lacking real-time feedback and hands-on experience, which makes it difficult for trainees to apply safety knowledge flexibly in real work situations. Rodrigues et al. [2] further demonstrated that OHS training through simulation and interactive learning can significantly enhance participants' safety awareness and behavioral change, encouraging them to comply with safety regulations and make correct decisions in hazardous situations.

In recent years, Virtual Reality (VR) technology, characterized by immersion and interactivity, has opened new possibilities for OHS education and training. VR can simulate realistic workplace scenarios and compensate for the lack of situational engagement and feedback in traditional instruction, making it an innovative tool for safety education. Jensen et al. [3], in a quasi-experimental study conducted within the context of Industry 4.0, found that integrating VR into OHS training increased trainees' safety awareness by about 30%, significantly improving risk perception and self-efficacy, and fostering a proactive safety culture. Similarly, Mazur et al. [4], using surgical training as an example, confirmed that VR instruction substantially improved participants' safety performance, with safety behavior scores rising from 2.2 to 2.5 points and statistically significant differences observed in 90% of evaluation items.

Given the multiple potential hazards in port operations, such as working at heights, heavy machinery operation, container hoisting, and confined space activities, traditional lecture-based or video-based safety education can no longer meet practical demands. To strengthen workers' hazard recognition and emergency response capabilities, a port management company in southern Taiwan implemented VR technology in combination with OHS training. The company's Human Resources Department collaborated with an external information technology team to design and develop two VR-based training modules titled *Scaffolding Assembly Operations* and *Mobile Crane Lifting Operations*, tailored to the port's high-risk work environments.

The VR training system was developed using Unreal Engine, paired with VR headsets and hand sensors to deliver a 360° immersive simulation experience. This system enables trainees to perform loading and unloading tasks, identify potential hazards, operate machinery, and respond to emergencies within a virtual environment. The course adopts a staged, task-based learning design, progressing from environmental risk identification to safe operating procedures and finally to emergency response simulation, allowing trainees to gradually build a comprehensive safety behavior model.

The purpose of this study is to evaluate VR-based OHS education and training from an instructional effectiveness perspective. Specifically, it aims to:

1. Examine trainees' satisfaction with the VR OHS training program.
2. Analyze trainees' perceived learning outcomes, including operational skills and cognitive understanding.
3. Investigate the correlation between learning satisfaction and learning effectiveness in VR OHS courses.

2 Theoretical Discussion

The theoretical foundations of Virtual Reality (VR) in education can be discussed from four major perspectives: **constructivism, experiential learning theory, situated learning theory**, and **cognitive load theory**. These theories provide the pedagogical scaffolding that links VR technology to meaningful learning processes, emphasizing knowledge construction and learner engagement beyond technical innovation.

2.1 Constructivism

Constructivism posits that learners are not passive recipients of information but active constructors of knowledge through interaction with their environment, peers, and learning tasks [5]. From this perspective, VR can be viewed as a medium that promotes active exploration and problem solving. Dewey emphasized that education should occur through *learning by doing,* enabling learners to gain understanding through real or simulated experiences [6]. Because VR provides concrete, manipulable, and three-dimensional learning environments, it strengthens learners' ability to visualize and transform abstract concepts. Radianti et al. [7] found that VR learning environments align closely with constructivist principles, particularly in fostering inquiry-based learning and reflective thinking.

Furthermore, Bailenson [8] proposed the *transformative experience theory,* arguing that immersive virtual experiences can lead to genuine learning transformations. When learners engage in role-playing, problem solving, or conceptual exploration in VR, they can convert these experiences into long-term cognitive structures, suggesting that VR is not only a technological innovation but also a medium for deep learning.

2.2 Experiential Learning Theory

Kolb's experiential learning model identifies four sequential stages: concrete experience, reflective observation, abstract conceptualization, and active experimentation [9]. VR naturally supports this full learning cycle, allowing students to perform simulated tasks safely (concrete experience), reflect on outcomes (reflective observation), conceptualize underlying principles (abstract conceptualization), and then re-test their hypotheses (active experimentation). Such applications are particularly valuable in safety training, where risk-free practice is essential.

Makransky and Mayer [10] reported that VR learning environments enhance learners' sense of presence and engagement, which, in turn, reinforce cognitive involvement. When students actively explore immersive settings, their reflective and abstract reasoning abilities are strengthened, validating the relevance of Kolb's model in VR-based instruction.

2.3 Situated Learning Theory

Situated learning theory emphasizes that knowledge acquisition must be embedded within authentic social and physical contexts [11]. The immersive nature of VR allows for the simulation of real-world environments, enabling learners to apply knowledge within highly relevant and contextualized tasks. For example, students can manipulate hazardous chemicals in a virtual laboratory or experience construction safety procedures in a simulated worksite, thereby strengthening knowledge transfer and problem-solving abilities.

Wu et al. [12] found that *situational authenticity* and *presence* are two core variables influencing learning outcomes in VR. When virtual tasks are closely connected to real-world professional practices, learners' situational engagement and intrinsic motivation are significantly enhanced, leading to more effective knowledge transfer.

2.4 Cognitive Load Theory and Presence

Cognitive load theory reminds instructional designers to balance the limits of working memory during learning [13]. Although VR provides rich sensory stimuli, overly complex designs may increase extraneous cognitive load and reduce learning efficiency. Makransky and Petersen [14] found that poorly controlled interactivity or visual complexity in VR environments can distract learners and diminish learning outcomes.

Meanwhile, presence, a key psychological dimension of VR, refers to the extent to which learners feel that they are truly being there in a virtual environment. Slater and Sanchez-Vives [15] argued that presence enhances emotional engagement and memory retention, yet its educational value depends on how well it aligns with specific learning objectives. Therefore, effective VR instructional design must balance immersion and cognitive load to achieve optimal learning outcomes.

The development of the VR OHS training courses in this study was explicitly grounded in the theoretical perspectives discussed earlier. Constructivist principles informed the interactive design, encouraging learners to actively construct understanding through exploration and reflection. Experiential learning theory shaped the hands-on simulation structure, allowing participants to learn by doing and engage in iterative cycles of experience and feedback. The authenticity of the simulated workplace environments reflected the tenets of situated learning theory, providing realistic scenarios where safety knowledge could be directly applied. Additionally, cognitive load theory guided the instructional design to maintain an optimal balance between immersion and cognitive demand, thereby maximizing learning efficiency.

3 Research Method

3.1 Research Design

This study adopts a quantitative questionnaire approach to collect data on employees' satisfaction with VR-based Occupational Health and Safety (OHS) training courses and their learning effectiveness, which includes operational skills and cognitive understanding. The overall research framework is illustrated in Fig. 1. The two major research variables are defined as follows:

1. Course satisfaction: Refers to participants' level of satisfaction with the training course, including their evaluations of course design, instructional content, interactivity, and technical support.

2. Learning effectiveness: Comprises two subdimensions, operational skills and cognitive understanding. The former refers to learners' self-perceived improvement in practical abilities (skill domain), while the latter concerns learners' self-perceived enhancement of conceptual and theoretical understanding (knowledge domain).

At the statistical analysis level, in addition to examining the independent effects of these two primary variables, this study also investigates the degree of association between them.

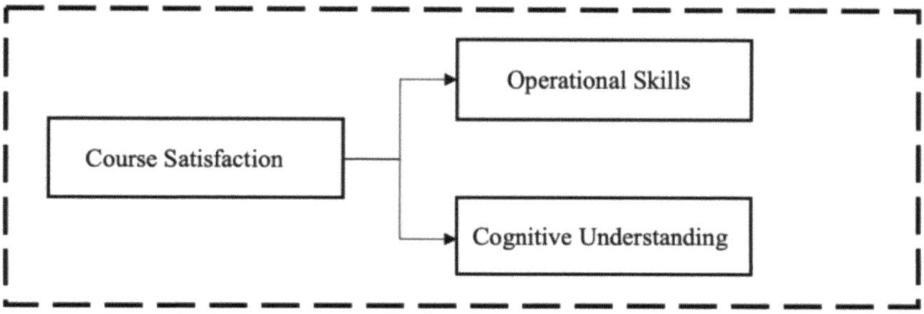

Fig. 1 The research design of the study

3.2 Research Participant

The participants of this study were 50 employees from a port management company in Taiwan. These employees had no prior experience using virtual reality and had long been trained through conventional occupational safety and health programs. According to company policy, each employee was required to attend two VR based OHS training courses, "Scaffolding Assembly Operations" and "Mobile Crane Lifting Operations," within a specified period in the company's training center. Each VR training session lasted approximately 50 min. Upon completion, participants were asked to immediately complete a post-training feedback form to assess their self-perceived course satisfaction and learning effectiveness.

3.3 VR Training Content

Two VR course content was offered in the study:

1. Scaffolding assembly operations: This course simulates scaffolding construction at a building site. Learners perform key operational and safety procedures in a virtual construction environment.
2. Mobile crane lifting operations: This course simulates the complete lifting operation process using a mobile crane. Learners practice safe equipment inspection and lifting operations under various conditions.

3.4 Assessment Tool

The post-training feedback questionnaire consisted of three dimensions: operational skills, cognitive understanding, and satisfaction. A five-point Likert scale was used, ranging from 1 (strongly disagree) to 5 (strongly agree). To ensure the validity of the instrument, three education experts reviewed the questionnaire items. Based on their evaluations, inappropriate items were removed, resulting in a final version containing 15 items, with five items for each dimension.

To assess internal consistency reliability, Cronbach's α coefficients were calculated for both the entire questionnaire and each dimension. The overall Cronbach's α value was 0.973, indicating an exceptionally high level of reliability and demonstrating that the questionnaire possessed excellent stability and internal consistency.

4 Findings

4.1 Trainees' Perceived Satisfaction and Learning Outcomes

Based on the questionnaire analysis results, the overall performance across the three dimensions was remarkably high, as shown in Table 2.

Table 2 Overall performance across three dimensions

Dimension	Mean	SD
Operational Skills	4.67	0.56
Cognitive Understanding	4.58	0.63
Course Satisfaction	4.69	0.52

The mean scores of all three dimensions ranged between 4.5 and 4.7, indicating that participants generally held highly positive perceptions of the VR-based Occupational Health and Safety (OHS) training.

First, the operational skills dimension achieved a mean score of 4.67, suggesting that most participants believed the VR simulation effectively enhanced their practical skills. Through repeated practice in simulated scaffolding assembly and crane-lifting operations, participants became more familiar with proper safety procedures and operational techniques. This result demonstrates that VR is particularly beneficial for skill-oriented training.

Second, the cognitive understanding dimension showed a slightly lower mean score of 4.58, though still at a high level. This finding indicates that participants perceived VR as helpful in improving their understanding of safety concepts and regulations. The immersive and interactive nature of VR allowed learners to receive real-time feedback and experience multi-sensory engagement, which facilitated deeper conceptual comprehension.

Finally, the course satisfaction dimension achieved the highest mean score (4.69), suggesting that participants were highly satisfied with the course design, interactivity, instructional content, and technical support. This reflects the motivational and engaging aspects of VR-based learning, which can enhance learner participation and enjoyment throughout the training process.

Overall, the results indicate that VR-based OHS training was highly effective in both practical skill development and conceptual understanding, with an exceptionally high level of learner satisfaction. The findings suggest that incorporating immersive VR technology into safety training can not only improve operational proficiency and risk awareness but also overcome the passivity often seen in traditional training, thereby promoting active engagement and deeper learning.

4.2 Correlation Between Learning Satisfaction and Learning Effectiveness

This study further employed Pearson's product moment correlation analysis to examine the relationship between satisfaction and learning effectiveness. The results are presented in Table 3. The statistical analysis revealed a significantly strong positive correlation between the satisfaction dimension and the operational skills dimension ($r = 0.721$, $p < .001$). This finding indicates that participants who reported higher satisfaction with the VR based training also perceived greater improvement in their practical and task related skills. In other words, when trainees found the course content, instructional design, and interactive features of the VR training system engaging and useful, they were more likely to develop confidence in performing work related safety operations. This suggests that satisfaction plays an important motivational role in facilitating skill acquisition within immersive learning environments.

Similarly, a strong positive correlation was found between the satisfaction dimension and the cognitive understanding dimension ($r = 0.839$, $p < .001$). This result demonstrates that participants who expressed higher satisfaction with the overall training experience also perceived a greater enhancement in their conceptual understanding of safety procedures and principles. The immersive and interactive nature of VR allows learners to connect abstract safety concepts with realistic scenarios, thereby promoting meaningful learning and cognitive retention. The strong association between satisfaction and cognitive understanding further highlights that affective engagement, such as enjoyment and perceived relevance, can substantially reinforce cognitive learning processes.

Table 3 Pearson's product moment correlation analysis

Dimension	Operational Skills	Cognitive Understanding
Course Satisfaction	$r = 0.721$ ($p < 0.001$)	$R = 0.839$ ($p < 0.001$)

Since learning satisfaction showed a significant positive correlation with both cognitive understanding and operational skills, this study further conducted regression analyses to examine the predictive effects among these variables. The results indicated that the satisfaction dimension had a significant positive predictive effect on operational skills ($R = 0.721$, $R^2 = 0.520$, $p < .001$), as well as on cognitive understanding ($R = 0.839$, $R^2 =$

0.703, $p < .001$). However, in terms of predictive strength, learning satisfaction demonstrated the highest level of accuracy in predicting cognitive understanding, explaining approximately 70% of its variance

4.3 Discussion

The results of this study indicate that VR-based Occupational Health and Safety (OHS) training effectively enhances both practical and conceptual learning outcomes. Participants expressed high satisfaction with the courses and reported noticeable improvement in operational skills and cognitive understanding. The analysis revealed strong positive relationships between satisfaction and both learning dimensions, suggesting that learners who were more satisfied with the VR experience also perceived greater gains in their skills and knowledge.

To further examine these relationships, regression analyses were conducted to test the predictive effects of satisfaction on learning outcomes. The findings confirmed that learning satisfaction positively influenced both operational skills and cognitive understanding. In particular, satisfaction showed a stronger predictive effect on cognitive understanding, suggesting that learners who felt more engaged and content with the VR training were also more likely to develop deeper conceptual insights. These results indicate that satisfaction functions not only as an emotional response to learning but also as a critical factor driving overall learning effectiveness.

These findings support the constructivist perspective that learning occurs through active engagement and interaction with the environment [5, 6]. The VR simulations provided realistic and manipulable contexts, enabling participants to construct understanding through exploration and reflection rather than passive reception. This is consistent with Kolb's experiential learning theory, which highlights the importance of concrete experience and reflective observation in knowledge development [9, 10]. Learners' satisfaction with the authenticity and interactivity of the VR environment likely enhanced their motivation and promoted meaningful experiential learning.

The results also align with situated learning theory, which emphasizes that knowledge is most effectively acquired within authentic contexts [11, 12]. By immersing participants in lifelike safety scenarios, the VR environment enabled them to connect theoretical knowledge with real workplace practices. When learners perceived the content and scenarios as relevant and engaging, they were more likely to internalize and transfer safety concepts to real-world situations.

Furthermore, the findings correspond with cognitive load theory and the concept of presence [13–15]. The VR training appeared to achieve a balance between immersion and cognitive processing, allowing learners to feel present in the environment without being overwhelmed by excessive visual or interactive stimuli. Such presence enhances emotional engagement and memory retention when aligned with clear learning goals [15].

In summary, the regression findings and theoretical interpretations collectively demonstrate that learner satisfaction is not only an outcome of effective VR instructional design but also a powerful predictor of learning effectiveness. The results confirm that immersive, interactive, and context-rich learning environments—grounded in constructivist, experiential, and situated learning theories—can foster deeper understanding, higher motivation, and more confident skill application in OHS training.

5 Conclusion

This study examined the integration of Virtual Reality (VR) into Occupational Health and Safety (OHS) education and its influence on course satisfaction and learning effectiveness. The results demonstrate that VR-based training effectively enhances learners' perceived operational skills, cognitive understanding, and overall satisfaction. The strong relationships among these dimensions indicate that learner satisfaction plays a pivotal role in promoting both practical skill development and conceptual learning. Regression analyses further confirmed that satisfaction not only correlates with learning outcomes but also serves as a significant predictor, underscoring its importance as a driving force in effective safety education.

From a theoretical perspective, the findings reinforce the pedagogical value of constructivism, experiential learning, and situated learning theories in VR-based training. By providing authentic, interactive, and immersive experiences, VR enables learners to actively construct knowledge, engage in meaningful reflection, and apply conceptual understanding to real-world safety contexts. Furthermore, through appropriate management of cognitive load, VR environments can maintain learners' motivation, enhance focus, and promote long-term retention of safety knowledge.

Practically, this study provides empirical evidence that VR is a powerful and pedagogically sound tool for improving OHS training outcomes. Organizations seeking to strengthen safety education should consider incorporating VR into blended learning strategies to enhance engagement, knowledge transfer, and hands-on competence. Future research could build upon these findings by examining long-term learning effects, exploring cross-industry implementations, and integrating physiological or behavioral indicators to capture authentic learning performance in immersive environments.

References

1. Robson, L.S., et al.: A systematic review of the effectiveness of occupational health and safety training. Scand. J. Work Environ. Health. **38**(3), 193–208 (2012)
2. Rodrigues, M.A., Vale, C., Silva, M.V.: Effects of an occupational safety pro gramme: a comparative study between different training methods involving secondary and vocational school students. Saf. Sci. **109**, 353–360 (2018)
3. Al-Hamad, A., Wedyan, M., Gilányi, A.: Virtual reality safety training and auditing in warehouse environments: AHP and critical thinking approach. Cogn., Technol. Work. **27**(3), 503–524 (2025)
4. Mazur, L., et al.: Effect of immersive virtual reality teamwork training on safety behaviors during surgical cases: nonrandomised intervention versus controlled pilot study. JMIR Med. Educ. **11**, e66186 (2025)
5. Piaget, J.: The Psychology of the Child. Basic Books (1972)
6. Dewey, J.: Experience and Education. Macmillan (1938)

7. Radianti, J., Majchrzak, T.A., Fromm, J., Haugstvedt, A.C.: A systematic review of immersive virtual reality applications for higher education: design elements, lessons learned, and research agenda. Comput. Educ. **147**, 103778 (2020)
8. Bailenson, J.N.: Experience on Demand: What Virtual Reality Is, how it Works, and What it Can Do. W. W. Norton & Company (2018)
9. Kolb, D.A.: Experiential Learning: Experience as the Source of Learning and. Development. Prentice Hall (1984)
10. Makransky, G., Mayer, R.E.: Benefits and pitfalls of immersive VR instruction: a cognitive and affective review. Educ. Psychol. Rev. **34**(4), 2117–2144 (2022)
11. Lave, J., Wenger, E.: Situated Learning: Legitimate Peripheral Participation. Cambridge University Press (1991)
12. Wu, B., Yu, X., Gu, X.: Effectiveness of immersive virtual reality using head-mounted displays on learning performance: a meta-analysis. Br. J. Educ. Technol. **51**(6), 1991–2005 (2020)
13. Sweller, J.: Cognitive load during problem solving: effects on learning. Cogn. Sci. **12**(2), 257–285 (1988)
14. Makransky, G., Petersen, G.B.: The cognitive and motivational effects of immersive virtual reality in education. Comput. Educ. **163**, 104099 (2021). https://doi.org/10.1016/j.compedu.2020.104099
15. Slater, M., Sanchez-Vives, M.V.: Enhancing our lives with immersive virtual reality. Front. Robot. AI. **3**, 74 (2016)

From Immersion to Learning? Evaluating Objective and Subjective Outcomes in VR-Based Healthcare Training

Leonie Kopahs(✉) and Matthias Schumann

Georg-August-University, Platz der Göttinger Sieben 5, Göttingen 37073, Germany
leonie.kopahs@uni-goettingen.de

Abstract. Immersive virtual reality (VR) is increasingly used in healthcare education, yet evidence on its impact on measurable learning outcomes remains mixed. This study evaluates a configurable VR training system for intravenous infusion preparation using a quantitative pre–post design. Sixty-one participants completed objective knowledge tests before and after a single training session, along with measures of subjective learning and user experience. Although user evaluations were positive, no significant short-term gains in procedural knowledge were observed, and perceived learning was not associated with objective improvement. These findings suggest that immersive design should be carefully aligned with evidence-based instructional principles and rigorous evaluation strategies in healthcare training.

Keywords: Immersive Virtual Reality · Healthcare Education · Learning Effectiveness · User Experience · Educational Technology Evaluation

1 Introduction

Simulation-based training plays a central role in healthcare education, enabling learners to acquire procedural knowledge and clinical skills while minimizing risks to real patients [1]. Increasing procedural complexity, heightened patient safety requirements, and persistent resource constraints in educational institutions have intensified the demand for scalable and effective training solutions. In response, immersive digital learning technologies, particularly virtual reality (VR), have emerged as promising tools to complement traditional simulation-based instruction [2, 3].

Immersive VR enables interactive, contextualized procedural training and is widely regarded as an innovative supplement to simulation-based education [4, 5]. In healthcare education, VR applications have been implemented in nursing training, emergency medicine, and procedural skill acquisition, often reporting positive effects on engagement, motivation, and perceived preparedness [6, 7]. These characteristics position VR as an innovative learning technology capable of enhancing experiential training formats.

However, empirical evidence regarding the effectiveness of immersive VR for improving objective learning outcomes remains mixed. While experiential benefits such

C.-J. Lin et al. (Eds.): ICITL 2026, LNCS 16841, pp. 283–292, 2027.
https://doi.org/10.1007/978-3-032-32112-1_28

as presence, enjoyment, and perceived learning are frequently documented, measurable improvements in knowledge and performance are less consistently observed [3, 8, 9]. Meta-analytical findings suggest that immersive technologies do not automatically lead to superior learning outcomes and that instructional design, learner characteristics, and contextual conditions critically shape their educational impact [1, 10].

A particular challenge in immersive learning research lies in distinguishing between subjective and objective learning outcomes. Discrepancies between perceived and measurable learning outcomes have been reported in immersive training contexts [8, 10]. In healthcare education, such discrepancies are especially consequential, as perceived competence without sufficient procedural accuracy may have implications for patient safety and professional practice [11]. Consequently, integrated evaluation approaches that combine performance-based measures with subjective user experience assessments are increasingly recommended in educational technology research.

Furthermore, prior domain knowledge has been identified as a key moderator of immersive learning effectiveness. According to Cognitive Load Theory, immersive environments may impose additional cognitive demands that differentially affect novice and experienced learners [12]. While experienced learners may benefit from contextualized practice, novices may experience increased extraneous cognitive load due to navigation, interaction complexity, and unfamiliar task structures [10, 13]. Nevertheless, empirical investigations that simultaneously examine objective learning, subjective experience, and prior-knowledge effects within the same VR-based training context remain limited.

Against this background, the present study evaluates an immersive VR training system for intravenous infusion preparation in healthcare education. The system is an innovative, configurable learning technology that enables guided procedural training in a high-fidelity virtual clinical environment. The study adopts a pre–post evaluation design that combines objective knowledge assessments with validated measures of subjective learning and user experience.

The study is guided by the following research questions:

RQ1: To what extent does immersive VR-based training lead to measurable short-term improvements in objective procedural knowledge in healthcare education?
RQ2: How are subjective learning perceptions and user experience related to objective learning outcomes, and how does prior domain experience influence these relationships?

This study evaluates cognitive and experiential outcomes in a configurable VR learning environment, advancing healthcare digital education. It offers insights into designing immersive systems that balance experiential richness with effective learning.

2 Related Research

Immersive Learning and VR in Healthcare. Simulation-based training is a core instructional approach in healthcare education, enabling learners to develop procedural knowledge and clinical skills in safe and controlled environments [1, 11]. While traditional simulation formats such as mannequin-based training provide valuable experiential learning opportunities, they are often resource-intensive, infrastructure-dependent, and limited in scalability [1]. Immersive VR has emerged as an innovative extension of simulation-based learning, offering interactive, high-fidelity virtual clinical environments that can be flexibly deployed across educational settings [2, 3].

Empirical research consistently reports positive effects of immersive VR on engagement, motivation, and learner satisfaction [6, 14]. However, evidence regarding objective learning outcomes remains inconsistent. Meta-analyses suggest that immersive VR does not reliably outperform traditional instructional approaches and that its effectiveness depends strongly on instructional design, task complexity, and learner characteristics [1, 3, 9]. These findings indicate that immersion alone does not guarantee learning effectiveness and that the educational value of VR must be examined in relation to pedagogical integration and contextual factors.

Cognitive Load and the Role of Prior Knowledge. Cognitive Load Theory provides a useful theoretical lens for understanding why immersive environments may produce variable learning outcomes [12]. Immersive VR introduces rich visual stimuli, spatial interaction demands, and novel interfaces that may increase extraneous cognitive load if not carefully designed [10]. While experiential richness can support contextualized learning, it may also divert attention from task-relevant information, particularly in complex procedural domains.

Prior knowledge plays a critical moderating role in this context. Experienced learners may benefit from immersive practice that reinforces existing mental models, whereas novices may experience cognitive overload when simultaneously processing procedural content and system interaction [12, 13]. Consequently, instructional scaffolding, structured workflows, and guided task progression are considered essential design elements in immersive training systems [10, 15].

Subjective Versus Objective Learning Outcomes. A persistent challenge in educational technology research concerns the divergence between subjective perceptions of learning and objective performance measures [8]. Learners frequently report high levels of satisfaction, presence, and perceived learning in immersive environments, yet these perceptions often show weak correlations with measurable knowledge gains [9]. In immersive VR contexts, heightened engagement may amplify this dissociation by fostering a compelling sense of progress without necessarily improving procedural accuracy.

In healthcare education, this distinction is particularly critical, as inflated perceptions of competence may not correspond to safe and accurate task execution [11]. Scholars, therefore, emphasize the need for integrated evaluation approaches that combine objective performance measures with subjective experience indicators to comprehensively assess the educational value of immersive technologies [1, 3].

3 Methodology

3.1 Educational Context and VR Training System

The study was conducted in the context of vocational and higher healthcare education, where simulation-based training is widely used to support the acquisition of procedural skills while minimizing patient risk [1, 11]. Immersive VR represents an innovative extension of traditional simulation approaches by enabling scalable, repeatable, and interactive learning environments [3].

The evaluated system, V + Care, is a high-fidelity immersive VR training application designed for intravenous infusion preparation. The procedure requires sequential decision-making, strict adherence to hygiene protocols, and coordinated material handling, making it suitable for structured simulation-based learning [6].

The system places learners in a virtual patient room where all relevant materials and medical devices are represented as interactive 3D objects. Users interact via a head-mounted display and handheld controllers, allowing spatial object manipulation and embodied task execution [16]. Figure 1 illustrates the virtual training environment and the procedural workflow implemented in the V + Care system.

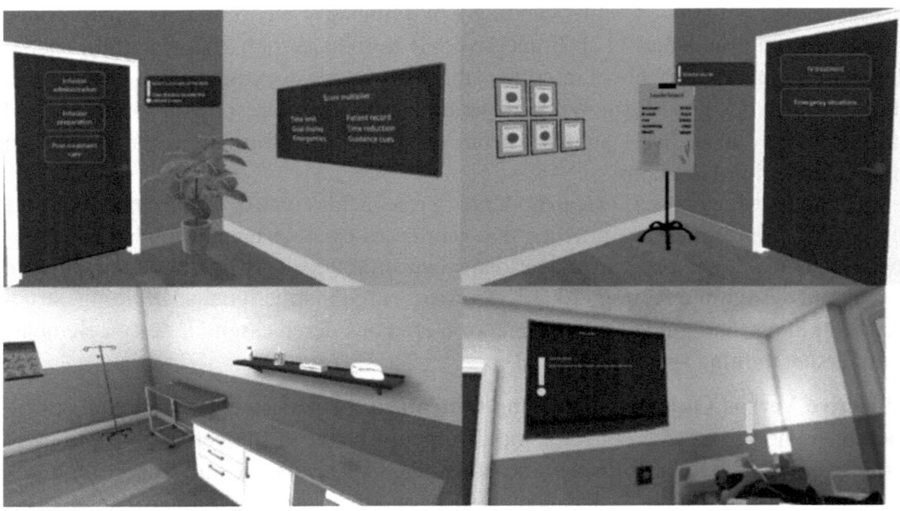

Fig. 1. VR Training Environment

The training scenario follows a predefined procedural workflow. Task progression is supported through visual guidance elements, including highlighted objects, task markers, and contextual cues indicating required actions. These features aim to reduce extraneous cognitive load while maintaining learner autonomy [10]. The system provides immediate procedural cues when required actions are omitted or performed incorrectly but does not include adaptive tutoring or structured debriefing components.

Importantly, the system allows configurable instructional settings, including the activation or deactivation of hints, task guidance, and time pressure. For this study, the scenario was configured without time constraints and with active visual guidance to ensure standardized learning conditions and to minimize additional cognitive load across learners with varying prior knowledge.

3.2 Study Design and Data Analysis

A quantitative pre–post evaluation design was employed to assess the short-term learning effects of the immersive VR training. Participants completed (1) a pre-test assessing procedural knowledge, (2) a single VR training session, (3) a post-test using the same knowledge instrument, and (4) a questionnaire measuring subjective learning and user experience. To examine the moderating role of prior knowledge, participants were categorized into two groups based on self-reported prior domain experience (with vs. without).

Data were analyzed using R. Pre–post learning gains were examined using paired-samples t-tests. Given deviations from normality, Wilcoxon signed-rank tests were conducted as robustness checks [17]. Effect sizes were calculated using Cohen's d [18]. Internal consistency of questionnaire scales was assessed using Cronbach's alpha [19]. Group differences in subjective learning and user experience were analyzed using independent-samples t-tests. Correlation analyses examined associations between subjective learning perceptions and objective knowledge gains. Sensitivity analyses, including outlier inspection and comparisons of parametric and non-parametric tests, were conducted to assess robustness.

4 Results

A total of 65 participants took part in the study. Four cases were excluded due to incomplete data, resulting in a final sample of 61 participants. Participants were predominantly young adults (M = 23.9 years, SD = 4.6) with a relatively balanced gender distribution (59% female). Demographic characteristics were comparable across participants with and without prior domain experience (Table 1).

Table 1. Sample Characteristics

Characteristic	Overall Sample (N = 61)	With Prior Experience (N = 29)	Without Prior Experience (N = 32)
Age (years), M (SD)	23.9 (4.6)	23.1 (3.9)	24.6 (5.1)
Female (%)	59%	62%	56%
Male (%)	41%	38%	44%

4.1 Objective Learning Outcome

Across the full sample, objective procedural knowledge increased slightly from pre-test (M = 10.32) to post-test (M = 10.62), corresponding to an average improvement of 0.30 points. This difference was not statistically significant, $t\ (60) = -1.29$, $p = .202$, with a negligible effect size ($d = 0.17$). When examining the subgroups separately, participants without prior domain experience improved on average by 0.47 points (from 9.27 to 9.73).

In contrast, participants with prior experience improved by 0.15 points (from 11.47 to 11.62). However, neither subgroup showed statistically significant improvements (both $p > .05$). Effect sizes were small to negligible.

As shown in Table 2, participants with prior experience entered the study with substantially higher baseline scores. Specifically, their pre-test performance averaged 11.47 out of 13 possible points (≈88% of the maximum score), indicating restricted variance and limited potential for measurable improvement. Even among participants without prior experience, baseline performance averaged 9.27 points (≈71% of the maximum score), suggesting moderate prior knowledge. Given the relatively small number of knowledge items and the limited score range, the instrument's restricted variance reduces its sensitivity to detect short-term learning gains, particularly among experienced learners.

Table 2. Pre–Post Comparisons

Group	N	Pre-Test Mean	Post-Test Mean	Mean Difference	t(df)	p-value	Cohen's d
Overall Sample	61	10.32	10.62	0.30	−1.29	.202	0.17
Without Prior Experience	29	9.27	9.73	0.47	−1.17	.254	0.28
With Prior Experience	32	11.47	11.62	0.15	−0.58	.567	0.12

4.2 Subjective Learning and User Experience

Participants generally evaluated the VR training positively. Mean scores indicate favorable perceptions of interaction quality, realism, usability, and subjective learning (Table 3).

Internal consistency was acceptable to good for most constructs (Cronbach's $\alpha = .70$–$.87$). Lower reliability was observed for immersion and spatial presence ($\alpha \approx .55$–$.63$), which should be considered when interpreting these subjective constructs.

No statistically significant differences emerged between participants with and without prior experience across any subjective learning or user experience construct (all $p > .05$). Effect sizes were small, indicating largely comparable perceptions across both groups. Although the differences were not statistically significant, participants with prior experience tended to report higher scores on realism- and presence-related constructs. However, effect sizes remained small to moderate, indicating limited practical differentiation between groups.

Correlation analyses further revealed no significant association between subjective learning ratings and objective pre–post knowledge gains. Thus, perceived learning was not predictive of measurable performance improvement.

Robustness checks, including non-parametric analyses and outlier inspection, did not materially alter the overall pattern of results. For realism and presence, participants with prior experience reported descriptively higher values (d = 0.41), indicating a small-to-moderate effect. Although this difference did not reach statistical significance, it suggests that experienced learners may have perceived the virtual environment as slightly more authentic or contextually meaningful.

Table 3. Subjective Learning and User Experience

Construct	With Prior Experience M (SD)	Without Prior Experience M (SD)	t(df)	p	Cohen's d	Cronbach's Alpha
Interaction Quality	1.27 (0.53)	1.11 (0.58)	1.14	.260	0.29	.70
Realism and Presence	0.41 (0.82)	0.04 (0.96)	1.58	.119	0.41	.81
Spatial Presence	0.66 (0.68)	0.60 (0.71)	0.30	.769	0.08	.58
Immersion	0.23 (0.61)	0.18 (0.73)	0.31	.759	0.08	.55
Experience – Workflow	0.31 (0.64)	0.23 (0.78)	0.43	.667	0.11	.61
Experience – Usability	0.60 (0.91)	0.47 (0.92)	0.54	.589	0.14	.87
Subjective Learning	0.54 (0.91)	0.61 (0.78)	−0.34	.738	−0.09	.79

5 Discussion

This study makes three key contributions. Firstly, it indicates that positive experiential outcomes in immersive healthcare training may not always correspond to immediate measurable knowledge improvements. Secondly, it highlights the importance of considering both subjective and objective indicators when assessing immersive learning technologies. Thirdly, it derives concrete design implications, including the integration of structured scaffolding, performance-contingent feedback, repeated practice opportunities, and guided debriefing phases to better align immersive affordances with evidence-based instructional principles in safety-critical educational settings.

The research explored the short-term learning effectiveness and experiential aspects of an immersive VR system for intravenous infusion preparation. The results present a nuanced, somewhat cautious view on the educational benefits of immersive technologies in healthcare. Although participants experienced positive usability and perceived learning benefits, there were no significant short-term gains in objective procedural knowledge. This mismatch between experiential quality and measurable learning outcomes emphasizes an ongoing challenge in immersive learning research: engagement alone does not guarantee cognitive improvement.

The absence of significant objective learning gains should be interpreted cautiously, as the findings may partly reflect limitations of the single-session design and assessment sensitivity rather than the ineffectiveness of immersive VR itself. Although small descriptive increases in knowledge scores were observed, effect sizes remained negligible to small. This pattern aligns with prior research suggesting that immersion and engagement alone may not necessarily lead to measurable cognitive learning gains, especially when instructional exposure is brief and outcome measures primarily capture declarative knowledge. It raises the critical question of whether the pedagogical integration of immersive affordances was sufficiently aligned with the intended learning objectives.

In addition, the interpretation of the null findings must take into account the characteristics of the knowledge assessment. Participants with prior experience entered the training with high baseline scores ($\approx$88% of the maximum), indicating limited variance and limited room for measurable improvement. Even among novices, baseline performance averaged 70% or more of the maximum score. Given the limited number of knowledge items and the relatively narrow score range, the instrument may have had reduced sensitivity to detect small short-term changes, particularly among experienced learners. Consequently, the absence of statistically significant gains should be interpreted with caution, as measurement constraints may have contributed to the observed pattern. In addition, the VR training primarily targeted procedural skill development, whereas the evaluation relied on a procedural knowledge test. As a result, the assessment may not have fully captured behavioral or performance-based learning outcomes.

The evaluated procedure required strict sequencing, adherence to hygiene protocols, and coordinated interaction with virtual objects. Such complexity may impose additional cognitive demands in immersive environments, where learners must simultaneously manage task requirements, spatial orientation, system feedback, and unfamiliar interaction mechanics [11, 19]. These findings are consistent with increased extraneous cognitive load during initial immersion. Under these conditions, meaningful consolidation may require repeated practice, structured reflection, or adaptive feedback beyond a single training session.

Prior domain experience contextualizes findings. Although it didn't statistically influence learning outcomes, patterns suggest that participants without prior experience showed larger gains, while experienced participants had higher baseline scores, indicating ceiling effects. These patterns align with theories that prior knowledge affects cognitive resources and how learners benefit from scaffolding. The lack of measurable gains among experienced learners should therefore not be interpreted as evidence of ineffectiveness, as subtle procedural improvements may not have been captured by the short-term assessment. No significant differences in user experience or perceived learning emerged between groups, indicating that the workflow and guidance supported diverse learners. However, positive evaluations across groups highlight the need to distinguish between perceived instructional quality and actual learning effectiveness. A key finding is the disconnect between perceptions and objective outcomes. Participants felt the training was engaging and effective, but these benefits weren't reflected in measurable knowledge gains. This is common in simulation and immersive learning, where confidence and presence can surpass actual performance. In safety-critical areas like healthcare education, this discrepancy is significant. Realism and presence may boost confidence without ensuring competence if instructional design and assessment aren't carefully aligned. Overall, the findings suggest that immersive VR should not be evaluated solely based on engagement or self-reported learning perceptions. Future research should therefore incorporate longer or repeated interventions, performance-based assessments, and more explicit pedagogical integration, including structured feedback and debriefing elements. Effective evaluation should include both subjective and objective measures. Limitations include the single-session design, the lack of a control group, and the use of short-term assessments. Future research should examine long-term retention and skill transfer to advance the evidence-based use of VR in healthcare education.

6 Conclusion

This study evaluated an immersive VR training system for intravenous infusion preparation in healthcare education. While learners reported positive user experiences and high levels of perceived learning, no statistically significant short-term improvements in objective procedural knowledge were observed.

The findings suggest that immersive engagement alone may not necessarily guarantee measurable short-term learning gains within the present study design. The effectiveness of VR-based training may depend on instructional design, assessment alignment, and learner characteristics. The observed dissociation between perceived and objective learning underscores the importance of integrated evaluation approaches in educational technology research. In innovation-oriented learning contexts, the results suggest that immersive VR is a promising yet design-sensitive tool. When carefully aligned with pedagogical principles and supported by appropriate assessment strategies, immersive environments can contribute to scalable, safe healthcare training. However, future research should further investigate how structured instructional mechanisms and assessment strategies can better support measurable competence development in immersive environments.

Overall, this study contributes to a more critical and evidence-based understanding of immersive learning technologies and provides practical guidance for the responsible integration of VR into healthcare education.

References

1. Cook, D.A., et al.: Technology-enhanced simulation for health professions education: a systematic review and meta-analysis. JAMA. **306**, 978–988 (2011). https://doi.org/10.1001/jama.2011.1234
2. Barteit, S., Guzek, D., Jahn, A., Bärnighausen, T., Jorge, M.M., Neuhann, F.: Evaluation of e-learning for medical education in low- and middle-income countries: a systematic review. Comput. Educ. **145**, 103726 (2020). https://doi.org/10.1016/j.compedu.2019.103726
3. Radianti, J., Majchrzak, T.A., Fromm, J., Wohlgenannt, I.: A systematic review of immersive virtual reality applications for higher education: design elements, lessons learned, and research agenda. Comput. Educ. **147**, 103778 (2020). https://doi.org/10.1016/j.compedu.2019.103778
4. Slater, M.: Place illusion and plausibility can lead to realistic behaviour in immersive virtual environments. Philos. Trans. R. Soc. Lond. Ser. B Biol. Sci. **364**, 3549–3557 (2009). https://doi.org/10.1098/rstb.2009.0138

5. Makransky, G., Lilleholt, L.: A structural equation modeling investigation of the emotional value of immersive virtual reality in education. Educ. Tech. Res. Dev. **66**, 1141–1164 (2018). https://doi.org/10.1007/s11423-018-9581-2
6. Liu, K., Zhang, W., Li, W., Wang, T., Zheng, Y.: Effectiveness of virtual reality in nursing education: a systematic review and meta-analysis. BMC Med. Educ. **23**, 710 (2023). https://doi.org/10.1186/s12909-023-04662-x
7. Seymour, N.E., et al.: Virtual reality training improves operating room performance: results of a randomized, double-blinded study. Ann. Surg. **236**, 458–463.; discussion 463-4 (2002). https://doi.org/10.1097/00000658-200210000-00008
8. Sitzmann, T., Kraiger, K., Stewart, D., Wisher, R.: The comparative effectiveness of web-based and classroom instruction: a meta-analysis. Pers. Psychol. **59**, 623–664 (2006). https://doi.org/10.1111/j.1744-6570.2006.00049.x
9. Makransky, G., Terkildsen, T.S., Mayer, R.E.: Adding immersive virtual reality to a science lab simulation causes more presence but less learning. Learn. Instr. **60**, 225–236 (2019). https://doi.org/10.1016/j.learninstruc.2017.12.007
10. Makransky, G., Petersen, G.B.: Investigating the process of learning with desktop virtual reality: a structural equation modeling approach. Comput. Educ. **134**, 15–30 (2019). https://doi.org/10.1016/j.compedu.2019.02.002
11. Issenberg, S.B., McGaghie, W.C., Petrusa, E.R., Lee Gordon, D., Scalese, R.J.: Features and uses of high-fidelity medical simulations that lead to effective learning: a BEME systematic review. Med. Teach. **27**, 10–28 (2005). https://doi.org/10.1080/01421590500046924
12. Sweller, J., Ayres, P., Kalyuga, S.: Cognitive Load Theory. Springer, New York, Dordrecht, Heidelberg, London (2011)
13. Kalyuga, S.: Knowledge elaboration: a cognitive load perspective. Learn. Instr. **19**, 402–410 (2009). https://doi.org/10.1016/j.learninstruc.2009.02.003
14. Jensen, L., Konradsen, F.: A review of the use of virtual reality head-mounted displays in education and training. Educ. Inf. Technol. **23**, 1515–1529 (2018). https://doi.org/10.1007/s10639-017-9676-0
15. Clark, R.E. (ed.): Learning from Media. Arguments, Analysis, and Evidence. Perspectives in Instructional Technology and Distance Learning, vol. 1. IAP, Greenwich, Conn (2001)
16. Mütterlein, J.: The three pillars of virtual reality? investigating the roles of immersion, presence, and interactivity. In: Bui, T. (ed.) Proceedings of the 51st Hawaii International Conference on System Sciences. Proceedings of the Annual Hawaii International Conference on System Sciences. Hawaii International Conference on System Sciences (2018). https://doi.org/10.24251/HICSS.2018.174
17. Field, A.: Discovering Statistics Using IBM SPSS Statistics. SAGE, Los Angeles, London, New Delhi, Singapore, Washington DC, Melbourne (2018)
18. Cohen, J.: Statistical Power Analysis for the Behavioral Sciences. Lawrence Erlbaum Associates publishers, Hillsdale, NJ (1988)
19. Nunnally, J.C., Bernstein, I.H.: Psychometric Theory. McGraw-Hill, New York, NY (1994)

Developing GenAI-Enhanced Virtual Reality for Learning of Ocean Sustainability

Silvia Wen-Yu Lee(✉) and Tai-Sheng Hung

National Taiwan Normal University, 106 Taipei, Taiwan
swylee@ntnu.edu.tw

Abstract. This study examined how a GenAI-enhanced virtual reality (VR) learning activity on ocean sustainability supported college students' dispositions toward agency in the Anthropocene (DAA), connectedness to nature (CtN), and environmental action planning. Particular attention was given to students' learning engagement and sense of agency. Thirty-five college-level students participated in the activity. Data were collected through pre- and post-questionnaires measuring DAA and CtN, as well as post-questionnaires measuring engagement and sense of agency in VR learning. Students' environmental action plans and their interactions with a customized GenAI assistant were also collected and analyzed. Quantitative analyses included paired-sample t-tests and Pearson correlation analyses, while qualitative data were examined through content analysis. The results showed significant improvements in students' DAA and CtN after the activity. Correlation analyses further indicated that DAA was positively associated with cognitive and emotional engagement, whereas CtN demonstrated broader associations with cognitive engagement, emotional engagement, learning agency, attentional agency, and actional agency. Analysis of students' environmental action plans revealed that most students identified government or policymakers, consumers, educators, and media as key actors, suggesting their ability to differentiate stakeholder roles and connect them to corresponding actions. However, their governance imagination remained largely government-led, with limited attention to civic participation and co-governance. Nearly half of the students revised their plans through interaction with AI by elaborating ideas, addressing limitations, and reconsidering unintended consequences. These findings suggest the potential of integrating VR and GenAI to support sustainability learning and environmental action design.

Keywords: virtual reality · agency · connectedness to nature · engagement

1 Introduction

Ocean sustainability has become an increasingly important issue in education, as students need not only scientific knowledge but also the competence and willingness to respond to complex environmental challenges. Virtual reality (VR) offers strong potential for sustainability education because it can provide immersive and meaningful learning experiences that make environmental problems more concrete and personally relevant. Recent studies suggest that VR can support environmental and climate-change

C.-J. Lin et al. (Eds.): ICITL 2026, LNCS 16841, pp. 293–298, 2027.
https://doi.org/10.1007/978-3-032-32112-1_29

learning by enhancing ecological literacy, environmental empathy, knowledge, and pro-environmental behavioral intentions [1, 2]. For example, prior work has shown positive effects of immersive technologies on marine conservation learning, climate-change adaptation intentions, waste-sorting behavior, and environmental empathy or skill transfer. However, this line of research has focused primarily on outcomes such as knowledge, attitudes, empathy, and behavioral intention, while giving much less attention to how learners develop **agency** in sustainability learning, how they **conceptualize stakeholder roles and actions** [3]. In addition, although connectedness to nature is increasingly recognized as an important outcome of environmental education, evidence regarding how immersive virtual experiences foster it remains limited and mixed.

The effectiveness of VR depends on how learning tasks are designed. A problem-based design may be especially valuable because it encourages learners to identify issues, make decisions, and propose solutions, thereby promoting engagement and agency. In addition, the integration of generative artificial intelligence (GenAI) may further support students by helping them elaborate, revise, and refine their action plans. Against this background, this pilot study examined the effects of a GenAI-enhanced VR learning environment on college students' sustainability competence and connectedness to nature, as well as the relationships among engagement, agency, and connectedness to nature in AI-supported ocean sustainability learning.

In the study, we posed the following research questions:

- What effects does a problem-based virtual reality learning design have on college students' dispositions toward agency in the Anthropocene and their connectedness to nature?
- What are the relationships among students' engagement, perceived agency in learning with VR, sustainability competence, and connectedness to nature in a virtual reality learning environment focused on ocean sustainability?
- How do students conceptualize and combine stakeholder roles when designing actions for ocean sustainability?
- How do students use AI to support the revision and refinement of their environmental action plans?

2 Methods

In this pilot study, a one-group pretest–posttest design was employed in this study to examine the effects of a problem-based virtual reality (VR) learning environment on students' ocean sustainability learning. The participants were 35 college students. The VR learning materials were developed using a problem-based navigation design that required learners to identify sustainability-related issues. A customized GenAI assistant was integrated to support students in decision-making and in generating potential solutions. Students were required to assume three different roles and identify corresponding actions for each role. The GenAI assistant then evaluated these actions as a whole and generated predictions of possible future outcomes. Based on this feedback, students could determine whether to revise any of the roles or the associated actions.

Data were collected through questionnaires administered before and after the intervention. Sustainability competence and connectedness to nature were measured as pretest and posttest variables. The Dispositions toward Agency in the Anthropocene (DAA) Questionnaire was developed by our research team based on the Agency in the Anthropocene by OECD, focusing on students' capacity to understand, care about, and act on environmental issues [4]. The sustainability competence questionnaire was a Likert scale including 15 items. The validity and reliability were examined and reported elsewhere. The Connectedness to Nature (CtN) questionnaire, also with Liker scale items, was adapted and translated from Musitu-Ferrer et al.'s research [5]. Following the VR learning experience, students also completed questionnaires assessing learning engagement and students' agency. The Learning Engagement Questionnaire [6] focused on learners' behavioral, cognitive and emotional engagement. The Sense of Agency in VR Learning Questionnaire [7] was used to examine three dimensions of agency experienced during the learning process, namely learning agency, attention agency, and behavioral agency.

Paired-sample t-test analyses were conducted to determine whether students showed significant changes in sustainability competence and connectedness to nature after the intervention. Correlation analyses were used to examine the associations among connectedness to nature, engagement, and agency variables. Finally, student-GenAI responses were also analyzed using content analyses. The analyses focused on the different roles and their associated environmental actions. In the analyses, we also focused on students' willingness to revise their action plans.

3 Results

3.1 Results of Sustainability Competence and Connectedness to Nature

Paired-sample t-tests were conducted to examine changes in students' dispositions toward agency in the Anthropocene (DAA) and connectedness to nature (CtN) before and after the GenAI-enhanced VR learning activity (see Table 1). The results showed that students' DAA significantly increased from pretest to posttest ($t(34) = 5.47, p < .001$) with a small-to-medium effect size (Cohen's $d = 0.412$). Students' CtN also significantly increased from pretest to posttest ($t(34) = 5.96$, $p < .001$) with a small effect size (Cohen's $d = 0.255$). These findings suggest that the GenAI-enhanced VR learning activity had a positive impact on students' DAA and CtN.

Table 1. Comparisons pre- and post- intervention results.

	Pre-test		Post-test		*t*	df	*p*	*Cohen's d*
	Mean	*SD*	*Mean*	*SD*				
DAA	3.47	0.56	3.85	0.55	5.47	34	<.001	.412
CtN	4.06	0.63	4.31	0.59	5.96	34	<.001	.255

3.2 Results of Correlation Analyses

Correlation analyses showed that both DAA and CtN were associated with students' engagement in the VR learning experience, but they differed in their relationships with learning agency. Specifically, DAA was significantly correlated with cognitive engagement ($r = .420, p = .012$) and emotional engagement ($r = .521, p = .001$), but not with behavioral engagement ($r = .083$, $p = .636$). Similarly, connectedness to nature was significantly correlated with cognitive engagement ($r = .441, p = .008$) and emotional engagement ($r = .715$, $p < .001$), while its correlation with behavioral engagement was positive but marginally non-significant ($r = .327$, $p = .055$). However, only CtN was significantly associated with the three dimensions of VR learning agency, including learning agency ($r = .445$, $p = .007$), attentional agency ($r = .478$, $p = .004$), and behavioral agency ($r = .477$, $p = .004$). In contrast, disposition toward agency in the Anthropocene was not significantly related to any subscales of agency in learning with VR.

3.3 Analyses of Students-GenAI Responses to Environmental Action

Overall, among the 35 students' final role selections, the most frequently identified role was government/policymakers (33 students, 94.3%), followed by consumers (28 students, 80.0%), media/education (22 students, 62.9%), fishery workers/fishers (15 students, 42.9%), and environmental/civic groups (7 students, 20.0%). The most common role combination was government - consumers - media/education (16 students), suggesting that many students conceptualized ocean sustainability through the interconnected dimensions of institutional regulation, market behavior, and social communication. The second most common combination, government - consumers - fishers (9 students), indicates that some students were able to link the policy, demand, and production dimensions of the issue, reflecting a more systemic supply-chain perspective. Within the given task structure, most students were able to differentiate role functions and connect them to corresponding actions. Nevertheless, their governance imagination remained largely government-led, with comparatively limited evidence of collaboration among different stake holders.

Among the 35 students, 17 students (48.6%) made at least one revision, with the highest number of revisions reaching four. The questions students posed to the AI could be further categorized into three themes: requests for the AI to elaborate on or extend the written content, inquiries about how to address limitations or gaps in their proposed plans, and requests for revisions in response to potential negative consequences. This suggests that students perceived the AI not merely as a generator of future predictions, but also as an interactive resource that supported the revision, refinement, and further development of their role-action designs.

4 Discussion

Students showed significant improvement in both dispositions toward agency in the Anthropocene (DAA) and connectedness to nature (CtN), suggesting that the GenAI-enhanced VR learning experience may have supported both sustainability-oriented dispositions and affective connection to environmental issues. However, the correlational results revealed different patterns between the two constructs. Both DAA and CtN were associated with cognitive and emotional engagement, indicating that students who were more intellectually and emotionally involved in the VR activity also tended to report stronger sustainability-related dispositions and stronger connection to nature. Nevertheless, only CtN was significantly related to the three dimensions of sense of agency in VR learning, including learning agency, attentional agency, and actional agency. This finding may be explained by the more experiential and affective nature of CtN [8, 9]. In contrast, DAA represents a broader disposition toward socio-ecological understanding, scientific reasoning, respectful perspectives, and hopeful agency in the Anthropocene. Although this disposition is important for sustainability learning, it may be less directly tied to students' moment-to-moment sense of control and action during VR learning.

The results of students-GenAI responses indicated that nearly half of the students used GenAI as a tool for elaborating, reconsidering, and refining their environmental action plans. However, it also suggests that more than half of the students accepted the AI-generated responses without further revision. This pattern may reflect students' tendency to perceive AI feedback as a finalized or authoritative response, rather than as a prompt for further inquiry and critical evaluation [10, 11]. Therefore, future GenAI-supported sustainability learning environments should provide more structured guidance to help students engage critically with AI output. For example, the AI assistant could be designed to ask follow-up questions, require students to compare multiple possible actions, identify trade-offs or unintended consequences, and justify why they accept or reject AI suggestions.

References

1. Hurrell, C., Chai, A., Green, H., Bradley, G.: Virtual reality facilitates pro-environmental behavioural intentions. Environ. Educ. Res. **30**(10), 1856–1883 (2024). https://doi.org/10.1080/13504622.2024.2342942
2. Nikhanbayeva, A., Issakov, Y., Ussenov, N., Gajić, T., Dénes Dávid, L.: Understanding nature through digital technologies: a systematic review of virtual learning of environmental content in geography. Cogent Educ. **13**(1) (2026). https://doi.org/10.1080/2331186X.2026.2616843
3. Stenberdt, V.A., Makransky, G.: Mastery experiences in immersive virtual reality promote pro-environmental waste-sorting behavior. Comput. Educ. **198**, 104760 (2023). https://doi.org/10.1016/j.compedu.2023.104760
4. White, P., et al.: Agency in the Anthropocene: Supporting document to the PISA 2025 Science Framework, OECD Education Working Papers, No. 297, OECD Publishing, Paris (2023). https://doi.org/10.1787/8d3b6cfa-en
5. Musitu-Ferrer, D., Esteban-Ibañez, M., León-Moreno, C., García, O.F.: Is school adjustment related to environmental empathy and connectedness to nature? Psychosoc. Interv. **28**(2), 101–110 (2019). https://doi.org/10.5093/pi2019a8
6. Tu, H.-Y., Lee, S.W.-Y.: Curiosity, interest, and engagement: unpacking their roles in students' learning within a virtual game environment. J. Educ. Comput. Res. **62**(8) (2025). https://doi.org/10.1177/07356331241277904
7. McGivney, E.: Interactivity and identity impact learners' sense of agency in virtual reality field trips. Br. J. Educ. Technol. **56**(1), 410–434 (2025). https://doi.org/10.1111/bjet.13513
8. Lumber, R., Richardson, M., Sheffield, D.: Beyond knowing nature: contact, emotion, compassion, meaning, and beauty are pathways to nature connection. PLoS One. **12**(5), e0177186 (2017). https://doi.org/10.1371/journal.pone.0177186

9. Mayer, F.S., Frantz, C.M.: The connectedness to nature scale: a measure of individuals' feeling in community with nature. J. Environ. Psychol. **24**(4), 503–515 (2004). https://doi.org/10.1016/j.jenvp.2004.10.001
10. Favero, L., Pérez-Ortiz, J.A., Käser, T., Oliver, N.: Enhancing critical thinking in education by means of a Socratic chatbot (2024). https://doi.org/10.48550/arXiv.2409.05511
11. Guan, R., Raković, M., Chen, G., Gašević, D.: How educational chatbots support self-regulated learning? A systematic review of the literature. Educ. Inf. Technol. **30**, 4493–4518 (2025). https://doi.org/10.1007/s10639-024-12881-y

Application of a Virtual Reality Social Skills Teaching System for Students with Autism Spectrum Disorder: An Evaluation of Daily Performance, Emotional Awareness, and Empathic Response

Ying-Ru Meng[1], Chia-Chi Yeh[2(✉)], Tung-Kuang Wu[3], and Ching-Jung Chiu[4]

[1] Department of Special Education, National Tsing Hua University, Hsinchu City, Taiwan
[2] Department of Education Psychology and Counseling, National Tsing Hua University, Hsinchu City, Taiwan
patma320@gmail.com
[3] Department of Information Management, National Changhua Normal University, Changhua City, Taiwan
[4] Taiwan Institute of Economic Research, Research Division II, Taipei City, Taiwan

Abstract. With the continuous refinement of diagnostic systems for Autism Spectrum Disorder (ASD), the number of identified students has risen significantly, highlighting the urgent need for specialized social skills training in special education. This study developed a Virtual Reality (VR) social skills teaching system designed to leverage students with ASD's strengths in visual thinking. Centered on the theme "An Artistic Journey with Classmates," the system aligns with the "Social Skills" component of the 12-Year National Basic Education Curriculum. Four immersive scenarios—including a classroom, a gallery ticket office, a restaurant, and a park—were developed to provide intervention for eight K-12 students with ASD and social functional difficulties over six sessions. The results, analyzed through descriptive statistics, t-tests, and ANOVA, indicated that all participants showed stable improvement in "Conversation Response Speed" and "Expressive Effectiveness." Although a slight decline in behavioral compliance was observed mid-course due to increased familiarity with the environment, overall social performance improved. Group comparisons revealed that while the Social Difficulty group had higher baseline scores, the ASD group demonstrated more consistent progress across all dimensions, with a statistically significant reduction in inappropriate social behaviors ($p = .090$*). Furthermore, both groups showed significant improvement in empathy scale scores ($p < .013$**), and behavioral experiments confirmed enhanced emotion recognition in the Social Difficulty group. Parent surveys further corroborated these findings, indicating increased flexibility and environmental adaptability in the students' daily lives. This research demonstrates that VR-based instruction effectively enhances social cognition, emotional awareness, and empathic responses in students with special needs.

Keywords: Virtual Reality (VR) · Autism Spectrum Disorder (ASD) · Social Skills · Empathy · Situated Learning

C.-J. Lin et al. (Eds.): ICITL 2026, LNCS 16841, pp. 299–308, 2027.
https://doi.org/10.1007/978-3-032-32112-1_30

1 Introduction

This study aims to address the issues of social skills deficits and emotional regulation among students with autism by utilizing story-driven Virtual Reality (VR) to teach social skills. Through interaction and simulation of real-life scenarios with peers, students can achieve effective learning outcomes in social skills, meeting the needs of students with autism in school group settings and their eventual integration into society.

Many scholars have pointed out that individuals with autism often face challenges in social interactions and require training in interpersonal communication, employment, and social adaptation. Vygotsky's (1978) [1] learning theory suggests that the cognitive development of children with disabilities may be hindered by the deprivation of normal interaction. Hence, in Taiwan's early intervention processes, group therapy is commonly used to improve social interaction among individuals with autism.

Research (Volkmar & Wiesner, 2009) [2] indicates that group-based social skills training can help address social skills deficits in individuals with autism. However, some participants exhibit resistance to group therapy. This is often due to their fear of unfamiliar environments and crowds, requiring more time to overcome psychological barriers. These difficulties make it challenging for individuals with autism to engage in group interactions during the early stages of intervention, thus affecting the initial effectiveness of therapy.

Given the limitations of current training methods in Taiwan, which fail to meet the specific learning needs of such students, reducing the fear of unfamiliar environments and crowds for individuals with autism becomes a key area for improvement in autism therapy.

1.1 The Instruction and Implementation of Virtual Reality for Autism

In recent years, assistive technology has greatly benefited students' learning. For the training of individuals with autism, integrating VR into their curriculum and training materials helps reduce anxiety caused by adapting to different scenarios during the training process. It stimulates their interest in learning, making it an undoubtedly viable path for future special education teaching.

VR interactive technology allows users to interact with virtual characters, objects, and environments created by computers using their body movements. This provides autistic individuals the opportunity to engage in activities they previously could not participate in. VR technology enhances motor control and motivation, making it an excellent tool for improving overall physical coordination for autistic individuals who struggle with motor control. Furthermore, once a VR training environment is established, it offers multiple advantages, such as repeated training opportunities, outcome testing, low costs, and the ability for users to perform activities independently. These characteristics enable repeated strengthening of autistic students' social scenario construction abilities.

Therefore, this study aims to integrate interdisciplinary subjects to provide more diverse teaching tools in special education by constructing a VR-based special education teaching environment. Manju et al. [3] conducted a study that demonstrated the superiority of their VR program over established methodologies in enhancing social skills among participants. Their findings revealed that the VR program not only improved social interactions but also facilitated more effective communication and behavioral outcomes. On the one hand, it explores the development and feasibility of VR technology applications in real-world special education settings; on the other hand, creating such environmental materials aims to address the disadvantages faced by individuals with autism in social interactions. Offering multiple opportunities for repeated training helps increase and accumulate their experience in social interactions, ultimately enhancing their social skills [4].

2 Materials and Methods

2.1 Virtual Reality Social Skills Course System

The system design of this study is categorized into basic and advanced scenarios based on the "Art Tour with Classmates" theme, focusing on a progressive learning curve for social interaction. In the basic scenarios, students navigate four standard environments—the classroom, exhibition venue, restaurant, and park—to establish foundational social routines such as pre-trip discussions, ticket purchasing, and dining etiquette. These initial modules are designed to familiarize students with the sequential nature of social outings while introducing unexpected situational triggers that adapt to the learner's progress, thereby cultivating their fundamental real-time response capabilities.

Building upon this foundation, the advanced scenarios utilize the same four environments but introduce complex social conflicts and higher-order problem-solving tasks to challenge the students' adaptive reasoning. For instance, the classroom setting requires students to brainstorm ways to help a peer persuade their parents, while the exhibition and restaurant scenes involve managing social infractions like line-cutting or handling menu unavailability through alternative decision-making. In the final park scenario, the focus shifts toward emotional regulation and empathy, where students must practice soothing a friend's disappointment and providing social reassurances, thus moving beyond mere routine toward sophisticated interpersonal support.

The implementation of this virtual reality teaching follows a structured pedagogical flow that transitions from traditional media to immersive experience over a 40-minute session. Each intervention begins with a 15-minute introductory phase consisting of course content overview and a themed picture book narration, followed by a 10-minute preparatory activity to prime the students for the virtual environment. The core of the session involves 10 min of active engagement in the virtual reality scenario, followed by a 5-min classroom assessment to evaluate immediate learning outcomes and trigger-based performance.

2.2 Research Methods and Participants

The participants in this study included four students with high-functioning autism and four students with social functional difficulties, all of whom fall under the Autism Spectrum Disorder (ASD) category (see Table 1). The virtual reality intervention was conducted between May and July 2024. During this period, each student participated in six sessions. Both before and after the intervention, the social skills development of the participants was assessed through a multi-informant approach, including observations by school teachers, parental evaluations of social status, and student self-assessments. Additionally, participants completed relevant tests and the Social Skills Behavioral Characteristics Checklist to evaluate the overall progress and behavioral changes.

Table 1. Participant Demographics and Characteristics

Participant ID	Age	IQ Score	Gender	Category
01	9	109	M	Asperger
02	11	77	M	HFA
03	11	92	M	HFA
04	11	82	M	HFA
05	9	86	M	HFA
06	13	115	M	Asperger
07	12	97	M	Asperger
08	12	100	M	Asperger
Mean	11	95.75	8 M	**4 Asperger; 4 HFA**

2.3 Analysis Tools

2.3.1 Elementary and Junior High School Students Social Skills Behavior Scale (Version Used by Teachers)

This scale was evaluated by a tutor familiar with the subject. There are 56 questions on the topic. The answers to each question include "always," "often," "sometimes," "seldom," and "never." The five items are divided into 1, 2, 3, 4, and 5 points (the higher the score, the more frequent the behavior).

2.3.2 Descriptive Statistics for Self-Developed Social Skills Performance Rating Scale

The main scoring project in this study contains" Response Speed in Conversation," "Effectiveness of Conversation Expression," "Sentence Structure Integrity," and "Conversation Etiquette." The scoring method for each item is as follows.

Numbered lists can be added as follows:

1. Response Speed in Conversation: The time needed for thinking and answering after the students hear the questions raised by the avatars. The time calculation starts from the time the avatar asks the question. The time calculation starts from the time the avatar asks the question and ends with the subject articulating the first word of his/her response. Five points in 0 ~ 3 s, four points in 3–5 s (more than 3 s, including 5 s), three points in 5–8 s (more than 5 s, including 8 s), and two points for more than 8 s. Those who did not answer the questions got one point. The faster students answer, the higher their score.

2. Effectiveness of Conversation Expression: This project includes volume control, the appropriateness of the tone, the manner of speaking, speaking speed, the expression of body language, etc.
3. Sentence Structure Integrity: This project considers whether each sentence answered by the student contains a subject, a verb, an adjective, a noun, an adverb, or even an active invitation or courage to ask a question through a complete sentence. The basic score of this project is 3 points. If the structure of the sentence answered by the subject is more complete, he/she can get a higher score.
4. Conversation Etiquette: There are five items in this section, including the participant's attention during the dialogue process (eye focus/behavioral performance), whether the conversion process has been interrupted or given an irrelevant answer, meaningless vocabulary or soliloquizing in the conversation, reiteration of the answer, etc. If all five of the above projects have been performed well, the subject gets five points. Poor performances in one of the items result in four points, three points for poor performances in two items, two points for poor performances in three items, and one point for poor performances in four or more items. If no response was made to any items, the subject also gets one point for this project.

The Likert Scale scored all items in this study. This assessment form is filled in by the researcher (also the examiner). Since teaching style and personal teaching methods could easily affect the accuracy of the research process and results, all teaching was performed by one researcher. The researcher observed each student's performance in lessons and rated them on the same criteria.

2.3.3 Social Skills Effectiveness Survey

The questionnaire is mainly based on the training objectives set in this study. The questionnaire is designed through the social skills curriculum in special education for 12 years. The content of the social skills course is divided into three aspects, including "accommodating with oneself", "communicating with others", "accommodating the environment", and sorting out the first level as situation 1 - discussing with the students before the trip, the main instructions Courage to express and accept meaning; the second level is situation 2 - with the classmates to the exhibition to see the exhibition, the main training to deal with advance and retreat and timely speech; the third level for the situation 3 - with the classmates to the restaurant, the main training flow waiting and self-choice; the fourth level is situation 4 - say goodbye to the class-mates and end the journey, mainly to teach emotional management and situational transformation. The Likert Scale scored all items in this study. The choice is Strongly Disagree to get 1 point, Disagree to get 2 points, Neutral to get 3 points, Agree to get 4 points, or Strongly Agree to get 5 points; the answer is obtained through the parents after the student completes the 8-week course to help fill out. As at this stage, parents spend the most time with students. Therefore, through the observation of parents to complete this questionnaire.

2.3.4 Empathy Scale

"Empathy" is one of the key competencies within social skills. To understand the progress of students' social skills after receiving instruction through the VR system, this scale was employed for assessment. Parents assisted in completing the scale to evaluate the differences in students' performance before and after the intervention. The assessment consists of ten items, with each item scored on a 5-point Likert scale ranging from 1 to 5 (from "Strongly Disagree" to "Strongly Agree").

2.3.5 Behavioral Experiment Task: Emotion Awareness Ability

This task evaluates students' emotion recognition through the use of facial expression images, with both pre-test and post-test assessments conducted. A total of 16 emotion images are included, covering eight primary categories: (1) Happiness, (2) Disgust, (3) Sadness, (4) Fear, (5) Contempt, (6) Surprise, (7) Anger, and (8) Neutral. Students observe these expressions and judge the correct emotion. The experiment utilizes E-Prime 3.0 as the tool for both image presentation and data collection.

3 Results

3.1 Social Skills Performance Rating Table

Based on the scores from the self-developed Social Skills Performance Rating Scale, a steady upward trend was observed across all participants in "Conversation Response Speed" and "Expressive Effectiveness." However, "Sentence Structure Integrity" showed a slight decline during the fourth session, and "Speaking Etiquette" regressed during the third session before gradually recovering. The maintenance effect for etiquette was less stable; as students became more familiar with the virtual environment over time, some transitioned from initial caution to exhibiting less rule-governed or impolite behavior. These findings indicate that while overall performance generally improved, students required occasional external reminders to maintain focus and execute tasks once they habituated to the environment. This suggests that learning performance across all social skill dimensions may not always yield continuous or stable outcomes (as shown in Table 2).

Table 2. Descriptive Statistics for Self-Developed Social Skills Performance Rating Scale in VR Social Skills Advanced Course (Session 1–6)

Item	Response Speed in Conversation			Effectiveness of Conversation Expression			Sentence Structure Integrity			Conversation Etiquette		
Session	Mean	Std Dev	N	Mean	Std Dev	N	Mean	Std Dev	N	Mean	Std Dev	N
First	3.747	0.656	8	2.942	0.565	8	2.902	0.254	8	4.406	0.404	8
Second	4.177	0.575	8	3.332	0.389	8	3.015	0.220	8	4.262	0.561	8
Third	4.451	0.646	8	3.595	0.441	8	3.339	0.353	8	3.849	0.779	8
Fourth	4.693	0.314	8	3.671	0.480	8	3.302	0.449	8	4.080	0.772	8
Fifth	4.697	0.182	8	3.806	0.210	8	3.346	0.238	8	3.960	0.921	8

(continued)

Table 2. *(continued)*

Item	Response Speed in Conversation			Effectiveness of Conversation Expression			Sentence Structure Integrity			Conversation Etiquette		
Sixth	4.738	0.136	8	3.735	0.508	8	3.372	0.483	8	4.143	0.760	8

3.2 Social Skills Effectiveness Opinion Survey

In this section, parents assisted in completing the Social Skills Effectiveness Opinion Survey to observe changes in the students' daily lives after the six-session virtual reality (VR) intervention. Based on the descriptive statistics presented in Table 3, parents perceived improvements across all assessed items, with progress scores ranging approximately from 0.125 to 0.625 points following the completion of the curriculum. The most significant change was observed in the "Interpersonal Interaction dimension, which showed a statistically significant difference between the pre-test and post-test results (see Table 4). This indicates that parents believe their children's interpersonal manners and social conduct improved after participating in the VR social skills courses. Furthermore, in contrast to the significant difficulties and unfamiliarity regarding the "Environmental Interaction" dimension found in previous studies, parents in this study reported that the widespread use of technology and mobile devices has mitigated the extreme maladaptation children previously experienced in unfamiliar settings. Consequently, most parents indicated in the survey that information technology now serves as a supportive tool to help children cope with environmental unfamiliarity.

Table 3. Training Objectives of the VR Advanced Social Skills Course and Results of the Social Skills Effectiveness Opinion Survey

Variables (Dimensions)	N	Pre-test Mean (M pre)	Post-test Mean (M post)	Pre-test SD (SD pre)	Post-test SD (SD post)	Mean Difference (ΔM)
Self-Interaction	8	2.729	3.25	0.597	0.864	0.521
Interpersonal Interaction	8	2.577	3.202	0.541	0.94	0.625
Environmental Interaction	8	3.792	3.917	0.853	0.718	0.125

Table 4. Training Objectives and Pre-test/Post-test Differences in Social Skills Effectiveness for the VR Advanced Course

Variables (Pairs)	Mean Difference	SD	Std. Error Mean	*t*	df	Sig. (2-tailed)
Self-Interaction (Pre/Post)	−0.521	1.013	0.358	−1.454	7	0.189
Interpersonal Interaction (Pre/Post)	−0.625	0.804	0.284	−2.199	7	0.064*
Environmental Interaction (Pre/Post)	−0.125	1.154	0.408	−0.307	7	0.768

$p < 0.05$**, $p < 0.1$*

3.3 Social Skills Effectiveness Survey

The mean scores for all students (regardless of group) showed that the pre-test scores were higher than the post-test scores, with a pre-test mean total of 169.714 and a post-test mean total of 159.857. This indicates that school teachers perceived a reduction in students' inappropriate social behaviors following the virtual reality social skills intervention (as shown in Table 5). Further analysis using a Paired Sample t-test revealed that while students' inappropriate behaviors improved (with undesirable behavior scores decreasing by approximately 9.857), the overall effectiveness did not reach statistical significance, yielding a two-tailed t-test p-value of 0.183 (as shown in Table 6). However, when examining the groups separately, a significant difference in inappropriate social behaviors was found within the Autism Spectrum Disorder (ASD) category, with a p-value of 0.090* (see Table 7). This suggests that the virtual reality instruction had a relatively more impactful effect on students with autism. Note: The sample size for this section is 7. One student with social difficulties was excluded from this analysis because they graduated from elementary school during the study. As a result, the parent was unable to request the original teacher to complete the post-test observation and rating scale.

Table 5. Comparison of Pre-test and Post-test Scores: Social Skills Behavioral Characteristics Checklist (Teacher Version)

Category	Mean (M)	Standard Deviation (SD)
Pre-test Total Score	169.714	15.207
Post-test Total Score	159.857	20.31

Table 6. Paired Samples T-Test for Overall Performance on the Social Skills Behavioral Characteristics Checklist

Item	N	Correlation	*t*	Sig. (2-tailed)
Pre-test Mean vs. Post-test Mean	7	0.555	1.504	0.183

$p < 0.05$**, $p < 0.1$

Table 7. Paired Samples T-Test for Students with ASD on the Social Skills Behavioral Characteristics Checklist

Item	N	Correlation	*t*	Sig. (2-tailed)
Pre-test vs. Post-test Mean (ASD Group)	7	0.804	2.468	0.090*

$p < 0.05$**, $p < 0.1$

4 Conclusion

Based on the analysis of the research data, the experimental results are summarized as follows:

1. Improvement in school-based social skills through VR-based unexpected social situation training.

The results from the Social Skills Behavioral Characteristics Checklist (Teacher Version) indicate that the six-session virtual reality (VR) intervention effectively enhanced students' social skills in the school environment. There was a significant improvement in social performance and a reduction in social interference behaviors.

2. Significant enhancement in overall social skill performance through VR experimental teaching.

The results demonstrate that the VR social skills curriculum led to improvements in "Conversation Response Speed," "Expressive Effectiveness," "Sentence Structure Integrity," and "Speaking Etiquette."

Conversation Response Speed: This dimension showed the most significant progress. Repeated practice enabled students to increase their response speed even as situational contexts changed.

Expressive Effectiveness: Improvements were noted in volume and speed control, body language, and tone/intonation adjustment. Observation during the experiment showed greater progress in volume and speed control compared to non-verbal cues.

Sentence Structure Integrity: Through repeated drills, students gradually refined the completeness of their spoken content, eventually developing their own coherent conversational structures.

Speaking Etiquette: This area showed high individual variability. It encompasses issues such as lack of attention (eye contact), interrupting, inappropriate responding, and self-talk. Initially, students were more rule-governed due to the unfamiliarity of the environment. However, as they became comfortable, some exhibited off-task behaviors (e.g., focusing on virtual objects or rushing the virtual characters). Nevertheless, with instructor reminders, students' adherence to rules and attentive attitudes recovered and improved, as reflected in the score fluctuations.

3. Enhanced adaptability in "Interpersonal Interaction" following VR training.

According to the Social Skills Effectiveness Opinion Survey completed by parents, the most substantial change observed in students' daily lives was in their ability to interact and get along with others (the "Interpersonal Interaction" dimension). While unfamiliar environments still cause stress, parents noted that modern technology and visual aids allow children to familiarize themselves with new settings in advance. This suggests that the primary concern for parents has shifted from general environmental unfamiliarity to specific long-term transitions, such as changing schools or classes.

4. Superior effectiveness of the VR social curriculum for students with Autism.

While the Social Skills Behavioral Characteristics Checklist scores showed a reduction in inappropriate social behaviors for both groups, the overall effect did not reach statistical significance for the entire sample. However, group-specific t-test results revealed that the reduction of inappropriate behaviors was more pronounced and effective for students with Autism (ASD) compared to those with general social difficulties. This indicates that while the curriculum is beneficial for both, it is particularly impactful for the ASD population. Future iterations of the curriculum should be adjusted to better meet the specific needs of students with general social difficulties to further enhance their social skill development.

References

1. Vygotsky, L.S.: Mind in Society: the Development of Higher Psychological Processes. Harvard University Press, Cambridge (1978)
2. Volkmar, F.R., Wiesner, L.A.: A Practical Guide to Autism: What every Parent, Family Member, and Teacher Needs to Know. Wiley, Hoboken, NJ (2009)
3. Manju, T., Magesh, P., Durairaj, S.: Increasing the social interaction of autism child using virtual reality intervention (VRI). In: ACM Transactions on Asian and Low-Resource Language Information Processing (2023). https://doi.org/10.1145/3592855
4. Yeh, C.-C., Meng, Y.-R.: Effectiveness of virtual reality social skills training for students with autism and social difficulties observed through behavior and brain waves. Appl. Sci. **15**(9), 4600 (2025). https://doi.org/10.3390/app15094600

Applying a Scaffolding-Informed Mixed Reality System to Vehicle Engine Disassembly Instruction

Bo-Yuan Cheng[1(✉)], Sheng-Chin Lin[2], and Chia-Ching Lin[3]

[1] Languages Center, National Pingtung University of Science and Technology, Pingtung City, Taiwan
Oakley.cheng@mail.npust.edu.tw

[2] Department of Vehicle Engineering, National Pingtung University of Science and Technology, Pingtung City, Taiwan

[3] Graduate Institute of Science Education and Environmental Education, National Kaohsiung Normal University, Kaohsiung City, Taiwan

Abstract. This study examined the effectiveness of a Mixed Reality-Based Vehicle Assisted Learning System (MRVALS), developed on the basis of scaffolding theory, in supporting vehicle engine disassembly instruction. The system incorporated three forms of scaffolding support, namely step-by-step procedural guidance, strategic prompts, and spatially aligned visual cues, to assist students in performing hands-on tasks within a mixed reality learning environment. A quasi-experimental design was employed to compare students' learning perceptions under MR-supported instruction and traditional instruction. Forty students participated in the study, with 20 assigned to the experimental group using MRVALS and 20 to the control group receiving teacher demonstration and manual-based instruction. The results indicated that students in the MRVALS group reported significantly lower levels of intrinsic and extraneous cognitive load than those in the traditional instruction group. No significant between-group differences were found in germane cognitive load, self-efficacy, or learning satisfaction. These findings suggest that scaffolding-informed mixed reality instruction may reduce students' perceived learning difficulty in engine disassembly tasks by supporting procedural understanding and minimizing unnecessary cognitive burden. Future research should extend the intervention period and incorporate direct measures of learning performance to further evaluate the instructional value of scaffolding-based mixed reality learning in technical and vocational education.

Keywords: Mixed Reality · Vehicle Practicum · Cognitive Load · Self-Efficacy · Learning Satisfaction

1 Introduction

Within technical and vocational education, vehicle practicum is a core course that helps students connect academic learning with industrial practice. As vehicle technologies become increasingly complex, students are expected to develop advanced hands-on

C.-J. Lin et al. (Eds.): ICITL 2026, LNCS 16841, pp. 309–318, 2027.
https://doi.org/10.1007/978-3-032-32112-1_31

competencies, including engine disassembly, engine assembly, and system diagnostics. However, instruction in many traditional training environments still relies heavily on an apprenticeship-style demonstration model. Under imbalanced teacher–student ratios, instructors typically demonstrate procedures to the whole class, after which students practice independently with printed manuals. This approach often limits timely individualized feedback and makes it difficult to provide instructional support equitably across learners.

In such settings, students often rely on manuals to learn engine disassembly and assembly procedures. Because the manual and the physical engine components are spatially separated, learners must repeatedly shift their visual attention between the two sources of information, which may create a split-attention effect. Previous research has shown that when learners must divide attention across spatially separated but interrelated sources of information, extraneous cognitive load increases and learning efficiency decreases [1]. In addition, static images and textual descriptions often fail to clearly represent the sequential and spatial features of complex mechanical disassembly. As a result, students may perform operations based on intuition or partial understanding, increasing the likelihood of procedural errors, component damage, or deviations from standard operating procedures (SOPs).

To address these challenges, Mixed Reality (MR) technology has shown considerable potential for instructional applications. A key advantage of MR is its ability to integrate virtual information with the physical environment and spatially align digital content with real objects, thereby enabling situated guidance during task performance [2]. Previous studies have shown that MR can provide contextualized, real-time guidance and feedback in authentic operational settings [3]. When designed appropriately, such features may help learners understand procedures more clearly, reduce unnecessary search and coordination demands, and support hands-on learning in complex operational tasks [4]. In addition, a systematic review [10] suggested that augmented reality (AR) and MR technologies may help reduce learners' extraneous cognitive load in multistep skill-based learning contexts. Together, these studies indicate that AR- and MR-based instructional support may benefit learners not only by improving task guidance but also by helping them manage the cognitive demands of procedural learning.

Nevertheless, the effectiveness of MR in education does not depend on technology alone, but also on how instructional support is designed. From the perspective of scaffolding theory, learning support should assist students in completing tasks that may otherwise be difficult for them to perform independently, especially in unfamiliar or cognitively demanding situations [5, 6]. In practical learning contexts, scaffolding can provide learners with structured guidance, strategic cues, and timely support that help them connect conceptual understanding with procedural action. In this sense, MR offers a promising environment for implementing scaffolding because digital information can be embedded directly into the physical task context, allowing learners to receive support at the moment and location where it is needed.

Accordingly, this study adopted scaffolding theory as the instructional foundation for designing a Mixed Reality-Based Vehicle Assisted Learning System (MRVALS). The system was developed to provide scaffolded support during engine disassembly through step-by-step procedural guidance, strategic prompts, and spatially aligned visual cues in a mixed reality environment. Accordingly, the present study examined whether MR-supported instruction could provide more effective learning support than traditional instruction for vehicle engine disassembly. The specific research objectives were as follows:

1. To examine differences in cognitive load between learners receiving MRVALS and those receiving traditional instruction.
2. To examine differences in self-efficacy between learners receiving MRVALS and those receiving traditional instruction.
3. To examine differences in learning satisfaction between learners receiving MRVALS and those receiving traditional instruction.

2 Research Methods

2.1 Development of the Mixed Reality-Based Vehicle Assisted Learning System (MRVALS)

According to scaffolding theory, instructional support should provide learners with temporary assistance that enables them to accomplish tasks beyond what they can complete independently. In the context of engine disassembly, learners are required not only to understand the procedural sequence of the task, but also to make appropriate operational decisions and accurately identify target components within a complex mechanical structure. Therefore, in this study, scaffolding was operationalized into three forms—procedural, strategic, and spatial scaffolding—to address these instructional demands. Specifically, procedural scaffolding was designed to support learners' understanding of the disassembly sequence and key procedures; strategic scaffolding was intended to assist learners in selecting appropriate tools and methods at each stage; and spatial scaffolding was developed to support the identification of target components within the physical engine. These forms of scaffolding were embedded into MRVALS through different functional zones in the mixed reality environment.

Learning Content Development. The MRVALS developed in this study was designed for the Vehicle Practicum course offered by the Department of Vehicle Engineering at a national university in southern Taiwan. The primary objective of this course is to cultivate students' practical skills in automobile engine maintenance. Given the broad scope of the course, this study focuses specifically on engine disassembly procedures, with 21 key engine components selected as the main instructional targets. Although the complete instructional content covered 21 key engine components, the present experiment focused on a seven-component disassembly task from the initial engine state to the intake and exhaust manifold stage.

For the development of the digital learning materials, an experienced course instructor was invited to perform a standardized demonstration of the procedures, and the entire disassembly process was recorded as a series of instructional videos. For each disassembly step, the system incorporated corresponding explanations of tool selection and professional operational tips. These materials were then transformed into interactive MR learning materials, including instructional videos, tool prompts, procedural guidance, and spatial visual cues, to guide students through complex engine disassembly tasks step by step.

Scaffolding-Based Learning Support Design. The system was developed in Unity3D and implemented on the Meta Quest 3 head-mounted display (HMD). With passthrough cameras, spatial positioning, and hand-tracking interaction, the system overlaid digital information onto the physical environment to support mixed reality learning during engine disassembly. To operationalize the three forms of scaffolding, MRVALS provided three types of support: procedural scaffolding through instructional videos and sequential guidance, strategic scaffolding through tool prompts and technical information panels, and spatial scaffolding through dynamic three-dimensional visual cues indicating component locations and disassembly directions. These features embedded scaffolding directly into the hands-on learning context and allowed learners to access task-relevant support while performing unfamiliar procedures.

Learning Interface and Interaction Workflow These three functional zones correspond to procedural, strategic, and spatial scaffolding, respectively. To facilitate learners' understanding of each step in the disassembly procedure, MRVALS organizes digital information into three core functional zones that are spatially anchored within the learners' operational field of view. The instructional content is displayed in front of the physical engine so that students can readily compare the virtual information with the actual engine structure during hands-on operation. The design rationale and functions of each zone are described as follows:

1. *Video Instruction Zone*

As shown in Fig. 1a, this zone represents the procedural scaffolding component of MRVALS and was designed to support learners' understanding of the disassembly sequence and key operational procedures. Using high-definition demonstration videos recorded by experts, the system provides step-by-step explanations of the disassembly process and highlights the structural features of each component. In addition, video playback control functions allow students to pause, replay, or skip sections based on their individual learning pace, which may support procedural understanding during hands-on disassembly.

2. *Strategic Scaffolding Zone*

As shown in Fig. 1b, this zone represents the strategic scaffolding component of MRVALS and was designed to support learners in making appropriate operational decisions during engine disassembly. After students finish watching the video, the system presents concise guidelines for each stage, including the required tools, disassembly methods, and related operational information. These guidelines may assist learners in identifying the relevant tools, component locations, and procedures during hands-on operation.

3. *Visual Guidance Zone*

As shown in Fig. 1c, this zone represents the spatial scaffolding component of MRVALS and was designed to support learners in locating the target component within the physical engine structure. Once students have selected the appropriate tool and are ready to begin disassembly, the system displays a dynamic three-dimensional arrow model on the target part to indicate its exact location. This spatially aligned visual cue may assist learners in identifying the intended disassembly object and reduce potential errors in spatial perception during hands-on operation.

Accordingly, the system supports a step-by-step learning process in which learners first comprehend the procedure, then confirm the required tools and technical details, and finally perform the disassembly task with spatial guidance.

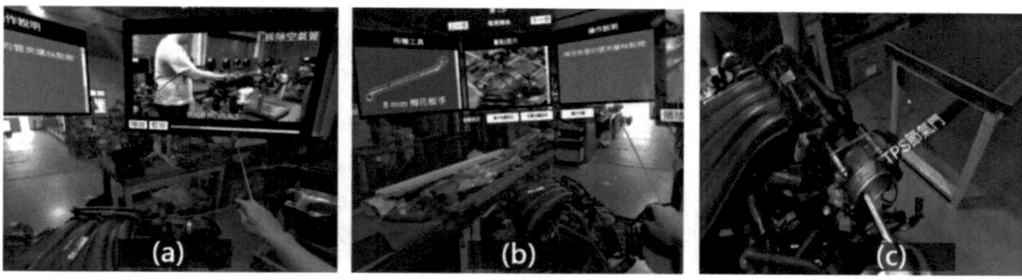

Fig. 1. Three functional zones of MRVALS: (a) Video Instruction Zone, (b) Strategic Scaffolding Zone, and (c) Visual Guidance Zone.

2.2 Experiment Participants

This study recruited 40 sophomore students from the Department of Vehicle Engineering at a university of science and technology in southern Taiwan. The participants were drawn from two different semesters of the same course, with students in the first semester assigned to the control group and those in the second semester assigned to the experimental group. None of the participants had previously taken a vehicle practicum course. Therefore, a quasi-experimental design was employed, with 20 students included in each group.

Both groups participated in a 3-h instructional activity and completed the learning task in pairs. To ensure experimental consistency, the task was limited to disassembling an automobile engine from its initial state to the intake and exhaust manifold stage, involving seven components, although the full MRVALS content covered 21 key engine components.

The control group received traditional instruction, in which the teacher first demonstrated the engine disassembly procedures and students then learned by consulting an automotive repair manual during the hands-on activity. By contrast, the experimental group received MR-based scaffolded support through MRVALS, including instructional videos, tool prompts, operational highlights, and spatially aligned visual cues. As shown in Fig. 2, students in the experimental group worked in pairs and shared one MR device while collaboratively completing the disassembly activity. They could take turns wearing and operating the MR device according to the progress of the task, while working together to complete the required procedures. In the control group, students collaborated under the same pair-based arrangement, but without MR support.

After the instructional experiment, questionnaire surveys were administered to both groups to collect data on their perceptions of cognitive load, self-efficacy, and learning satisfaction. Because students in the experimental group shared one MR device within each pair, the degree and duration of direct interaction with the system may not have been identical for every participant, which should be taken into account when interpreting the questionnaire results.

Fig. 2. Pair-based operation in the experimental group: students collaboratively completed the disassembly task while sharing the MR device during the activity.

2.3 Assessment Tools

Cognitive Load Scale This study adopted the Cognitive Load Scale [7] to measure the intrinsic, extraneous, and germane cognitive load experienced by students during the learning activity. The scale was developed based on Cognitive Load Theory and is designed to distinguish among these three types of cognitive load, thereby enabling a more precise assessment of the mental demands imposed by a learning task.

The scale consists of three dimensions, each containing two to three items, and uses a seven-point Likert scale ranging from 1 (strongly disagree) to 7 (strongly agree). The intrinsic cognitive load dimension assesses the inherent complexity of the learning content and the difficulty of understanding it. The extraneous cognitive load dimension measures cognitive burden caused by instructional design or the learning interface. The germane cognitive load dimension reflects the mental effort that learners invest in understanding and constructing knowledge. Previous research has shown that the scale has good construct validity and internal consistency reliability, with Cronbach's α values above .80 for all dimensions.

Self-Efficacy Scale. This study adopted the self-efficacy subscale of the Motivated Strategies for Learning Questionnaire (MSLQ) [8] to assess students' confidence in their ability to complete tasks and achieve learning goals during the learning activity. The interpretation of this construct was informed by Bandura's self-efficacy theory [11], which emphasizes that learners' beliefs in their own capabilities play an important role in shaping motivation and effort.

The scale consists of eight items rated on a five-point Likert scale ranging from 1 (strongly disagree) to 5 (strongly agree), with higher scores indicating higher levels of self-efficacy. In the present study, the internal consistency reliability of the self-efficacy subscale was acceptable, with a Cronbach's α of .86.

Learning Satisfaction Scale. This study used an adapted version of the Learning Satisfaction Scale [9] to assess students' satisfaction with the instructional approach adopted in this study. The original instrument included multiple dimensions related to learners' perceptions of situated mobile learning, such as user experience, system interaction, and learning satisfaction. In the present study, only the dimension related to satisfaction with the learning approach was adopted, as it was most relevant to the purpose of this study.

The selected dimension consists of nine items rated on a five-point Likert scale ranging from 1 (strongly disagree) to 5 (strongly agree), with higher scores indicating higher levels of learning satisfaction. Based on the design of the original study, this research retained the third dimension, degree of satisfaction with the learning approach, as the focus of assessment. The items cover aspects such as students' understanding of the learning tasks, the level of challenge presented by the learning approach, enjoyment of learning, and perceived improvement in observation and thinking abilities. In the present study, the scale demonstrated good internal consistency reliability, with a Cronbach's α of .89.

3 Results and Discussion

To investigate the effects of the two instructional approaches on students' learning perceptions, this study employed independent-samples t tests to compare the groups on cognitive load, self-efficacy, and learning satisfaction. The results are presented in Table 1.

Table 1. Summary of Cognitive Load, Self-Efficacy, and Learning Satisfaction

Variable	Group	*n*	*M*	*SD*	*df*	*t*	*p*	Cohen's *d*
Intrinsic Cognitive Load	Experimental Group	20	3.48	1.27	38	−2.06	.046*	−0.65
	Control Group	20	4.30	1.26				
Extraneous Cognitive Load	Experimental Group	20	2.93	1.15	38	−4.11	< .001***	−1.30
	Control Group	20	4.40	1.11				
Germane Cognitive Load	Experimental Group	20	5.58	0.82	38	0.44	.662	0.14
	Control Group	20	5.45	1.08				
Self-Efficacy	Experimental Group	20	3.79	0.67	38	−0.72	.475	−0.23
	Control Group	20	3.96	0.76				
Learning Satisfaction	Experimental Group	20	4.06	0.56	38	−0.70	.489	−0.22

(continued)

Table 1. *(continued)*

Variable	Group	*n*	*M*	*SD*	*df*	*t*	*p*	Cohen's *d*
	Control Group	20	4.20	0.70				

* $p < .05$, ** $p < .01$, *** $p < .001$

3.1 Cognitive Load Analysis

Regarding intrinsic cognitive load, the experimental group scored significantly lower than the control group (t(38) = −2.06, p = .046, Cohen's d = −0.65). This finding should be interpreted cautiously, as both groups completed the same seven-component engine disassembly task. Rather than indicating a reduction in task complexity, it may suggest that MRVALS helped learners perceive the task as more manageable and reduced the difficulty of processing task-related information.

Regarding extraneous cognitive load, the experimental group also scored significantly lower than the control group (t(38) = −4.11, p < .001, Cohen's d = −1.30), suggesting that MRVALS reduced unnecessary mental load during learning. Compared with conventional instruction, MRVALS provided task-relevant information directly in the real-world context, which may have reduced split attention and unnecessary search during operation. This result is consistent with previous studies showing that AR/MR can reduce extraneous cognitive load in multistep skill training contexts [10].

No significant difference was found in germane cognitive load between the two groups. This suggests that although MRVALS reduced learners' perceived task burden, its short-term use did not lead to greater deeper cognitive engagement than traditional instruction. A possible reason is that MR-based scaffolding mainly supported procedural understanding and task execution, whereas deeper knowledge construction may require longer practice and reflection.

3.2 Self-Efficacy Analysis

Regarding self-efficacy, no significant difference was found between the experimental group (M = 3.79, SD = 0.67) and the control group (M = 3.96, SD = 0.76), t(38) = −0.72, p = .475. This finding suggests that, under the conditions of the present study, MRVALS did not lead to significantly higher self-efficacy than traditional instruction. One possible explanation is that self-efficacy develops gradually through repeated mastery experiences and sustained feedback [11], which may not have been sufficiently supported within the short intervention period. Although MRVALS provided scaffolded support for understanding and performing the disassembly task, its short-term use may not have been enough to substantially influence learners' confidence in their own capabilities. Future research may further examine this issue by extending the duration of use and incorporating repeated practice and feedback opportunities.

3.3 Learning Satisfaction Analysis

Regarding learning satisfaction, no significant difference was found between the experimental group ($M = 4.06$, $SD = 0.56$) and the control group ($M = 4.20$, $SD = 0.70$), $t(38) = -0.70$, $p = .489$. This finding indicates that students reported comparable overall levels of satisfaction with MR-supported learning and traditional instruction. One possible explanation is that, although MRVALS provided scaffolded support through procedural guidance, strategic prompts, and spatially aligned cues, these advantages may have been more directly reflected in reduced cognitive burden than in students' overall judgments of learning satisfaction. In addition, satisfaction with a new learning environment may require a longer period of use for its benefits to become fully apparent. Future research may further examine this issue by extending the duration of use and exploring additional aspects of learner experience related to satisfaction and continued use intention.

4 Conclusion

This study examined the effects of applying MRVALS, designed on the basis of scaffolding theory, to vehicle engine disassembly instruction. The results showed that students in the MRVALS group reported significantly lower intrinsic and extraneous cognitive load than those in the traditional instruction group. However, the intrinsic cognitive load result should be interpreted cautiously, because both groups completed the same task. This finding may suggest that MRVALS helped learners perceive the task as more manageable, rather than reducing the inherent complexity of the task itself. No significant differences were found in germane cognitive load, self-efficacy, or learning satisfaction. Overall, the findings suggest that MRVALS can serve as a supportive tool for reducing learners' perceived cognitive burden in engine disassembly tasks.

Several limitations should be noted. Because a quasi-experimental design was adopted, pre-existing group differences cannot be fully ruled out. In addition, students completed the task in pairs, and those in the experimental group shared one MR device, which may have resulted in different levels of direct interaction. The study also relied mainly on self-report measures. Future research is recommended to adopt more rigorous designs and include objective measures such as task performance and procedural accuracy. Longer interventions may also help further examine the effects of MR-based scaffolding.

Acknowledgments. The authors would like to thank the National Science and Technology Council, Taiwan, for supporting this research under Grant No. NSTC 113-2410-H-020-003-.

Disclosure of Interests. The authors have no competing interests to declare that are relevant to the content of this article.

References

1. Chandler, P., Sweller, J.: The split-attention effect as a factor in the design of instruction. Br. J. Educ. Psychol. **62**, 233–246 (1992). https://doi.org/10.1111/j.2044-8279.1992.tb01017.x

2. Tang, Y.M., Au, K.M., Lau, H.C., Ho, G.T., Wu, C.H.: Evaluating the effectiveness of learning design with mixed reality (MR) in higher education. Virtual Reality. **24**(4), 797–807 (2020). https://doi.org/10.1007/s10055-020-00427-9
3. Maffei, A., Dalle Mura, M., Monetti, F.M., Boffa, E.: Dynamic mixed reality assembly guidance using optical recognition methods. Appl. Sci. **13**(3), 1760 (2023). https://doi.org/10.3390/app13031760
4. Yang, Z., et al.: Influences of augmented reality assistance on performance and cognitive loads in different stages of assembly task. Front. Psychol. **10**, 1703 (2019). https://doi.org/10.3389/fpsyg.2019.01703
5. Azevedo, R., Hadwin, A.F.: Scaffolding self-regulated learning and metacognition: implications for the design of computer-based scaffolds. Instr. Sci. **33**(5–6), 367–379 (2005). https://doi.org/10.1007/s11251-005-1272-9
6. van de Pol, J., Volman, M., Beishuizen, J.: Scaffolding in teacher–student interaction: a decade of research. Educ. Psychol. Rev. **22**, 271–296 (2010). https://doi.org/10.1007/s10648-010-9127-6
7. Klepsch, M., Schmitz, F., Seufert, T.: Development and validation of two instruments measuring intrinsic, extraneous, and germane cognitive load. Front. Psychol. **8**, 1997 (2017). https://doi.org/10.3389/fpsyg.2017.01997
8. Pintrich, P.R., Smith, D.A.F., Duncan, T., McKeachie, W.J.: A Manual for the Use of the Motivated Strategies for Learning Questionnaire (MSLQ). University of Michigan, National Center for Research to Improve Postsecondary Teaching and Learning, Ann Arbor (1991)
9. Chu, H.-C., Hwang, G.-J., Tsai, C.-C.: A two-tier test approach to developing location-aware mobile learning systems for natural science courses. Comput. Educ. **55**(4), 1618–1627 (2010). https://doi.org/10.1016/j.compedu.2010.07.004
10. Buchner, J., Buntins, K., Kerres, M.: The impact of augmented reality on cognitive load and performance: a systematic review. J. Comput. Assist. Learn. **38**(1), 285–303 (2022). https://doi.org/10.1111/jcal.12617
11. Bandura, A.: Self-Efficacy: the Exercise of Control. W. H. Freeman, New York (1997)

A Perceptual Gate for Iconic Gestures in Educational Virtual Reality

Renia Lopez-Ozieblo[1](✉), Daniel Jiandong Shen[2], Aru Nurgissayeva[2], and Paulina Pui Yun Wong[3]

[1] Department of English and Communication, The Hong Kong Polytechnic University, Hung Hom, Hong Kong, China
renia.lopez@polyu.edu.hk
[2] Soqqle Hong Kong Limited, Hong Kong, China
{dan,aru}@soqqle.com
[3] Lingnan University, Hong Kong, China
paulinawong@ln.edu.hk

Abstract. In social Virtual Reality (VR), avatars can use gestures to communicate, yet it remains unclear whether such movements are noticed and interpreted as intended. This study analysed free-text responses from 187 tertiary students who completed an educational VR task involving an avatar performing an iconic gesture. The results showed that participants most often described the avatar's movement in terms of interface use rather than as a communicative gesture, with the largest response cluster (64.3%) reflecting an interface-focused vocabulary. When the gesture was described in communicative terms, it was usually interpreted together with speech rather than as a separate source of information. A smaller subset of comments focused on movement quality, with mixed descriptions such as "smooth" and "robotic." Sentiment analysis revealed no significant differences across response clusters. Based on these findings, we propose a two-stage model in which gesture in educational VR must first pass a perceptual gate before it can be interpreted and evaluated. Overall, the findings indicate that iconic gestures in VR can support communication only after they attract attention, and that movement quality appears to matter chiefly for the smaller subset of users who attend to it.

Keywords: Virtual Reality · Iconic Gestures · Processing Gestures

1 Introduction

Humans are recognized as limited-capacity processors, a concept reflected in Baddeley's multicomponent model of working memory, which distinguishes between visual-spatial and auditory-verbal subsystems coordinated by a capacity-limited central executive [1]. In VR, gestures act as visual-spatial signals, while speech serves as auditory-verbal input, allowing for potential cross-modal support. However, the demands of interface use and task management may reduce resources for processing gestures, even when those gestures could aid comprehension [13]. Lavie's Load Theory suggests that under

C.-J. Lin et al. (Eds.): ICITL 2026, LNCS 16841, pp. 319–328, 2027.
https://doi.org/10.1007/978-3-032-32112-1_32

high task demand, stimuli not deemed essential are less likely to capture attention [8]. In VR, gestures are likely to be overlooked, especially when they are redundant with speech rather than providing new information.

2 Literature Review

2.1 Gesture Perception and Processing

Gesture scholars consider gesture and speech as parts of a single communicative act rather than separate channels [5, 12]. Kendon argues that the most meaningful phase of a gesture, the "stroke", coincides with the prosodic peak of speech [5]. McNeill's Growth Point hypothesis explains this coordination by proposing a unified idea unit that combines imagery and language before unfolding into synchronized speech and gesture [12]. McNeill also emphasizes the function of gesture in discourse, arguing that it often highlights new or especially meaningful elements within an utterance [12]. In this framework, iconic gestures are relevant because they depict concrete aspects of spoken meaning, such as action or movement, rather than merely pointing or representing abstract ideas [12]. A chopping motion accompanying the word "decomposition," for example, visually expresses part of the spoken meaning. Because of their concrete and semantically transparent nature, iconic gestures offer a valuable perspective for examining how visual-gestural information is perceived and integrated in virtual environments.

When explaining a complex process, a speaker may use an iconic gesture at the point where a key action or new idea is introduced, making the information more salient to the listener. In this sense, gesture is not simply redundant to speech. It can help organize information and draw attention to the most important parts of the message, thereby supporting mutual understanding and conversational grounding. In everyday face-to-face communication, listeners often incorporate gestural information into their understanding without being explicitly aware of the gesture itself [12]. By contrast, gestures are more likely to be missed when they repeat information already available in speech [3].

2.2 Gestures in Virtual Reality

In VR, an avatar's gestures may influence more than just information transfer; they can also shape rapport, engagement, and the overall quality of interaction. Recent studies have also highlighted the importance of realistic avatar movement [14]. Using full face and body motion capture, Fraser et al. [4] showed that richer nonverbal animation improves perceived realism and the quality of VR social interactions. At the same time, technical limitations may create a mismatch between natural human motion and avatar animation, weakening the coherence of the interaction. This issue is captured by the Congruence-Plausibility framework [6], which asserts that believable VR experiences rely on consistency between sensory input and user expectations. From this perspective, plausibility hinges not only on an avatar's appearance but also on whether its movement seems appropriate and convincing in context.

2.3 Modality and Visual Competition

An additional challenge in VR gesture perception is speech modality. When speech is shown as on-screen text alongside audio, users may divide visual attention between reading and observing the avatar's movements [1]. This competition may make gestures less noticeable, especially when text and gesture appear together. Multimedia learning research similarly suggests that redundant on-screen text can split attention and hinder visual processing [10]. Thus, audio-only speech may leave more visual resources for gesture processing, whereas adding text may create a design-induced bottleneck. This modality effect remains underexamined in VR gesture research and is addressed in the present study.

2.4 Individual and Task Differences

Individual differences in VR experience may shape gesture perception. Novice users often devote more attention to basic interaction, such as controller use and navigation, leaving fewer resources for noticing avatar gestures [13]. Task complexity, including topic domain and educational level, may similarly affect attention to social cues. However, these moderators remain underexamined in VR gesture research, which often relies on relatively homogeneous samples [4]. The present study uses a heterogeneous sample across three institutions and topics, allowing exploratory examination of these factors.

A related limitation concerns cognitive load measurement. Although Load Theory [8] and Cognitive Load Theory [13] suggest that higher task demands may reduce gesture noticeability, most VR gesture studies infer load from task design rather than measuring it directly. Direct measures such as NASA-TLX, secondary-task probes, or physiological indicators remain uncommon. The current study therefore follows this inferential approach while acknowledging the need for direct cognitive load measurement in future research.

2.5 The Current Study

Previous research suggests that people perceive and process gestures differently [3], raising an important question for avatar design: how necessary are natural-looking arm and hand movements in instructional VR? Avatar gestures may enhance presence [6], and motion-captured avatars can support realistic and comfortable social interaction in VR [4]. However, it remains unclear whether users actually notice and interpret specific avatar gestures during educational tasks. This study therefore examines whether participants noticed a specific iconic gesture, how they interpreted it, and how they evaluated its movement quality.

The study addressed four aims. First, it examined whether participants noticed the avatar's iconic gesture and how often this occurred (RQ1). We expected that the demands of a novel VR environment would cause many users to miss even a salient gesture (H1), challenging assumptions from face-to-face communication [5, 12]. Second, it explored how the gesture was processed when noticed (RQ2). We expected participants to describe the gesture together with the accompanying speech as one communicative unit (H2), consistent with McNeill's Growth Point hypothesis [12].

Third, the study examined evaluations of the gesture's movement quality (RQ3). We expected quality-related comments to occur less often than simple noticing reports (H3), and to focus mainly on naturalness or links to interface control [4, 6]. Fourth, the study explored whether gesture perception and processing were related to affective response (RQ4). We expected successful gesture processing to be associated with more positive responses (H4) [6].

3 Methodology

3.1 Participants

This study employed a multimethod analytic design, combining quantitative analysis with computational analysis of open-ended survey responses.

A total of 251 participants took part in the VR activity; 187 completed the survey and consented to take part in the study. The sample comprised tertiary students from Malaysia (61 completed surveys out of 123 taking part in the activity, master's level, topic: communication), Singapore (98 of 98, undergraduate level, topic: consumer behavior), and Hong Kong (28 of 30, master's level, topic: sustainability). Survey completion in Malaysia declined due to a technical issue affecting the form on Day 1. Overall, 71.31% of participants were female. Participants were native speakers of Malay, English, Mandarin, or Cantonese, with English as a second language for most. We did not collect data on prior VR experience, which represents a limitation acknowledged in the Discussion. Ethical approval was obtained from The Hong Kong Polytechnic University Institutional Review Board, and all participants provided consent. The sample was intentionally heterogeneous, allowing gesture perception to be examined across a broad tertiary student population rather than a narrow group of experienced VR users.

3.2 Procedure

In all scenarios, participants completed four to six tasks involving interactions with multiple avatars through the VR platform Classlet, a VR-enabled system for scenario-based learning that supports quest-based task flow and NPC interactions and has been examined in prior research on technology adoption [2, 9]. Two of these interactions involved the same avatar, which performed the "decomposition" gesture; the other avatars did not gesture. The gesture appeared twice during separate interactions, with slightly different accompanying wording, but in both cases referred to the idea of decomposition. It involved a chopping movement of the right hand above the left hand to illustrate the breakdown of a larger entity into smaller parts (see Fig. 1). Avatar speech was delivered both aurally and through on-screen text. The task took about 15 min and was completed using headsets and handheld controllers.

After a brief introduction to the VR environment and the consent procedure, participants completed the task individually during class time and then filled in a post-task survey. The survey asked whether they remembered the avatar's gesture and, if so, to describe it. It also included measures of self-reported cybersickness, presence, confidence with new technologies, perceived usefulness, ease of use, behavioral expectancy, and intention to use [2, 9]. No direct measure of cognitive load (e.g., NASA-TLX) was administered; inferences about cognitive load are therefore theory-based rather than directly measured.

Fig. 1. Iconic gesture performed by the avatar. The avatar performs a chopping motion with his hands to illustrate the idea of 'breaking' down a larger entity into pieces.

3.3 Gesture Perception

To answer RQ1, "Do participants perceive the gesture, and if so, how often?", we reviewed survey responses about the avatar's movement and coded whether the gesture was perceived. Responses were coded as gesture perception if they referred to any hand or arm movement by the avatar, even vaguely, using verbs such as *move*, *wave*, *chop*, or *show*. Responses were coded as non-gesture only when participants explicitly stated that they did not remember the gesture or referred solely to system controls, such as pressing a button or using a joystick. For example, "right hand moves onto the left hand" was coded as an observed gesture, whereas "press the button on your index finger" was not.

To address RQ2, "How is the gesture described, revealing its processing (content vs. interface related)?", and RQ3, "How is the gesture's kinematic quality appraised?", we analysed participants' free-text comments. Responses were preprocessed using standard NLP steps, including lowercasing, removal of URLs and social media handles, expansion of contractions, lemmatization with the *udpipe* package, and stop-word removal. The median response length was two tokens, meaning that the linguistic data available for analysis were extremely brief. This limits the granularity of clustering and sentiment analysis, a caveat we return to in the Discussion. We then constructed a TF-IDF weighted response-term matrix, normalized responses for comparison, and applied k-means clustering to the processed comments. The resulting clusters partially aligned with the predefined coding categories (CAT1–CAT6), indicating that participants' language broadly reflected the conceptual distinctions in the coding scheme. To answer RQ4, "What is the resulting affective response when attentional resources are successfully allocated to the gesture?", we analyzed the sentiment of each comment using the *sentimentr* package in R. We aggregated sentence-level scores into a single sentiment score per comment and linked these scores to the six gesture categories, assigning comments to all relevant categories.

To operationalize the two-stage model that emerged from our findings, we defined *perceptual access* as the participant's ability to verbally recall any hand or arm movement by the avatar in an open-ended survey question. Operationally, this was coded dichotomously (present/absent) based on mention of movement-related verbs (e.g., *move, wave, chop, show*) regardless of whether the movement was interpreted as communicative or interface-related. *Post-perceptual response* refers to how participants who demonstrated perceptual access described the movement. These descriptions were categorised into three broad types: (1) *gesture-focused interpretation* (linking the movement to speech, meaning, or explanation), (2) *interface-focused interpretation* (linking the movement to VR controls, buttons, or task actions), and (3) *movement-focused description* (commenting on kinematic quality, e.g., "smooth," "robotic," without clear interpretation). These operational definitions guided the coding and clustering analyses reported in the Results section.

4 Results

Of the 187 survey responses, 140 contained at least one usable token after preprocessing and were included in the clustering analysis; 47 were excluded.

We represented the comments using a TF-IDF weighted document-term matrix, normalized the matrix by row, and applied k-means clustering ($k = 6$) to identify lexical groupings in how participants described the avatar's movement. The average silhouette width for the six-cluster solution was 0.10, indicating weak separation between clusters and suggesting that the solution identifies broad lexical tendencies rather than sharply distinct thematic groups. Given the low silhouette values across all solutions, we do not claim that $k = 6$ is statistically optimal; we report it because it aligns with our predefined coding categories, allowing comparison between computational and human coding. Readers should therefore interpret the resulting clusters with caution.

The resulting six-cluster solution was unevenly distributed. The six clusters varied considerably in size. The largest, Interface focus, movement interpreted as a control-related action (CAT6), comprised 90 comments (64.3%) and described the movement using interface-related vocabulary such as "press," "grab," and "movement." Four smaller clusters captured various forms of gesture-related responses: Gesture-speech integration, creating meaning together (CAT4, $n = 14$, 10.0%), Movement description, description of bodily movement without interpretation (CAT5, $n = 12$, 8.6%), Uncertain recall of the gesture (CAT2, $n = 11$, 7.9%), and Gesture noticed (CAT3, $n = 5$, 3.6%). The smallest cluster, No recall (CAT1, $n = 8$, 5.7%), reflected no memory of the gesture.

The cluster solution aligns with the distinction between *perceptual access* and *post-perceptual response*. CAT1 and CAT2 indicate perceptual access failure or uncertainty, while CAT3 to CAT6 represent various forms of post-perceptual response, including gesture-focused interpretation, interface-focused interpretation, and movement-focused description.

We examined whether the tone of participants' comments differed across the six lexical clusters by conducting sentiment analysis on the cleaned document texts. Mean sentiment scores varied across clusters, with Cluster 4 showing the highest average sentiment ($M = 0.106$) and Cluster 3 the lowest ($M = -0.058$). These differences were minor. A Kruskal–Wallis test revealed that sentiment did not significantly differ across clusters ($\chi^2(5) = 3.75$, $p = .585$). The effect size was negligible (epsilon$^2 \approx 0$, computed value = −0.009). While some clusters appeared more positive or negative, the data do not support a meaningful difference in sentiment across the six lexical groupings. Given the very short response length (median = 2 tokens), sentiment scores should be interpreted with caution, as brief texts may not fully capture affective tone.

5 Discussion

This study investigated how attention is allocated to a virtual avatar's iconic gesture within a demanding educational VR task. Our findings show that the effectiveness of gestural communication is limited by the user's attentional resources. Consistent with Cognitive load theory [13] and Load Theory [7, 8], alongside broader models of attention and working memory [11], the novelty of the VR environment and the demands of the task likely increased cognitive load, which may have reduced the attentional resources available for processing the avatar's gestures. This suggests that gesture must first pass a perceptual bottleneck before any downstream benefits can be realized.

5.1 Gesture Perception

Our most important finding was that participants seldom described the avatar's movement as a gesture. Only 3.6% of comments fell into the *Gesture noticed* cluster and 10.0% into the *Gesture-speech integration* cluster, whereas 64.3% were classified as *Interface focus*. However, given the weak cluster separation (silhouette = 0.10) reported in Results, these percentages should be interpreted as heuristic approximations rather than precise categorical distinctions. This pattern might suggest that many participants understood the movement mainly in relation to using the VR system rather than as a communicative cue. One likely reason is that the task demanded a great deal of attention. As a result, attention appears to have been directed more toward task-related actions than toward the gesture itself.

Competition for visual attention may have played a role. Although the avatar's speech was delivered aurally, it also appeared as on-screen text. As a result, participants had to divide their visual attention between reading the text and noticing the gesture. Presenting both at the same time may have increased visual processing demands [1]. This may help explain why some participants referred to actions such as "pressing buttons" or "using the joystick" when the avatar performed a chopping motion. Instead of being interpreted mainly as a communicative teaching cue, the movement was often understood in relation to interface demands and task-related actions.

5.2 Processing the Gesture

To address RQ2, we examined how participants described the gesture after the task. When participants referred to the gesture, they often described it alongside the avatar's speech rather than as a separate stream of information. This indicates that the main challenge was noticing the gesture, not integrating it with speech. Comments in this cluster often regarded the movement and the spoken explanation as part of the same communicative event. This pattern aligns with McNeill's Growth Point Hypothesis [12] and suggests that gesture–speech integration can occur in human–avatar interaction when the gesture receives adequate attention.

Only a small subset of comments focused on movement quality, with mixed descriptions ranging from "smooth" to "robotic." This supports the view that movement quality matters mainly after the gesture has first been noticed, consistent with the Congruence-Plausibility framework [6].

5.3 Sentiment Analysis

As reported in Results, sentiment did not differ significantly across the six clusters (Kruskal-Wallis, $p = .585$). Contrary to H4, we found no evidence that gesture processing was associated with positive or negative affect. Null results should be interpreted with caution given the very short response length (median = 2 tokens). This limited sentiment effect is important when considering the design implications of avatar movement. Although more natural-looking movement may support a more positive response for some users, it is unlikely to matter unless the gesture is first noticed. In this sense, noticeability and movement quality should be treated as related but distinct design concerns. Despite advances in avatar appearance [4], much less is known about how movement quality shapes user response. The present findings suggest that improving movement quality may be most worthwhile in cases where users are already attending to the gesture—but this remains a hypothesis for future research, not a conclusion supported by our sentiment data.

5.4 Theoretical Implication: a Conceptual Model

These findings support a two-stage model of gesture processing in educational VR (Fig. 2). The first stage, *perceptual access*, involves users consciously noticing the avatar's gesture amid competing cognitive and interface demands; consistent with H1, many participants did not report the gesture. The second stage, *post-perceptual response*, concerns how noticed movements are interpreted and evaluated, including gesture-focused interpretation, interface-focused interpretation, and movement-focused description. CAT4 provided support for H2 by suggesting that gesture-related descriptions were often linked to speech, while the relatively small movement-description cluster supported H3. However, the weak cluster separation (silhouette = 0.10) means that this model should be viewed as an exploratory framework requiring validation in future studies with larger text corpora or alternative methodologies (e.g., interviews, behavioral tracking).

5.5 Limitations

Several factors limit the generalizability of our findings and should be considered when interpreting the two-stage model. First, the avatar's speech was delivered both aurally and as on-screen text. This design choice likely increased visual competition, potentially reducing gesture noticeability compared to an aural-only condition. Our findings therefore generalize most directly to VR scenarios with redundant on-screen captions; they may underestimate gesture perception in audio-only environments.

As we did not measure participants' prior VR experience, it is possible that novice users may have allocated more attention to basic interaction (e.g., controller use, navigation) than experienced users, potentially reducing gesture noticeability. Future research should include measures of VR familiarity to examine whether experience moderates the perceptual gate effect. In addition, participants' responses were brief (median = 2 tokens). Only a minority of users actively evaluated the kinematic fidelity of an avatar's movements, and the use of descriptive adjectives for kinematic quality was limited, as users prioritized conveying what the avatar did over how it was done. Ongoing studies by the team are adding post-treatment interviews that will collect more data.

We inferred cognitive load from task design rather than measuring it directly. Direct measures—such as the NASA-TLX, secondary task probes, or physiological indicators—remain an important direction for future research to establish causal links between load and gesture perception.

A key question raised by our two-stage model is whether perceptual access to gestures translates into measurable educational benefits. The present study was not designed to answer this question; we collected only short-term, self-reported data and did not assess learning outcomes (e.g., comprehension, retention, transfer). Therefore, the claim that gestures "support communication" or "enhance learning" remains theoretical in the context of this study. Future research should employ longitudinal designs or performance-based measures to test whether gestures that pass the perceptual gate actually improve educational outcomes.

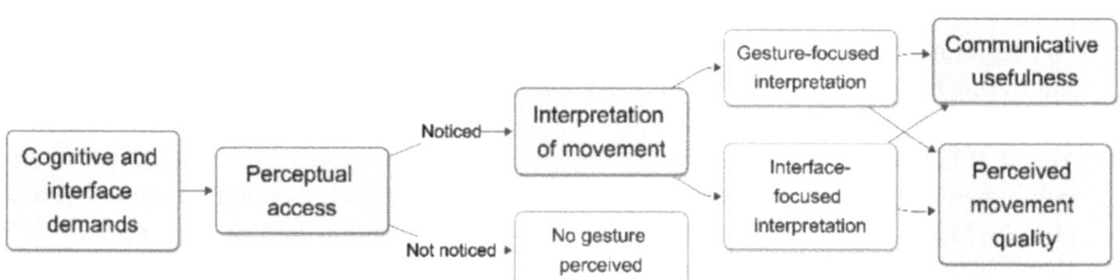

Fig. 2. Conceptual model of gesture processing in educational VR. Gesture must first achieve perceptual access under cognitive and interface demands. Once noticed, responses divide into interpretation and evaluation.

Acknowledgments. We are very grateful to all our participants.

This project was funded by the Teaching and Learning Committee of the Department of English and Communication of The Hong Kong Polytechnic University and the University Grants committee Hong Kong TDLEG-IICA led by Lingnan University (#102746).

Renia Lopez-Ozieblo is a member of the Research Centre for Professional Communication in English (RCPCE) of the Department of English and Communication of The Hong Kong Polytechnic University under which mission this project was developed.

Disclosure of Interests Daniel Shen Jiandong reports a relationship with Soqqle Hong Kong Limited that includes equity or stocks.

References

1. Baddeley, A.: The episodic buffer: a new component of working memory? Trends Cogn. Sci. **4**(11), 417–423 (2000). https://doi.org/10.1016/S1364-6613(00)01538-2
2. Choi, H., et al.: Uncovering the drivers of intent to use the metaverse: diverse experiences in sustainability education. Discov. Sustain. **6**, 152 (2025). https://doi.org/10.1007/s43621-025-00903-9
3. Dargue, N., Sweller, N., Jones, M.P.: When our hands help us understand: a meta-analysis into the effects of gesture on comprehension. Psychol. Bull. **145**(8), 765–784 (2019). https://doi.org/10.1037/bul0000202
4. Fraser, A.D., Branson, I., Hollett, R.C., Speelman, C.P., Rogers, S.L.: Do realistic avatars make virtual reality better? Examining human-like avatars for vr social interactions. Comput. Human Behav. Artif. Humans. **2**(2), 100082 (2024). https://doi.org/10.1016/j.chbah.2024.100082
5. Kendon, A.: Gesture: Visible Action as Utterance. Cambridge University Press, Cambridge (2004)
6. Latoschik, M.E., Wienrich, C.: Congruence and plausibility, not presence: pivotal conditions for xr experiences and effects, a novel approach. Front. Virtual Reality. **3**, 694433 (2022). https://doi.org/10.3389/frvir.2022.694433
7. Lavie, N.: Distracted and confused?: selective attention under load. Trends Cogn. Sci. **9**(2), 75–82 (2005). https://doi.org/10.1016/j.tics.2004.12.004
8. Lavie, N., Hirst, A., De Fockert, J.W., Viding, E.: Load theory of selective attention and cognitive control. J. Exp. Psychol. Gen. **133**(3), 339 (2004). https://doi.org/10.1037/0096-3445.133.3.339
9. Lopez-Ozieblo, R., Wong, W.C.G., Shen, J.D.: Enhancing vr education: a tam- based study on predicting student engagement and intent to use virtual reality. In: Cheng, E.C.K. (ed.) Innovating Education with AI. Lecture Notes in Educational Technology. Springer, Singapore (2025)
10. Mayer, R.E., Fiorella, L.: Principles for reducing extraneous processing in multimedia learning: coherence, signaling, redundancy, spatial contiguity, and temporal contiguity principles. In: Mayer, R.E. (ed.) The Cambridge Handbook of Multimedia Learning, pp. 279–315. Cambridge University Press, Cambridge (2014)
11. McLaughlin, B., Rossman, T., McLeod, B.: Second language learning: an information-processing perspective. Lang. Learn. **33**(2), 135–158 (1983). https://doi.org/10.1111/j.1467-1770.1983.tb00532.x
12. McNeill, D.: Hand and Mind: What Gestures Reveal about Thought. University of Chicago Press (1992)
13. Sweller, J.: Cognitive load theory. In: Psychology of Learning and Motivation, vol. 55, pp. 37–76. Academic (2011). https://doi.org/10.1016/B978-0-12-387691-1.00002-8
14. Wolfert, P., Robinson, N., Belpaeme, T.: A review of evaluation practices of gesture generation in embodied conversational agents. IEEE Trans. Human-Mach. Syst. **52**(5), 375–387 (2022). https://doi.org/10.1109/THMS.2022.3149173

Context Assessment for the Development of a Virtual Reality (VR) Exhibition Based on a Constructivist Approach to Enhance Creative Problem-Solving in High-Energy Physics and Quantum Technology Related to Clean Energy for Upper Secondary School Students

Ponlapat Thongsong[1], Charuni Samat[2(✉)], Suchat Wattanachai[3], and Ganigar Chen[4]

[1] Center of Excellence in Coding Manpower Development and Digital Citizenship, Faculty of Education, Khon Kaen University, Khon Kaen 40002, Thailand
[2] Faculty of Education, Khon Kaen University, Khon Kaen 40002, Thailand
scharu@kku.ac.th
[3] Faculty of Veterinary Medicine, Khon Kaen University, Khon Kaen 40002, Thailand
[4] National Science Museum, Technopolis, Khlong 5, Khlong Luang, Pathum Thani 12120, Thailand

Abstract. This study is part of a larger developmental research project aimed at designing and developing a Virtual Reality (VR) exhibition based on a constructivist approach to enhance creative problem-solving (CPS) in high-energy physics and quantum technology related to clean energy for upper secondary school students. This paper focuses specifically on Phase 1: Context Assessment, a critical foundational stage conducted prior to the design and development of the exhibition. The target group comprised 60 Grade 12 students, 2 science teachers, and 3 measurement and evaluation experts from Tessaban Wat Klang School. Data were collected using a student context survey, a teacher context survey, and an environmental context survey. Data analysis employed basic descriptive statistics (mean, standard deviation, and percentage) and analytical narration. Quantitative findings revealed that: (1) 80% of students had a GPA above 3.00 but only 41.67% had prior exposure to clean-energy content, and none had used immersive VR for learning; (2) students' baseline CPS performance averaged 11.67/30 (S.D. = 3.25), well below the 80% criterion, with the weakest sub-process being Acceptance Finding ($\bar{x} = 1.83$); (3) both teachers (mean teaching experience $>$ 10 years) relied predominantly on lecture-based instruction yet held very-high readiness for technology integration; and (4) the school's ICT infrastructure (WiFi coverage $>$90%, projector, stable bandwidth) was adequate for VR deployment. These findings informed the synthesis of a five-base theoretical framework and a seven-component VR exhibition design framework, presented here with supporting figures and an explicit comparison to prior VR-in-physics studies (2019–2025).

C.-J. Lin et al. (Eds.): ICITL 2026, LNCS 16841, pp. 329–338, 2027.
https://doi.org/10.1007/978-3-032-32112-1_33

Keywords: Context Assessment · Virtual Reality Exhibition · Constructivism · Creative Problem-Solving · High-Energy Physics · Quantum Technology · Cognitive Load · Generative AI

1 Introduction

In the current era of Thailand's "Thailand 4.0" policy, developing human resources with advanced scientific capabilities has become an urgent national priority, particularly in the fields of High-Energy Physics (HEP) and Quantum Technology, which are directly linked to the development of clean-energy solutions to address the global climate crisis [1, 2]. These disciplines, however, remain highly abstract and difficult for secondary-school students to access through traditional lecture-based teaching alone.

Museum and exhibition-based learning is widely recognised as a high-potential learning environment that bridges abstract science content and real-world experience [3, 4]. In science museums in particular, hands-on, interactive exhibits have been shown to support inquiry, observation, and the construction of conceptual understanding of phenomena that learners cannot otherwise see, such as particle interactions, quantum behaviour, or nuclear processes [5]. Hein's [3] "Constructivist Museum" and Falk and Dierking's [4] Contextual Model of Learning are routinely used as the pedagogical foundation for science-museum exhibits on topics such as high-energy physics, particle accelerators, and clean-energy technologies.

Virtual Reality (VR) technology has emerged as a powerful tool for enhancing science learning by simulating phenomena that cannot be observed in real life [6, 7]. Recent empirical work on VR in physics education has demonstrated three consistent benefits relevant to this study. First, immersive VR significantly increases learners' sense of presence, motivation, and engagement compared with screen-based media [6, 8]. Second, 3D virtual learning environments allow students to manipulate abstract physical variables (e.g., electric and magnetic fields, particle trajectories) and observe their consequences in ways that conventional laboratories cannot afford, particularly for schools with limited equipment budgets [7, 9].

immersive environments shows that adaptive, dialogue-based agents can personalise scaffolding, model expert problem-solving, and reduce the need for constant teacher intervention [10, 11]. The Coaching component of the proposed framework is informed by this line of work, even though the present Phase 1 paper does not yet evaluate a generative-AI coach empirically.

Creative Problem-Solving (CPS) — the six-process framework developed by Treffinger and colleagues [15, 16] — represents an essential competency for 21st-century learners and is increasingly seen as the higher-order outcome that science exhibitions and VR experiences should target [17].

2 Research Objective

To assess the learner, instructor, and environmental contexts as a foundation for designing a constructivist-based Virtual Reality (VR) exhibition to enhance creative problem-solving in high-energy physics and quantum technology related to clean energy for upper secondary school students.

3 Literature Review

3.1 Constructivist Theory and Museum-Based Learning

Constructivist theory proposes that learning occurs when learners actively build knowledge through interaction with their environment rather than passively receive information. Vygotsky [19] emphasised social interaction and introduced the Zone of Proximal Development (ZPD), while Hein [3] applied constructivist principles to museums via the "Constructivist Museum". Falk and Dierking [4] developed the Contextual Model of Learning, which posits that museum learning experiences arise from the intersection of three dimensions: the personal context (motivation, prior knowledge, interests), the social context (interactions with visitors, guides, peers), and the physical context (architecture, object arrangement, facilities). Recent applications of this model to science-museum exhibits on physics and energy topics confirm that authentic, problem-based artefacts and peer dialogue are essential for moving learners beyond surface recall toward conceptual change [5, 17].

3.2 Virtual Reality for Learning, Especially in Physics

A substantial body of research confirms VR's potential to enhance science learning. Makransky and Lilleholt [6] found that immersive VR significantly increases learners' sense of presence and motivation. Bogusevschi et al. [7] demonstrated that 3D virtual environments allow students to engage actively with content such as the water cycle and laboratory experiments, and reported gains of approximately 65% in low-achieving classrooms after VR-supported instruction. Optimisation studies on physics-specific VR applications report normalised learning gains around 0.80 relative to traditional teaching [8].

3.3 Creative Problem-Solving (CPS)

The CPS framework [15, 16] consists of six sequential processes: (1) Mess Finding — recognising and identifying a problematic situation; (2) Data Finding — gathering relevant information; (3) Problem Finding — analysing data to define the underlying problem; (4) Idea Finding — brainstorming diverse, novel solutions; (5) Solution Finding — evaluating and selecting the most appropriate solution; and (6) Acceptance Finding — planning for implementation and gaining stakeholder buy-in. Recent classroom and pre-service-teacher studies confirm that Idea Finding and Acceptance Finding are typically the weakest sub-processes in Thai secondary settings [21], a pattern that the present context assessment also replicates.

3.4 Constructivist VR Exhibition Model

Samat [22] developed a web-based constructivist learning environment model to promote creative thinking, incorporating seven components: Problem Base, Resources, Cognitive Tools, Collaboration, Creative Problem-Solving Centre, Scaffolding, and Coaching. This model aligns with Hannafin's [23] principles for Open Learning Environments (OLEs), which emphasise learner-centred, resource-rich, tool-supported knowledge construction. The present study extends this model to a fully immersive VR exhibition and embeds the six-process CPS pipeline inside the Creative Problem-Solving Centre component.

4 Research Methodology

4.1 Participants

Participants for Phase 1 were selected through purposive sampling and consisted of three groups, as detailed in Table 1.

Table 1. Participant groups for Phase 1: Context Assessment.

Participant group	*n*	Purpose
Grade 12 students	60	To examine learner context: demographics, learning experience, technology use, baseline CPS, and learning needs
Science teachers	2	To examine instructional context and teaching practices
Measurement & evaluation experts	3	To validate the quality of the data-collection instruments

4.2 Instruments

Five instruments were used for Phase 1 data collection: (i) a document review form; (ii) a student context survey covering demographics, GPA band, learning experience, and digital-tool use; (iii) a teacher context survey covering teaching method, attitudes toward instructional innovation, and CPS-related practice; (iv) an environmental context survey covering classroom, lighting, sound, climate, ICT infrastructure, and network stability; and (v) a theoretical-framework synthesis record. All surveys were developed on the basis of the contextual-study framework of Richey and Klein [18] and validated by three measurement and evaluation experts prior to deployment.

4.3 Data Collection

A systematic literature review was carried out to examine the relevant theories, principles, and prior studies. A contextual study was then conducted by administering the on-site surveys to 60 Grade 12 students during one class period and to 2 science teachers. The environmental survey was administered by the researcher through direct observation of classrooms and ICT facilities. Finally, data from all stages were integrated to synthesise the theoretical framework and the VR exhibition design framework.

4.4 Theoretical Framework

The theoretical framework was synthesised from five foundational bases: (1) Contextual Base (National curriculum, Learner profile, Teacher profile and Content scope) (2) Psychological Base (Constructivism Theory and Cognitivism) (3) Pedagogical Base (Constructivist Learning, Environment Model Instructional, Design Model (SOI Model), Open Learning Environments (OLEs), Model Situated Learning and Cognitive Apprenticeship); (4) Media and Technology Base (media symbol systems and VR technology) and (5) Creative Problem Solving Base (Mess Finding, Data Finding, Problem Finding, Idea Finding, Solution Finding and Acceptance Finding). Figure 1 visualises how each base maps onto the seven exhibition components.

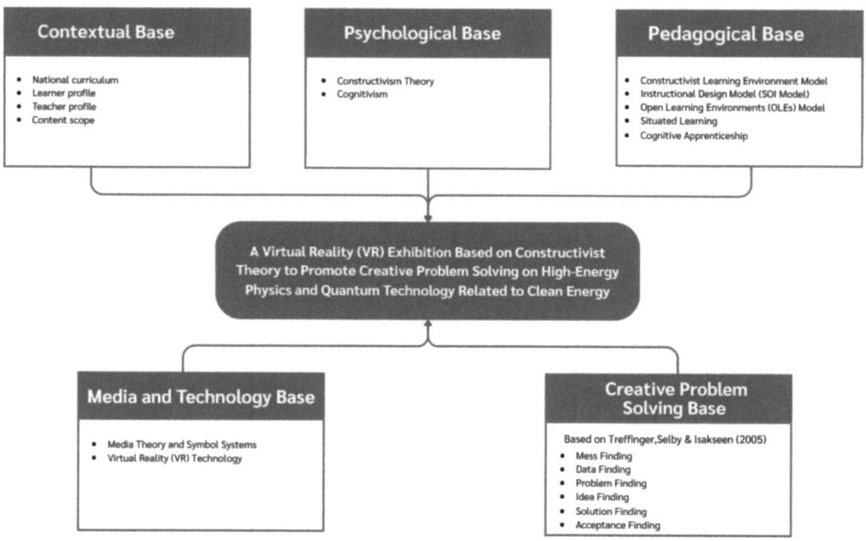

Fig. 1. Theoretical framework: mapping of the five foundational bases (left) through their generative principles (centre) to the seven VR-exhibition components (right). Adapted from Thongsong [24].

5 Results

5.1 Learner Context (N = 60)

Demographics and Academic Background. The student sample comprised 25 male (41.67%) and 35 female (58.33%) Grade 12 students. Eighty percent reported a GPA above 3.00, and the remaining 20% reported a GPA between 2.50 and 2.99; no students fell below GPA 2.50. Although 100% of students had studied general science content aligned with the Revised Basic Education Core Curriculum (2017), only 41.67% reported any prior exposure to clean-energy content, and familiarity with HEP and quantum-technology topics was minimal.

Table 2. Baseline (pre-exhibition) CPS sub-process scores (n = 60; 5 points per sub-process; total 30).

CPS sub-process	Mean ($\bar{x}$)	S.D.	% of criterion
1. Mess Finding	1.97	0.76	39.33%
2. Data Finding	1.97	0.67	39.33%
3. Problem Finding	1.97	0.72	39.33%
4. Idea Finding	2.00	0.69	40.00%
5. Solution Finding	1.93	0.69	38.67%
6. Acceptance Finding	1.83	0.65	36.67%
Total (/30)	11.67	3.25	38.89%

As Table 2 shows, every sub-process scored below the 80% criterion. The weakest sub-process was *Acceptance Finding* ($\bar{x}$ = 1.83, 36.67%), followed by *Solution Finding* ($\bar{x}$ = 1.93, 38.67%). No student met the 80% criterion on the pre-test. This pattern — strong general digital competence but very weak ability to evaluate, select, and operationalise solutions to authentic problems — directly motivated the inclusion of a dedicated Creative-Problem-Solving Centre and a structured Coaching component in the proposed exhibition design.

Learning Needs. Students expressed strong interest in clean-energy and modern-technology content, and clearly preferred active, hands-on, situated learning over passive lecture-based instruction.

5.2 Instructor Context (N = 2)

Profile. The two science (physics) teachers were 38 and 45 years of age, with more than 10 years of teaching experience. Both reported prior experience designing brain-based science instruction, prior exposure to VR media, and prior practice of CPS-style activities (Design Thinking).

Primary teaching method. Both teachers predominantly employed lecture-based instruction supplemented by laboratory demonstrations. Some digital media (slides, video) were used, but no immersive or fully virtual learning environments had been deployed for HEP or quantum-technology topics.

5.3 Environmental Context

The environmental survey revealed that Tessaban Wat Klang School possesses sufficient ICT infrastructure to support VR-based learning. Classrooms were well-lit, kept at 25–27 °C, and arranged for group activities. WiFi coverage exceeded 90% of the school area with very-good stability, and each room included a projector, screen, and amplifier. The main constraint was a limited number of available VR headsets (Meta Quest 2). This constraint informed the decision to adopt a small-group learning model; the optimal group size was determined empirically in Phase 2 to be six students per group.

5.4 Synthesised Design Framework

Drawing on the five theoretical bases (Sect. 4.4) and the three context findings above, the design framework was synthesised into a seven-component VR exhibition, summarised in Table 3 and visualised in Fig. 2-4.

Table 3. Components and theoretical principles of the constructivist VR exhibition.

No	Component	Function and theoretical basis
1	Problem Base	Simulates real-world contexts to stimulate problem awareness (Mess Finding). Based on constructivist theory and CPS [15, 16].
2	Resources	Supports information retrieval (Data Finding). Based on Information Processing [25], SOI Model [26], and Cognitive Load Theory [13, 14].
3	Cognitive Tools	Supports thinking processes and knowledge construction. Based on OLEs Processing Tools [23]: Seeking, Collecting, Organising, Integrating, Generating.
4	Collaboration	Promotes cognitive schema expansion through social interaction. Based on social constructivism [19].
5	Creative Problem-Solving Centre	Practises all six CPS processes: Mess → Data → Problem → Idea → Solution → Acceptance Finding.
6	Scaffolding	Supports learners who cannot construct knowledge independently. Based on ZPD [19] and Scaffolding OLEs [23]: Conceptual, Metacognitive, Procedural, Strategic.
7	Coaching	Stimulates thinking and extends problem-solving approaches; teacher acts as coach rather than lecturer. Based on cognitive apprenticeship principles; compatible with generative-AI coaching agents [11].

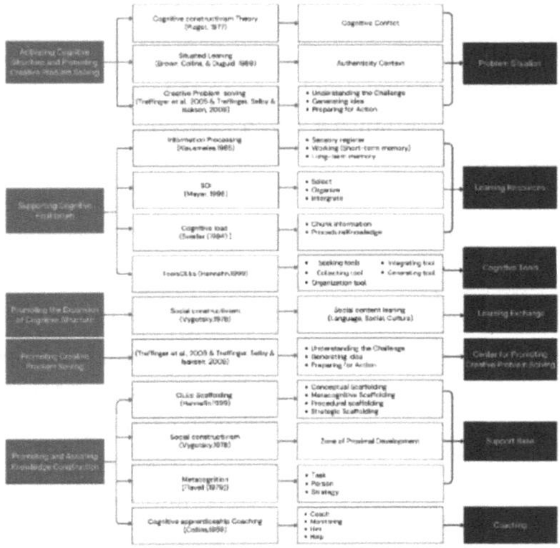

Fig. 2. Seven-component VR-exhibition design framework, derived from the five theoretical bases of. Adapted from Thongsong [24].

6 Discussion

The context-assessment findings revealed several interrelated issues that justified the design decisions taken in this study. These are discussed in light of the most recent VR-and-physics literature (2020–2025).

Lack of higher-order thinking stimulation. The teacher survey confirmed that lecture-based instruction remains the dominant mode for HEP and quantum-technology content, consistent with Rodriguez Calderon [9], who argued that traditional physics instruction is inadequate for abstract content and that VR holds significant potential for transforming such learning. Bogusevschi et al. [7] and Wei et al. [10] reach the same conclusion using more recent samples and instruments, reporting gains in motivation and performance once immersive simulations replace static media. The proposed exhibition addresses this gap by making the Coaching component, rather than direct lecturing, the primary mode of teacher interaction.

Below-criterion CPS skills. Students' baseline CPS total of 11.67/30 (S.D. = 3.25) was particularly weak in Acceptance Finding ($\bar{x} = 1.83$) and Solution Finding ($\bar{x} = 1.93$). This is consistent with Kochapong [21] for pre-service teachers and confirms the need for a learning environment that provides structured opportunities for both systematic ideation and realistic operationalisation. The Creative-Problem-Solving Centre component, which guides learners through all six Treffinger processes inside an authentic clean-energy scenario, was designed specifically to address this deficit. Phase 3 of this project subsequently confirmed that 86.67% of students met the 80% CPS criterion after exposure to the exhibition [24].

Cognitive load and immersive design. Recent reviews [13, 14] caution that immersive VR can easily exceed working-memory capacity, particularly when learners are new to the medium. Since the present sample reported only "fair" prior VR experience and zero use of VR in physics, three CLT-aligned design rules were embedded in every scene: chunked information, fading procedural scaffolds, and clear visual separation of decorative and instructional elements. This approach is consistent with Markowitz and Bailenson [11], who report that the quality of presence — not the volume of stimuli — is the most reliable predictor of VR-mediated learning gains.

7 Conclusions

Phase 1 Context Assessment proved to be a highly valuable foundational stage in the development of a VR learning exhibition. Quantitative findings established that, in the target setting, students hold strong general digital competence (mean GPA > 3.00 in 80% of the sample; very-good ratings on six common digital tools) but very weak immersive-VR experience and CPS performance (total 11.67/30, with Acceptance Finding the weakest sub-process at 36.67% of criterion). Teachers showed high technology readiness but defaulted to lecture-based instruction for abstract HEP content, and the school's ICT infrastructure was sufficient for VR deployment with the constraint that small-group use is required.

The framework synthesised during this phase serves as a theory-grounded blueprint for the subsequent design and development of the VR exhibition. This Theory-Based Design approach, as advocated by Richey and Klein [18], enhances both the effectiveness and the credibility of learning innovations. The seven-component VR exhibition derived from this framework was subsequently evaluated in Phase 2 (Quality Evaluation) and Phase 3 (Validation), where it was shown to significantly enhance CPS among Grade 12 students, with 86.67% meeting the 80% CPS criterion and 93.33% meeting the 80% learning-achievement criterion [24].

References

1. UNEP: Emissions Gap Report 2019. United Nations Environment Programme, Nairobi (2019).
2. International Energy Agency: World Energy Outlook 2020. IEA, Paris (2020)
3. Hein, G.E.: Learning in the Museum. Routledge, London (1998)
4. Falk, J.H., Dierking, L.D.: Learning from Museums: Visitor Experiences and the Making of Meaning. AltaMira Press, Walnut Creek (2000)
5. Allen, S., Gutwill, J.: Designing science museum exhibits with multiple interactive features: five common pitfalls. Curator Mus. J. **47**(2), 199–212 (2004)
6. Makransky, G., Lilleholt, L.: A structural equation modeling investigation of the emotional value of immersive virtual reality in education. Comput. Educ. **121**, 112–122 (2018)
7. Bogusevschi, D., Muntean, C., Muntean, G.M.: Teaching and learning physics using 3D virtual learning environment: a case study of combined virtual reality and virtual laboratory in secondary school. J. Comput. Math. Sci. Teach. **39**(1), 5–18 (2020)
8. Villada Castillo, J.F., Bohorquez Santiago, L., Martínez García, S.: Optimization of physics learning through immersive virtual reality: a study on the efficacy of serious games. Appl. Sci. **15**(6), 3405 (2025)
9. Rodriguez Calderon, R.: Physics instruction using virtual learning environments. Int. J. Sci. Educ. **41**(12), 1604–1624 (2019)
10. Wei, X., Zhang, Y., Li, H.: Embodied presence and its role in VR learning outcomes: a meta-analytic review. Comput. Educ. X Real. **4**, 100074 (2025)

11. Markowitz, D.M., Bailenson, J.N.: Decades of VR research through the lens of natural language processing: presence as a central organising construct. Front. Virtual Real. **6**, 1452318 (2025)
12. Pinker, S.: Virtual realities and the psychology of perception. Trends Cogn. Sci. **29**(2), 121–134 (2025)
13. Sweller, J., van Merriënboer, J.J.G., Paas, F.: Cognitive architecture and instructional design: 20 years later. Educ. Psychol. Rev. **31**, 261–292 (2019)
14. Frederiksen, J.G., et al.: Cognitive load and performance in immersive virtual reality versus conventional virtual reality simulation training of laparoscopic surgery. Surg. Endosc. **34**(3), 1244–1252 (2020)
15. Treffinger, D.J.: Creative problem solving: overview and educational implications. Educ. Psychol. Rev. **7**(3), 301–312 (1995)
16. Treffinger, D.J., Selby, E.C., Isaksen, S.G.: Understanding individual problem-solving style: a key to learning and applying creative problem solving. Learn. Individ. Differ. **18**(4), 390–401 (2008)
17. Liu, T.Y., Tan, T.H., Chu, Y.L.: QR code and augmented reality-supported mobile English learning system. In: Jin, J.S., Xu, C., Xu, M. (eds.) Mobile Multimedia Processing LNCS, vol. 5960, pp. 37–52. Springer, Heidelberg (2010)
18. Richey, R.C., Klein, J.D.: Design and Development Research: Methods, Strategies, and Issues. Routledge, New York (2007)
19. Vygotsky, L.S.: Mind in Society: the Development of Higher Psychological Processes. Harvard University Press, Cambridge (1978)
20. Mikropoulos, T.A., Natsis, A.: Educational virtual environments: a ten-year review of empirical research (1999–2009). Comput. Educ. **56**(3), 769–780 (2011)
21. Kochapong, N.: Development of a psychological learning management model to enhance creative problem-solving for pre-service teachers. Ph.D. dissertation, Srinakharinwirot University, Bangkok (2018)
22. Samat, C.: Development of a web-based constructivist learning environment model to enhance creative thinking for undergraduate students. Ph.D. dissertation, Khon Kaen University, Khon Kaen (2009)
23. Hannafin, M.J., Land, S., Oliver, K.: Open learning environments: foundations, methods, and models. In: Reigeluth, C.M. (ed.) Instructional Design Theories and Models, vol. 2, pp. 115–140. Lawrence Erlbaum, Mahwah (1999)
24. Thongsong, P.: Development of a Virtual Reality (VR) Exhibition Based on a Constructivist Approach to Enhance Creative Problem-Solving in High-Energy Physics and Quantum Technology Related to Clean Energy for Upper Secondary School Students. Master's thesis, Khon Kaen University, Khon Kaen (2026)
25. Klausmeier, H.J.: Educational Psychology, 5th edn. Harper & Row, New York (1985)
26. Mayer, R.E.: Learning strategies for making sense out of expository text: the SOI model for guiding three cognitive processes in knowledge construction. Educ. Psychol. Rev. **8**(4), 357–371 (1996)
27. Liu, G., Gomez, R., Samdal, C.: Multi-strategic learning environments in technology-enhanced constructivist education. Educ. Tech. Res. Dev. **57**(3), 201–220 (2009)

Reducing Nurses' Anxiety in Sexual Assault Evidence Collection Training Through Digital Game-Based Learning

Wei-Ching Chen and Han-Yu Sung(✉)

Department of Allied Health Education and Digital Learning, National Taipei University of Nursing and Health Science, Taipei, Taiwan
hanyu.sung@gmail.com

Abstract. The increasing complexity and sensitivity of sexual assault evidence collection present significant challenges for emergency nurses, often leading to elevated anxiety and decreased confidence in clinical practice. Traditional training approaches, such as lectures and video-based instruction, are limited by low interactivity and insufficient opportunities for repeated practice. To address these limitations, this study developed a scenario-based digital game to provide an immersive and low risk learning environment for training in sexual assault evidence collection procedures. A quasi-experimental design was employed to evaluate the effectiveness of the intervention. The results demonstrated a statistically significant reduction in nurses' anxiety levels following the intervention. These findings indicate that digital game-based learning can effectively alleviate anxiety in high-pressure clinical training contexts by offering a safe, interactive, and repeatable learning experience. This approach shows promise for enhancing psychological readiness in nursing education.

Keywords: sexual assault evidence collection · digital educational game · anxiety

1 Introduction

Recent statistics from the Department of Protective Services, Ministry of Health and Welfare (2023) indicate a steady increase in reported sexual assault cases [1]. Emergency department nurses are often the first professionals to encounter victims and are required to perform multiple complex tasks, including forensic evidence collection, adherence to legal protocols, provision of psychological support, and coordination of subsequent social services. These responsibilities demand not only technical competence but also emotional resilience. Without adequate preparation, nurses may experience uncertainty and stress when managing such cases, which can negatively affect both their performance and confidence in clinical decision-making. Therefore, structured training is essential to support nurses in developing both procedural accuracy and psychological readiness.

In Taiwan, however, specialized forensic nurse roles are not yet widely established, and most hospitals rely on in-service training to prepare emergency nurses for these

C.-J. Lin et al. (Eds.): ICITL 2026, LNCS 16841, pp. 339–344, 2027.
https://doi.org/10.1007/978-3-032-32112-1_34

responsibilities. Although asynchronous instructional videos provided by the Ministry of Health and Welfare serve as foundational educational resources, many of these materials are dated and primarily based on international clinical contexts. Consequently, they may not fully align with local legal regulations, cultural considerations, or clinical workflows. This mismatch may create cognitive gaps for learners, making it more difficult to transfer knowledge into practice and potentially increasing learning-related anxiety [2].

Moreover, conventional instructional approaches, such as linear videos and static materials, are typically characterized by one-way information delivery. These formats often lack interactivity and immediate feedback, limiting learners' opportunities to actively engage with the content. As a result, learners may remain passive recipients of information, which can reduce motivation, hinder sustained attention, and weaken the development of procedural competence [3]. Notably, the absence of a safe environment for repeated practice may further contribute to learners' apprehension when facing real clinical situations. However, there remains a lack of training approaches that integrate interactive design, real-time feedback, and context-specific clinical scenarios tailored to local practice.

Accordingly, the development of a contextually grounded, interactive digital learning game tailored to local clinical practices may provide an effective approach to reducing learning-related anxiety, enhancing engagement, and improving the accuracy of procedural performance among emergency nurses.

2 Literature Review

With the increasing demand for medical services related to sexual assault cases, emergency department nurses are required to perform complex and sensitive tasks under high-pressure conditions. These tasks include forensic evidence collection, adherence to legal procedures, and the provision of psychological support. Such responsibilities require not only procedural accuracy but also emotional resilience. For nurses with insufficient training, these situations may lead to uncertainty and heightened anxiety, which may negatively affect their confidence and clinical performance.

Existing training approaches often combine theoretical instruction, simulation, and clinical immersion. While these methods can enhance learners' competence and confidence, they are often resource-intensive and difficult to scale. In addition, the unpredictable occurrence of sexual assault cases limits opportunities for repeated practice in real clinical settings [4]. Conventional instructional methods, such as lectures and video-based learning, are more accessible but often lack interactivity and immediate feedback, which may reduce learner engagement and hinder procedural skill development. Without sufficient opportunities for safe and repeated practice, learners may experience increased anxiety when facing real clinical situations. This issue may be particularly pronounced in contexts where training resources are limited or not fully aligned with local clinical practices.

In response to these limitations, digital game-based learning (DGBL) has emerged as a promising approach in nursing education. By incorporating goal-oriented tasks, progressive challenges, and real-time feedback, DGBL can enhance learner engagement and support skill acquisition [5, 6]. DGBL also provides a low-risk, interactive environment where learners can repeatedly practice clinical procedures and receive immediate feedback, thereby improving their confidence and reducing anxiety.

Despite these advantages, there is still a lack of training approaches that effectively integrate interactive design, real-time feedback, and context-specific clinical scenarios tailored to local practice. Therefore, this study proposes the use of a contextually grounded digital educational game as an instructional intervention to enhance emergency nurses' motivation, reduce learning-related anxiety, and improve procedural performance in sexual assault evidence collection training.

3 Method

This study developed a digital educational game using the RPG Maker platform. The platform was selected for its event-driven system and scripting flexibility, which allow the construction of multi-stage scenarios and interactive learning sequences.

The game was designed as a scenario-based, task-oriented learning environment that simulates the workflow of sexual assault evidence collection. By integrating narrative elements, character interaction, and goal-oriented challenges, the system provides learners with an immersive and low-risk environment in which they can repeatedly practice clinical procedures. This design aims to support procedural understanding while reducing learning-related anxiety and enhancing learner engagement.

The game incorporates structured scenarios that reflect real clinical procedures, including obtaining informed consent, environmental assessment, evidence collection, and documentation. Narrative elements and character dialogue guide learners through decision-making processes, allowing them to experience realistic clinical situations in a safe environment. This approach supports repeated practice and helps reduce learners' uncertainty when applying knowledge in real-world contexts. The game content is aligned with local clinical guidelines and legal regulations, including standardized reporting procedures and relevant policies. By incorporating locally relevant cases, the game bridges the gap between theoretical knowledge and real-world practice, thereby facilitating learning transfer and increasing learners' confidence in applying their skills.

The game adopts a mission-based structure in which learners navigate a virtual environment and complete a series of scenario-driven tasks across seven levels, each corresponding to a key component of the sexual assault evidence collection process. Learners can progress at their own pace and revisit levels for repeated practice, enabling flexible and self-directed learning. Each level integrates both procedural knowledge and decision-making; early stages focus on understanding the overall workflow and obtaining informed consent, while later stages require learners to identify appropriate evidence types, apply correct collection procedures, and ensure proper documentation. Through interactive tasks and guided decision-making, learners engage in experiential learning and receive immediate feedback on their actions. This structured progression is designed to foster a sense of control and achievement, which are essential for promoting motivation and facilitating flow experience. Moreover, by providing a low-risk environment without real-world consequences, the game reduces performance pressure and learning-related anxiety, while supporting the gradual development of learners' confidence and clinical competence.

3.1 Participants

This study employed a quasi-experimental design to examine the effects of a digital game-based learning intervention on nurses' anxiety in sexual assault evidence collection training. The intervention integrates scenario-based simulation and interactive tasks to create an immersive learning environment, aiming to reduce uncertainty and alleviate anxiety during clinical decision-making. Participants were recruited from the emergency department of a medical center in northern Taiwan. A total of 36 registered nurses participated in the study.

Prior to data collection, the research team conducted an on-site briefing to introduce the study purpose, procedures, data collection methods, and potential risks and benefits. Participation was voluntary, and written informed consent was obtained from all participants before inclusion in the study. All procedures were conducted in accordance with ethical research guidelines.

3.2 Experiment Design

The experimental procedure consisted of four sequential stages designed to examine the effects of the digital game-based learning intervention on nurses' anxiety. First, participants completed a pre-test using the anxiety scale to assess their baseline anxiety levels prior to the intervention. Second, participants attended an orientation session, during which the instructor introduced the learning objectives, instructional activities, and operational guidelines of the digital educational game. This step ensured that participants were familiar with the system interface and learning tasks, thereby reducing initial uncertainty. Third, participants engaged in the digital game-based learning activity, which simulated the process of sexual assault evidence collection. Through scenario-based tasks, interactive decision-making, and immediate feedback, participants practiced clinical procedures in a low-risk environment. Finally, after completing the intervention, participants completed a post-test using the same anxiety scale to measure changes in their anxiety levels. The pre- and post-test results were then compared to evaluate the effectiveness of the intervention on anxiety reduction.

3.3 Measuring Tools

The anxiety measure used in this study was adapted from Tsai and Chen (1996) [7]. The original scale demonstrated high internal consistency (Cronbach's $\alpha = 0.93$) and consisted of four dimensions: personal response, work concerns, competence, and inability to complete personal tasks, with a total of 47 items. As this study focuses on professional clinical practice, the work concerns dimension was selected for adaptation. This dimension reflects nurses' perceived stress and expectations regarding their professional roles and originally consisted of 13 items. The items were revised to align with the context of sexual assault evidence collection in emergency departments. The adapted scale was used to assess nurses' anxiety when performing related clinical tasks. All items were measured using a five-point Likert scale, ranging from 1 (strongly disagree) to 5 (strongly agree). Sample items included statements such as "I have difficulty effectively communicating with physicians during sexual assault evidence collection" and "I am unable to respond to patients' or family members' questions."

4 Experimental Results

The results of this study indicate a significant reduction in nurses' anxiety levels following the use of the digital game-based learning intervention. A paired-samples t-test was conducted to compare anxiety levels before and after the intervention. The post-test anxiety scores (M = 3.59, SD = 1.08) were significantly lower than the pre-test scores (M = 4.14, SD = 0.68), with a t-value of −2.89 and a p-value of .007.

This finding suggests a statistically significant decrease in anxiety, indicating that the digital game-based learning approach effectively supported nurses in managing anxiety associated with sexual assault evidence collection tasks. The reduction in anxiety highlights the value of incorporating interactive and low risk learning environments into healthcare training, particularly in high-pressure and emotionally demanding clinical contexts (Table 1).

Table 1. t-test result of the pre- and post-learning anxiety scores

Anxiety	N	Mean	S.D.	t	p
Post-test	36	3.59	1.08	-2.89^{**}	.007
Pre-test	36	4.14	0.68		

$^{**}p < .01$

5 Conclusions

This study demonstrated that a digital game-based learning approach effectively reduced nurses' anxiety in performing sexual assault evidence collection tasks. By providing an interactive, scenario-based, and low-risk learning environment, the game enabled nurses to engage in repeated practice and guided decision-making, thereby alleviating uncertainty associated with complex clinical procedures.

The findings indicate that digital game-based learning can serve as an effective training strategy for reducing anxiety in high-pressure clinical contexts. Compared with traditional instructional approaches, this method offers greater interactivity, immediate feedback, and opportunities for self-paced learning, which contribute to a more supportive and psychologically safe learning experience.

As healthcare systems increasingly seek efficient and scalable training solutions, technology-enhanced learning approaches such as digital educational games have the potential to improve both learning experiences and emotional readiness in clinical practice.

Future research should explore the long-term effects of game-based learning on clinical performance and anxiety management in real-world settings. Expanding the sample size and including diverse clinical contexts may provide further insights into its effectiveness and generalizability. Overall, this study highlights the potential of digital game-based learning in supporting anxiety reduction and enhancing training outcomes in nursing education.

References

1. Department of Protective Services, Ministry of Health and Welfare: Statistics on reported sexual assault cases. Ministry of Health and Welfare. https://dep.mohw.gov.tw/DOPS/lp-1303-105-xCat-cat02.html (2023).
2. Yesodharan, R., Jose, T.T., Nirmal Krishnan, M., Anitha, S., Nayak, V.C.: Looking through the lens of a sexual assault examiner: novel trends and approaches in forensic photography. Egypt. J. Forensic Sci. **11**(1), 27 (2021)
3. Palaigeorgiou, G., Papadopoulou, A.: Promoting self-paced learning in the elementary classroom with interactive video, an online course platform and tablets. Educ. Inf. Technol. **24**(1), 805–823 (2019)
4. Nathan, S., Moret, J.D.: Sexual assault forensic examiner recruitment and retention: using simulation to teach a trauma-informed interview. J. Forensic Nurs. **18**(1), 54–58 (2022)
5. Prensky, M.: Digital natives, digital immigrants part 2: do they really think differently? On Horizon. **9**(6), 1–6 (2001)
6. Prensky, M.: Digital Game-Based Learning. McGraw-Hill (2007)
7. Tsai, S.L., Chen, M.L.: A test of the reliability and validity of nurse stress checklist. Nurs. Res. (Chinese Version). **4**(4), 355–362 (1996)

Exploring the Effect of GAI in VR-Based Learning

Chang-Zhi Chen[1], Qing Tan[2], Jiann-Liang Chen[1], and Yueh-Min Huang[1](✉)

[1] Department of Engineering Science, National Cheng Kung University, Tainan City, Taiwan
N98131512@gs.ncku.edu.tw, lchen@mail.ntust.edu.tw, huang@mail.ncku.edu.tw

[2] Athabasca University, Athabasca, AB, Canada
qingt@athabascau.ca

Abstract. While Virtual Reality (VR) provides highly immersive environments for self-regulated learning, the lack of real-time human guidance often leaves learners susceptible to excessive cognitive load and social isolation. Traditional VR feedback mechanisms, which are predominantly static and unidirectional, struggle to provide adequate psychological and cognitive support. This study investigates the effectiveness of integrating a Generative Artificial Intelligence (GAI) voice assistant to enhance learners' basic psychological needs, intrinsic motivation, and academic performance in a VR embedded systems course. A randomized controlled trial was conducted with 62 university students, who were randomly assigned to either an experimental or a control group. The experimental group interacted with a real-time, dynamic GAI voice tutor, while the control group received traditional, preset feedback. The results revealed that the experimental group demonstrated significantly higher levels of autonomy ($p < .05$), competence ($p < .01$), and relatedness ($p < .001$) compared to the control group. Furthermore, the GAI voice assistant significantly boosted learners' intrinsic learning motivation ($p < .01$) and, after controlling for prior knowledge, significantly improved their post-test scores ($p < .05$). These findings indicate that by synergizing dynamic cognitive scaffolding with anthropomorphic emotional support, GAI voice tutors effectively fulfill learners' basic psychological needs. This fulfillment acts as a crucial psychological buffer, transforming learners' cognitive appraisals of technical challenges, and ultimately driving sustained growth in learning motivation and academic achievement within immersive learning environments.

Keywords: Virtual Reality · Generative Artificial Intelligence · Self-Determination Theory · Intrinsic Motivation

1 Introduction

With the proliferation of digitalization and technology, educational paradigms are shifting from collective, standardized instruction toward personalized, self-regulated learning [1]. In this transition, Virtual Reality (VR) is regarded as a core technological medium

C.-J. Lin et al. (Eds.): ICITL 2026, LNCS 16841, pp. 345–354, 2027.
https://doi.org/10.1007/978-3-032-32112-1_35

for supporting personalized exploration due to its ability to provide high-fidelity, contextualized experiences [2]. However, despite its high level of immersion and interactivity, learners in VR self-learning environments—which often lack the real-time guidance of a human instructor—frequently suffer from excessive cognitive load or a profound sense of learning isolation [2]. Consequently, the design focus of VR learning environments has evolved from mere visual immersion and content interaction to the design of effective feedback mechanisms [3]. In self-learning environments devoid of external constraints, a learner's ability to maintain stable intrinsic motivation is a critical factor determining learning effectiveness [4].

The stimulation of intrinsic motivation depends heavily on the satisfaction of three basic psychological needs: autonomy, competence, and relatedness [4]. Therefore, effective self-learning systems must demonstrate supportiveness toward the learner, ensuring that students feel they have choices, possess the ability to solve problems, and establish emotional connections during the exploration process. Examining current VR learning environments reveals several issues that may restrict learners' intrinsic motivation. First, regarding autonomy, while VR's interactivity and immersion are expected to enhance learner autonomy, the learning paths in most current VR research are typically linear or tree-structured, confining learners' choices to preset options. Once a student develops an interest in a non-prescribed concept or wishes to explore deeper, the system cannot generate relevant supplemental content in real-time, leaving the need for high autonomy unmet [5]. Currently, empirical research on autonomy in immersive learning remains insufficient; more evidence is needed to understand how different media and designs enhance or diminish autonomy [6]. Second, in terms of competence, although VR offers opportunities for hands-on operation, its feedback mechanisms are often restricted to standardized (fixed and uniform) replies. This type of non-explanatory feedback fails to address personalized needs or help learners understand the root causes behind complex errors, making it difficult for them to establish a solid sense of competence when facing challenges [7]. Third, interactions within VR environments require improvement regarding relatedness. Currently, most virtual agents in VR environments rely on scripted or rule-based interaction models. This makes it difficult for them to demonstrate emotional depth, empathy, or conversational coherence, resulting in stiff, repetitive interactions that fail to establish the authentic sense of relatedness and social support that students crave [8].

The emergence of Generative Artificial Intelligence (GAI), particularly GAI tutors equipped with voice interaction capabilities, offers a turning point for VR self-learning environments [9]. Unlike traditional AI based on rules or preset scripts, GAI possesses powerful content generation, complex reasoning, and natural language interaction capabilities, which can make learning environments more personalized, inclusive, and interactive [10]. First, learners can receive real-time, personalized supplemental course content generated within the VR curriculum, thereby maximizing their capacity for autonomous choices. Second, GAI can provide explanatory feedback and offer learning scaffolding (such as posing questions, offering perspectives, providing feedback, or assisting in decision-making) to support learners' competence development in a more nuanced manner. Third, by simulating interactions characterized by empathy and a personalized tone, it can effectively establish a sense of relatedness. This enables GAI voice tutors to serve as a technological vehicle capable of comprehensively satisfying the three psychological needs within a VR self-learning environment. Therefore, this study aims to systematically deconstruct how GAI voice tutors drive learners' intrinsic motivation in VR self-learning environments by fulfilling their basic psychological needs.

This study explores three research hypotheses:

- H1: In a VR self-learning environment, the group receiving GAI voice tutor feedback will perceive significantly higher levels of autonomy, competence, and relatedness compared to the traditional feedback group.
- H2: In a VR self-learning environment, the group receiving GAI voice tutor feedback will demonstrate significantly higher intrinsic motivation than the traditional feedback group.
- H3: In a VR self-learning environment, the group receiving GAI voice tutor feedback will achieve significantly higher learning outcomes than the traditional feedback group.

2 Literature Review

2.1 Self-Learning and Intrinsic Motivation in Virtual Reality

In the current evolution of educational technology, Virtual Reality (VR) is regarded as a revolutionary tool for promoting self-regulated learning; its advantage lies in providing learners with an exploratory space characterized by a high sense of presence and embodied cognition [11]. In such non-linear learning environments, learners are no longer passive recipients of knowledge but must actively regulate their own learning pace, pathways, and decision-making [12]. From the perspective of Achievement Goal Theory, research by Ames and Archer [13] exploring students' learning strategies and motivational processes indicates that learners driven by intrinsic motivation and oriented toward mastery goals tend to view challenges as opportunities to enhance their abilities rather than as threats to their competence. Extending this theoretical mechanism to VR learning contexts reveals that when students possess high intrinsic learning motivation, they not only actively employ deeper cognitive strategies but, when facing potential initial discomfort or operational bottlenecks with equipment, are also more inclined to perceive these technical obstacles as part of the learning process. Consequently, students demonstrate higher engagement and continue to invest cognitive resources to overcome technical and knowledge barriers; conversely, if motivation is lacking, the students' sense of disorientation, frustration, and the high visual load of VR will lead to a disruption in learning engagement. An empirical study by Wang, Lee [6] exploring self-regulated VR learning environments points out that immersive environments highly depend on learners' self-regulation abilities; when low-motivation learners are placed in a VR environment lacking appropriate learning support mechanisms, they are highly susceptible to becoming lost in complex virtual tasks due to a lack of clear learning goals, and may even divert their limited cognitive resources and attention toward negative emotions such as anxiety [14].

2.2 The Evolution of Generative AI Voice Tutors in Education

Unlike traditional chatbots that restrict learner autonomy through rigid decision trees, Large Language Model (LLM)-driven Generative AI (GAI) provides real-time, customized instructional scaffolding. Empirical studies demonstrate that LLMs not only reduce cognitive load and foster deeper autonomous learning [15], but also dynamically optimize tailored learning activities [16]. However, utilizing solely text-based GAI in immersive VR significantly increases extraneous cognitive load [17]. To address this, integrating voice interaction is crucial. Voice-enabled GAI facilitates intuitive communication while conveying empathy and social presence through anthropomorphic vocal cues, effectively mitigating the isolation of VR self-learning [18]. In summary, by synergizing dynamic cognitive scaffolding with anthropomorphic emotional support, GAI voice tutors emerge as a transformative intervention capable of reshaping learners' psychological and educational pathways.

3 Method

3.1 Participants and Experimental Design

This study employed a between-subjects randomized design with 62 university students aged 19 to 22 ($M = 19.7$, $SD = 0.73$). Participants were randomly assigned to an experimental group ($n = 32$; 17 males, 15 females) and a control group ($n = 30$; 16 males, 14 females). All participants provided informed consent with the right to withdraw at any time. Both groups used VR head-mounted displays to engage in the learning tasks.

3.2 Materials and VR Learning Environment

In terms of instructional materials, the learning tasks for the embedded systems course were designed based on Bloom's taxonomy [19], dividing the learning content into three modules (as shown in Table 1). The first module introduces foundational knowledge related to I/O sensors and electronic circuits. The second module focuses on the correlation between programming code and electronic circuits, allowing learners to understand how programming logic interfaces and interacts with the development board. The third module explains how to integrate multiple electronic components through programming to realize Internet of Things (IoT) applications.

Table 1. VR Learning Unit and Tasks

Classification	Task and Course
Remember	Introduces knowledge related to electronic circuits and the Internet of Things (IoT), including multiple I/O sensors.
Understand	During this stage, learners will acquire fundamental Python programming logic and complete tasks involving circuit wiring and hardware configuration.
Apply	Explains the integration logic and applications of various hardware components.

3.3 GAI Voice Assistant

This study implemented two distinct feedback mechanisms within the virtual reality (VR) learning environment. First, the experimental group integrated a Generative Artificial Intelligence (GAI) voice assistant. Regarding the interaction mechanics, participants could use VR hand controllers to intuitively grab, move, and manipulate all virtual objects on the workbench. Simultaneously, the system interface incorporated a floating information panel to guide the workflow of the learning tasks and provide system feedback (as shown in Fig. 1). Voice input could be directly triggered via a button on the controller, which also opened a text box displaying the responses from the GAI voice assistant (as shown in Fig. 2). The voice assistant's interactive capabilities were realized through OpenAI's Speech-to-Text (STT) and Text-to-Speech (TTS) technologies. The underlying language model employed was GPT-5 mini, paired with specific prompts to design the assistant's conversational style.

In contrast, the control group utilized a VR learning environment equipped with a traditional feedback mechanism. While its basic functionalities were similar to those of the experimental group and were applied across all learning modules and tasks, a key difference existed: upon receiving feedback or task instructions, learners could not engage in further interaction with the system. The feedback was strictly unidirectional. Learners could only adjust their learning strategies based on these preset responses, which included error feedback, instructional feedback, and motivational feedback.

Fig. 1. Screenshot of the VR environment

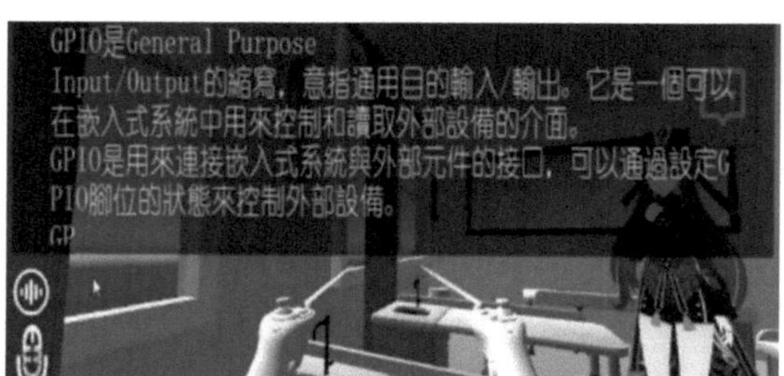

Fig. 2. Voice Interaction Interface of the GAI VOICE ASSISTANT System

3.4 Experimental Procedure

The participants in this study were undergraduate students (ranging from freshmen to seniors) from the Department of Engineering Science at a university in southern Taiwan. All participants volunteered for the study and were informed that their participation would not affect their academic grades. Students spent 15 min completing a pre-test questionnaire and a demographic information survey, followed by a 15-min introduction to the course, equipment, and usage instructions. Subsequently, students wore head-mounted displays to participate in the learning activities (divided into three task modules). Considering visual load and extraneous cognitive load, each module was limited to 20 min and conducted over three consecutive weeks. After the experiment, participants spent 25 min completing a post-test questionnaire. The experimental procedure is illustrated in Fig. 3.

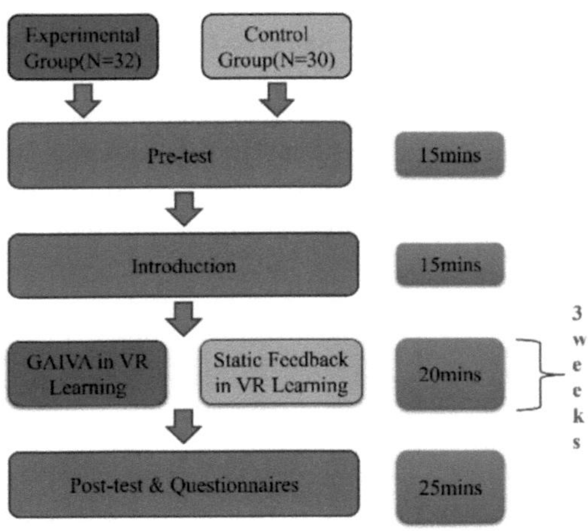

Fig. 3. Experimental Procedure

3.5 Questionnaires and Measurements

The measurement tools in this study assessed knowledge level, intrinsic motivation, and psychological need satisfaction. The knowledge test comprised 20 questions (true/false, multiple-choice, and open-ended; max 100 points) covering IoT, electronic circuits, and Python programming. It was validated by two domain experts, yielding an inter-rater reliability (Cronbach's α) of 0.81. Intrinsic motivation was measured using the 4-item subscale of the Situational Motivation Scale (SIMS) [20] on a 7-point Likert scale (Cronbach's $\alpha = 0.91$). Lastly, the satisfaction of basic psychological needs (Autonomy, Competence, and Relatedness) was evaluated using the 12-item Technology-based Experience of Need Satisfaction-Task (TENS-Task) [21] on a 5-point Likert scale (Cronbach's $\alpha = 0.82$).

4 Results

4.1 SDT Basic Psychological Needs

To address the first research question, an independent samples t-test (Table 2) revealed that the experimental group (EG) scored significantly higher than the control group (CG) across all three SDT basic psychological needs: autonomy ($t = 3.13$, $p < .05$), competence ($t = 6.25$, $p < .01$), and relatedness ($t = 8.39$, $p < .001$). These findings demonstrate that the GAI Voice Assistant effectively enhances learners' psychological needs within VR environments.

Table 2. Independent sample t-test for Autonomy Competence Relatedness.

	Group	Mean	SD	t	Effect size
Autonomy	EG	14.45	2.21	3.13*	0.72
	CG	12.70	2.27		
Competence	EG	15.42	2.28	6.25**	1.43
	CG	12.27	2.35		
Relatedness	EG	16.35	2.12	8.39***	2.03
	CG	12.27	2.26		

Note: *$p < 0.05$, **$p < 0.01$, ***$p < 0.001$. Bold values represent significant difference.

4.2 Intrinsic Motivation

To address the second research question, an independent samples t-test (Table 3) revealed that the experimental group (EG) demonstrated significantly higher intrinsic motivation than the control group (CG) ($t = 4.52$, $p < .01$). These findings suggest that the GAI Voice Assistant effectively enhances intrinsic motivation within VR instructional environments.

Table 3. Independent sample t-test for Intrinsic motivation.

	Group	Mean	SD	t	Effect size
Intrinsic motivation	EG	21.18	3.21	4.52**	1.05
	CG	16.72	3.15		

Note: *$p < 0.05$, **$p < 0.01$, ***$p < 0.001$. Bold values represent significant difference.

4.3 Learning Outcomes

To address the third research question, an ANCOVA was conducted to compare post-test learning outcomes, using pre-test scores as a covariate. The assumption of homogeneity of variances was met (Levene's test: $F(1, 60) = 0.08, p = .78$). Results (Table 4) revealed that after adjusting for initial differences, the experimental group (M = 70.08, SD = 11.23) achieved significantly higher learning outcomes than the control group (M = 58.80, SD = 10.96), $F = 5.71, p < .05$, partial $\eta^2 = .076$.

Table 4. Results of ANCOVA and descriptives of Learninig outcomes

			Pre-test			Post-test			
		M	SD	F	Partial η^2	M	SD	F	Partial η^2
Score	EG	30.68	7.12	35.21	.338	70.08	11.23	5.71*	.076
	CG	27.71.	6.85			58.80	10.96		

Note: *$p < 0.05$, **$p < 0.01$, ***$p < 0.001$. Bold values represent significant difference.

5 Discussion

The experimental results demonstrate a clear sequential pathway where the GAI Voice Assistant significantly enhances basic psychological needs, intrinsic motivation, and overall learning outcomes in complex STEM VR environments. According to Self-Determination Theory (SDT), the GAI effectively fulfilled learners' needs for relatedness (p < .001) through empathetic, anthropomorphic companionship that mitigated VR-induced social isolation. It enhanced competence (p < .01) via step-by-step interrogative guidance that reduced extraneous cognitive load during trial-and-error processes, and promoted autonomy (p < .05) by returning the agency of debugging to the learner through open-ended natural language interactions. The adequate satisfaction of these three fundamental needs served as a crucial psychological buffer, triggering a shift toward active exploration and significantly boosting intrinsic motivation. Aligning with Achievement Goal Theory, this heightened motivation altered learners' cognitive appraisals; instead of viewing technical errors as threats to their abilities, they embraced them as valuable learning opportunities. Ultimately, compared to the rigid, one-size-fits-all feedback of traditional systems, the GAI's real-time dynamic scaffolding successfully translated this robust psychological resilience into sustained engagement and significantly superior learning outcomes. In summary, the GAI Voice Assistant acts as a vital catalyst in immersive learning, seamlessly bridging psychological support and cognitive scaffolding to drive both motivational growth and academic achievement.

Despite the positive outcomes, several limitations should be noted. First, the short intervention duration (60 min over three weeks) suggests that the significant gains in motivation and psychological needs might be partially driven by the novelty effect of the GAI technology. Future longitudinal studies are needed to verify if these motivational benefits persist over time.Second, the exceptionally large effect size for relatedness (d = 2.03) warrants caution. According to SDT, need satisfaction and need frustration are distinct mechanisms. The control group's complete lack of social interaction in an isolated VR environment may have actively triggered "need frustration," making it asymmetrical to the experimental group's "need satisfaction." Future research should include a baseline virtual agent (non-GAI) to isolate the true value of GAI.Finally, a discrepancy exists between the profound psychological impacts and the more moderate learning outcomes. Given the maximum score of 20 for TENS-Task subscales, the experimental group's high relatedness mean (16.35) indicates a potential "ceiling compression effect," which may have artificially inflated the psychometric effect sizes. Future studies should utilize measurement tools with higher discriminatory power and report full data distributions to validate these findings.

References

1. Laas, N.I., Romanova, I.A., Gurova, E.V.: DIGITAL TRANSFORMATION OF EDUCATION: A MODERN VIEW ON SELF-DEVELOPMENT. Management of the Personnel and Intellectual Resources in Russia 4 (2022)
2. Zhang, H., et al.: Investigating high school students' perceptions and presences under VR learning environment. In: Cross Reality (XR) and Immersive Learning Environments (ILEs) in Education, pp. 97–117. Routledge (2023)
3. Paulsen, L., Dau, S., Davidsen, J.: Designing for collaborative learning in immersive virtual reality: a systematic literature review. Virtual Reality. **28**, 63 (2024)
4. Deci, E.L., Ryan, R.M.: Conceptualizations of intrinsic motivation and self-determination. In: Intrinsic Motivation and Self-Determination in Human Behavior, pp. 11–40. Springer (1985)
5. Skulmowski, A.: Ethical issues of educational virtual reality. Comput. Educ. X Reality. **2**, 100023 (2023)
6. Wang, W.S., Lee, H.Y., Lin, C.J., Li, P.H., Huang, Y.M., Wu, T.T.: Enhancing students' learning outcomes in self-regulated virtual reality learning environment with learning aid mechanisms. Br. J. Educ. Technol. **56**, 366–387 (2025)
7. Qorbani, S., Dalili, S., Arya, A., Joslin, C.: Assessing learning in an immersive virtual reality: a curriculum-based experiment in chemistry education. Educ. Sci. **14**, 476 (2024)
8. Martella, A.M., et al.: Systematically reviewing the rigour of immersive virtual reality research in STEM education: a deep dive into threats to internal validity. J. Comput. Assist. Learn. **42**, e70165 (2026)
9. Wang, W.-S., Lin, C.-J., Lee, H.-Y., Huang, Y.-M., Wu, T.-T.: Integrating feedback mechanisms and ChatGPT for VR-based experiential learning: impacts on reflective thinking and AIoT physical hands-on tasks. Interact. Learn. Environ. **33**, 1770–1787 (2025)
10. Lang, Q., Wang, M., Yin, M., Liang, S., Song, W.: Transforming education with generative AI (GAI): key insights and future prospects. IEEE Trans. Learn. Technol. **18**, 230–242 (2025)
11. Conrad, M., Kablitz, D., Schumann, S.: Learning effectiveness of immersive virtual reality in education and training: a systematic review of findings. Comput. Educ. X Reality. **4**, 100053 (2024)
12. Wang, C.-H.: Education in the metaverse: developing virtual reality teaching materials for K–12 natural science. Educ. Inf. Technol. **30**, 8637–8658 (2025)
13. Ames, C., Archer, J.: Achievement goals in the classroom: Students' learning strategies and motivation processes. J. Educ. Psychol. **80**, 260 (1988)
14. Chen, C.-Z., Wang, W.-S., Huang, Y.-M.: Designing adaptive feedback for hands-on learning in VR: feedback intervention theory. Educ. Inf. Technol., 1–25 (2026)
15. Poupard, M., Larrue, F., Sauzéon, H., Tricot, A.: A systematic review of immersive technologies for education: learning performance, cognitive load and intrinsic motivation. Br. J. Educ. Technol. **56**, 5–41 (2025)

16. Gong, Y., Wang, M., He, L., Xu, C., Yu, Y.: Asking, playing, learning: investigating large language model-based scaffolding in digital game-based learning for elementary artificial intelligence education. J. Educ. Comput. Res. **64**, 311–343 (2026)
17. Makransky, G., Terkildsen, T.S., Mayer, R.E.: Adding immersive virtual reality to a science lab simulation causes more presence but less learning. Learn. Instr. **60**, 225–236 (2019)
18. Dang, B., Huynh, L., Gul, F., Rosé, C., Järvelä, S., Nguyen, A.: Human–AI collaborative learning in mixed reality: examining the cognitive and socio-emotional interactions. Br. J. Educ. Technol. **56**, 2078–2101 (2025)
19. Bloom, B.: Bloom's taxonomy (1956)
20. Guay, F., Vallerand, R.J., Blanchard, C.: On the assessment of situational intrinsic and extrinsic motivation: the situational motivation scale (SIMS). Motiv. Emot. **24**, 175–213 (2000)
21. Peters, D., Calvo, R.A., Ryan, R.M.: Designing for motivation, engagement and wellbeing in digital experience. Front. Psychol. **9**, 300159 (2018)

Author Index

C.-J. Lin et al. (Eds.): ICITL 2026, LNCS 16841, pp. 355–356, 2027.
https://doi.org/10.1007/978-3-032-32112-1

MIX
Papier aus verantwortungsvollen Quellen
Paper from responsible sources
FSC® C105338

If you have any concerns about our products,
you can contact us on
ProductSafety@springernature.com

In case Publisher is established outside the EU,
the EU authorized representative is:
Springer Nature Customer Service Center GmbH
Europaplatz 3, 69115 Heidelberg, Germany

Printed by Libri Plureos GmbH
in Hamburg, Germany